THE FATHERS
OF THE CHURCH

A NEW TRANSLATION

VOLUME 18

THE FATHERS OF THE CHURCH

A NEW TRANSLATION

Founded by
LUDWIG SCHOPP

EDITORIAL BOARD

ROY JOSEPH DEFERRARI
The Catholic University of America
Editorial Director

RUDOLPH ARBESMANN, O.S.A.
Fordham University

BERNARD M. PEEBLES
The Catholic University of America

STEPHAN KUTTNER
The Catholic University of America

ROBERT P. RUSSELL, O.S.A.
Villanova College

MARTIN R. P. MCGUIRE
The Catholic University of America

ANSELM STRITTMATTER, O.S.B.
St. Anselm's Priory

WILFRID PARSONS, S.J.
The Catholic University of America

JAMES EDWARD TOBIN
Queens College

GERALD G. WALSH, S.J.
Fordham University

SAINT AUGUSTINE

LETTERS

VOLUME II (83-130)

Translated by
SISTER WILFRID PARSONS, S.N.D.

THE CATHOLIC UNIVERSITY OF AMERICA PRESS
Washington, D. C.

NIHIL OBSTAT:

        JOHN M. A. FEARNS, S.T.D.
        Censor Librorum

IMPRIMATUR:

        ✠ FRANCIS CARDINAL SPELLMAN
        Archbishop of New York

February 9, 1953

The Nihil obstat and Imprimatur are official declarations that a book or pamphlet is free of doctrinal or moral error. No implication is contained therein that those who have granted the Nihil obstat and Imprimatur agree with the contents, opinions or statements expressed.

Library of Congress Catalog Card No.: 64-19948
ISBN-13: 978-0-8132-1559-4 (pbk)

Copyright © 1953 by
THE CATHOLIC UNIVERSITY OF AMERICA PRESS, INC.
All rights reserved
Reprinted, 1966
Reprinted, 1985
First paperback reprint 2008

CONTENTS

Letter   *Page*

Letter		Page
83	To Bishop Alypius	3
84	To Bishop Novatus	8
85	To Bishop Paul	9
86	To Caecilian	11
87	To Emeritus	12
88	To Januarius	22
89	To Festus	34
90	Nectarius to Augustine	41
91	To Nectarius	42
92	To Italica	50
92A	To Cyprian	55
93	To Vincent	56
94	Paulinus and Therasia to Augustine	106
95	To Paulinus and Therasia	115
96	To Olympius	124
97	To Olympius	126
98	To Bishop Boniface	129
99	To Italica	139
100	To Donatus, Proconsul	141
101	To Bishop Memorius	144
102	To Deogratias [Six Questions Answered for Pagans]	148

Letter		Page
103	Nectarius to Augustine	177
104	To Nectarius	180
105	To the Donatists	195
106	To Macrobius	211
107	Maximus and Theodore to Augustine	212
108	To Macrobius	213
109	Bishop Severus to Augustine	238
110	To Bishop Severus	241
111	To Victorian	245
112	To Donatus, Proconsul	254
113	To Cresconius	256
114	To Florentinus	257
115	To Bishop Fortunatus	258
116	To Generosus	260
117	Dioscorus to Augustine	261
118	To Dioscorus	262
119	Consentius to Augustine	294
120	To Consentius	300
121	Bishop Paulinus to Augustine	317
122	To His Brethren	334
123	St. Jerome to Augustine	336
124	To Albina, Pinian, and Melania	337
125	To Bishop Alypius	339
126	To Albina	344
127	To Armentarius and Paulina	356
128	To Marcellinus	365
129	To Marcellinus	369
130	To Proba	376

WRITINGS
OF
SAINT AUGUSTINE

VOLUME 10

INTRODUCTION

HE LETTERS IN THIS VOLUME (Numbers 83 to 130) were written in years 408 to 412. These five years were crowded and busy ones for Augustine, filled with the most varied problems of all sorts; he had, at times, to contend also with ill health. His conflict with Donatism reached its climax in the longed-for Conference between Catholics and Donatists held at Carthage in 411. Although it did not have the immediate effect of putting an end to the violent excesses of the Donatists, it did produce many conversions, and was, in fact, the beginning of the end for them. A contemporary event of terrifying importance was the sack of Rome by the Vandals under Alaric. This disaster drove many influential and wealthy Romans to Africa.

The list of his correspondents during these years is varied and impressive: bishops and priests, catechumens and deacons, public officials of high rank and authority, and, for the first time, women. St. Jerome does not figure in the correspondence of this period, except for an enigmatic fragment (123) which was formerly attached to Letter 195, but is now regarded by editors as part of an earlier letter than that one. Its tenor is so obscure that several widely varied interpretations of it are offered. There is no answer from Augustine. St. Paulinus of Nola is represented by one letter with the usual list of questions, which are painstakingly answered (94, 95);

and the same detailed attention is given by Augustine to a letter from Deogratias (102) containing six oddly assorted questions, as well as to one from Dioscorus (117), a young student of Cicero and of Greek philosophy, who seems to have regarded the Bishop of Hippo as a sort of companion to the classics.

The letters on Donatism include two addressed to the Donatist laity; one defending the penal laws recently enacted against them (105) and one giving them a true account of the Conference of Carthage, about which their own bishops were trying to keep them in the dark. In his earlier dealings with these schismatics, Augustine had aimed chiefly at drawing them into discussions where he could prove the fallacy of their position, in the belief that, once they were convinced of the truth, they would make their submission to the Church. He worked tirelessly at bringing about a general conference, in which the views of both sides should be discussed. As the Catholics had all the arguments and all the proofs, based on public records, on their side, the Donatists were understandably reluctant to engage in such a one-sided debate. They also stood to lose all the Church property which they had unlawfully annexed. In the end they were forced to this Conference by an imperial decree, for their cruel and inhuman excesses had by this time called forth the intervention of the secular power. Augustine had opposed this at the beginning, not because he denied the right of the state to intervene in a matter where public peace and order were at stake, but because he hoped that the more intellectual method of argument would succeed in putting an end to the schism. In the later years of the conflict he recognized the absolute need of suppression by the secular arm, and he set about to justify the repressive imperial enactments, while at the same time he urged a Christian moderation on public officials in applying the penalties. When the Donatists complained that the Catholics had appealed to the emperor against them, Augustine reminded them that they had done it first, when they appealed to Constantine at the beginning of the schism. His two letters to Macrobius (106, 108), a Donatist bishop in Hippo, use this argument. Several letters to Marcellinus (128, 129, 133, 139), the imperial legate in charge of the Carthage Conference, lay down the right of the state to intervene, but urge mildness in the intervention. The same moderation is urged upon the proconsul Donatus (100). To Vincent (93), head of the Rogatist sect—a schism from a schism—he expressed his joy at the many conversions brought about by the imperial laws, and justified the use of compulsion to make men good, not by forcing them to embrace the faith, but by restraining them from the madness which had led them astray. This controversy did not finally die out until 420, and will appear again in other letters.

The Letters of Class II end with Letter 123, and the first of Class III (124) introduces an incident that could have happened nowhere but in Africa. Toward the end of the year 410, the noble and wealthy widow, Albina, with her daughter, the younger Melania, and her son-in-law Pinian, left Rome then being besieged by Alaric, and reached Africa the following year, where they settled at Tagaste. They were most eager to meet Augustine, and, as he could not then go to them, they went to Hippo. While they were attending Mass in Augustine's church, the excitable people of his congregation, admiring Pinian's devout demeanor, and—as it was hinted afterward—attracted by his wealth, suddenly raised a shout demanding that he be ordained priest for their church. He refused vehemently and declared that, if he were forcibly ordained, he would leave Hippo and never come back. The people then made a tumultuous scene, and grew so threatening that he agreed to take an oath that he would not leave Hippo and that if he ever were ordained it would be nowhere but at Hippo. This pacified the congregation—Augustine had remained discreetly behind the scenes all this time—and they calmed down. The next day, Pinian and the two ladies returned to Tagaste, arguing that an oath extorted through fear is not binding. Augustine held that the danger had not been as real as they claimed and that, in any case, an oath is an oath. In Letter 124, Augustine had explained his inability to go to Tagaste on the score of his health and some troublesome diocesan affairs, not specified. After this letter, the visit to Hippo took place. In Letter 125, Augustine pours out to Alypius his deep hurt at the suspicion of Albina that the Hipponensians only wanted Pinian's wealth, and expresses his views on the binding force of an oath. In Letter 126 he writes tactfully and considerately to Albina, relating the whole incident in detail, repudiating her charge of mercenary aims against his flock, and even taking an oath himself that they had no such aims. He holds to the view that Pinian is bound to stay at Hippo, and that he will give scandal by repudiating his pledged word. Unfortunately, the letters leave this fascinating tale half-told, but we learn from other sources that Pinian lost his property, the people of Hippo forgot their enthusiasm, and later, the devout pair went to the Holy Land, where Pinian entered a monastery, and Melania became abbess of a convent.

Shortly after this, another matter of a vow was submitted to Augustine by Armentarius and Paulina (127), who had taken a vow of continence, and wanted to be released from it. They received an exhortation on the binding nature of a vow, and the moral harm suffered by the unfaithful soul. Only one condition could render a vow invalid, which had been taken jointly by a married pair: if one of the partners refused full consent. This condition had apparently not been present when the vow was made.

The first of Augustine's letters to woman correspondents

is addressed to Italica (92), a Roman widow, explaining to her the nature of the vision of God, and refuting the false notion that He can be seen with bodily eyes. In Letter 99, he tries to encourage her in the midst of the universal panic over the first siege of Rome by Alaric. Another Roman widow, Proba, was the recipient of some deeply spiritual teaching on prayer (130). This letter does not deal with methods of prayer, but with the conditions of soul requisite for prayer, and on the proper objects of the soul's petitions. In it Augustine makes an ingenious comparison between the virtues of faith, hope, and charity, the three admonitions to ask, seek, and knock, and the three pairs of objects mentioned in the parable on prayer: bread and stone, fish and serpent, egg and scorpion. In an unexpected accommodation of Scripture he identifies the egg of the parable with the virtue of hope, because the living chick is not yet seen but is hoped for, and the hope which is seen is not hope.

One series of letters deals with the kidnaping of an unfortunate tenant-farmer named Faventius, who had aroused the anger of an unnamed 'very rich man' and had taken sanctuary in a church at Hippo, while Augustine undertook to intercede for him. He grew somewhat careless of his safety and went out to dine with a friend. On his way home he was arrested by a certain Florentinus, a sort of police officer, and was carried off and held incommunicado. Augustine went to great lengths to have him set free so that the grievance, whatever it was, might be handled legally. To this end he wrote to Cresconius (113), official in charge of the coast guards, to Florentinus (114), to the Bishop of Cirta (115), and to Generosus (116), Governor of Numidia, before whom Faventius would have to appear. One can only hope and suppose that these letters had their effect and that Faventius had his day in court.

There is much in these Letters that has a modern ring, and

it is not hard to imagine that, were St. Augustine living, he would approach the problems of today in the same thorough and straightforward manner, basing his arguments on Scripture and human reason, making no compromise with principle, but showing an inexhaustible compassion for erring human nature forever confronted with the mystery of evil.

LETTERS

83-130

Translated
by
SISTER WILFRID PARSONS, S.N.D.
Emmanuel College
Boston, Mass.

83. *Augustine and the brethren who are with me give greeting in the Lord to the most blessed lord and respectfully loved and cherished brother and fellow priest, Alypius,[1] and the brethren who are with him (405)*

The sad state of the church at Thiave[2] allows my heart no rest until I hear that they have been restored to their former good relations with you, which ought to be done quickly. For, if the Apostle was exercised about one individual only, saying: 'Lest such a one be swallowed up by overmuch sorrow,'[3] and again: 'that we be not possessed by Satan, for we are not ignorant of his devices,'[4] how much more is it incumbent on us to watch carefully that we do not have to make this plaint over a whole flock, and especially over those who have recently joined the Catholic peace,[5] and whom I cannot abandon. But, because the shortness of time we had together did not allow us to work out a carefully planned statement, I send your Holiness what has come to my mind, after long thought, since our departure and, if you agree, have the letter which I have written in our joint name sent to them without delay.

---

1 Cf. Letters 24, 29. Alypius was Bishop of Tagaste, and the monastery was in his diocese.
2 This must have been a small town or hamlet in the diocese of Hippo, but it is not found in the atlas under this name.
3 2 Cor. 2.7.
4 Cf. 2 Cor. 2.11.
5 This seems to indicate a reconciliation of Donatists to the Church, subsequent to the laws against them in 405.

You said that they should have half,[6] and that I should provide the other half for them from some undescribed source. But I think that, if the whole were taken from them, there would be grounds for saying that we are interested not so much in money as in justice. When we concede them half, and patch up a peace with them in this fashion, it would give the impression that our interest was entirely financial, and you can see what harm would result from that. For we shall seem to have brought them a half which was someone else's property, and they will seem to us to have accepted it dishonestly and unfairly, so as to be helped by a half which was entirely the portion of the poor. Your words, 'we must be careful not to cause greater wounds by trying to remedy a doubtful situation,' will have just as much weight if half is allowed them; since for that half, those whose conversion we want to secure will put off the sale of their own goods, by all sorts of excuses and delays, so that they may be dealt with after this precedent. After that, is it any wonder if the whole people should be scandalized by this dubious transaction when they think that their bishops, whom they hold in great esteem, are tainted with base avarice, and all this because we do not avoid the appearance of evil?[7]

Whenever anyone is converted to monastic life, if he is

---

6 There was question of some money, which a priest of Thiave, who had been a monk at Tagaste, had left. The monks of Tagaste thought it should be theirs, and had evidently made themselves disagreeable about it, so Alypius had proposed as a compromise that it should be divided and half given to the monks; half, to the church at Thiave. Augustine thought this was a merely mercenary arrangement, and that according to the law of inheritance, what was left by a priest belonged of right to his church. He is willing, however, to give the monks money from another source to ease their disappointment, if certain conditions are met. 'They,' in this part of the letter, are the monks.

7 This wrong would be his avoiding the relinquishment of his worldly goods which his conversion to the religious life requires. Augustine thinks the proposed compromise would be a bad precedent.

converted with his whole heart, he does not think of that, because he is sternly warned how wrong that would be. But, if he is not sincere and 'seeks the things that are his own, not the things that are Jesus Christ's,'[8] he would surely not have charity, and 'what does it profit him if he should distribute all his goods to the poor and deliver his body to be burned?'[9] An additional consideration, as we have already agreed, is that it is possible to avoid this difficulty for the future and to deal with the one who is converted, by not permitting him to join the society of the brethren until he has stripped himself of all his possessions, and is directed in the way of peace, once his property has ceased to be his. But this death[10] of the weak, and this great obstacle to the salvation of those whom we labor so earnestly to win to the Catholic fold, cannot otherwise be avoided unless they understand very clearly that we are not at all concerned about money in such cases. They will never understand this unless we leave to their use the money which they have always thought belonged to the priest; if it was not his, they should have known this from the beginning.

It seems to me, then, that this is the rule to be followed in situations of this sort: Whenever a cleric possesses property by the usual law of possession, the property belongs to the church in which he has been ordained, wherever that may be. Therefore, we must deal with that property of the priest Honoratus,[11] which is in question, by this same rule. As he was not only ordained elsewhere, but had previously been a member of the monastery at Tagaste, if he died without selling his property or transferring it to someone else by an attested gift, only his heirs have a right to inherit it, as brother

---

8 Cf. Phil. 2.21.
9 Cf. Cor. 13.3.
10 I.e., the death of the soul. Such scandal might result in apostasy in those of weak faith.
11 This is the priest who had been a monk and whose property was claimed by the church at Thiave and the monastery at Tagaste.

Aemilian[12] fell heir to those thirty soldi[13] of brother Privatus. These precautions must be taken beforehand, but, if they have not been taken, it will be advisable to follow the laws which have been enacted to regulate the possession or non-possession of such property according to the usages of civil society. As far as it is possible for us, let us refrain not only from the actuality but even from the appearance of wrongdoing, so as to guard the good reputation so indispensable to our ministry. Your holy Prudence should take note of how harmful that appearance can be. Leaving to one side their disappointment, which we have experienced, and to avoid being led astray myself, as is apt to happen when I am too prone to follow my own erroneous opinion, I told the whole story to our brother and colleague Samsucius,[14] not at first saying what I thought, but rather adding what we both decided when we first opposed them. He was greatly horrified, and he was surprised at our approving this, being chiefly moved by the appearance of something base in it, something most unworthy not only of ours, but of anybody's life and character.

Therefore, I beg you not to delay in sending the letter which I have written, signed with our joint names. And if, by scrutinizing it carefully, you perceive that this is just, do not let the weak be forced to learn now what I myself do not yet understand, but let what the Lord said be applied to them in this case: 'I have many things to say to you but you cannot bear them now.'[15] No doubt, it was in consideration of such

---

12 This was probably one of those stock examples used to solve cases of canon law.
13 The solidus was a gold coin introduced by the emperors and worth about twenty-five denarii. The whole sum in question would be $120.
14 Bishop of Turres, a Numidian town. Cf. Letter 62.
15 John 16.12.

weakness that He said this about paying the tribute: 'Then the children are free: but that we may not scandalize them'[16] and the rest, when He sent Peter to pay the tax which was then required. For He was acquainted with another law by which he owed no such tax, but He had Peter pay the tribute for Him by the same law by which we said that the heir of the priest Honoratus would have inherited from him, if he died before he could either give away or sell his property. Moreover, even in the law of the Church the Apostle Paul is considerate of the weak and does not exact the tithes due, although assured by his conscience that he could exact them with perfect justice,[17] but he avoided even so much as a suspicion which could taint the good odor of Christ. He refrained from anything which could give the appearance of avarice in those places where he knew it was wise to do so, and perhaps even before he had experienced the harshness of men. But let us remedy, somewhat late and after experience, what we should have provided against at first.

Finally, because I fear everything and I remember what you suggested at our departure, that the brothers of Tagaste should hold me responsible for half of that sum, if you see clearly that such an arrangement is just, I do not refuse, except on the condition that, when I have the money, I will pay it, and that will be when a similar sum accrues to the monastery at Hippo, provided it can be done without pinching, and that an equal part of that sum shall be deducted in proportion to the number of monks living there, and shall accrue to ours.

---

16 Matt. 17.25,26.
17 1 Cor. 9.1-15.

84. Augustine and the brethren who are with me give greetings in the Lord to the blessed lord and esteemed and cherished brother and fellow priest, Novatus,[1] and the brethren who are with you (c. 405; before 411)

I also feel how hard-hearted I seem to be, and I can scarcely bear my own conduct in not sending to your Holiness your brother, the deacon Lucillus, my son,[2] and allowing him to be with you. But, when you also begin to assign to the necessities of churches located far from you some of your dearest and sweetest nurslings, then you will feel with what pangs of longing I am torn, because some of those who are bound to me by ties of the strongest and sweetest friendship are not physically present with me. Suppose I send your relative far away; however much the tie of blood prevails, it does not surpass the bond of friendship, by which brother Severus[3] and I are joined, yet you know how seldom it falls to my lot to see him. Certainly it is neither by his will nor mine, but because we sacrifice the needs of our own time to the requirements of Mother Church, in view of the life to come where we shall be together forever. How much more reasonable is it for you to bear the absence, for the sake of the same Mother Church, of the brother with whom you have not fed in the Lord's pasture as long as I have with my most sweet fellow citizen Severus, who converses with me only now and again in scanty little notes. And even those too full of other cares and transactions to be the bearers of any fruit of our meadows in the sweetness of Christ!

Hereupon you will probably say: 'What of it? Will my brother not be as useful to the Church here with me, or do I

---
1 Bishop of Sitif, a town on the border of Mauretania.
2 I.e., his spiritual son. He evidently belonged to the diocese of Hippo.
3 Bishop of Milevis. Cf. Letter 62.

long to have him with me for any other reason?' Obviously, if his presence seemed as useful to me there as here, for gaining or ruling over the sheep of the Lord, anyone might justly blame me for my hardness of heart, not to say my injustice. But when it is a case of speaking Latin,[4] and the ministry of the Gospel is greatly hampered by a scarcity of that ability in our part of the world—where you are, its use is general—do you think it is right for us, who have to provide for the welfare of the people of the Lord, to send that ability there and take it away from here, where its lack causes us great grief of heart? Be indulgent to me, then, because I am acting against my own feelings as well as against your desire, and it is my burden of care which forces me to do it. The Lord, upon whom you have set your heart, will grant that your own labors will be such as to reward you for this generosity; you will be the one who has given the deacon Lucillus to the burning thirst of our lands, and you will win no little reward by not burdening me further with any request in this matter. So I shall seem no more than merely too severe to your respected and holy Benevolence.

85. *Augustine gives greeting in the Lord to Paul,[1] sincerely beloved lord, brother, and fellow priest, whose happiness he seeks in all his prayers (c. 405)*

You would not call me so unyielding if you did not think I was a liar. For, what else do you think of my dispositions when you write such things to me, except that there is in me

---

4 The reference to the ability to speak Latin points to a general use of Punic in Numidia at this time.

1 Bishop of Cataqua, an obscure African town, whose conduct was at variance with his sacred profession. Augustine here exhorts him to forsake worldly aims and return to a simple and austere life.

a knot of discord, and a detestable hatred against you, as if I were not in reality on my guard, 'Lest preaching to others, I myself be found a castaway,'[2] or that I should so wish to pluck the mote from your eye as to maintain a beam in my own?[3] It is not as you think. See, I tell you again, and I call God to witness, that if you wished for yourself all the good that I wish for you, you would long since have been living secure in Christ, and you would rejoice His whole Church in the glory of His Name. See how I have now written that you are not only my brother, but my colleague, also, and it would not be possible for any bishop of the Catholic Church to be my colleague, of whatever sort he were, if he were under any ecclesiastical censure. But there is no reason for my not communicating with you except that I cannot flatter you. Indeed, I am greatly in your debt, because I begot you in Christ Jesus through the Gospel, by truthfully chiding you with the life-giving sting of charity. My joy that many have been won by you to the Catholic Church by the help of the Lord is tempered by the grief consequent on so many being lost from it. For you have so wounded the Church at Hippo that, unless the Lord sets you free from all your worldly cares and burdens and calls you back to the true life and diet of a bishop, such a wound cannot be healed.

But, when you continue, even after your renunciation, to involve and implicate yourself more and more deeply in the things which you have renounced—something which cannot be excused in any way even according to human laws—and when the frugality of your Church does not satisfy your wants in that profession by which you are supposed to live, why do you seek close relations with me when you are not ready to listen to my chiding? Perhaps whatever you do is to be blamed on me by men whose complaints I cannot bear? It is useless

---
2 1 Cor. 9.27.
3 Matt. 7.4.; Luke 6.41,42.

for you to suspect that those who opposed you even in your former life are your detractors. That is not so, nor is it any wonder that many things are kept from you. But, even if it were true, there ought to be nothing in your conduct which they could find to criticize, and thereby blaspheme the Church. You still think, perhaps, that I say these things because I have not accepted your atonement, but I tell you that I would not be able to atone to God for my own sins if I passed over yours in silence. I know that you have a heart, but it is slothful and irresponsible when it is in heaven, and a wide-awake heart is nothing when it is on earth. The episcopate is not a device for passing through life on false pretenses. The Lord God will teach you what I say; He has closed to you all the ways on which you wished to travel by using Him for your purposes, so as to direct you, if you understand Him, into that way on which you are to travel, by means of the holy burden which is laid on you.

86. Augustine, the bishop, gives greeting in the Lord to Caecilian,[1] excellent lord, son truly and deservedly honored and cherished in the charity of Christ
(405)

The purity of your government, and the fame of your virtues, the praiseworthy diligence, also, of your Christian piety and your faithful uprightness—divine gifts granted you for your joy by Him from whom you hope for higher ones—have encouraged me to share with your Excellency the stormy state of my affairs. We are truly happy that you have provided for the restoration of Catholic unity with remarkable success in other parts of Africa, but we are equally grieved that Hippo

---

[1] Prefect of the Province of Africa. From the honorary titles given him it appears that the office must have been a high one.

Regius[2] and other territories of Numidia adjacent to it have not yet deserved to be helped by enforcement of your prefectural edict,[3] excellent lord, son truly and deservedly honored and cherished in the charity of Christ. I have thought it best not to conceal this from your Magnificence, so as not to be blamed for my negligence, since I bear the burden of being Bishop of Hippo. From my brothers and colleagues, who will be able to give the details to your Sublimity, or from the priest whom I have sent with letters, if you will deign to listen, you will learn the extent of the bold presumption of the heretics in the country of Hippo. And by the help of the Lord our God you will undoubtedly take measures to cure the swelling of this accursed pride, by the repression of fear, so as not to have to cut it out by measures of vengeance.

87. Augustine to his cherished and beloved brother Emeritus[1]
(c. 405; before 411)

When I hear that someone endowed with a good mind and trained in the liberal studies—although the salvation of the soul does not depend on that—has a view different from what truth requires on a very easy question, I both wonder and ardently desire to know the man and talk with him, or, if I cannot do that, I long at least to meet his mind and be met by his through letters which fly afar. I hear that you are such a man, and I grieve that you are severed and separated from the Catholic Church, which is spread through the whole world, as it was foretold by the Holy Spirit.[2] I do not know

---

2 Augustine's diocesan city.
3 For the suppression of the Donatists.

1 Emeritus of Caesarea in Mauretania, a Donatist bishop, one of the seven chosen to represent their sect at the Council of Carthage in 411.
2 Ps. 2.8.

why. For it is certain that a large part of the Roman world, not to mention the barbarian tribes to which the Apostle said he was also a debtor,[3] with whose Christian faith our own is intertwined, knows nothing of the sect of Donatus, nor have they any idea when or from what cause that dissension arose. Assuredly, unless you admit that all those Christians are innocent of the charges which you make against the Africans, you are forced to say that all of you are guilty of the evil deeds of all, since there lurk among you, to put it mildly, some abandoned characters. You do not expel anyone, or at least you only expel him when he has done something worthy of expulsion. Or is it that you do not condemn a man who has been in hiding for some time and is afterward betrayed and convicted? I ask, therefore, whether he contaminated you during the time he was in hiding? You will answer: 'Not at all.' Then, if he remained in hiding always, he would not contaminate you at all, for it often happens that after people die their deeds come to light, but this is no harm for the Christians who lived in contact with them during their lifetime. Why, then, have you, by a rash and accursed schism, cut yourselves off from communion with innumerable Eastern churches, which knew nothing of what happened in Africa according to what you teach or pretend?

Whether what you say is true is another question, while we prove your facts to be false by much more authoritative documents, and we hold that this is proved even better by your own documents, in regard to the charges which you make against us. But, as I said, this is another question, one to be taken up and discussed when need arises. Turn the attention of your mind now upon this: that no one can be contaminated by the unknown crimes of unknown people.[4] From this

---
3 Rom. 1.14.
4 The Donatists were the Puritans of their time, and the reason they alleged for their separation from the Catholic Church was the sup-

it is clear that you are separated by a sacrilegious schism from communion with the rest of the world, to which the charges, true or false, which you make against the Africans are completely unknown and have always been unknown. At the same time we must not fail to point out that even known malefactors do no harm to the good in the Church if there is no authority for excommunicating them, or if some consideration of keeping the peace has a prior claim. Who were those in the Prophet Ezechiel[5] who deserved to be marked with a sign before the slaughter of the wicked, and who escaped unharmed while the slaughter was going on, except those, as is clearly shown, who sighed and moaned over the sins and abominations of the people of God which were committed in their midst? For the same reason the Apostle Paul bore with false brethren; he was not speaking of unknown persons when he said: 'For all seek the things that are their own, not the things that are Jesus Christ's;'[6] and he shows that they were with him. Of what sort were those who preferred to offer incense to idols or to deliver up the sacred books rather than die, if they were not of those who 'seek the things that are their own, not the things that are Jesus Christ's'?

I pass over many proofs from the Scriptures, in order not to make my letter too long for its purpose, and I leave many things to your own learning, to be thought over by you privately. But I ask you to look into them adequately. If so many wicked men in the single people of God did not make those who testified against them[7] such as they were them-

---

posed corruption of the Church in Africa, or of some of its ministers or members. They thought to maintain their own 'purity' by separation, claiming that they were contaminated by the acts of others. Augustine easily demolishes their contention by a *reductio ad absurdum*.
5 Ezech. 9.4-6.
6 Phil. 2.21.
7 2 Esdras 9.30.

selves; if that band of false brethren[8] did not make the Apostle Paul, who formed part of the same Church with them, one who sought the things that were his own, not the things that were Jesus Christ's—it is evident that a man is not changed because some sinner approaches the altar of God with him; and this is true even if the sinner is not unknown, provided he is not approved, and that he is held at a distance by the displeasure of a good conscience. Obviously, then, to run with a thief[9] is nothing else than to steal with him, or to receive his stolen goods with pleasure. We say this to do away with endless and pointless questions about the deeds of men which do not affect our argument.

But all of you, unless you agree to this, will become such as you know Optatus[10] was—a fate which I hope will not come upon a man of such character as Emeritus, and others like him, because I am sure there are some who are far removed from conduct like this. The only charge we make against you is that of schism, which you have brought about by a wrong persistence in heresy. Read, as I am sure you have read, what account divine judgment makes of that crime. You will find that Dathan and Abiron, and all who agreed with them, were swallowed up by a chasm in the earth, and consumed by fire which rose in their midst.[11] By immediate punishment, the Lord God pointed out an example to be avoided, but in such way as to show what final judgment He reserves for those whom He now treats with the utmost patience. If you are such as rumor makes you out to be, and God knows I believe and wish it so, we do not blame your motives, if at the time when Optatus was boasting of the unbridled fury of his power, when the lamentation of all Africa was his accuser, with you for additional mourners—no, we

---

8 Gal. 2.4; 2 Cor. 11.26.
9 Ps. 49.18.
10 Cf. Letter 51, Vol. 1, p. 241.
11 Num. 16.27-35.

do not blame you for not wishing to excommunicate him at that time, lest he should drag many with him in his excommunication, and rend your communion with the violence of schism. But what stands against you in the judgment of God, brother Emeritus, is this: that, when you saw it was so great an evil for the sect of Donatus to be torn asunder, that it seemed better to tolerate Optatus in your communion rather than admit this, you still persisted in that evil which was committed by your predecessors when they broke away from the Church of Christ.

Here, perhaps, under the compulsion of making some answer, you will defend Optatus. Do not do it, my brother, I beg of you; do not do it. It does not befit you, and, if it were fitting for anyone else by any chance, if it were even fitting for bad men to defend anything, it certainly is not fitting for Emeritus to defend Optatus. But perhaps it is not fitting to accuse him. That may be. Follow a middle course and say: 'Everyone bears his own burden.'[12] 'Who art thou that judgest another man's servant?'[13] If, then, according to the testimony of all Africa, nay, rather, of the whole world, wherever the fame of Gildo[14] blazed, as soon as he had become known, you never dared to judge Optatus, how is it that we can or ought finally to bring a rash sentence—at least according to your testimony—on those who have lived before us, and that it is not enough for you to accuse the unknown, but we must also judge the unknown? Even supposing Optatus was a victim of false hatred, you are not defending him but yourself when you say: 'I do not know what he was like.' How much less does the Eastern world know what the Africans were like, whom you accuse, though quite unknown! Yet you cut yourselves off, by a wicked dissension, from

---
12 Gal. 6.5.
13 Rom. 14.4.
14 Count of Africa, called the Tyrant, who favored the Donatists and was in collusion with Optatus.

those churches whose names you have in your books, and which you read aloud. If your notorious and ill-famed bishop of Tamugada[15] was not known to his contemporary colleague of Sitif,[16] not to mention Caesarea,[17] how could the betrayers among the Africans,[18] whoever they may have been, have been known to the churches of the Corinthians, the Ephesians, the Colossians, the Philippians, the Thessalonians, the Antiochenes, the Pontians, the Cappadocians and people of the other parts of the world, evangelized by the Apostles and brought to Christ, or how did they deserve to be condemned by you if they could not have been known? Yet you are not in communion with them, and you say that they are not Christians, and you attempt to rebaptize them. What more is to be said? It makes me want to complain and to cry out. If I am speaking to a man of fine feeling, I share with you the darts of my indignation, for you undoubtedly see what I would say if I were willing to say it.

But, perhaps your elders held a council among themselves, and condemned all of the Christian world except themselves? Has your credit in the matter fallen so low that the council of the Maximianists,[19] which was a schism from your schism, and very few in comparison with you, did not prevail against you, yet your council prevails against the Gentiles, the inheritance of Christ and the utmost parts of the earth His possession?[20] I marvel how anyone who has blood in his body does not blush at this. Answer these arguments, please; for I have heard from some persons whom I cannot but believe that you will answer if I write to you. I sent you one letter some time ago, but whether you received it and have an-

---
15 Numidian town, of which Optatus was the Donatist bishop.
16 A Mauretanian town.
17 The town in Mauretania of which Optatus was the Donatist bishop.
18 This supposed vice of betrayal of the sacred books under persecution, not proved, was the alleged reason for the Donatist schism.
19 Cf. Letter 43, Vol. 1, p. 205.
20 Cf. Ps. 2.8.

swered it—I have not received yours—I do not know. But I ask you now, in the meantime, not to refuse to answer this, according to your opinion. But do not raise up other questions, for that would be the beginning of a most complicated investigation into the origin of the schism.

Even the secular powers, when they prosecute schismatics, protect themselves by the rule formulated by the Apostle: 'He that resisteth the power, resisteth the ordinance of God. And they that resist, purchase to themselves damnation; for princes are not a terror to the good work, but to the evil. Wilt thou then not be afraid of the power? Do that which is good; and thou shalt have praise from the same: for he is God's minister to thee for good. But if thou do that which is evil, fear; for he beareth not the sword in vain. For he is God's minister, an avenger to wrath upon him that doth evil.'[21] Therefore, the whole question is whether schism is not evil, or whether you have not made a schism, so that you resist the powers for a good work, not for an evil, by which you might purchase to yourselves damnation. Consequently, it was most providential that the Lord did not say: 'Blessed are they that suffer persecution' only, but added: 'for justice' sake.'[22] If you acted for justice' sake when you accomplished that dissension, in which you persist, according to what I said above, I should like to know it from you. But, is it an injustice to condemn the Christian world without a hearing, either because it has not heard what you have heard, or because what you believe without reason and assert without documentary evidence has not been proved to it? Is it an injustice, therefore, to wish to rebaptize so many churches founded by the preaching and labor of the Lord Himself in the flesh and of His Apostles? Is it allowed you not to know your wicked African colleagues, living at the same time with you, and administer-

---
21 Rom. 13.2-4.
22 Matt. 5.10.

ing the sacraments, or to know, but to tolerate them, so as to prevent division in the sect of Donatus, while those established in the most remote part of the world are not to be allowed not to know what you either know or believe or have heard or imagine about the Africans? What perversity is so great as to love one's own wickedness and to lay the blame on the severity of the powers?

'But it is not allowed Christians to prosecute the wicked.' Very well, suppose it is not allowed; does that make it right to oppose the powers which are set up for that purpose? Or shall we erase the Apostle? Do your books contain what I quoted a while ago? 'But,' you will say, 'you ought not to be in communion with such persons.' What then? Were you not in communion with Flavian,[23] formerly vicar, a man of your sect, when, to keep the law, he killed some whom he found doing harm? You will say: 'But you appealed to the Roman rulers against us.' No; rather, you appealed to them against yourselves when you dared to wound the Church with schism—the Church of which they are now the members, as was foretold long ago, 'And all the kings of the earth shall adore him,'[24]—and you still persist in rebaptizing. But ours seek protection from the legitimate powers against the lawless and secret violence of yours, something which you, who do not do such things, grieve and lament over. And they do it, not to persecute you, but to defend themselves, as the Apostle Paul acted against the Jews who were conspiring to kill him, before the Roman Empire was Christian, when he asked to be given the protection of an armed guard.[25] But those rulers above-mentioned, knowing, on any given occasion, the wickedness of your schism, enact against you what they will, in accord with their responsibility and power. For they bear not

---

23 The vicar of prefects, who, although a Donatist, carried out the imperial laws requiring all basilicas to be given up to the Catholics.
24 Ps. 71.11.
25 Acts 23.12-24.

the sword in vain, they are the ministers of God, avengers unto wrath against those who do evil. Finally, if any of ours act in this matter with an unchristian lack of moderation, it does not please us. But we do not on that account leave the Catholic Church, because we are not able to cleanse the threshing floor before the last time of the winnowing,[26] whereas you did not leave the sect of Donatus because of Optatus, when you did not dare to expel him.

'But why do you want us to be joined to you if we are wicked?' Because you are still living and capable of correction, if you wish it. For, when you are joined to us, that is, the Church of God, the inheritance of Christ, whose possession is the ends of the earth,[27] then you are corrected so as to live in the root. The Apostle has this to say of broken branches: 'For God is able to graft them in again.'[28] You therefore are changed from that sect by which you are separated, although the sacraments which you have are holy, since they are the same in all. That is why we wish you to be won away from your false position, so that your cut-off branches may be again rooted. The sacraments, which you have not changed, are approved by us as you have them; so, when we wish to correct your aberration, we must guard against doing a sacrilegious wrong to those mysteries of Christ which have not been vitiated by your vice. For, Saul did not vitiate the anointing which he had received, when King David, the devout servant of God, did such honor to it.[29] We do not rebaptize you when we wish to restore you to the root, because we approve the form of the lopped-off branch, if it is not changed, which, however, even when intact, is anything but fruitful without a root. It is one question about the persecutions which you say you suffered even under our mildness and tolerance, when

---

26 Matt. 3.12.
27 Ps. 2.8.
28 Rom. 11.23.
29 2 Kings 1.1-16.

your adherents individually committed such gravely unlawful acts, but baptism is another question, since we do not look to see where it is, but where it is validly. Wherever it is, it is itself, but the one who receives it is not himself wherever he is. Therefore, in schism, we detest the individual wickedness of men, but we honor the baptism of Christ everywhere; so, for example, if deserters from an army carry off with them the standards of their commander, if the standards have remained safe they are recovered whether the deserters have been condemned to punishment or won back by clemency. If there is to be a more searching examination into this matter, that, as I said, is another question. In dealing with these things we are to follow the practice of the Church.

It is asked whether your church or ours is the Church of God. You should ask your leader why you have fallen into schism. If you do not answer me, I shall have no further responsibility before God, as I believe, because I have sent peaceful letters to a man who, as I have heard, is a good man—except for schism—and a well-educated one. You will have to see what you can answer to Him whose praiseworthy patience you now experience, but whose sentence you will have to fear at the end. If you will answer with the same care with which you see this is written, the mercy of God will not be wanting, and the error which now separates us will fade away because of our love of peace and respect for truth. Remember that I have said nothing about the Rogatists,[30] who are said to call you Firmians,[31] just as you call us Macarians.[32] And I do not mention your bishop of Rusucada,[33] who is

---

30 A Mauretanian sect, split off from the Donatists, of mild character, which did not use violence. They were followers of Rogatus of Cartenna, and were persecuted by Optatus.
31 Followers of Firmus, a Mauretanian chieftain who revolted against the Roman power, proclaimed himself emperor, and allied himself with the Donatists (366-372).
32 Cf. Letter 23, Vol. 1, p. 63.
33 A Numidian town.

reported to have bargained with Firmus for the safety of his own flock, as the price of opening the gates and betraying the Catholics to slaughter, and innumerable other instances. Cease, then, to magnify the deeds of men, either heard or known, into general statements, for you see that I pass over your deeds, so as to argue the case about the origin of the schism, which is the heart of the whole question. May the Lord God breathe peaceful thoughts into you, beloved and desired brother. Amen.

88. The Catholic clergy of the region of Hippo Regius to Januarius[1] (406)

Your clerics and Circumcellions[2] are raging against us with a persecution of a new sort and of an unspeakable cruelty. If ours were to return evil for evil, they would act thus against the law of Christ; but now, comparing your actions and ours, we are found to suffer what is written: 'They repaid me evil for good,'[3] and in another psalm: 'With them that hated peace, I was peaceable: when I spoke to them, they fought against me without cause.'[4] But, since you have now reached such an advanced age, we think that you must know perfectly well that the sect of Donatus, which was first called the sect of Maiorinus[5] at Carthage, made a gratuitous accusation against Caecilian,[6] then Bishop of Carthage, to the emperor of that time, Constantine. But, fearing that your Gravity

---

1 Donatist bishop of Casae Nigrae in Numidia, primate among Donatist bishops. Although this letter is written in the name of the clergy of Hippo, it is believed to be Augustine's composition, and the style is his.
2 Cf. Letter 23 n. 13.
3 Ps. 34.12.
4 Ps. 119.6.
5 Cf. Letter 43, Vol. 1, p. 183.
6 *Ibid.*

might have forgotten this, or should pretend that you know it, or even—which we do not believe—that it happens that you do not know it, we are enclosing in our letter a copy of the account given by Anulinus, then proconsul, whom the faction of Maiorinus appealed to at that time, with the request that the charges which they were making against Caecilian be sent by the same proconsul to the above-mentioned emperor.

'Anulinus, of consular rank, proconsul of Africa, to our emperors.

'My devotion has been careful to include among the acts of my insignificance the divine decrees[7] of your Majesty, which have been received and communicated to Caecilian, and those who serve under him, who are called clerics; and I have urged them to bring about unity by general agreement, and, making full use of every privilege of your Majesty's kindness, to show themselves free to devote themselves to the divine service, with all due reverence, and with regard for the sanctity of Catholic law. But a few days later there arose certain ones, who had gathered a crowd of people around them, who thought that Caecilian should be opposed, and who offered to my reverence[8] a document sealed in a pouch, and a booklet not sealed, and they asked very earnestly that I should direct it to the sacred and venerable court of your Divinity. With Caecilian remaining in his position, and the acts thereof hereunto appended, my insignificance has taken steps to send these, so that your Majesty may judge of all. The two documents transmitted are: one in a pouch inscribed thus: "Docu-

---

7 According to these decrees of Constantine (313), all clerics were to be freed of all public duties and burdens, so as to be able to apply themselves to their priestly duties. The use of the word 'divine' here, as of 'divinity' below, in speaking of the emperor, shows that the terminology used by and of the pagan emperors had not yet been discontinued.
8 A title used by an inferior to a superior, but not commonly used by an official in speaking of himself.

ment of charges against Caecilian of the Catholic Church, offered by the sect of Maiorinus"; the other without seal, attached to the same pouch. Given on the fifteenth day of April, at Carthage, in the third consulship of our lord Constantine.'[9]

After this account had been sent to him, the emperor ordered both sides to come to Rome to have a hearing before a court of bishops. The ecclesiastical annals tell how the case was tried and completed, with Caecilian declared innocent. That was surely the time, after a peaceful settlement by a court of bishops, for all the persistent quarreling and hatred to be extinguished. But your predecessors went back again to the emperor and complained that the whole case had not been heard, and that the decision was unjust. Thereupon he granted them another court of bishops to be held at Arles, in the state of Gaul, and after their vain and diabolical dissension had been condemned, many of yours returned to agreement with Caecilian, but others, extremely persistent and quarrelsome, appealed to the same emperor. Under this compulsion he put an end to the case, as tried by the bishops and recognized by both sides, and for the first time issued a law against your sect, that the places of worship of your congregations should be confiscated. But, if we were to include the reports of all these actions, we should make our letter much too long. However, there is one thing which must by no means be passed over, and that is the way in which the case of Felix of Aptunga[10] was discussed and settled by a public verdict. He is the one whom your founders held to be the source of the whole trouble, when a council was held at

---

9 This was the year 313. Even after the disappearance of the Republic, the Romans went on counting by consulships. The document ends here.
10 Cf. Letter 43, Vol. 1, p. 184.

LETTERS 25

Carthage, on the call of Secundus of Tigisis,[11] the primate, at the time when yours were putting pressure on the emperor. For the above-mentioned emperor testified in his letters that yours had been the accusers and constant appellants in this case. We hereinafter add copies of these.

'Flavius Constantine Maximus and Valerius Licinianus, Emperors and Caesars,[12] to Probianus, proconsul of Africa.[13]

'While the most excellent Verus, vicar of prefects,[14] was incapacitated by ill health, Aelianus, your predecessor, exercised authority over those territories, and, among other things, he believed that this business or ill will which seems to have been stirred up about Caecilian, a bishop of the Catholic Church, should also be referred to his inquiry and authority. Therefore, when he had commanded the presence of Superius, the centurion,[15] Caecilian, the city-ruler of Aptunga,[16] Saturninus, the former city clerk,[17] and Calibius the younger, city clerk of

---

11 *Ibid.* He was primate in Numidia. This was in 315.
12 Diocletian had introduced the principle of co-emperors. Two highest were to be called Augusti, two lesser ones were Caesars. These latter had active leadership in the army. The system was finally abolished when Constantine became sole ruler.
13 Petronius Probianus, Governor of Africa in 315.
14 A Roman official in charge of several provinces. In Africa this was at least six. The Empire had been organized by Diocletian into 101 provinces, each under a governor; these were grouped into seventeen dioceses, each under a vicar of prefects; these in turn were grouped into four prefectures, each under an Augustus or a Caesar, and a praetorian prefect.
15 A military commander. He was probably called because the civil rulers had used military help in forcing the Christians to give up the sacred books.
16 Not Bishop Caecilian. This one was Alfius Caecilianus, a member of a two-man municipal government in Aptunga during the persecution. His letter to Felix is the one in question.
17 The ex-curator, probably a sort of clerk of records, is otherwise called Calidius or Claudius Saturianus. Here is an instance of the breaking down of the old Roman family names. Calibius Junior is also called Calidius Gratianus. He was curator in 314.

the same city, and the civil servant Solus,[18] he held a valid hearing, with the result that, when it was objected against Caecilian that the episcopacy had seemingly been conferred on him by Felix, who was accused of an alleged betrayal and burning of the sacred Scriptures, it appeared that Felix was innocent of that charge. Finally, when Maximus[19] charged that Ingentius,[20] a municipal senator of the city of Ziquensis,[21] had forged a letter of Caecilian, the former city-ruler, we discovered by the records which were at hand that the same Ingentius had been removed, but had not been tortured, because he admitted that he was a senator of Ziquensis. Therefore, we wish that you send the same Ingentius, under a suitable escort, to the court of Constantine Augustus, so that it may be possible, in the hearing and presence of those who appear before us and do not cease daily to appeal, to make it clear and to publish that they have tried in vain to stir up ill will against Bishop Caecilian and to revolt against him. So it will happen that, by putting an end to all disturbances of this sort, the people without any dissension may apply themselves to the practice of their own religion with due reverence.'

When you see the facts, how it is that you can stir up ill will against us about the edicts of the emperors which are enacted against you, when you first did this whole thing yourselves? If emperors ought not to take any action in these matters, if Christian emperors ought not to have anything to do with these things, who forced your predecessors to send the case of Caecilian to the emperor through the proconsul? Who forced them again to accuse the bishop to the emperor—after they

---

18 He was probably called at this time to take down the minutes of what occurred. This Solus is also called Solon. These civil servants could serve in almost any capacity.
19 Probably the investigator.
20 A decurion or member of a municipal senate or commission.
21 A city in the Province of Africa.

had in a sense already passed sentence on him in his absence? And when his ordaining Bishop Felix had been declared innocent, who forced them to manufacture other false charges against him to the same emperor? And now, what else but the verdict of the great Constantine himself stands against your sect, a verdict which your predecessors chose, which they extorted by continued appeals, which they preferred to the verdict of the court of bishops? If the imperial decrees displease you, who first roused the emperors to set these in motion against you? When you cry out against the Catholic Church because the emperors issue edicts against you, it is as if those who first wanted Daniel to be devoured by the lions should cry out against him because, when he had been delivered, they were thrown in to be devoured by the same lions,[22] for it is written: 'There is no difference between the threats of a king and the anger of the lion.'[23] His evil-hearted enemies had Daniel thrown into the lions' den; his innocence prevailed over their wickedness. He was drawn out unharmed; they were thrown in and destroyed. In like manner, your predecessors exposed Caecilian and his congregation to the king's wrath to be consumed by it; when his innocence had been set free, you suffered the same things from the same kings which yours wanted them to suffer, since it is written: 'He that prepareth a pit for his neighbor, shall himself fall into it.'[24]

You have no complaint to make of us, and the mildness of the Church would even have allowed these decrees of the emperors to remain inactive, if your clerics and Circumcellions had not forced their revival and renewal against you, because of your inhuman cruelties and raging violence, which disturb and ravage our peace. For, before these more recent

---

22 Dan. 6.16-24.
23 Cf. Prov. 19.12.
24 Cf. Eccli. 27.29.

laws of which you complain had come into Africa, your people had laid traps along the roads for our bishops; they had beaten our fellow clerics with monstrous blows; they had inflicted horrible wounds on our laymen also and set fire to their buildings. And when a certain priest, of his own free will, had chosen the unity of our communion, they tore him from his house, beat him savagely without let or hindrance, rolled him in a muddy ditch, made a display of him, clothed in a mat of rushes—an object of grief to some, of mirth to others—as if to boast of their crime; dragged him around according to their whim, and let him go after something like twelve days. Then, according to the city records, Proculeianus[25] was summoned by our bishop, and, when they had made excuses to be let off from an investigation into their case, and he was summoned again and again, he announced that he would say nothing more than was in the records. Those who did this are today your priests, and they are still terrorizing and persecuting us to the utmost of their power.

Nevertheless, our bishop did not complain to the emperors of these wrongs and persecutions which the Catholic Church in our territory then bore. But he decided to hold a council,[26] so as to meet your followers peaceably, and if possible to provide for a general meeting with you, to remove your error and allow fraternal charity to rejoice in the bond of peace.[27] Let the public records enlighten your Gravity as to what Proculeianus first answered: namely, that you would hold a council and would see what you ought to answer; but, afterward, when he had been summoned again in virtue of his promise, he expressed himself, according to the records, as being opposed to a peaceful meeting. In the next place, when the savagery of your clerics and Circumcellions, only too well

---
25 Cf. Letter 33.
26 At Carthage in 403.
27 Eph. 4.3.

known to all, did not cease, an accusation was filed against Crispinus,[28] and he was adjudged a heretic,[29] but the fine of ten pounds of gold prescribed by the emperors was not permitted to be levied against him, by reason of the Catholic policy of mildness. In spite of this, he saw fit to appeal to the emperors. This was the reply to the appeal; was it not the previous violent behavior of your sectaries, and their own appeal that brought down this penalty on them? But, even after this answer, he did not have to pay the fine in gold, because of the intervention of our bishops with the emperor. Our bishops then agreed to send envoys to the court, to ask that not all the bishops and clerics of your sect should be subject to the fine of ten pounds of gold which was prescribed against all heretics, but only those in whose localities the Catholic Church had had to suffer acts of violence from your people. But when the envoys came to Rome, the fresh and shocking scars of the Catholic Bishop of Bagai[30] so affected the emperor that laws were again passed such as had been passed previously. But, when these came into Africa, at a time when you were beginning to be persuaded to good rather than to evil, what else was there for you to do but to send to our bishops and arrange to have a meeting with them, as you had yourselves just met, and so allow the truth to appear by an open discussion?

But you were so far from doing it that your people are now doing even worse things to us. They not only beat us with

---

28 A Donatist bishop, the first to be declared heretic as well as schismatic.
29 Up to this time the Donatists had been considered schismatics, or separatists, but not heretics. The former did not deny or question dogma, but resisted authority in the Roman Catholic Church. For this reason, their conferring of Orders was considered valid, and their reconciliation with the Church was a fairly simple matter. Heretics were regarded as enemies of the state as well as of the Church, hence the penalty inflicted by the secular power.
30 Maximian; not to be confused with the schismatic who gave his name to the Maximianists.

clubs and stab us with swords, but, with an unspeakable refinement of cruelty, they try to blind us by throwing into our eyes lime mixed with vinegar. They pillage our homes, and they have made for themselves dangerous and terrible weapons, armed with which they run here and there, threatening and breathing out murder, rapine, fire, blindness. We have been forced by these excesses to complain first to you, that your Gravity may consider how many of yours—or even all of you—who say that you suffer persecution under these supposedly terrible laws of the Catholic emperors are now living in safety in your possessions—and those of others—while we suffer such indescribable wrongs at your hands. You say that you suffer persecution, and we are beaten by your armed bands with clubs and swords; you say that you suffer persecution, and our homes are robbed and ravaged by your armed bands; you say that you suffer persecution, and our eyes are put out by your armed bands with lime and vinegar; besides, if yours meet death at their own hands,[31] it is because they wish to bring hatred to us and glory to you. What they do to us they do not blame on themselves; what they do to themselves, they blame on us. They live as brigands, they die as Circumcellions, they are honored as martyrs—yet we have never heard that those whom they robbed had blinded the brigands. They bear the slain away from the light;[32] they do not take light away from the living.

Meanwhile, if ever we hold any of yours, we preserve them unharmed with great affection; we speak to them and read to

---

[31] The Circumcellions frequently committed suicide by throwing themselves over precipices or into fire or water, or even by hiring or forcing people to kill them. Their adherents tried to make out that this kind of death was martyrdom, and they attempted to honor them as martyrs. The practice went to such extremes that the Donatists themselves had to forbid their sectaries to honor the supposed relics of such false martyrs.

[32] I.e., bury them. Burying the dead is one of the corporal works of mercy.

them whatever can prove the error which separates brother from brother; we do what the Lord commanded through the Prophet Isaias: 'Hear the word of the Lord, you who tremble; say: "you are our brothers" to those who hate you and curse you; that the name of the Lord may be glorified, and he may appear to them in their joy; but let them blush.'[33] Thus we welcome some of them who consider the evidence of truth and the beauty of peace to the charity of the Holy Spirit and the body of Christ; not by baptism, since they had already received its royal mark, but as deserters returned to the faith which was lacking to them. For it is written: 'Purifying their hearts by faith,'[34] and it is likewise written: 'Charity covereth a multitude of sins.'[35] But, if they refuse to join the unity of Christ through excessive hardness of heart, or through shame at facing the insults of those with whom they uttered so many false charges against us, and thought up so many abusive acts, or, even more, through fear of suffering at our hands the same sort of things they inflicted on us, we let them go as unharmed as we held them. We urge the same course on our laymen, as far as we can: to hold them unhurt and bring them to us to be corrected and instructed. Some of them listen to us and do that, if they can; others deal with them as with robbers, because that is truly the way they act; some ward off their blows from their own bodies by threatening to strike back if they are hit by them; others catch them and bring them to the judges, and show them no mercy, even when we intercede for them, because they fear to suffer such inhuman injuries from them. In all these cases they do not forswear the conduct of brigands, yet they expect the honor due to martyrs.

This, then, is our great desire, which we make known to

---
33 Cf. Isa. 66.5.
34 Acts 15.9.
35 1 Peter 4.8.

your Gravity through these letters, and through the brothers whom we are sending: first, if possible, that you consult peaceably with our bishops, and where error is found, the error, not the man, should be removed; that your people should not be punished, but corrected; that you now join in a meeting which you have previously scorned to do. How much better for you to do this among yourselves, and to send a written and sealed account to the emperor of what you have done, rather than allow it to be settled by the secular power, which can only enforce the laws it has already passed against you! For your colleagues, who traveled across the sea, said before the prefects that they had come to be heard, and they named our holy father, the Catholic Bishop Valentine,[36] who was then at court, saying that they wished to be heard by him; but the judge could not grant them this according to the laws which had been enacted against you. Besides, he had not come for that purpose, nor had he received any such mandate from his fellow bishops. How much better will the emperor himself, who is not subject to the same laws and who has it in his power to enact other laws, be able to judge of the whole case, when your report has been read to him, even though the actual pleading of the case will be over! But our reason for wanting to confer with you is not to end the case a second time, but to prove to those who do not know it that it is indeed ended. And if our bishops should not wish to meet you, what do you lose thereby, or do you not rather gain, by making known your good will, and avoiding blame for your lack of confidence? Of course, you do not think such a meeting unpermissible, since you are not unaware that the Lord Christ spoke about the Law even with the Devil,[37] and that Paul

---

36 Probably one of the bishops who accompanied the Catholic group to Rome for this inquiry. There were to be ten from each side. The demand of the Donatists to have as judge one who was not officially appointed as such has the appearance of delaying tactics on their part.
37 Matt. 4.1-10.

conversed not only with the Jews, but also with Gentile philosophers of the sect of Stoics and Epicureans.[38] Perhaps those laws of the emperor do not allow you to meet our bishops? See, here in the meantime are our bishops, in the territory of Hippo, where we endure such wrongs from your people, meet them! How much more freely and licitly will your writings come to us through your delegates than their weapons have done!

Finally, through those same brothers of ours whom we have sent to you, send us back an answer in the same tone. But, if you refuse to do this, at least hear us, together with your own adherents, from whom we suffer so much. Show us the truth, for the sake of which you say that you suffer persecution, while we suffer such unbounded cruelty from you. If you prove us to be wrong, perhaps you will do us the favor of not rebaptizing us, in the belief that you may well grant to us—who were baptized by men never condemned by you—what you granted to those whom Felician of Musti and Praetextatus of Assur had baptized over so long a period; at the time when you were trying by judicial orders to drive from their basilicas those who were in communion with Maximian, men condemned by you explicitly and by name, at the Council of Bagai.[39] We can show you all these facts in the court and city records, where you suborned your own council, trying to prove to the judges that you were expelling schismatics from your schism from the basilicas. Yet, you who made a schism from the very seed of Abraham, in whom all nations are blessed,[40] would not be driven from the basilicas by judges, as you drove your own separatists, but by the very kings of the earth who adore Christ, in fulfillment of the prophecy, from

---
38 Acts 17.18.
39 Cf. Letter 51, Vol. 1, pp. 239-240.
40 Gen. 22.18.

whose presence you went back defeated when you accused Caecilian.

If, then, you will neither hear us nor teach us, come, or send someone to us in the territory of Hippo, to look upon that armed force of yours, although no soldier has ever added to his assortment of arms lime and vinegar for the eyes of barbarians. If you will not do this, at least write to them to put a stop to their murder, pillage, and blinding of us. We do not wish to say, 'Condemn them,' but you will see how it is possible that the brigands, whom we have just pointed out in your communion, do not defile you, yet the betrayers, whom you have never been able to prove, do defile us. Choose which of these alternatives you like, but, if you disregard our complaints, we shall still not regret having tried to act by peaceful means. The Lord will be with His Church, to make you regret having despised our humility.

89. Augustine gives greeting in the Lord to Festus,[1] beloved lord, honored and esteemed son (406)

If men make such efforts in behalf of their error and accursed dissension and false teaching—even when completely refuted—that they do not cease to threaten the Catholic Church and to lay snares for her, though she seeks only their

---

1 From the title Benignity used by Augustine—a title commonly used to laymen of rank or official position—from the various references in the letter to responsibility and authority, it appears that Festus was an official charged with the duty of putting into effect the imperial decrees against the Donatists. He was evidently not a purely local official and may have been Governor of the Province of Numidia or his deputy. From the controversial tone of the letter, it almost seems as if he were not a Catholic, or at least not a convinced one. However, he may merely have been unable to hold his own in argument against the Donatists, and the purpose of the letter is evidently twofold: to urge him to exercise his authority and to furnish him with material to use in argument.

salvation, how much more reasonable and even obligatory is it for those who spread the truth of Christian peace and unity —so evident, though all malign and restrain it—to work constantly and untiringly not only for the strengthening of those who are Catholics, but also for the correction of those who are not. For, if obstinacy aims at having unsurpassed strength, how great should be that of constancy which carries through its good work steadily and untiringly, and knows that it is pleasing to God and assuredly not displeasing to men of prudence!

Is there anything more unprofitable or more deliberately wrong than the conduct of the Donatists, who boast that they suffer persecution; who refuse to be abashed by the compulsion brought on them by their own wrong-doing, and even seek praise for it; and who are either strangely and wilfully blind, or with an execrable perversity pretend they do not know that true martyrs are those who suffer for a cause, not those who pay a penalty for crime? And I would say this even against those who are merely wrapped in the fog of heretical error, for which sacrilege they must pay a richly deserved penalty, though they may not have dared to harm anyone with mad violence. But what shall I say against those whose baneful perversity is either restrained by the fear of damnation or taught by exile how widespread the Church is, as was foretold, although they would rather attack than acknowledge it? And if what they suffer under a most merciful authority were to be compared with the acts which their unbridled fury commits, it would be easy to see who are to be called persecutors. The more a father and mother love their children, the more they oblige them to a good life, without any pretense; so, also, bad sons are shown by their abandoned life, which makes them persecute the faith of their parents more rabidly, even though they do not lay violent hands on them.

There are in existence, in the public records, most authentic documents, which you can read, if you will—in fact, I ask and urge you to read them—in which there is proof that the predecessors of those who first separated themselves from the peace of the Church dared gratuitously to accuse Caecilian to Emperor Constantine, through the agency of Anulinus, the governor. If they had won their case, what punishment would Caecilian have suffered from the emperor, other than the one which he decreed against them after they had lost it? But, no doubt, if their charges had been sustained, Caecilian and his colleagues would have been driven from the churches which they held—for the royal censure could not overlook the defeated party, if they went on resisting—and then those others[2] would have boasted of their foresight and their anxious care for the Church, as something worthy of public praise. But, now that they have lost because they could not prove their charges, they call it persecution when they are punished for their wickedness; they set no limit to their unchained fury; they even claim the glory of martyrdom, as if, indeed, the Christian Catholic emperors[3] were applying any other law against their obstinate malice than the verdict of Constantine. It was to his authority that the accusers of Caecilian appealed voluntarily; they so far preferred it to that of all the overseas bishops that they submitted an ecclesiastical case not to them but to him; and, when he allowed them a court of bishops at Rome and they first lost their case, they made a second accusation to him and were given a second trial by a court of bishops at Arles. From this they appealed to him personally, and, when the decision finally went against them, they persisted in their insubordination. I believe that, if the Devil himself had been so often adjudged wrong by the authority of a judge whom he had voluntarily chosen, he would not so shamelessly have persisted in his case.

---

2 The Donatists.
3 Honorius and Arcadius.

But, let us suppose that these were human decisions, and that possibly they were reached by connivance or misinformation or even by bribery; why, then, is the Christian world still accused and branded with charges of alleged betrayal? Surely, it neither could nor should give credence to defeated litigants in preference to properly selected judges! Those judges have their case before God, for good or ill, but what did the world-wide Church do—and this is why those others insist on rebaptism—except believe that in a case where it could not decide where the truth lay it was better to trust those who were capable of judging than those who refused to yield, even after they lost their case? O monstrous crime of all nations, which God promised should be blessed in the seed of Abraham,[4] and, as He promised, performed! When with one voice they said: 'Why do you wish to rebaptize us?' the answer was: 'Because you do not know who the betrayers of the sacred books were in Africa, and because in your ignorance you preferred to believe judges rather than accusers.' If a man is not attainted by another's crime, what is it to the rest of the world if someone commits a crime in Africa? If an unknown crime does not incriminate anyone, how could the world know the crime of either the judges or the accused? You who have a heart, give judgment. Is this the justice of heresy, that, because the world does not condemn an unknown crime, the sect of Donatus condemns the world without a hearing? Surely it is enough for the world to hold to the promises of God, and to see them fulfilled in itself, as the Prophets foretold so long ago, and to recognize the Church in the same Scriptures in which Christ its King is recognized. When we read in the Gospel the fulfillment of the prophecies of Christ, we perceive there, also, the fulfillment in the world of the prophecies concerning the Church.

Perhaps someone of the prudent will be impressed by the

---
4 Gen. 22.18.

common saying about baptism, that, when it is given by a good
man, it is the true baptism of Christ; whereas the Church of
the world holds to this most evident truth of the Gospel,
where John says: 'He who sent me to baptize with water,
said to me: He upon whom thou shalt see the Spirit descending as a dove and remaining upon Him, He it is that baptizeth with the Holy Spirit.'[5] Hence, the Church securely
puts her hope not in a man, lest she fall upon that sentence
in which it is written: 'Cursed be everyone that puts his hope
in man,'[6] but she puts her hope in Christ who took on the
form of a slave without losing the form of God,[7] of whom it
is written: 'He it is that baptizeth.' Therefore, whatever kind
of man is the minister of baptism and whatever burden he
bears, it is not he, but the One upon whom the dove descends,
He it is that baptizes. But those who hold foolish views fall
into such contradiction that they cannot escape from an absurd conclusion. For, when they admit that a baptism is valid
and true if administered by a person stained with crimes, but
whose guilt is concealed, we say to them: 'Who, then, baptizes?' and they can only say: 'God,' for they cannot assert
that an adulterer sanctifies anybody. So we answer them: 'If,
when a good man baptizes, he sanctifies, but when a man of
hidden guilt baptizes, it is not he but God who sanctifies, then
people who are baptized ought to wish rather to be baptized
by bad men whose guilt is hidden than by known good men;
for it is better to have God as sanctifier than any man, however good. If it is absurd that a person to be baptized should
choose to have it done by an adulterer of undisclosed guilt
rather than by a manifestly chaste man, the conclusion is unavoidable that baptism is valid whatever the character of the

---
5 Cf. John 33.1.
6 Cf. Jer. 17.5.
7 Phil. 2.6,7.

men who administer it, because 'He upon whom the dove descends, He it is that baptizes.'[8]

Yet, when a truth so clear strikes the ears and hearts of men, they are involved in such a whirlpool of evil habit that they choose to resist every sort of authority and reason sooner than submit. They resist in two ways: either by savagery or by inaction. What remedy can the Church then apply, seeking with maternal love the salvation of all, but buffeted about between the frenzied and the apathetic? Is it possible for her to despise them? Ought she leave them to themselves? She must necessarily be irksome to both groups, because she is hostile to neither. The frenzied are averse to being restrained, the apathetic do not want to be aroused; but her loving care continues to chastise the frenzied, to goad the indifferent, and to cherish both. Both are offended, but both are loved; both are angry at being disturbed as long as they are sick, but both, when healed, are grateful.

Finally, we do not, as they think and boast, receive them as they were, but entirely changed, because they do not begin to be Catholics until they have ceased to be heretics. And their sacraments, which they have in common with us, are no stumbling-block to us, because they are not human but divine. Their distinctive error, which they wrongly made their own, has to be removed, but not the sacraments which they have received as we have, but which they have and transmit to their own punishment, because they have them unworthily. Still, they do have them. Therefore, when their error has been renounced, and the wrongfulness of their separation has been corrected, they come over from heresy to the peace of the Church, which they did not have, and without which all that

---

8 They could make this choice voluntarily, because infant baptism was not insisted on in the early Church, and many people deferred baptism until late in life. Augustine himself was over thirty when he was baptized.

they had was ruinous to them. But, if their conversion is not sincere, the judgment on that is not ours but God's; as a matter of fact, some who were thought to be insincere, on the ground that they had come over to us through fear of the government edicts, were later proved in various trials, and came out better than some Catholics of long standing. Immediate action is not necessarily unprofitable action. The wall of hard custom is not breached by merely human terrors; the faith and understanding of the mind have to be strengthened by divine authority and reason.

In view of all this, your Benignity will know that your people who are in the territory of Hippo are still Donatists, and that your letters have not had any effect on them. There is no need of writing why they have not been effective, but, send one of your servants or friends on whose fidelity you can rely, and do not let him go to those places, but come first to us without their knowing anything about it, and after we have talked over a plan between us, let him, with the Lord's help, do whatever it will seem best to do. And what we do when we do it is to be not only for them, but also for ours who have just become Catholics, and who are endangered by their nearness to those others. That is why we cannot overlook them. I have been able to write only thus briefly, but I wanted you to have a letter from me so that you would know the reason for my anxiety, and also that you might have something to answer to anyone who might try to dissuade you from working toward the correction of your people, or calumniate us for wishing such measures taken. If my effort is useless because you have either heard all this already, or thought it out for yourself, or if I have been an annoyance, interrupting one so occupied with public cares, with a long-winded letter, I ask your pardon, provided you do not spurn what I have asked and suggested. May the mercy of God keep you.

LETTERS

90. Nectarius[1] to Bishop Augustine, illustrious lord and deservedly cherished brother (408; after June 1)

You know how great is the love of country, so I say nothing of it. It is the only love which rightly surpasses that for parents. If there were any limit or legitimate restriction on our duty to serve our country,[2] we might honorably retire from public office. But, since our love and devotion to the state grows with each day, we have a greater desire, as life draws to its end, to leave our fatherland safe and in flower. Therefore, I am especially glad that my plea is being made to a man so well versed in learning. In the colony of Calama[3] there are many things which we have good reason to love, either because we were born there or because we seem to have fulfilled important duties there. This city, illustrious and deservedly honored Sir, has fallen, through no slight fault of its people. But, if we are to be weighed in the strict scale of public law, we should be subject to a too severe penalty.

It is right for bishops, however, to secure salvation for men, to be their advocate on the better side in their trials, and to merit from Almighty God pardon for the sins of others. Therefore, I beg you, with the most earnest prayer I can make, to see that the guiltless be defended, if any defense has to be

---

1 A pagan of the colony of Calama, obviously a former official, now retired and nearing the end of his life. He writes to ask Augustine to use his influence to secure a remission or commutation of penalty for his fellow pagans who had violated the laws of Honorius against pagan worship. As a pagan, he speaks most respectfully of the Christian God.
2 Cicero, *De re publica*, frag. 4.7.7.
3 In the later Roman Empire, colonies were provincial towns made up largely of landowners. Originally, these colonies were settlements made by Rome in conquered territory, to serve as focal points for the enforcement of Roman authority. The land grants were made—of confiscated land—to veterans of retirement age, or to Roman citizens who 'gave in their names' for one or another place. Roman customs persisted longer in these places than elsewhere, and it is not surprising that Calama, a Numidian town not far from Hippo, should have clung to pagan practices after the Empire had become officially Christian.

made, and that harm be kept from the innocent. Grant me this, which you can see is a request after your own heart. An appraisal of damages can easily be made; we ask only to be let off corporal punishment. May you be always more pleasing to God, illustrious Sir, deservedly cherished brother.

91. *Augustine to Nectarius, excellent Sir, deservedly honored brother (408)*

I do not wonder that your heart glows with love of your country as old age slows down your body, and I praise you, both for remembering and for showing forth in your life and character that there is no limit or legitimate restriction to our duty to serve our country. This I admit without objection, or, rather, wholeheartedly. But there is a certain heavenly country, for whose holy love, according to our modest ability, we struggle and toil among those whom we are helping to attain it; of it we should like to see you such a devoted citizen that you should think no limit or restriction of service possible, for one who travels on this earth to reach its portal. In proportion as you pay in advance your services due to this better country, you become better yourself; in its eternal peace you will find no end of joy, if in your labors on earth you have set no limit of service.

But until this happens—and I do not despair of your being able to attain that fatherland, and you may even now be thinking of laying hold on it, as the father who begot you to this one has preceded you to that one—until that happens, as I said, forgive us if, when we consider our own fatherland, which we do not wish to leave at all, we are saddened at yours, which you wish to leave in flower. If we differ with your Prudence about its flowers, there is no danger of your being easily persuaded—something which is not likely to happen—of the best way for the state to flower. That great poet of your far-famed literature wrote something of the flowers of Italy,[1] but we have not experienced in your fatherland 'the manhood with which that country bloomed,' so much as the 'arms with which it was aglow'; not aglow with arms, but ablaze with flames. Do you think you will leave your country in bloom if such a crime is left unpunished, with no adequate amendment of the wrong-doers? No flowers for fruit are these, but for thorns! Choose now whether you would prefer your country to bloom with respect for authority or with lawlessness; with good behavior or with unrestrained daring; compare these and see whether you surpass us in love of your country; whether your wish to see it bloom is greater or truer than ours.

Look for a little at those books on the Republic[2] from which you drew that ideal of the most devoted citizen: that there should be no limit or legitimate restriction on his service. Look, I beg you, and notice with what high praise frugality and temperance are there spoken of, as well as fidelity to the marriage bond, and chaste, honorable, and upright conduct. When a state excels in these it can truly be said to bloom. But in churches in growing numbers all over the world, as in holy gatherings of peoples, these principles are taught and learned; above all, the devotion by which the true and truth-giving God is worshiped, who not only commands these principles to be kept, but gives them fulfillment. It is by these that the human mind is prepared and made fit for the divine society, and for its habitation in the eternal heavenly country. Hence He has foretold that the images of the many false gods would be overturned, and has commanded them to be overturned.[3] Nothing, indeed, makes men so unfit for society, by a

---
1 Vergil, *Aeneid* 7,643-645: 'Now tell . . . with what manhood kindly Italy bloomed, with what arms she was aglow.'
2 Cicero, *De re publica*, frag. 4.7.7.
3 Lev. 26.30; Ezech. 6.4; 30.13; Osee 10.2; 3 Kings 15.11-13; 2 Paral. 23.17; 31.1; 33.5; 34.3,4.

depraved life, as the imitation of those gods as they are described and praised in their literature.

In the next place, those learned men of eminence who tried to discover by private discussions, and who described what the republic of the earthly city should be like, and who then organized and formed it by their public life, proposed as objects of imitation for the instruction of the youthful character men whom they considered outstanding and praiseworthy, but not gods. As a matter of fact, the youth in Terence[4] who looked at the wall fresco, where the adultery of the king of the gods was pictured, was incited to lust by the example of such an authority, but he would never have fallen by desiring, nor been entrapped by committing that base act, if he had chosen to imitate Cato[5] rather than Jupiter. But, how could he do this when he had to worship Jupiter, not Cato, in the temples? Perhaps we should not take these examples from comedy, which only serves to confirm the immorality of the irreligious and their sacrilegious superstition. Read or recall

---

4 Terence, *Eun.* 584-591. The youth was Chaerea, who says: 'During the preparations the girl sat in the room looking at a picture on the wall. The subject was the story of Jove's sending down a shower of gold into Danae's bosom. I fell to gazing at it, too, and the fact that he had played a like game long ago made me exult all the more: a god's turning himself into a man and stealing onto another man's roof tiles, and what a god, too! He "whose thunder shakes the highest realms of heaven." Was I a mere manikin, not to imitate him? Imitate I would, and like nothing better.' The passage is well chosen to prove Augustine's argument. In *Confessions* 1.16, he uses the same passage for the same purpose.

5 Two of this name were famous to the Romans; Cato the Censor (232-147 B.C.) is probably the one intended here. He was the very type of the old Roman character: frugal, abstemious, hard-working, patriotic, and violently opposed to the Greek influence in literature and art which was beginning to be felt in Rome. His *De re rustica* is one of the earliest examples of Latin prose.

The second of the name, Cato Uticensis, was a great-grandson of the former. He lived 93-45 B.C. He also was a model of the stern, upright life, and was opposed to the innovations that were undermining Roman society. He opposed Caesar, and committed suicide rather than see the death of the old republic.

from those same books[6] how wisely it is laid down that the words and actions of comedies cannot be welcomed except by those whose conduct accords with them. Thus, on the authority of famous men excelling in the state and arguing about the state, it is affirmed that wicked men become worse by imitating the gods—the false and fictitious gods, not the true One.

Oh, but all those things which were written long ago of the lives and conduct of the gods are to be understood and interpreted by the wise. Yes, no doubt, and when the people gathered in the temples we heard harmless explanations of this sort yesterday and the day before. I ask you: Is the human race so blind to the truth as not to recognize such obvious and manifest nonsense? In so many places, Jupiter, in the act of committing such adulteries, is painted, cast, beaten, carved, written, read, acted, sung, danced; what good would it do for anyone to read of him as forbidding such things, least of all in his own temple on the Capitoline? If these misdeeds, full of impurity and impiety, are approved among the people with no one to prevent; are adored in the temples, and laughed at in the theatres, while the sheepfold of the poor man is despoiled to supply victims for the worship of such gods, and the inherited wealth of the rich is lavished on singers and dancers representing their immorality, is this to be called a state in bloom? The mother of flowers like these is not the fertile earth, not some fruitful power, but the goddess Flora, a worthy parent, indeed, whose stage plays are performed with such unbounded, debased licentiousness that anyone can understand what sort of demon that is, which is not placated by birds or four-footed beasts, or even by human blood, but by nothing else than the much more accursed sacrifice of human shame.

I have said this because of what you wrote; namely, that as your life draws near its end you desire to leave your father-

---

6 Cicero's *Republic,* extant only in fragments.

land safe and in flower. Let us drop all these useless and foolish ideas; let men be converted to the worship of the true God, and to a chaste and religious life. Then you will see your country in bloom, not with the opinions of fools, but with the truth of the wise. Then this earthly country of yours will be a part of that country to which we are born by faith, not by flesh; where all the saints and faithful servants of God will bloom in an unending eternity, after the wintry toils of this life. Therefore, it is our dearest wish not to give up the policy of Christian mildness, but, on the other hand, not to leave in that city an example which would be harmful to others. God will see how we can do this, if He is not too deeply angry with them. Otherwise, the mildness which we wish to preserve, and the discipline which we aim to use in moderation, can be hampered, if God has some other secret design; or if He judges that this evil should be chastised with a heavier scourge; or if, as a sign of His greater wrath, He wills this evil to go unpunished for a time, because they have not been corrected or converted to Him.

Your Prudence writes to us in a certain way of the role of a bishop, and you say that your country has fallen, through no slight fault of its people, but 'if we were to be weighed in the strict scale of public law, we should be subject to too severe a sentence,' but, you say, 'it is right for bishops to secure salvation for men, to be their advocate on the better side in their trials, and to merit from Almighty God pardon for the sins of others.'[7] This we certainly try to guard against, that no one is subject to too severe a penalty, either by us or by any other at our intervention; and we do desire to secure salvation for men, but this is found in the happiness of right living, not in the security of evil-doing. We do strive to win pardon, not only for our own but for others' sins, also, but we cannot obtain it unless they amend their lives. You add the sentence:

---

7 These passages are quoted from Letter 90.

LETTERS   47

'I beg you, with the most earnest prayer I can make, to see that the guiltless be defended, if any defense is to be made, and that harm be kept from the innocent.'

Hear in a few words what acts were committed, and distinguish for yourself the guilty from the innocent. Contrary to the recent laws[8] of June 1, an idolatrous worship was carried out at a pagan festival, without interference from anyone, and with such insolent daring that a most wanton band of dancers came into the neighborhood of the Church and even to the very doors, something which had not happened in the times of Julian.[9] When the clerics tried to put a stop to this most lawless and unseemly performance, the church was stoned. Then, about a week later, when the bishop had called the attention of public authority to these very well-known laws, and while the latter were making a semblance of enforcing the edicts, the church was stoned again. The next day, when ours were powerless to impose fear, as it seemed, and when they wished to make a public protest, they were refused their rights. Then came a hail of stones,[10] but the offenders were so far from being frightened by celestial prodigies that, as soon as it was over, they at once engaged in a third stoning, and finally threw fire on the church roofs, and on men. They killed one of the servants of God, who lost his way and ran into them. Of the rest, some hid wherever they could, and some ran away wherever they could, and when the bishop had hidden himself, crowded and squeezed into a certain place, he heard their voices calling for his death, and upbraiding him because they could not find him, and were thereby prevented from committing a further crime. This went on

---

8 These laws were enacted by Honorius. The date, June 1, serves to place this letter.
9 The Apostate, emperor from 361 to 363, who attempted to restore and revive a dying paganism.
10 This was a natural phenomenon which never failed to terrify pagan Rome, as Livy testifies in many places.

from the tenth hour[11] until late in the night. Not one of those whose authority could have prevailed tried to restrain them; not one tried to help the victims, except one stranger who rescued several servants of God from the hands of those who were trying to kill them, and recovered a good deal of property from looters. From his act it is quite clear that it would have been easy to prevent these happenings entirely, or to stop them at the beginning, if the citizens, and especially the officials, had forbidden them to be done or to be continued.

From this you may be able to distinguish in that whole city, not the innocent from the guilty, but the less guilty from the more guilty. Those of minor guilt are the ones who were prevented from giving aid by fear of offending those whom they knew to be powerful in that town, and to be enemies of the Church, but all are guilty, even those who took no part in it, did not instigate it, but only allowed it to go on; more guilty are the perpetrators, most guilty the instigators. We think that we have a suspicion of this instigation, but no truth; so let us not discuss things which cannot be found out in any other way than by putting to torture those who could be examined.[12] Let us then pardon those who thought it was better to pray to God for the bishop and his attendants than to offend the powerful enemies of the Church. But the others who remain, do you judge that they should be restrained by no discipline, and do you favor letting such a monstrous instance of outrage go unpunished? We have no desire to feed our anger by taking vengeance for the past, but we are anxious to provide for the future by mercy. There are ways in which evil men

---

11 About 4 P.M.
12 It was common practice to inflict pain on witnesses to extort truth from them, because it was believed that otherwise they would not tell the truth. This practice, dating back into early pagan times, had not been abolished in the early fifth century. In fact, it took the Church several centuries to train men away from these and other barbarous customs.

are open to punishment by Christians, but only out of kindness, and to their own benefit and improvement. They have their bodily integrity, they have the means of livelihood, they have the means of living wickedly. Let the first two of these remain intact, so that there may be some to repent: this we pray for, this we work for with all our might. But in the third, if God wills to cut it off like something rotten and decayed, He will show great mercy in His punishment. And if He wills something more or does not even permit this, surely the reason for His higher and more just plan is His own. We have to use our care and authority, as far as He grants us to see, by praying to Him to approve our intention, by which we wish what is best for all, and asking Him not to allow us to do anything which, He knows far better than we, would not be good for us or for the Church.

When we were at Calama recently—and we went there to comfort our people in their great sorrow, and to moderate their anger at their injuries—we arranged with the Christians, to the best of our ability, what we thought was most opportune to do. Then we sought out the pagans themselves, the source and cause of the wrong, and we took advantage of the occasion to advise them what they had better do if they are wise, not only for the sake of doing away with their present anxiety, but also for attaining eternal salvation. They heard much from us; they asked much; but we are not such slaves—far from it!—that we should be delighted to have requests made of us by people who make no requests of our Lord. With your quick mind you perceive that our aim in preserving Christian mildness and moderation is either to prevent others from imitating the vile conduct of these, or to induce others to imitate their amendment. The losses which have been caused are either endured by Christians or made good by Christians. The gains we desire are those of souls, and we yearn to gain these even at the cost of blood. That is the kind of gain we seek in that place, and we hope not to be hampered in other places by their example. May the mercy of God grant us to rejoice in your salvation.

92. Augustine, bishop, gives greeting in the Lord to the excellent and deservedly renowned lady, his daughter Italica,[1] worthy of honor in the charity of Christ (408)

I have learned from your letter, as well as from the statement of the bearer that you ardently desire a letter from me, in the belief that it will bring you the greatest consolation. I must not refuse or delay this letter, but you will have to see what good you can draw from it. Let the faith and hope and charity, which are diffused through the hearts of the faithful by the Holy Spirit,[2] be your consolation. We receive a little of it in this life as a pledge[3] to make us learn how to long for its fullness. You must not think of yourself as left alone, since in the interior life you have Christ,[4] present in your heart by faith.[5] And you should not grieve as the heathen do who have no hope, because we have hope, based on the most assured promise, that as we have not lost our dear ones who have departed from this life, but have merely sent them ahead of us, so we also shall depart and shall come to that life where they will be more than ever dear as they were closer to us, and where we shall love them without fear of parting.

In this life, however intimately you knew your husband,

---

1 A Roman lady of rank who had lost her husband. St. John Chrysostom also addressed a letter to her. This is the first of Augustine's letters to women correspondents.
2 Rom. 5.5.
3 2 Cor. 1.22; 5.5.
4 Eph. 3.16,17.
5 1 Thess. 4.12.

through whose loss you are called widow, he was better known to himself than to you. And how was this possible, since you saw his bodily countenance, which he certainly did not see himself, except that our knowledge of our interior self is more authentic, and 'no one knows the things of a man but the spirit of a man that is in him'?[6] But, when 'the Lord shall come and shall both bring to light the hidden things of darkness and make manifest the counsels of the heart,'[7] then nothing will be hidden between us and our dearest, then there will be nothing for anyone to reveal to his own, or to hide from strangers, for none will be strangers. As for that light by which all these things which are now hidden in hearts will be revealed, what tongue can describe what or how great it is, or who can even grasp it with his limited mind? Doubtless, that light is God Himself, since 'God is light and in Him there is no darkness,'[8] but He is the light of purified minds, not of these bodily eyes. For then the mind will be capable of seeing that light, which now it is not yet able to do.

But the bodily eye cannot see Him either now or then. It is a fact that every object which can be perceived by bodily eyes must necessarily occupy some space, yet its whole is not everywhere, but with its smaller part it takes up a smaller space, and a larger space with a larger part. The invisible and incorruptible God is not like that, 'Who only hath immortality and inhabiteth light inaccessible, whom no man hath seen nor can see.'[9] This means that He cannot be seen by man with the faculty by which man in the flesh sees corporeal things. For, if He were inaccessible to the minds of holy men, it would not be said of Him: 'Come ye to him and be enlightened,'[10] and if He were invisible to holy minds it would not

---
6 1 Cor. 2.11.
7 Cf. 1 Cor. 4,5.
8 1 John 1.5.
9 1 Tim. 6.16.
10 Ps. 33.6.

be said: 'we shall see Him as He is.' Look at that entire verse in the Epistle of John: 'Dearly beloved,' he says, 'we are the sons of God and it hath not yet appeared what we shall be. We know that when he shall appear we shall be like him, because we shall see him as he is.'[11] We shall see Him then in so far as we shall be like Him, because now we do not see Him in so far as we are unlike Him. We shall see Him then by being like Him. Who is so utterly lacking in intelligence as to say that in the body we either are or will be like God? Consequently, that likeness is in the inner man, 'who is renewed in the knowledge of God according to the image of him that created him.'[12] And the more we become like Him, the more we advance in the knowledge and love of Him, because, 'though our outward man is corrupted, yet the inward man is renewed day by day.'[13] Consequently, in this life, however advanced a man's age might be, he would be far removed from that perfection of likeness which is required for seeing God, as the Apostle says, 'face to face.'[14] Obviously, if by these words we wish to understand a bodily face, the conclusion will be that God has such a face, and that there is a space between ours and His when we see Him face to face; if there is a space, there would surely be a limit and a definite outline of physical members, and other details too absurd to utter and too impious to think. By such vain deceits the 'sensual man, not perceiving the things that are of the spirit of God,'[15] is mocked.

Some of those who babble such things—at least, as far as I have been able to find out—say that we see God now with our mind, but then we shall see Him with fleshly sight, and they go so far as to assert that even the wicked will see Him in

---
11 1 John 3.2.
12 Cf. Col. 3.10.
13 2 Cor. 4.16.
14 1 Cor. 13.12.
15 Cf. 1 Cor. 2.14.

like manner. See to what lengths of evil they go, while their unrestrained prating goes wandering about here and there, without regard for fear or shame. Formerly they used to say that Christ had granted this unique power to His own flesh of seeing God with bodily eyes; then they added that all the saints would see Him in the same way when they regained their bodies at the resurrection, but now they have conceded this possibility even to the wicked. By all means let them grant as much as they like and to whom they like, for who would gainsay men giving what is their own? 'Who speaketh a lie, speaketh of his own.'[16] But you, joining with those who hold the true doctrine, must not venture to adopt any of those beliefs as your own, and when you read: 'Blessed are the clean of heart, for they shall see God,'[17] understand that the wicked will not see Him, for the wicked are neither blessed nor clean of heart. Likewise, when you read: 'We see now through a glass in a dark manner, but then face to face,'[18] understand that we shall then see face to face in the same way as we now see through a glass in a dark manner. Both of these are attributes of the inward man, whether he walks by faith in that journey in which he uses a glass in a dark manner, or whether, in his true country, he beholds Him in a vision, and this manner of seeing is called face to face.

Let the flesh, drunk with its carnal thoughts, take heed: 'God is a spirit, and therefore they that adore God must adore Him in spirit and in truth.'[19] If they must so adore, how much more must they so see Him! Who would dare to affirm that the substance of God can be seen corporally, when He does not will to be adored corporally? But they imagine they are arguing cleverly and pressing their point home when they ask: 'Was Christ able to grant to His flesh the power of seeing His

---
16 John 8.44.
17 Matt. 5.8.
18 1 Cor. 13.12.
19 Cf. John 4.24.

Father with bodily eyes, or was He not able?' Thus, if we should answer that He was not able, they would claim that we had belittled the onnipotence of God, but, if we should agree that He was able, they would consider their argument proved by your reply. Others fall into a more pardonable error who assert that our flesh will be changed into the substance of God and will become that which God is, for they at least would make the flesh fit to see God, and not removed from Him by its unlikeness. This fallacy I suppose those others put far from their faith and perhaps even from their ears. Yet, if they were faced by a similar set of alternatives about this—whether God can do this or cannot do it—will they belittle His power if they say that He cannot, or, if they admit that He can, will they conclude that this is what will happen? In the same way, then, that they get out of someone else's trap, let them get out of their own. Again, why do they insist that this power is granted only to the eyes of Christ's Body and not to the other senses? Will God then be sound so as to be perceived by His ears? And will He be breath so as to be felt by His nostrils? And will He be some kind of liquid so as to be able to be drunk? And will He be matter so as to be able to be touched? 'No,' they say. What, then? Can God be this and not that? If they say He cannot, why do they belittle His almighty power? If they answer that He can but He does not wish to, why do they favor the eyes alone and discriminate against the other senses of the Body of Christ? Or is that as far as they want their folly to go? We could do better not to put any bounds to their foolishness, but we do not want it to go any further.

Many arguments can be adduced to refute that madness. But if at any time they assail your ears with it, read this to them and do not fail to write me as best you can what answer they make. It is for this that our hearts are purified by faith[20]

---

20 Acts 15.9.

because the sight of God is promised to us as a reward of faith. But, if this is achieved by the eyes of the body, then the mind of the saint is fruitlessly trained to behold it, or, rather, the mind, acting so wrongly, is not exercised in itself but is wholly in the flesh. For, where will it dwell more steadily and surely except where it thinks it will see God? I leave to your understanding to recognize what a great misfortune that would be, and I will not labor to explain it at greater length. May your heart abide ever in the protection of the Lord, excellent and deservedly illustrious lady, daughter to be honored in the charity of Christ. I greet again, with the respect owed to your merits, your honored sons with you, beloved by us in the Lord.

92A. Augustine gives greeting in the Lord to his most truly upright and holy brother and fellow priest, Cyprian[1]

I have sent a letter to our blessed daughter, Italica, and I ask you to be so kind as to take it to her yourself. In it I said something against the opinion of those who can hope nothing of God except what they experience in the body, although they do not dare to say that God is a corporeal being. However, they state this another way when they assert that He can be seen by bodily eyes, which he created for seeing corporeal objects only. Truly, it seems to me that they do not know what a body is, nor how far from a body is a God who is a spirit. I thought she certainly deserved to be consoled, and, taking advantage of that, I did not wish to forego mention of the source where true comfort

---

1 Evidently a priest who was traveling to Rome. In letter 71 there is mention of 'our son, the deacon Cyprian' who was to carry that letter to St. Jerome. That was in 403, and by 408 he could have been an ordained priest. This letter is not found in Migne. A note in the textual apparatus of the Vienna Corpus text states that it is found in only one codex and is published for the first time.

for all of us in our pilgrimage is to be found. I tried also to refute in a few words what they might say to the contrary, and I hope your Holiness will not find it too much to write to me, in case her modesty should shrink from undertaking that sort of controversy on someone else's objection. At least, your Charity might succeed in getting those who hold this opinion, and who do not stop spreading it around and trampling it in, to write to me in reply to what I have written. Then it can be taken up with them later, and your holy Prudence must see, with me, that it ought to be so taken up. It is no wonder that the rational soul, fed on such fantasies, should be imprisoned and deeply cast down, so as not to perceive that supreme and unchanging good. If its faith is based on Him, so as to enjoy this in advance . . .[2] I thank your Kindness for sending me the reading matter which I had asked.

93. *Augustine to his beloved brother, Vincent*[1] *(408)*

I have received a letter which it seemed to me was not improbably yours, for the one who brought it to me, as he was evidently a Catholic Christian, would, I think, not venture to lie to me. But if, by any chance, the letter is not yours, I still think the writer ought to be answered, although I am now a more eager seeker for peace than I was when you knew me as a young man in Carthage, during the lifetime of Rogatus, to whom you have succeeded. But the Donatists are much too active, and it seems to me it

---

2 The letter ends abruptly here, and the ending seems almost to belong to another letter.

1 Rogatist, member of a Mauretanian sect of mild character, set up by Rogatus of Cartenna. Cf. Letter 88. Vincent succeeded Rogatus, as schismatic bishop of Cartenna, a Mauretanian town.

would be advisable for them to be restrained and corrected by the powers established by God. For we now rejoice over the correction of many who hold to Catholic unity, defend it so sincerely, and are so happy over their freedom from their former error that we wonder at them with great thankfulness. However, a strange force of habit makes some of them think that they cannot be changed for the better except under the influence of this fear, and then they turn their anxious minds to consider truth. If they were to bear these temporal trials with a useless and unprofitable patience, not for the sake of justice, but through persistence in wrong and reliance on man, they would afterward meet from God the punishments due to the wicked, because they had despised His gentle warning and His fatherly scourges. But, when once they had become submissive after reflecting on that thought, they would find the Church promised to all nations, not in calumnies and in man-made fables, but in the sacred Books, and they would see it set before their eyes. Then they would not doubt that Christ, as promised in those Books, though unseen, is now above the heavens. Why in the world, then, should I begrudge them salvation, by recalling my colleagues from this sort of fatherly duty, when it is through this that we see many renouncing their former blindness? Yet, some who believed, without seeing, that Christ is raised above the heavens, still denied His glory over all the earth, which they did see, although the Prophet, with strong significance, included both in one sentence when he said: 'Be thou exalted, O God, above the heavens, and thy glory over all the earth.'[2]

So, then, if we should despise and bear with those sometimes savage enemies of ours, who so deeply trouble our peace and quiet by various sorts of violence and craft, and if we made no plans and placed no blame such as could

---
2 Ps. 107.6.

avail to frighten and correct them, then indeed we should
return evil for evil. If anyone were to see an enemy, delirious
with dangerous fever, running headlong, would he not be
returning evil for evil if he let him go, rather than if he
took means to have him picked up and restrained? Yet he
would then seem to the man himself most hateful and most
hostile when he had proved himself most helpful and most
considerate. But, when he recovered his health, his thanks
would be lavish in proportion to his former feeling of injury at not being let alone. Oh, if I could show you, from
the very ranks of the Circumcellions, how many now become
active Catholics, condemn their former life and the
wretched error which made them think they were doing a
service to the Church of God when they thus rashly disturbed the peace! Yet they would not have been brought
to this state of health if they had not been restrained, like
the fever-stricken, with the shackles of those laws[3] which
are displeasing to you. And what of that other kind of deadly
illness which afflicts those who had no impulse to make
trouble, but who sank down, under the weight of long in-
ertness, saying to us: 'What you say is true; we have no
answer for it; but it is hard for us to leave the way of life
of our forefathers'? Should they not, for their own good, be
roused by a set of temporal penalties, so as to make them
come out of their lethargic sleep and awake to the health
of unity? How many of these, too, who now rejoice with us,
blame the former weight of their deadly custom, and con-

---

[3] These were old laws penalizing the Donatists by fines, and requiring them to give up their churches, which had often been taken
from the Catholics. These laws had been allowed to lapse, but were
reaffirmed by Honorius in 405. Originally, Augustine had been
opposed to the use of force by the secular arm in the solution of
the Donatist schism, and he had hoped to win back the dissidents
by argument and persuasion. This letter shows that he had been
forced by recent excesses to change his opinion, and was now
ready to justify the oppressive measures.

fess that it was right for us to disturb them and so prevent them from perishing in that sleep of seeming death and that disease of long-standing habit.

But with some those measures do not succeed, you say. Is a remedy, then, to be discontinued because the illness of some patients is incurable? You are looking at those who are so hardened that they are not affected by such correction. Concerning these it has been written: 'In vain have I struck your children; they have not received correction.'[4] I think, however, that they have been struck in love, not in hatred. But you ought to look at the many over whose salvation we rejoice. For, if they were frightened but not taught, the compulsion would seem unjust. Again, if they were taught but not frightened, they would remain hardened in their inveterate custom, and would be sluggish in rousing themselves to set out on the way of salvation. Indeed, there are many, as we know well, who have been convinced by our reasoning, and have recognized the truth as revealed by divine testimony, and who replied to us that they wished to come over into communion with the Catholic Church, but feared the violent hatred of desperate men. No doubt they ought to have despised this for the sake of justice and eternal life, but, until they are made strong, the weakness of such men is a matter of tolerance, not of despair. We must not forget that the Lord Himself said to Peter, when he was still weak: 'Thou canst not follow me now, but thou shalt follow hereafter.'[5] But when the saving doctrine is added to useful fear, so that the light of truth drives out the darkness of error, and at the same time the force of fear breaks the bonds of evil custom, then, as I said, we rejoice in the salvation of many who bless God with us, and give Him thanks because, by fulfilling the prophecy in which He

---
4 Jer. 2.30.
5 John 13.16.

promised that the kings of the earth would serve Christ,[6] He had thus cured the sick and healed the weak.

Not everyone who spares is a friend, nor is everyone who strikes an enemy. 'Better are the wounds of a friend than the proffered kisses of an enemy.'[7] Love mingled with severity is better than deceit with indulgence. It is more profitable for bread to be taken away from the hungry, if he neglects right living because he is sure of his food, than for bread to be broken to the hungry, to lead him astray into compliance with wrong-doing. The one who confines the madman, as well as the one who rouses the lethargic, is troublesome to both, but loves both. Who could love us more than God does? Yet He continually teaches us sweetly, as well as frightens us for our good. Often adding the most stinging medicine of trouble to the gentle remedies with which He comforts us, He tries the patriarchs, even good and devout ones, by famine;[8] He chastises a stubborn people with heavier punishments; He does not take away from the Apostle the sting of the flesh, though asked three times, so as to perfect strength in weakness.[9] Let us love our enemies, by all means, because it is right and God commands it, 'that we may be the children of our Father who is in heaven, who maketh his sun to rise upon the good and bad, and raineth upon the just and unjust.'[10] But, while we praise those bounties of His, let us think of His scourges inflicted on those whom He loves.

Do you think no one should be forced to do right, when you read that the master of the house said to his servants:

---

6 Dan. 7.27.
7 Prov. 27.6.
8 Gen. 12.10 (Abraham); 26.1 (Isaac); 41.54 (Joseph); 42.1 (Jacob); 43.1 (sons of Jacob).
9 2 Cor. 12.7-9.
10 Cf. Matt. 5.44,45.

'Whomever you find, compel them to come in';[11] when you read also that Saul himself, afterward Paul, was forced by the great violence of Christ's compulsion to acknowledge and hold the truth?[12] Do you think that money, or any other possession, is more precious than that light which was taken from his eyes? Thrown to the ground by that voice from heaven, he did not recover the sight so suddenly lost until he became a member of the holy Church. Or do you think that no force should be used to free a man from destructive error, when you see, by the most convincing examples, that God Himself does this—and no one loves us more advantageously than He does—and when you hear Christ saying: 'No man comes to me except the Father draw him'?[13] This happens in the hearts of all who turn to Him through fear of the divine anger. You know, too, that a thief sometimes sets out food to lead the flock astray, and that the shepherd sometimes calls the wandering sheep back to the fold by using the lash.

Did not Sara readily punish her rebellious handmaid, when the authority was given her?[14] Yet she obviously did not hate her cruelly, since she had previously done her the kindness of allowing her the opportunity of becoming a mother, but she restrained the pride of the maid for her own good. You know that those two women, Sara and Agar, and their two sons, Isaac and Ismael, are figures of the carnal and the spiritual, and although we read that the handmaid and her son suffered harsh treatment from Sara, the Apostle Paul says that Isaac suffered persecution from Ismael: 'But as then he that was born according to the flesh persecuted him that was after the spirit, so also it is

---
11 Cf. Luke 14.21-23.
12 Acts 9.3-18.
13 Cf. John 6.44.
14 Gen. 16.1-6.

now.'[15] Let those who are able understand that it is rather the Catholic Church which suffers persecution through the pride and wickedness of the carnal-minded, and that it attempts to correct these through temporal penalties and fears. Surely, in whatever the true and legitimate mother does, even if it is felt to be harsh and stern, she is not rendering evil for evil, but is using the good effect of punishment to drive out the evil of wickedness, and she does it in order to heal by love, not to injure by hatred. When both the good and the bad do the same things and suffer the same things, they are to be distinguished by their intentions, not by their acts and penalties. Pharao oppressed the people of God with hard labors;[16] Moses afflicted the same people, who had fallen into idolatry, with severe punishments;[17] they did the same things, but they did not aim at the same result; the former was puffed up with pride of power, the latter was animated by love. Jezabel killed the prophets; Elias killed the false prophets.[18] I think there was a difference in merit between the doers as between the victims.

Consider now the time of the New Testament, when that mildness of charity was not only to be preserved in the heart, but to be displayed in full light; when the sword of Peter was ordered by Christ back into its scabbard,[19] and it was made clear that it should not have been drawn from the scabbard, nor used in defense of Christ. We read both that the Jews beat the Apostle Paul,[20] and that the Greeks beat the Jew Sosthenes instead of Paul.[21] Does not the

15 Gal. 4.28-29.
16 Exod. 5.6-18.
17 Exod. 32.25-28.
18 3 Kings 18.4; 40.
19 Matt. 26.51-52; John 18.10,11.
20 Acts 15.22,23.
21 Acts 18.17.

likeness of the deed seem to join them, though the unlikeness of the cause distinguishes between them? Doubtless, God 'spared not his own Son, but delivered him up for us all';[22] doubtless, it is said of the Son, 'who loved me and delivered himself for me';[23] doubtless, it is also said of Judas that Satan entered into him that he 'might deliver up Christ.'[24] Therefore, when the Father delivered up the Son, and Christ Himself delivered up His Body, and Judas delivered up His Master, why, in that delivering up, is God good and man guilty, except that though they all did the same thing, they did not do it for the same reason? There were three crosses in one place: on one, a thief was to be pardoned; on another, a thief was to be damned; between them, Christ was to pardon one and damn the other. What more alike than those crosses? What more unlike than those who hung on them? Paul was delivered up to be imprisoned and fettered,[25] but Satan certainly is worse than any prison guard; yet Paul delivered a man up to him 'for the destruction of the flesh that the spirit may be saved in the day of the Lord Jesus.'[26] What shall we say of this? See how the cruel betrayer hands over to a more merciful jailer, and the merciful betrayer hands over to a more cruel jailer. Let us learn, brethren, when actions are alike, to distinguish the intentions of the actors; otherwise, if we shut our eyes to this, we might judge falsely, and we might accuse well-wishers of doing us harm. Likewise, when the same Apostle says that he delivered up certain men to Satan, 'that they may learn not to blaspheme,'[27] did he render evil

---

22 Rom. 8.32.
23 Gal. 2.20.
24 John 13.2.
25 Acts 16.22-24; 21.33,34.
26 1 Cor. 5.5.
27 1 Tim. 1.20.

for evil, or did he, rather, judge that it was a good work to correct evil men even by evil?

If it were always praiseworthy to suffer persecution, it would have been enough for the Lord to say: 'Blessed are they that suffer persecution,' without adding: 'for justice sake.'[28] Similarly, if it were always blameworthy to persecute, it would not be written in the sacred Books: 'The man that in private detracted his neighbor, him did I persecute.'[29] Sometimes, then, the one who suffers it is unjust and the one who does it is just. It is clear that the bad have always persecuted the good, and the good have persecuted the bad; the former to do harm unjustly, the latter to bring about amendment by punishment; the one unboundedly, the other within bounds; those as slaves of passion, these out of love. The one who kills does not mind how he butchers his victim, but the one who cures watches carefully how he cuts; he has health as his aim, the other destruction. Impious men killed the Prophets; the Prophets also killed impious men. The Jews scourged Christ, and Christ scourged the Jews. The Apostles were delivered up by men to the civil rulers, and the Apostles delivered up men to the power of Satan. In all these cases, what else is to be noted except to ask which of them served the cause of truth, which that of sin; which one wished to injure, which one wished to convert?

No instance is found in the Gospels or the Apostolic writings of any help being asked of the kings of the earth for the Church against the enemies of the Church.[30] Who says one is found? That prophecy was not yet fulfilled: 'Receive instruction, you that judge the earth. Serve ye the Lord in fear.'[31] But, up to the present, that other earlier

---

28 Matt. 5.10.
29 Ps. 100.5.
30 This is another objection which Augustine is answering.
31 Ps. 2.10,11.

passage in the same psalm was fulfilled, in which it is said: 'Why have the gentiles raged and the people devised vain things? The kings of the earth stood up and the princes met together against the Lord and against his Christ.'[32] If past events in the prophetic books were a figure of future ones, in the king named Nabuchodonosor[33] both periods were foreshadowed: that under the Apostles, and the present one in which the Church is now living. Thus, in the times of the Apostles and martyrs, that part was fulfilled which was foreshadowed when the king forced devout and upright men to adore an idol, and, when they refused, had them thrown into the fire; but, now, that part is fulfilled which was prefigured in the same king, when he was converted to the true God, and decreed for his realm that whoever blasphemed the God of Sidrach, Misach, and Abdenago should suffer due penalties. Therefore, the first part of that king's reign signified the earlier periods of infidel kings, when Christians suffered instead of the impious, but the latter part of that king's reign signified the period of later faithful kings under whom the impious suffered instead of the Christians.

But, severity evidently is mitigated and greater gentleness shown in the case of those who are led astray by evil men and who wander off under the name of Christ, lest, perhaps, the sheep of Christ should wander off, too, and have to be called back in some other way. Thus, by the coercion of exile and loss of goods, they are led to reflect on what they are suffering and why, and they learn to prefer the reading of the Scriptures to the rumors and false tales of men. Who of us, who of you does not praise the laws passed by the emperors against pagan sacrifices? Yet, a much more serious penalty is there enacted—indeed, the

---
32 Ps. 2.1,2.
33 Dan. 3.1-21, 91-96.

death penalty is prescribed for that impiety. But, in correcting and restraining you, a method is used rather to warn you to give up your error than to punish you for a crime. Perhaps the same thing can be said of you that the Apostle said of the Jews: 'I bear them witness that they have a zeal of God, but not according to knowledge; for they, not knowing the justice of God, and seeking to establish their own justice, have not submitted themselves to the justice of God.'[34] What else but your own justice do you seek to establish when you say that none are saved except those who have been able to receive baptism from you? But in this statement of the Apostle, which he uttered about the Jews, you differ from the Jews in this, that you have the Christian sacraments which they still lack. Whereas, when he says: 'Not knowing the justice of God and seeking to establish their own,' and that: 'they have a zeal of God, but not according to knowledge,' you are exactly like them, always excepting, of course, those among you who do know what is true, but who war against the truth so well known to them, through the hatred arising from their own debased conduct. I should not wonder if the impiety of these surpassed even idolatry. And because all cannot easily be brought into subjection—for this evil lies deep in their mind—you are chastised with less severity, as being not too far removed from us. This I would say either of all heretics who are well versed in Christian practices, yet are separated from the truth or unity of Christ, or I would say it of all Donatists.

As far as you are concerned, you not only share with them the general name of Donatists, from Donatus, but you are more properly called Rogatists from Rogatus, and you seem to be of milder character, since you do not commit cruelties with monstrous gangs of Circumcellions; but

---
34 Cf. Rom. 10.2,3.

no wild beast is called tame merely because it has neither teeth nor claws, and does not hurt anyone. You say you do not wish to act cruelly; I think you are not able. You are so few in number that you would not dare to act against opponents who are more numerous than you, even if you wished. But let us suppose that you do not want to do what you are not strong enough to do; let us suppose that you understand the Gospel teaching where it says: 'If a man will take away thy coat and contend with thee in judgment, let go thy cloak also unto him,'[35] and that you so understand and hold to it that you think you should not only do no injury to those who persecute you, but that you should not even oppose them by law. Certainly, your founder Rogatus did not have this understanding of it, or at least he did not follow it out, since, as you say, he fought about certain things with unyielding obstinacy, even by means of civil suits. If he had been asked: 'Who of the Apostles in the service of the faith ever defended his possessions by public law?'—as you put in your letter: 'Who of the Apostles in the service of the faith ever appropriated anyone else's property?'—he would indeed find no instance of this course of action in the divine writings. Still, he would perhaps find some true defense if he held to the true Church, and did not shamelessly possess something under the name of the true Church.

As to the advisability of requesting or extorting decrees from the secular powers against heretics or schismatics, those, indeed, from whom you broke away, were extremely active both against you[36] and the Maximianists,[37] as far as

---

[35] Cf. Matt. 5.40.
[36] The Rogatists had seceded from the Donatists, who did not tolerate schism from their own ranks, and treated the separatists with cruelty.
[37] Followers of Maximian, a Donatist deacon of Carthage who separated from his bishop Primian and set up a schism from a schism.

we have been able to discover, and we can prove this by trustworthy records of their doings. Still, you had not yet completed your separation from them when they said in their petition to the Emperor Julian that he was the sole depositary of justice. Now, they certainly knew him as an apostate and saw him as one given up to idolatry; consequently, they were thereby either asserting that idolatry is justice or they were guilty of a vile lie—and this they cannot deny—when they said of a man in whose life idolatry held the chief place, that he was the sole depositary of justice. Granted that the mistake was in their words, what have you to say about their course of action? If no form of justice is to be asked of an emperor, why was Julian asked for what was considered justice?

Or is this appeal to be made in order to recover one's own property, but not to lay a charge against anyone which would subject him to the emperor's punishment? Meanwhile, by this appeal for the recovery of one's property, there is a departure from the example of the Apostles, since not one of them is known to have done this. Moreover, when your predecessors laid a charge before the Emperor Constantine, through the proconsul Anulinus,[38] against that same Caecilian, then Bishop of the Church at Carthage, with whom they would not hold communion, they were not claiming lost property, but were slandering an innocent man by their attack; at least we think so, and the outcome of the trial proved it. Could they have done anything worse than that? But if, as you wrongly think, they were handing over a really guilty man to be judged by the secular powers, why do you reproach us for what the boldness of your followers did first? We would not blame them for doing it if they had acted with the intention of bringing about amendment and

---

38 Proconsul of Africa in the time of Constantine, whose report to the emperor is quoted in Letter 88.

correction, and not out of jealousy and the wish to hurt. But we do most undeniably blame you, to whom it seems a crime to make any complaint to a Christian emperor about the enemies of our communion, whereas your predecessors delivered a document to the proconsul Anulinus to be forwarded to the Emperor Constantine, entitled as follows: 'Document of charges against Caecilian of the Catholic Church, offered by the sect of Maiorinus.' And we blame more sharply those who accused Caecilian to the emperor without cause, when they should have proved their charges before the court of their overseas colleagues,[39] although the emperor himself took the more lawful course of referring a case concerning bishops to the judgment of bishops, even after it had been appealed to him. Then, when the case went against them, they refused to make peace with their brethren; again they went to the same emperor, and this time they accused to a secular ruler not only Caecilian, but also the bishops who had been appointed judges of the case; again they appealed from another court of bishops to the same emperor, and when he decided between the parties and gave a verdict, they would not yield either to truth or to peace.

What further decrees would Constantine have made against Caecilian and his party, if they had lost the case to your prosecuting predecessors, than those he issued against these latter, who had made gratuitous charges, had not been able to prove them, and, when they lost the case, had refused to submit to the truth? That emperor first decreed in this case that the property of the plaintiffs, defeated and obstinately refusing to submit, should be confiscated. No doubt, if your prosecuting forefathers had won their case, and the emperor had issued such a decree against the com-

---

39 The Gallic and Italian bishops who first passed on the validity of Caecilian's consecration. Cf. Letter 43.

munion of Caecilian, you would claim the titles of stewards of the Church, defenders of peace and unity. But, when the self-appointed accusers could prove nothing against him, and refused to accept the embrace of peace offered to them as a refuge and means of amendment, and when such decrees are made by emperors, they cry out at such a horrible deed; they declare that no one should be forced into unity, and that evil should not be rendered for evil to anyone. This is exactly what someone wrote of you: 'What we wish is holy.'[40] And now it ought not to be a great or difficult thing to reflect and to realize that the verdict and sentence of Constantine is in force against you; the same one which was pronounced against your predecessors who so often accused Caecilian to the emperor and never won their case; the same one which successive emperors, especially Catholic Christian ones, have been forced to put into effect whenever the compulsion of your obstinacy has brought something down on you.

It would be easy to draw those conclusions, and to say to yourselves once in a while: 'If Caecilian was innocent, or could not be proved guilty, what offense was committed in this matter by the worldwide Christian community? Why are those whom Christ sowed in His field, that is, in this world, and whom He instructed to grow among the cockle until harvest-time[41]—why are so many thousands of the faithful in all nations, whose number the Lord compared to the stars of heaven and the sands of the sea,[42] to whom He promised and granted that they should be blessed in the seed of Abraham, why are they refused the name of Christians, because in this controversy, which they took

---
40 An epigram of Tychonius, a Donatist theologian who was finally excommunicated in 380, by his own sect. His Seven Keys, or method of interpreting Scripture, was admired by St. Augustine.
41 Matt. 13.24-30.
42 Gen. 22.17,18.

no part in discussing, they preferred to believe judges whose verdict would have imperilled their own conscience if it had been unjust, rather than the defeated litigants? Surely, no one is tainted by a charge of which he is ignorant. How could the faithful, dispersed throughout the whole world, have known the charge against the betrayers, when the accusers could not prove it even if they knew it? Surely, their very ignorance of the charge clearly shows them innocent of it. Why, then, are the innocent accused on false charges because they did not know whether others' charges were false or true? What room is left for innocence, if there is personal guilt in not knowing of others' guilt? Moreover, if that ignorance of so many nations, as it is said, shows their people to be innocent, what a great crime it is to be separated from communion with those innocent people! For, the deeds of guilty men, which cannot be proved to the guiltless nor be believed by them, do not taint anyone even if they are known and tolerated for the sake of the fellowship of the innocent. The good are not to be abandoned because of the bad, but the bad are to be borne with because of the good, as the Prophets bore with those against whom they made such bitter reproaches. They did not refuse to take part in the religious rites of that people, just as the Lord Himself bore with the guilty Judas, even to his accursed end, and allowed him to share in the sacred banquet with the innocent. So, also, the Apostles tolerated those who preached Christ out of envy,[43] which is the sin of the Devil himself; so Cyprian[44] bore with the avarice of his colleagues, which, following the Apostle, he calls the service of idols.[45] Finally, whatever was done at that time by those bishops, even if it was known to some—not to

---
43 Phil. 1.15.
44 Cyprian, *Ep.* 55.27, cited by Migne.
45 Eph. 5.5.

make a distinction of persons—is now known by none. Why, then, is peace not loved by all? You should be able to think this out very easily, and perhaps you are thinking it out now. But it would be better for you to agree to the known truth through love of your worldly possessions and fear of losing them, than to love the vain esteem of men so much that you think you will lose it if you do agree to the known truth.

You see now, I think, that the point to be considered is not whether anyone is being forced to do something, but what sort of thing he is being forced to do, whether it is good or bad. Not that anyone can be good against his will, but, by fear of enduring what he does not want, he either gives up the hatred that stands in his way, or he is compelled to recognize the truth he did not know. So, through fear, he repudiates the false doctrine that he formerly defended, or he seeks the truth which he did not know, and he willingly holds now what he formerly denied. It would perhaps be useless to say this in any number of words if it were not shown by so many examples. We see that not only these or those men, but many cities which were formerly Donatist are now Catholic, now detest the diabolical separation, and now ardently love unity. These became Catholic by the effect of that fear which displeases you, through the laws of the emperors from Constantine, to whom yours first accused Caecilian without cause, to the present emperors.[46] And these with perfect justice order that Constantine's sentence be enforced against you, since you took him for judge and preferred his decision to that of the court of bishops.

I have, then, yielded to the facts suggested to me by my colleagues, although my first feeling about it was that no

---

46 Honorius and Arcadius.

one was to be forced into the unity of Christ, but that we should act by speaking, fight by debating, and prevail by our reasoning, for fear of making pretended Catholics out of those whom we knew as open heretics. But this opinion of mine has been set aside, not because of opposing arguments, but by reason of proved facts. First of all, the case of my own city[47] was set before me, which had been wholly Donatist, but was converted to Catholic unity by the fear of imperial laws, and which now holds your ruinous hatred in such detestation that one could believe it had never existed there at all. Similarly, many other cities were recalled to me by name, and by these examples I recognized how truly the word of Scripture could be applied to this case: 'Give an occasion to a wise man, and he will be wiser.'[48] How many there are—as we know for a fact—who have been for a long time wishing to be Catholics, drawn by such manifest truth, but who kept delaying from day to day through fear of offending their families! And how many are held by the heavy bond of inveterate custom rather than by truth—something on which you have never relied —and thus fulfill that divine saying: 'A stubborn slave will not be corrected by words, for, even if he shall understand, he will not obey.'[49] How many thought that the sect of Donatus was the true church because security made them too slothful, contemptuous, and unconcerned to acknowledge Catholic truth! How many were debarred from entering the Church by the reports of the evil-minded who kept saying that we place some unnamed thing on the altar of God! How many believe that it makes no difference to what section of Christianity a man belongs, and remain in the Donatist sect because they were born there and no

---

47 Hippo.
48 Cf. Prov. 9.9.
49 Cf. Prov. 29.19.

one forced them to leave it and come over to the Catholic faith!

For all these, the fear of the laws promulgated by temporal rulers who serve the Lord in fear[50] has been so beneficial that some now say: 'This is what we wanted all along, but thanks be to God who has given us an opportunity to act at once, and has cut off all our little delays and postponements!' Others say: 'We have known long since that this is true, but we have been held back by some force of habit; thanks to the Lord who has broken our bonds and brought us under the bond of peace!' Others say: 'We did not know that truth was here, and we did not want to learn it; but fear has made us alert to recognize it, the fear of being struck with the possible loss of temporal goods without any gain of eternal goods; thanks to the Lord who shook off our sloth with the goad of fear, and made us seek in our anxiety for what we should never have troubled to know if we had been secure.' Others say: 'We were held back from entering the Church by false rumors which we could not know as false without entering, nor would we enter without being forced; thanks to the Lord who has removed our anxiety by this scourge, who has taught us by experience what vain and baseless stories lying rumor has circulated about His church; by this we now believe that those charges, too, are false which the originators of this heresy made, since their successors have invented falsehoods which are so much worse.' Others say: 'We thought it made no difference where we held the faith of Christ, but thanks to the Lord who has gathered us out of our separation, and has shown us that it befits one God that men should dwell in unity.'

Was I to resist or contradict my colleagues and thereby prevent these gains for the Lord, that the sheep of Christ,

---
50 Ps. 2.11.

wandering on your mountains and hills—that is, on the swellings of your pride—should not be gathered into the sheepfold of peace, where there is 'One fold and one shepherd'?[51] Ought I to have opposed this arrangement, to keep you from losing the property which you call yours, and thereby leave you to proscribe Christ without danger? Were you to safeguard your wills by Roman law, and break by slanderous accusations the testament safeguarded for the Fathers by divine law, where it is written: 'In thy seed shall all nations of the earth be blessed'?[52] Were you to have freedom of contract in buying and selling and then dare to divide for yourselves what Christ bought by being sold Himself? Should the gifts which you make to anyone have value, and what the God of gods gave to those called to be His sons 'from the rising of the sun even to the going down thereof'[53] have no value? Should you be saved from being sent into exile from your earthly land, yet attempt to make Christ an exile from the kingdom of His Blood, 'from sea to sea and from the river unto the ends of the earth'?[54] Rather, let the kings of the earth serve Christ even by making laws in behalf of Christ. Your forefathers exposed Caecilian and his companions to punishment by the kings of the earth on false charges; let the lions turn to break the bones of the calumniators, and let Daniel himself, proved innocent, not intercede for them, for he 'that diggeth a pit for his neighbor, himself shall justly fall into it.'[55]

Save yourself, brother, while you live in the flesh, from the wrath which is about to come upon the obstinate and the proud. When the temporal powers use fear to make

---
51 John 10.16.
52 Gen. 22.18; 26.4.
53 Ps. 49.1.
54 Ps. 71.8.
55 Cf. Prov. 26.27.

war on truth, it becomes a glorious test for the strong, but a dangerous temptation for the weak; when they use it to champion truth, it becomes a warning useful to prudent men when they go astray, but a meaningless chastisement to the unthinking. Nevertheless, 'There is no power but from God; therefore he that resisteth the power, resisteth the ordinance of God. For princes are not a terror to the good work, but to the evil. Wilt thou then not be afraid of the power? Do that which is good and thou shalt have praise from the same.'[56] If the power in defense of truth corrects anyone, it has praise from the same in that someone has been set right, but if it is hostile to truth and rages against anyone, it has praise from the same in that the victor is crowned. But you do not do good, so you do not win the reward of not fearing the power; unless, perhaps, it is good to sit down and not to speak against your brother,[57] although you are speaking against all the brethren established in all nations, to whom the Prophets, Christ, and the Apostles bore witness, as we read: 'In thy seed shall all nations be blessed,'[58] or again: 'From the rising of the sun to the going down, there is offered to my name a clean offering, for my name is great among the gentiles, saith the Lord.'[59] Listen to it: 'saith the Lord,'—not says Donatus or Rogatus or Vincent or Hilary or Ambrose or Augustine, but 'saith the Lord.' We read also: 'And in him shall all the tribes of the earth be blessed; all nations shall magnify him. Blessed be the Lord, the God of Israel, who alone doth wonderful things, and blessed be the name of his glory forever and ever, and the whole earth shall be filled with his glory. So be it, so be it.'[60] And you sit at Cartenna with

---
56 Rom. 13.1-3.
57 Cf. Ps. 49.20.
58 Gen. 22.18.
59 Mal. 1.11.
60 Cf. Ps. 71.17-19.

ten Rogatists who are left, and you say: 'Let it not be, let it not be.'

You hear the Gospel saying: 'All things must needs be fulfilled which are written in the law, and in the Prophets and in the Psalms concerning me. Then he opened their understanding that they might understand the Scriptures. And he said to them: Thus it is written and thus it behooved Christ to suffer and to rise again from the dead, the third day; and that penance and remission of sins should be preached in his name unto all nations, beginning at Jerusalem.'[61] You read also in the Acts of the Apostles how this Gospel began at Jerusalem where the Holy Spirit first filled the one hundred and twenty souls, and from there it went forth into Judea and Samaria and to all nations,[62] as He had said to them before His Ascension into heaven: 'You shall be witnesses unto me in Jerusalem and in all Judea, and Samaria, and even to the uttermost parts of the earth,'[63] because 'their sound hath gone forth into all the earth and their words unto the ends of the world.'[64] You contradict these divine testimonies, founded on such assurance, revealed with such clarity, and you try to outlaw the inheritance of Christ, and when, as He said, penance shall be preached in His name to all nations, if anyone shall be moved to penance in any part of the world, his sins can not be forgiven unless he seeks and finds Vincent of Cartenna, hiding in imperial Mauretania, or some one of his nine or ten companions. Such is the swelling pride of a skin-covered carcass! Such the depths of presumption into which flesh and blood hurls itself! Is this your good work which preserves you from fearing the power? 'Such a scandal thou

---

61 Cf. Luke 44.47.
62 Acts 1.15; 2.4.
63 Acts 1.8.
64 Ps. 18.5; Rom. 10.18.

didst lay against thy mother's son,'[65] when he was so evidently small and weak, 'for whom Christ hath died,'[66] not yet fit for his father's food, but needing to be fed still with his mother's milk.[67] And you reproach me with the books of Hilary,[68] going so far as to deny the spread of the Church among all nations, to the end of time, which, notwithstanding your unbelief, God promised with an oath. And although you would have been most unfortunate if you had withstood it when the promise was made, now, when it is being fulfilled, you deny it.

But, learned historian that you are, you have found an objection which you think can be offered against the testimony of God. For you say: 'If you consider the parts of the whole world, the part in which the Christian faith is recognized is small in comparison with the whole world,' but you will not notice, or pretend not to know, how many barbarous nations have even now received the Gospel in so short a time, so that even the enemies of Christ cannot doubt of the fulfillment in a short time of what He mentioned in His answer to the inquiries of the Apostles about the end of the world: 'And this gospel shall be preached in the whole world for a testimony to all nations, and then shall the end come.'[69] Go now, shout and proclaim as loud as you can, that even if the Gospel shall be preached in the Indies and Persia—where it has been preached this long time—if anyone hears it, he cannot in any way be cleansed of his sins unless he comes to Cartenna or its neighborhood. If you lack so loud a voice, do you fear to be laughed at, or if you do not lack it, do you refuse to weep?

---

65 Ps. 49.20.
66 1 Cor. 8.11.
67 1 Cor. 3.2.
68 Hilary of Poitiers (315-368), chief defender of orthodoxy in the West. Cf. Letter 75, Vol. 1, p. 364.
69 Cf. Matt. 24.14.

You imagine you are saying something clever when you derive the name Catholic,[70] not from its universal membership in the world, but from the observance of all divine commands and all the sacraments, as if we rely on the meaning of the word to prove that the Church is worldwide, and not rather on the promise of God, and on so many and such clear pronouncements of truth itself. Yet it does happen that the Church is called Catholic, too, because it embraces all truth, and there are even some fragments of this truth to be found in different heresies. But, no doubt, this is the sum of what you are trying to prove to us, that the Rogatists are the only ones left who are properly to be called Catholics, because of their observance of all the divine commands and all the sacraments, and you are the only ones in whom the Son of man will find faith when He comes.[71] Pardon us if we do not believe it. You may even go so far as to say that you are not to be reckoned as on earth but in heaven, so that the faith can be found among you which the Lord said He would not find on earth. For our part, the Apostle has put us on guard by teaching that though an angel from heaven should preach a gospel besides that which we have received, he ought to be anathema.[72] And how are we sure from the divine writings that we have received the true Christ, if we have not also received a true Church? Whatever handles and hooks anyone attaches to the simplicity of truth, whatever clouds of clever falsehood he pours out, that man will be accursed who shall say that Christ neither suffered nor rose again the third day, since we learn on the truth of the Gospel: 'It behooved Christ to suffer and to rise again from the dead the third day';[73] and he will be equally

---

70 Catholic means universal.
71 Luke 18.8.
72 Gal. 1.8.
73 Luke 24.46.

accursed who shall preach a church other than the communion of all nations, because we have learned in the subsequent passage 'that penance and remission of sins should be preached in his name unto all nations, beginning at Jerusalem'[74] and we ought to hold with unshaken belief that, 'if anyone preach to you a gospel besides that which you have received, let him be anathema.'[75]

Now, if we do not listen to the whole Donatist sect when it sets itself up in place of the Church of Christ, because it does not offer any evidence in its favor from the divine truths, as a basis of its teaching, I ask you how much less should we listen to the Rogatists, who will not try to apply to themselves that passage where it is written: 'Where dost thou feed? where dost thou lie at midday?'[76] If in this quotation, Africa in the sect of Donatus is to be understood by midday,[77] then all the Maximianists will surpass you because their schism blazed up at Byzantium[78] and Tripoli. But the people of Arzuga[79] could get up a conflict with them and claim that this refers more exactly to them. Still, Caesarean Mauretania is nearer to the western than to the

---

74 Luke 24.47.
75 Gal. 1.9.
76 Cant. 1.6.
77 There is a kind of play on the word *'meridies'*, which means *'south'* as well as *'midday'*. This is an example of the extremely literal accommodation of Scripture to a situation far from the original meaning.
78 This should perhaps be amended to read *'Byzacium.'* Byzantium on the Bosphorus is several degrees of latitude north of Africa and therefore does not fall in with Augustine's argument of a more southerly schism being more in accord with the words of the Canticle. The argument is a *reductio ad absurdum*. Byzacium, on the other hand, is a section of the province of Africa lying south of Carthage and Hippo, and is bordered by Tripoli. The Maximianist schism began in Carthage when Maximian, a Donatist deacon, quarreled with his bishop, Primian, and set himself up as head of a new sect. It seems unlikely that a relatively small group like this ever reached European Byzantium.
79 Evidently a small African town further south than Cartenna. It does not appear on the map.

southern part; since it does not wish itself to be called Africa, how will it boast about the south, I do not say against the world but against the sect of Donatus, from which the sect of Rogatus cut itself off—a very small bit from a larger part? Would anyone be so lacking in modesty as to apply to himself something expressed by an allegory, unless he had some clear indication to throw light on its obscure language?

What we are accustomed to say to all Donatists, we say with much greater insistence to you. If, by some impossible set of circumstances, a certain group had just reason for separating their communion from the communion of the world, and should call themselves the church of Christ because they had acted justly in thus separating themselves from the communion of all nations, how would you know, in a Christian society of such wide extent, whether another group, in a faraway land, might also have broken away for a just reason before you did, and how could the report of their justifiable action reach you? How could the Church be preferably in you rather than in them, who happened to cut themselves off before you did? Since you do not know this, it follows that you must be uncertain about yourselves, and this necessarily befalls all who found their sect not on divine authority but on their own. And you cannot say: 'If this had happened it could not remain unknown to us,' since, in Africa alone, you could not tell, if you were asked, how many factions have split off from the sect of Donatus—with this peculiarity, that those who break away claim that the fewer they are, and therefore the less known, the more likely they are to be in the right. For this reason you do not know whether some authentic group, small and therefore unknown, before the sect of Donatus severed its purity from the wickedness of the rest of men, may have broken away very early, and at a distance from the south of Africa, on the side of the north, and may itself be the Church of God, a sort of spiritual Sion, which forestalled all of you by a justifiable separation. And it may apply to itself what is written: 'Mount Sion, the side of the north, the city of the great king,'[80] with much greater reason than the sect of Donatus applies to itself: 'Where dost thou feed, where dost thou lie in the midday?'[81]

And yet you fear that, when you have been forced to unity by imperial laws, the name of God may the longer be blasphemed by Jews and pagans, as if the Jews do not know how the early people of Israel wanted to destroy in war the two tribes and a half that had received lands on the other side of the Jordan, because they believed they had withdrawn from union with their people.[82] But the pagans could more likely curse us because of the laws which Christian emperors have enacted against the worshipers of idols, yet many of them have been corrected and converted to the living and true God, and are daily being converted. But, surely, if the Jews and pagans thought the Christians were as few in number as you are—you who claim to be the only Christians—they would not bother to curse us, they would never stop laughing at us. If the Church of Christ is your handful, do you not fear that the Jews may say to you: 'Where is the church which your Paul recognized as yours, where it is said: "Rejoice, thou barren that bearest not: break forth and cry thou that travailest not, for many are the children of the desolate, more than of her that hath a husband," '[83] giving the people of the Christians precedence over the people of the Jews? Are you going to answer them thus: 'We are the more

---
80 Ps. 47.3.
81 Cant. 1.6.
82 Josue 22.9-12. The tribes were Ruben and Gad, and the half-tribe of Manasses.
83 Gal. 4.27, quoted by St. Paul from Isa. 54.1.

elect because we are so few?' and do you not expect them to answer: 'However many you say you are, you are not those of whom it is said, "Many are the children of the desolate," since you have remained such a small number'?

Here you will probably bring up the example of that just man, at the time of the flood, who, with his household, was the only one found worthy of being saved.[84] Do you see, then, how far you are from justice? As long as you remain exactly seven, to which you form the eighth, we do not say that you are a just man, if, as I said, someone before the sect of Donatus has forestalled that justice, and with seven of his, moved by some good reason, has separated himself in some far-off places and has escaped from the flood of this world. Since you do not know whether this happened and was unheard of by you, as the name of Donatus is unheard of by many Christian peoples settled in remote countries, you are not sure where the Church is. It will be there where that was first done which you did afterwards, if there could be any justifiable reason for which you could sever yourselves from union with all nations.

But we are sure that no one can sever himself justifiably from communion with all nations, because no one of us seeks the Church in his own justice, but in the divine Scriptures, and there he sees it realized according to the promise. Of the Church it is said: 'As the lily among the thorns, so is my love among the daughters,'[85] and they cannot be called thorns except for the dissoluteness of their behavior, nor daughters except by their participation in the sacraments. It is the Church herself who says: 'To thee have I cried from the ends of the earth when my heart was in anguish,'[86] and in another psalm: 'A fainting hath taken

---
84 Gen. 7.1-23.
85 Cant. 2.2.
86 Ps. 60.3.

hold of me, because of the wicked that forsake thy law,' and: 'I beheld the fools and I pined away.'[87] It is she who says to her spouse: '[Show me] where thou feedest, where thou liest at midday, lest I become as one hidden upon the flocks of thy companions,'[88] that is, as it is said elsewhere: 'Make thy right hand known to me and make us learned in heart and wisdom,'[89] among whom, shining with light and glowing with love, thou dost repose as at midday. Otherwise I might, as one covered, rush, not upon thy flock, but upon the flocks of thy companions, that is, the heretics. She here calls them companions, as she calls the thorns daughters because of their participation in the sacraments, of whom it is said elesewhere: 'But thou a man of one mind, my guide and my familiar, who didst take sweet meats together with me; in the house of the Lord, we walked with consent. Let death come upon them and let them go down alive to hell,'[90] like Dathan and Abiron, the impious inciters to separation.[91] It is she to whom the answer is straightway made: 'If thou know not thyself, O fair among women, go forth and follow after the steps of the flocks, and feed thy kids in the tents of the shepherds'[92]—truly the answer of the sweetest of spouses! He says: 'if thou know not thyself,' because, obviously, 'a city seated on a mountain cannot be hid,'[93] and therefore thou art not hidden so as to run upon the flocks of my companions, for I am 'the mountain prepared . . . upon the top of mountains, to which all nations shall come.'[94] If,

---

87 Ps. 118.53, 158.
88 Cf. Cant. 1.6.
89 Cf. Ps. 89.12.
90 Cf. Ps. 54.14-16.
91 Num. 16.1-33.
92 Cf. Cant. 1.7.
93 Matt. 5.14.
94 Isa. 2.2.

therefore, thou knowest not thyself, in the testimony of my books, but not in the words of liars; if thou knowest not thyself, because of thee it is said: 'Lengthen thy cords, and strengthen thy strong stakes; stretch out again and again to the right and to the left; for thy seed shall inherit the gentiles and thou shalt inhabit the cities which were desolate. There is no reason for thee to fear, thou shalt prevail; do not blush because thou hast been an object of hatred. Thou shalt forget the shame forever, thou shalt remember no more the shame of thy widowhood, for I am the Lord who made thee, the Lord is his name, and he who rescued thee shall be called the God of Israel over the whole earth.'[95] If thou know not thyself, O fair among women, because it is said of thee: 'The king hath desired thy beauty';[96] because it is said of thee: 'Instead of thy fathers, sons are born to thee; thou shalt make them princes over all the earth';[97] if thou know not thyself, go forth, I do not cast thee forth, but go thou forth, that it may be said of thee: 'They went out from us, but they were not of us.'[98] Go forth in the footsteps of the flocks, not in my footsteps, but in the footsteps of the flocks, not of one flock, but of the scattered and straying flocks. And feed thy kids, not as Peter, to whom it is said: 'Feed my sheep,'[99] but feed thy kids in the tents of the shepherds; not in the tent of the shepherd, where there is 'one fold and one shepherd.'[100] For he knows her very self, so that this may not happen to her, because it does happen to those who have not known themselves in her. She it is of whose fewness in comparison with the many wicked it is said: 'Narrow . . .

---

95 Cf. Isa. 54.2-5.
96 Cf. Ps. 44.12.
97 Ps. 44.17.
98 1 John 2.19.
99 John 21.17.
100 John 10.16.

and strait is the way that leadeth to life, and few there are that walk in it';[101] and again it is she of whose great number it is said: 'Thy seed shall be as the stars of heaven and as the sand of the sea.'[102] Likewise, the faithful who are holy and good are few in comparison with the larger number of the wicked, but considered in themselves, they are many, 'for many are the children of the desolate, more than of her that hath a husband';[103] and 'many shall come from the east and the west and shall sit down with Abraham and Isaac and Jacob in the kingdom of heaven';[104] and because God shows to Himself 'a numerous people, zealous for good works,'[105] and many thousands 'which no man could number' are seen in the Apocalypse, 'of every tribe and tongue, in white robes, with palms'[106] of victory. It is she who is sometimes darkened and, as it were, clouded over by the great number of scandals, when 'the sinners bend their bow to shoot in the dark of the moon the upright of heart,'[107] but even then she shines forth in her strongest members. And if any distinction is to be made in these divine words, perhaps it was not idly said of the seed of Abraham: 'As the stars of heaven and as the sand which is on the sea shore,' so that by the stars of heaven we might understand the few who are strong and eminent, but by the sand of the sea shore the great number of the weak and the carnal-minded, who sometimes, in time of peace, appear quiet and free, but are also sometimes disturbed and overwhelmed by the waves of trials and temptations.

---

101 Cf. Matt. 7.14.
102 Cf. Gen. 22.17; Dan. 3.36.
103 Gal. 4.27.
104 Matt. 8.11.
105 Cf. Titus 2.14.
106 Apoc. 7.9.
107 Cf. Ps. 10.3.

Such was the time of which Hilary¹⁰⁸ wrote, whose work you thought to use as a snare for so many divine proofs, as if the Church had perished from the earth. Can you, in the same way, say that the many churches of Galatia did not exist when the Apostle said: 'O senseless Galatians, who hath bewitched you?' and: 'whereas you began in the spirit, you would now be made perfect by the flesh'?¹⁰⁹ Thus you do an injury to a learned man who was earnestly rebuking the slothful and timid, of whom he was in labor again until Christ should be formed in them.¹¹⁰ Who does not know that many of the uninstructed had been deceived at that time by ambiguous words so as to think that the Arians believed what they themselves believed, while others had yielded through fear and had pretended to conform, but 'They walked not uprightly unto the truth of the gospel'?¹¹¹ When these were afterward converted, would you refuse them pardon when pardon was granted to them? Obviously, you do not know the word of God. Read what Paul wrote about Peter,¹¹² and what Cyprian thought about it,¹¹³ and do not be displeased at the mildness of the Church which gathers the scattered members of Christ but does not scatter what she has gathered, although of those also who were the strongest and best able to understand the deceitful words of the heretics—few, indeed, in comparison with the rest—of those very ones, some triumphed strongly for

---

108 Hilary of Poitiers had written against the Arians in his *De synodis*: 'Except for Eleusius and a few with him, the ten provinces of Asia, among which I take my stand, for the most part do not truly know God.'
109 Gal. 3.1-3.
110 Gal. 4.17.
111 Gal. 2.14.
112 Gal. 2.11-14.
113 Cyprian (210-258) was a convert from paganism who became bishop of Carthage in 249. He was a vigorous apologist and has left thirteen works besides his Letters. He suffered martyrdom for the faith under Decius. The reference here is to Letter 73, Vol. 1, p. 332.

the faith, but some went into hiding in different parts of
the world. So the Church, which increases among all
nations, has been preserved with the Lord's grain[114] and
will be preserved to the end, until it includes all nations,
even the barbarian ones. The Church is symbolized by the
good seed, which the Son of Man sowed, and of which He
foretold that it would grow, intermingled with cockle, until
the harvest time. The field indeed is the world, and the
harvest the end of the world.

Hilary was stating, therefore, that ten of the provinces
of Asia were either cockle and not good grain, or they were
good grain which was endangered by the falling away of
some; and he thought the usefulness of his argument would
be in proportion to its forcefulness. For the canonical Scriptures
have this method of making a statement by seeming
to speak in general, while referring to a certain group.
When the Apostle says to the Corinthians: 'How do some
among you say that there is no resurrection of the dead?'[115]
he shows plainly that not all of them were such, but he
bears witness that such men were not outside, but among
them. And shortly afterward he warned them not to be led
astray by those who held that opinion, saying: 'Be not
seduced; evil communications corrupt good manners. Be
sober, ye just, and sin not, for some have not the knowledge
of God. I speak it to your shame.'[116] But when he says: 'For
whereas there is among you envying and contention, are
you not carnal and walk according to man?'[117] he is speaking
as if to all, and you see how sternly he speaks. Moreover,
if we did not read in the same Epistle: 'I give thanks
to my God always for you, for the grace of God that is
given you in Christ Jesus, that in all things you are made

---

114 Matt. 13.24-30,38,39.
115 1 Cor. 15.12.
116 Cf. 1 Cor. 15.33,34.
117 1 Cor. 3.3.

rich in Him, in all utterance and in all knowledge; as the testimony of Christ was confirmed in you, so that nothing is wanting to you in any grace,'[118] we should think all the Corinthians carnal-minded and sensual, not discerning what is of the spirit of God, 'quarrelsome, envious, walking according to man.'[119] Therefore, 'the whole world is seated in wickedness,'[120] on account of the cockle which is everywhere in the world, and Christ is 'the propitiation for our sins, not for ours only, but also for those of the whole world,'[121] on account of the good grain which is everywhere in the world.

But the charity of many has grown cold[122] because of the prevalence of scandals, and as the Name of Christ is more and more glorified, even the evil-minded and altogether perverse are gathered into the participation of His mysteries, but like the chaff they are not to be removed from the Lord's threshing floor until the final winnowing.[123] They do not overwhelm the Lord's grain—of small quantity in comparison with them, but plentiful in itself—they do not blot out the elect of God who are to be gathered at the end of the world, as the Gospel says: 'from the four winds, from the farthest parts of the heavens to the utmost bounds of them.'[124] Theirs is the cry: 'Save me, O Lord, for there is now no saint, for truths are decayed from among the children of men,'[125] and of them the Lord says, in the abundance of iniquity: 'he that shall persevere to the end, he shall be saved.'[126] Finally, the subsequent verses show us

---

118 1 Cor. 1.4-7.
119 1 Cor. 2.14; 3.3.
120 1 John 5.19.
121 1 John 2.2.
122 Matt. 24.12.
123 Matt. 3.12; 13.30.
124 Matt. 24.11.
125 Ps. 11.2.
126 Matt. 24.13.

that not one man but many are speaking in the same psalm, where it says: 'Thou, O Lord, wilt preserve us, and keep us from this generation forever.'[127] And because of this abounding iniquity which the Lord foretold would come to pass, this is expressed: 'When the Son of Man cometh, shall He find, think you, faith on earth?'[128] The doubt of the All-Knowing prefigures our doubt in Him, when the Church, often deceived in many, of whom she had hoped much—whereas they have turned out otherwise than had been believed—becomes so distrustful of her own that she will scarcely believe anything good of anyone. However, it is not allowed us to doubt that they whose faith He will find on earth are growing with the cockle over the whole field.

This, then, is the very Church which swims with the bad fishes in the Lord's net,[129] but in heart and character is always separate and distinct from them so as to be presented to her spouse: 'Glorious . . . not having spot or wrinkle.'[130] But she awaits the physical separation on the sea shore,[131] that is, at the end of the world, converting those whom she can, bearing with those whom she cannot convert, but not forsaking her union with the good because of the malice of those whom she does not convert.

Therefore, brother, in the face of so many divine, clear, and incontestable proofs, do not try to gather misrepresentations from the writings either of our bishops, such as Hilary, or of those who antedated the schism of Donatus, such as Cyprian and Agrippinus,[132] because, in the first place, writings of this sort are to be distinguished from the

---

127 Ps. 11.8.
128 Luke 18.8.
129 Matt. 13.47.
130 Eph. 5.27.
131 Matt. 13.48,49.
132 Bishop of Carthage, one of Cyprian's predecessors in the see.

authority of canonical writings. For, anyone who reads them may differ from the proofs they offer, wherever they teach what is at variance with the requirements of truth. Certainly, we are in that class, and we do not refuse to apply to ourselves the word of the Apostle: 'and if in anything you be otherwise minded, this also God will reveal to you; nevertheless whereunto we are come . . . let us also continue in the same,'[133] namely, in that way which is Christ,[134] the way of which the psalm speaks thus: 'May God have mercy upon us, and bless us; may He cause the light of his countenance to shine upon us, that we may know thy way upon earth, thy salvation in all nations.'[135]

In the second place, you like the testimony of Cyprian, a holy bishop and illustrious martyr, which, indeed, as I said, we distinguish from the authority of canonical writings. Why do you not also like the fact that he held with firm affection to the unity of the whole world, and of all nations; that he defended it by his arguments; that he considered the self-righteous, who wished to separate from it, as utterly arrogant and proud? He even laughed at them for daring to arrogate to themselves what the Lord did not allow to the Apostles: that they should gather the cockle before the time; that they should separate the chaff from the good grain, as if it had been permitted them to carry off the chaff and clean the threshing-floor.[136] Cyprian showed also that no one can be stained by another's sins, something which all the authors of this accursed revolt allege as the sole cause of the separation, and he gave as his opinion that his colleagues who held views different from his in this very matter were not to be judged nor to be deprived of the right of communion with him. In that very letter

---
[133] Phil. 3.15,16.
[134] John 14.6.
[135] Ps. 66.2,3.
[136] Matt. 13.28-30; 3.12.

to Jubaianus which was first read in the council[137]—the one whose authority you cite in the matter of rebaptism—he confesses that in the past some were admitted to the Church who had been baptized elsewhere. These were not baptized again, so that some thought they were not baptized at all. In this does he not hold the peace of the Church so vital and so necessary that for the sake of it he does not believe that they are deprived of its gifts?

Thus—as far as I know your mind—you can easily see that your whole case is undermined and destroyed. For, if the world-wide Church was destroyed by sharing its sacraments with sinners, as you think—and this is why you separated from it—then it had already been totally destroyed when, as Cyprian says, some were admitted to it without baptism; and if not even Cyprian himself held this view of the Church in which he was reborn, how much less should your later founder and father Donatus hold it! But, if at that time when members were admitted to it without baptism, it was still the Church which produced Cyprian, and also produced Donatus, it is clear that the just are not defiled by the sins of others when they partake of the sacraments with them. Thus, you can offer no excuse for the separation by which you withdrew from unity, and in you is fulfilled this wise saying of Holy Scripture: 'A wicked son calls himself just, but he did not cleanse his going forth.'[138]

But, just as he does not compare in merit with Cyprian, who does not dare to rebaptize even heretics because they have the same sacraments, so whoever does not force the Gentiles to observe the Jewish law does not compare in merit with Peter. Now, that hesitation of Peter as well as his amendment is contained in the canonical Scriptures,

---
137 Council of Carthage, 256.
138 Prov. 24.35 (Septuagint).

while the fact that Cyprian held views about baptism different from the form and practice of the Church is not found in canonical writings, but in his own, and in the reports of a council. Still, we must not think it inconsistent in such a man to have changed his opinion, and it could even be that the change was suppressed by those who were too pleased with his erroneous views, and did not wish to be deprived of such strong support. There are some, too, who maintain that Cyprian did not hold this view at any time, but that a deceit was passed off under his name by presumptuous liars. For, the authenticity and correctness of the writings of one bishop, however famous, could not be guaranteed as the canonical Scripture, written in so many languages, is guaranteed by the order and succession of ecclesiastical observance. Yet, in spite of this, there have been writers who have passed off many vain imaginings of their own under the names of the Apostles, but without success, because the apostolic writings were so trustworthy, so widely diffused, and so well known. The infamous boldness of such an attempt shows what can happen to writings of no canonical authority, since it did not shrink from touching writings based on such a foundation of knowledge and renown.

For two reasons, however, we believe that Cyprian held that view: first, because his style has a certain peculiar quality by which it can be recognized; and second, because by it our case is shown to be invincible, and the underlying assumption of your separation, namely, that you feared to be stained by the sins of others, is easily refuted. It is clear from the letters of Cyprian that sacraments were shared with sinners when they were admitted to the Church, and that these, according to your view—and his, too, if you like —did not have baptism; yet the Church survived, and the good grain of the Lord, scattered over the world, retained the integrity of its own nature. Consequently, if any harbor is good to the storm-tossed, and you therefore take refuge in Cyprian, you see what a rocky shoal your error strikes upon; if you no longer dare to take refuge even in him, then you are sunk without a struggle.

To sum up, then, Cyprian either did not hold that view at all, as you say he did; or he retracted it afterward according to the rule of truth; or he covered over that supposed blemish with the overflowing charity of his most candid soul; since he most eloquently defended the unity of the Church, then spreading over the world; and he held most firmly to the bond of peace, for it is written: 'Charity covereth a multitude of sins.'[139] We must add, too, that the Father purged that most fruitful branch—if anything in him needed correcting—with the pruning knife of suffering, for the Lord said: 'the branch in me . . . that beareth fruit, my Father purgeth it that it may bring forth more fruit.'[140] And how does he do this except by clinging to the root in the pruning of the vine? For, even if he should deliver his body to be burned, and have not charity, it profits him nothing.[141]

Stay a little longer on the letters of Cyprian, and you will see how little excuse he leaves to the one who, on the pretext of his own righteousness, tries to break away from the unity of the Church, which God promised and fulfilled to all nations. You will understand better, too, the truth of that verse quoted by me just above: 'The wicked son calls himself just, but he did not cleanse his going forth.' He makes a point in one of his letters to Antonianus[142] very apposite to the matter we are now discussing, and it is better to give his exact words: 'Certain bishops of ours,'

---

139 1 Peter 4.8.
140 Cf. John 15.2.
141 Cf. 1 Cor. 13.3.
142 Cyprian, *Ep.* 55.21.

he says, 'who preceded us in our province, thought that absolution should not be given to adulterers, and they thus shut off every opportunity of repentance from adultery; yet they did not break off their relationship with their fellow bishops, nor rend the unity of the Catholic Church by their harshness and their unyielding refusal of pardon; nor did those who refused absolution separate from the Church because there were others who gave absolution to adulterers. Thus, each bishop regulated and directed his own conduct, with a view to his obligation of giving an account of his stewardship to the Lord, while the bond of unity was preserved and the personal character of the ministry in the Catholic Church was maintained.' What do you say to this, brother Vincent? Doubtless, you observe that this great man, this peace-loving bishop, this bravest of martyrs, accomplished his most active work in preventing the bond of unity from being broken. You see him in labor, not only that the little ones conceived in Christ may be born, but even that those already born may not die outside the bosom of their Mother.

Notice, moreover, the very point which he stresses against the impious separatists. If those who gave absolution to adulterers communicated with adulterers, then were those who did not do so defiled by their association with them? But if, as truth teaches and the Church reasonably holds, absolution was rightly given to repentant adulterers, then those who shut off the whole area of repentance from adulterers certainly acted wrongly, in that they refused healing to the members of Christ, and took away the keys of the Church from those who knocked for entrance, and in their harsh cruelty they said 'no' to the most merciful patience of God, who allowed these sinners to live precisely that they might be healed by the penitent sacrifice of an afflicted spirit and the offering of a contrite heart.¹⁴³ Yet, that monstrous error and impiety did not contaminate the merciful and the peace-loving, who partook of the Christian sacraments with them, and showed them tolerance within the nets of unity, until such time as they should be drawn to the shore and separated,¹⁴⁴ or, if it did contaminate them, then the Church has by this time been wiped out by contact with the wicked, and there was no Church to produce a Cyprian. But, if the Church has continued to exist—which is an established fact—it is equally an established fact that no one in the unity of Christ can be defiled by the sins of others, so long as he does not consent to the deeds of the wrong-doers, and in this case he would be contaminated by sharing in their sins. But, for the sake of the good he bears with the wicked, who are the chaff awaiting the final winnowing on the Lord's threshing floor.¹⁴⁵ In view of all this, what grounds have you for separation? Are you not wicked sons? You call yourselves just, but you do not cleanse your going forth.

Now, if I should wish to recall what Tychonius included in his writings—a man of your persuasion who wrote rather against you and in favor of the Catholic Church—to the effect that he broke away uselessly from communion with the Africans, as alleged traditors, for which admission alone Parmenianus¹⁴⁶ refutes him, what could you answer except what the same Tychonius said of you, as I quoted it awhile back: 'What we wish is holy.'¹⁴⁷ For that Tychonius, a man, as I said, of your persuasion, writes that a council of

---

143 Ps. 50.19.
144 Matt. 13.47-49.
145 Matt. 3.12; 13.29,30,38.
146 Successor to Donatus in the schismatic see of Carthage (355-391). He wrote five treatises against the Church 'of the Traditors,' and a letter to Tychonius. He was not an African, but either a Gaul or a Spaniard.
147 See above, note 40.

270 of your bishops was held at Carthage,[148] and that they set all past differences aside, and labored for seventy-five days over a decision and decree that if traditors, guilty of the worst crime, refused to be baptized, they should be received unconditionally. He says that Deuterius, a Macrimensian[149] bishop of your sect, had gathered a crowd of traditors, and had introduced them among his congregation, and, acording to the enactments of that council composed of 270 of your bishops, he had maintained constant communication with the traditors; and that Donatus had communicated constantly with the said Deuterius after this accomplishment, and not only with this Deuterius but even with all the bishops of Mauretania for forty years. And he says these kept in communion with the traditors, without rebaptism, until the persecution raised by Macarius.[150]

'But,' you say, 'who is that Tychonius?' He is that Tychonius whom Parmenianus silences by his answer, when he warns him not to write such things again; but he did not retract what he had written. In one point alone, as I said above, he presses him hard, namely, that although he said such things about the world-wide Church, and admits that no one in its unity is stained by another's sins, he nevertheless broke away from the alleged contamination of the African traditors, and joined the sect of Donatus. Parmenianus could have said that all of that was lies, but, as the same Tychonius relates, there were many still alive

---

148 No other reference is found to this council, which does not seem to have been held before 330. Cf. Migne, *PL* 33-342 n.
149 Macrimeni was a town in Numidia.
150 This was the name given by the Donatists to the repressive measures of the Emperor Constans in 348. Macarius was the official sent by the emperor to enforce his decrees. When the Donatists resisted, there was violence and many Donatists were killed by the soldiers of Macarius. The schismatics called these martyrs, and referred to the whole incident as the persecution of Macarius. Cf. Letter 44, Vol. 1, pp. 210-211.

by whom these facts could be proved to be only too true and too well known.

But I say nothing of this. Grant that Tychonius lied, I refer you back to Cyprian, whose name you brought in yourself. Obviously, according to the writings of Cyprian, if everyone in the unity of the Church is stained by another's sins, the Church ceased to exist long before Cyprian, and there was no Church from which Cyprian could come forth. But, if it is sacrilegious to think this, and it is evident that the Church continues to exist, then no one in union with her is stained by another's sins, and in vain do you, wicked sons, call yourselves just; you do not cleanse, you do not purify your going forth.

You say: 'Why do you seek us? Why do you receive us whom you call heretics?' See how easily and how briefly I answer. We seek you because you are lost; so that we may rejoice to find you, as we grieve over your loss. We call you heretics, but it is before you are converted to the Catholic fold, before you put off the error in which you are enmeshed. But, when you come over to us, you first leave behind what you were, so as not to be heretics when you come over to us. You say: 'Then baptize me.' I would do so if you had not been baptized, or if you had received the baptism of Donatus or Rogatus, not that of Christ. It is not the Christian sacraments that make you heretical, but your perverse and wrong ideas. Because of the evils that came forth from you, the good that remains in you is not to be denied, that good which you have to your own hurt, if you do not have it from the source of all good. All the sacraments of the Lord are of the Catholic Church, which you hold and administer as they were held and administered before you left the Church. You do not cease to have them because you are no longer where they originated as you have them. We do not change in you what you have in common with us, for you are with us in many things, and of such it is said: 'For among many they were with me';[151] but we do correct those things in which you are not with us, and we wish you to receive here what you do not have there, where you are. Now you are with us in baptism, in the Creed, in the other sacraments of the Lord, but you are not with us in the spirit of unity and the bond of peace,[152] or in the Catholic Church. If you would receive these, what you have will not merely be at hand, but will be for your advantage. We do not then receive your adherents, as you think, but by receiving them we make ours those who leave you to be received by us; in order to begin to be ours they first cease to be yours. For we do not enforce union with us of the workers of iniquity,[153] which we despise, but we wish them to join us so that they may cease to be what we despise.

'But,' you say, 'the Apostle Paul baptized after John.'[154] Did he do it after a heretic? Or, if perhaps you dare to say that the friend of the bridegroom[155] was a heretic and was not in the unity of the Church, I wish you would write that also. But, if it is complete madness either to think or to say that, then it is the duty of your Prudence to reflect on the reason why the Apostle Paul baptized after John. If he baptized after an equal, all of you ought to baptize after yourselves; if after a superior, you ought to baptize after Rogatus; if after an inferior, Rogatus should have done it after you, because you baptized as a priest. On the other hand, if the baptism which is now given is equally valid to those who receive it in spite of the unequal merit of those who give it, because it is the

---
151 Ps. 54.19.
152 Eph. 4.3.
153 1 Macc. 3.6.
154 Acts 19.1-5.
155 John 3.29.

baptism of Christ, not of those by whom it is administered, I think you now understand that Paul gave to some the baptism of Christ for the reason that they had received the baptism of John, but not that of Christ. It is expressly referred to as the baptism of John, as the divine Scripture testifies in many places, and the Lord Himself said: 'The baptism of John, whence was it? from heaven or from men?'[156] But the baptism which Peter gave was not Peter's, but Christ's, and that which Paul gave was not Paul's but Christ's, and the baptism which was given by those who preached Christ not sincerely but out of envy[157] was not theirs, but Christ's; and that given by those who, by crafty theft, stole property in the time of Cyprian and increased it by money-lending at high rates of usury[158] was not their baptism, but Christ's. And because it was Christ's, even though it was not given to them by their equals, it was equally effective to those who received it. If anyone were to receive a better baptism because of being baptized by a better person, then the Apostle was wrong in giving thanks that he had baptized none of the Corinthians except Crispus and Gaius and the household of Stephanas,[159] since their baptism would be of higher worth if they were baptized by Paul, a man of higher worth. Finally, when he says: 'I have planted, Apollo watered,'[160] he seems to have meant that he had preached the Gospel and Apollo had baptized. Was Apollo better than John? Why, then, did he not baptize after him as he did after John, except that the one baptism, no matter by whom given, was Christ's, but the other, no matter by whom given, was only John's, although he prepared the way for Christ?

---

156 Matt. 21.25.
157 Phil. 1.15-17.
158 Cyprian, *De lapsis* 6.
159 1 Cor. 1.14-16.
160 1 Cor. 3.6.

This seems an invidious saying: 'Baptism is repeated after John but not after heretics,' but this also could be an invidious saying: 'Baptism is repeated after John but not after drunkards.' It is better for me to mention this vice, which cannot be hidden by those addicted to it, and everybody who is not blind knows how many there are. Yet, among the works of the flesh—and those who practice them will not possess the kingdom of God—the Apostle includes this where he enumerates heresies. He says: 'The works of the flesh are manifest, which are fornication, uncleanness . . . luxury, idolatry, witchcrafts, enmities, contentions, emulations . . . quarrels, dissensions, sects, envies, drunkenness, revellings and such like, of which I foretell you, as I have foretold to you, that they who do such things shall not obtain the kingdom of God.'[161] For this reason, therefore, although baptism is given again after John, it is not given after a heretic; for this reason, although baptism is given again after John, it is not given after a drunkard, because both heresy and drunkenness will not obtain the kingdom of God. Does it not seem to you an unbearable insult that baptism should be repeated after one who prepared the way for the kingdom of God, and who not only used wine with moderation, but did not use wine at all, while it is not repeated after a drunkard who will not obtain the kingdom of God? What answer is there except that the former baptism was John's, and that the Apostle baptized after it with the baptism of Christ; but the latter is the baptism of Christ even though administered by a drunkard? Between John and a drunkard there is the difference of complete opposites; between the baptism of John and the baptism of Christ there is a great difference, but not that of opposites. Between an Apostle and a drunkard there is a great difference; between the baptism

---

161 Gal. 5.19-21.

of Christ given by an Apostle and the baptism of Christ given by a drunkard there is no difference. So, between John and a heretic there is the difference of opposites, and between the baptism of John and the baptism of Christ, given by a heretic, there is a great difference, but not that of opposites; between the baptism of Christ given by an Apostle and the baptism of Christ given by a heretic there is no difference. The nature of the sacraments is recognized as the same even when there is a great difference in the merits of men.

But I ask your pardon. I was wrong in trying to convince you with an argument of a drunkard baptizing; it slipped my mind that I was dealing with a Rogatist, not with any sort of Donatist. Possibly among your few colleagues and among your clerics you will not be able to find a drunkard. For you are the only ones who hold the Catholic faith, not only of the communion of the whole world, but even of those who observe all the precepts and all the sacraments. You are the only ones among whom the Son of Man will find faith when He shall come, and shall not find it on earth, because you are neither of the earth nor on earth, but you dwell in heaven as angels! Do you neither observe nor fear that 'God resisteth the proud and giveth grace to the humble?'[162] Does that place in the Gospel not strike home to you where the Lord says: 'The son of man when he cometh, shall he find, think you, faith on earth?'[163] And straightway, as if fore-knowing that some would arrogantly attribute this faith to themselves, he said: 'To some who seemed to themselves to be just and despised others, he spoke this parable: Two men went up into the temple to pray; the one a Pharisee and the other a publican,'[164]

---

162 James 4.6.
163 Luke 18.8.
164 Cf. Luke 18.9,10.

and the rest. Do you now answer to yourself for what follows. Inquire more carefully into those few adherents of yours, whether no drunkard baptizes among them. For, this curse has made such wide inroads in souls, and rules with such freedom that I should be greatly surprised if it had not entered into your little flock, although you boast that you have separated the sheep from the goats,[165] even before the coming of the Son of Man, the one Good Shepherd.[166]

Hear, at least through me, the voice of the Lord's grain, toiling amidst the chaff until the final winnowing on the Lord's threshing floor,[167] which is the wide world, where 'God hath called the earth from the rising of the sun even to the going down thereof,'[168] where even the children praise the Lord.[169] Hear this voice: Whoever by reason of this imperial edict persecutes you, not to correct you through love, but to show hatred to you as an enemy, displeases us. And although earthly goods are not rightly possessed by anyone except by divine law, by which the just possess all things, or by human law, which is the power of earthly kings, and since you wrongly call yours goods which you do not possess justly, and which you have been ordered by the laws of earthly kings to give up, it will be useless for you to say: 'We have toiled to amass them' when you read the text: 'The just shall eat the labors of sinners.'[170] However, if, by reason of this law which the kings of the earth, the servants of Christ, have enacted to restrain your impiety, anyone covets your lawful property, he displeases us. Finally, if anyone holds the goods of the poor, or the

---
165 Matt. 25.32,33.
166 John 10.11.
167 Matt. 3.12.
168 Ps. 49.1.
169 Ps. 112.1.
170 Cf. Prov. 13.22.

basilicas of the people, which you held under the name of the Church, which goods are owed exclusively to the Church, the true Church of Christ, and if he holds them through cupidity, not through justice, he displeases us. And if anyone receives a person cast out by you for some crime or wrong-doing, as those are received who have lived without blame among you, except for the error by which you separated yourselves from us, he also displeases us. But you cannot easily prove those points to us, and if you could, we still tolerate some whom we cannot correct or punish; we do not forsake the Lord's threshing floor because of the chaff,[171] nor burst the nets of the Lord because of the bad fishes,[172] nor abandon the flock of the Lord because of the goats, which are to be separated at the end,[173] nor do we leave the house of the Lord because of the vessels made unto dishonor.[174]

But you, brother, as it seems to me, if you do not regard the vainglory of men and despise the insults of fools who say: 'Why do it now?' you will undoubtedly come over to the Church, which I know you recognize as the true Church, nor need I look far for proof of that sentiment of yours. In the beginning of that letter of yours, which I am now answering, you yourself put these words: 'I know well,' you say, 'that you were for a long time separated from the Christian faith and given up to the study of literature, and that you were a promoter of peace and honorable conduct, and after your conversion to the Christian faith, as I have learned from the reports of many, you devoted yourself to legal disputes.' Certainly, if you sent me that letter, those are your words. So, when you admit that I was converted to the Christian faith, since I

---

171 Matt. 3.12.
172 Matt. 13.47,48.
173 Matt. 25.32,33.
174 2 Tim. 2.20.

was converted neither to the Donatists nor to the Rogatists, without doubt you prove that the Christian faith is something different from that of the Rogatists and the Donatists. The faith, then, as we say, is disseminated among all the nations which, according to the testimony of God, are blessed in the seed of Abraham,[175] so why do you hesitate to embrace what you believe, unless you are embarrassed at having believed at one time what you do not believe now, or at having defended it as if it were something else? And while you are ashamed to correct your error, why are you not ashamed to persist in your error, which is a much greater reason for shame?

This is a point on which Scripture is not silent. 'For there is a shame that bringeth sin and there is a shame that bringeth glory and grace.'[176] Shame brings sin when anyone is ashamed to change a wrong sentiment for fear of being thought fickle, or of being judged by his own evidence of long-continued error; so 'they go down alive into hell,'[177] that is, knowing their own destruction. They were prefigured long before by Dathan and Abiron and Core, who were swallowed up by the opened earth.[178] But shame brings grace and glory when anyone blushes for his own sin and changes for the better through repentance. This, however, is something which you shrink from doing, weighed down as you are by that false shame, and fearing that men who do not know what they are saying will reproach you with that saying of the Apostle: 'For if I build up again the things which I have destroyed, I make myself a prevaricator.'[179] If this could be said against those who after conversion preach the truth which they had

---
175 Gen. 22.18.
176 Eccli. 4.25.
177 Ps. 54.16.
178 Num. 16.31-33.
179 Gal. 2.18.

wrongly opposed, it would be said first of all against Paul himself, on whose account the Churches of Christ praised God when they heard that he was preaching the faith which once he had impugned.[180]

But do not think that anyone can pass from error to truth, or from any sin, whether great or small, to conversion, without repentance. And it is an unpardonable fault to wish to accuse the Church—which is proved by so many divine testimonies to be the Church of Christ—of discrimination in her treatment of those who leave her, but repent and are converted; and those have never been hers and who embrace her peace for the first time. The former she humbles profoundly, the latter she receives kindly, but she loves both, and by healing both she treats them with maternal charity. You now have a letter which is probably longer than you wanted. It would be shorter if I were thinking of you alone in my answer; but, indeed, if it does you no good, I think it will not be without effect for those who are careful to read it with fear of God and without distinction of persons. Amen.

94. Paulinus and Therasia,[1] sinners, to Augustine, bishop, holy and blessed lord, father, brother, master, uniquely dear and venerable and desirable to us
(408)

'Thy word is [always] a lamp to my feet and a light to my path.'[2] Thus, as often as I receive letters from your most blessed Holiness, I feel the darkness of my stupidity being

---

180 Gal. 1.23, 24.

---

1 Cf. Letters 24, Vol. 1, p. 66.
2 Ps. 118.105.

dispelled, and, as if the eyes of my mind had been anointed with the salve of enlightenment,³ I see more clearly, when the night of ignorance has been driven away and the mist of doubt has been scattered. I have felt this often on other occasions, when the boon of your letters has been bestowed on me, but most especially in that recent letter of which that blessed brother of the Lord, our deacon Quintus, was the welcome and worthy bearer. He came after a long time to the city,⁴ where I had gone after Easter, according to my custom, to venerate the Apostles and martyrs, and there he gave us the blessing of your words. And, indeed, forgetting the time which he had wasted at Rome, without my knowing he was there, as soon as I saw him, he seemed to me fresh from your presence, so that I could believe he had just come from you to me, and was offering me the full odor of your sweetness,⁵ in your words, fragrant with the purity of a heavenly ointment.⁶ I confess to your venerable Unanimity that I was not able to read that work as soon as I had received it at Rome, for there were such crowds there that I could not examine your gift with care, nor enjoy it as I longed to do, seeing that, if I had begun to read it, I should have had to study it thoroughly. Therefore, as usually happens, in the confident expectation of the banquet awaiting me, and with the sure hope of repletion, I curbed the hunger of my greedy mind, since I had in my hand the bread of my desire, ready to be devoured in the volume which was afterward most sweet in my mouth and in my stomach, as I fed on it; and I easily held my gluttony in check, gloating over the honeycomb⁷ of your letter, until I set out from the city. Then,

---

3 Apoc. 3.18.
4 The 'city' for Romans was always Rome.
5 Gen. 8.21.
6 Cant. 1.2.
7 Cant. 4.11.

as there was a day to be spent at a stopping place, which we had in the town of Formiae,[8] I planned to spend the whole of it on this work, and to feast on the spiritual delights of your letter, free from all the dust of care and the jostling of crowds.

What answer, then, shall I, lowly and earth-bound, make to the wisdom which is given to you from above, which this world does not receive[9] and which no one savors except the wisdom of God, and the man wise and eloquent in the word of God? Therefore, because I have 'a proof of Christ that speaketh'[10] in thee, 'in God I will praise [thy] words,'[11] and I 'shall not be afraid of the terror of the night'[12] because you have taught me in the spirit of truth how to exercise control over my mind in transitory and mortal things, such as you saw in that blessed mother and grandmother, Melania,[13] who wept over the earthly passing of her only son with a silent grief, but with a sorrow that did not restrain her maternal tears. Your spirit, closer and more akin to hers, understood more deeply her restrained and worthy tears, and from the similarity of your own heart you could gauge more adequately, and from an equally lofty viewpoint, the maternal heart of a woman, perfect in Christ, possessing the unassailable strength of a virile mind; you could behold her weeping, moved at first by natural affection, but afterward touched by a stronger motive; not so much the human one that she had lost in this present

---

8 An Italian town south of Rome, where travelers frequently broke their journey. Cf. Horace, *Satires* 1. 1.37.
9 John 14.17.
10 2 Cor. 13.3.
11 Ps. 55.5.
12 Ps. 90.5.
13 A Roman matron of the family of Valerii. Her granddaughter, the younger Melania, is venerated as a saint in the Church, and was well-known to Augustine and Alypius. The son of the older Melania, mentioned in this letter, was Publicola.

life, her only son who had paid the debt of his mortal nature, as that he had been cut off almost in the midst of worldly vanity, because his ambition to attain senatorial rank had not left him. Thus, the death was not in accord with the holy avarice of her prayers, which would have had him exchange the glory of earthly intercourse for that of resurrection, knowing that he would gain the same rest and crown as his mother, if, following the example of her life in this world, he had preferred sackcloth to the toga, and a monastery to the senate.

However, this same man, as I think I formerly related to your Holiness, died rich in good works, and if he did not show forth the nobility of his mother's humility in his dress, he manifested it in his mind. Thus, according to the word of the Lord, he was in conduct so 'meek and humble of heart'[14] that he can reasonably be believed to have entered into the rest of the Lord,[15] since 'there are remnants for the peaceable man,'[16] and 'the meek . . . shall possess the land,'[17] pleasing to God, 'in the land of the living.'[18] For, surely, he fulfilled the ideal of the Apostle, not only by the meekness of his inner disposition, but also by his devout conduct in his public duties; and although he ranked with the great of this world, and was their colleague in honor, he was not boastful, nor did he 'mind the high things' of earth, but as a perfect imitator of Christ he 'consented to the humble,'[19] and he continued to 'show mercy and to lend all the day long.'[20] Hence, 'his seed [has become] mighty on earth,'[21] among those who as 'strong gods of the

---
14 Matt. 11.29.
15 Heb. 3.11,18; 4.1; 3.10,11.
16 Ps. 36.37.
17 Matt. 5.4.
18 Ps. 114.9.
19 Rom. 12.16.
20 Ps. 36.26.
21 Ps. 111.2.

earth are exceedingly exalted,'²² so that even from the appearance of his family and his home the holy worth of the man is revealed. 'The generation of the righteous shall be blessed,'²³ said he; an unfading glory and an unfailing wealth shall be in his house, in his house which is built in heaven, not by the work of his hands, but by the holiness of his works. I say no more of the memory of a man so dear to me and so devoted to Christ, since, I repeat, I related many things about him in my earlier letters, and I can say of the blessed mother of this son, Melania, the root of equal worth with its holy branches, nothing better or holier than your Holiness has deigned to utter and express regarding her. For, I indeed a sinner, having 'unclean lips,'²⁴ could say nothing worthily of her, far removed as I am from the merits of her faith and the virtues of her soul; but you, as a man of Christ, a doctor in Israel of the Church of truth, helped on to better things by the grace of God, stand forth as a more fitting eulogist of her virile soul in Christ; and, as I said, with your spirit more akin to hers, you can appreciate her mind strengthened by divine virtue, and you can praise in more appropriate words her tenderness mingled with strength.

You did me the compliment of asking me what is likely to be the occupation of the blessed after the resurrection of the body, at the end of time. But I consult you, as a master and spiritual physician, about the present condition of my life, that you may teach me to do the will of God, to follow Christ in your footsteps, and to die that death of the Gospel, in which we anticipate our fleshly dissolution by a voluntary separation—not actual, but in intention—withdrawing from the life of this world which is all made

---

22 Ps. 46.10.
23 Ps. 111.2,3.
24 Isa. 6.5.

up of temptations, or, as you said to me once, is all temptation. How I wish that my paths may be directed in your footsteps, that, imitating you in loosing the old sandal from my feet,[25] I may break my bonds and may freely exult to run my course! May I attain that death by which you have died to this world, so as to live to God, while Christ lives in you, whose death and life are manifest in your body and heart and mouth, because your heart does not 'mind earthly things,'[26] nor does your mouth speak the works of men,[27] but the word of Christ dwells abundantly in your breast[28] and the spirit of truth[29] is poured forth on your tongue, with the force of the heavenly stream making the city of God joyful![30]

But what virtue produces this death in us, except 'love which is strong as death'?[31] For, it so blots out and destroys this world in us as to give the effect of death through the love of Christ, to which we turn when we are converted from the world, and for whom, though living, we die 'from the elements of this world.'[32] Yet, we judge concerning the sight and use of these as if we were not living, because the death of Christ is our portion, whose resurrection from the dead we do not attain in glory unless we imitate His death on the Cross by mortifying our bodies and our fleshly senses. Then we live, not according to our will, but according to His, whose 'will is our sanctification'[33] and who died for us and rose again that we should no longer live to

---

25 Exod. 3.5; Jos. 5.16; Acts 7.33.
26 Phil. 3.19.
27 Ps. 16.4.
28 Col. 3.16.
29 John 14.17; 15.26.
30 Ps. 45.5.
31 Cant. 8.6.
32 Col. 2.20.
33 1 Thess. 4.3.

ourselves but to Him who died for us and rose again,[34] and who gave us the pledge of his promise by His spirit,[35] just as He placed in heaven in His Body the pledge of our life which is our body. Consequently, the Lord is our expectation and our substance,[36] which was made by Him, and which exists by Him and in Him and through Him who was made like to the body of our lowness[37] so as to make us like to the body of His glory and bring us to dwell with Him in heaven. Therefore, those who are worthy of eternal life shall be hereafter in the glory of His kingdom, that they may be with Him, as the Apostle says, and may remain with Him,[38] and as the Lord Himself said to the Father: 'I will that where I am, they also . . . may be with me,'[39] the same thought, undoubtedly, which you find in the psalms: 'Blessed are they that dwell in thy house: they shall praise thee forever and ever.'[40] And I think that this praise is expressed by the voices of those who sing together, although the bodies of the risen saints are to be changed so as to be like the Body of the Lord when it appeared after the Resurrection, in which, certainly, a living image of the resurrection of man was shown, so that the Lord Himself, in the very Body in which He had suffered and had risen again, should be a kind of mirror of contemplation to all. Moreover, He often appeared and showed to the eyes and ears of men all the real activities of all His members, in the same flesh in which He had died and had been buried and had risen again. But, even if the angels, whose nature is simple and spiritual, are said to have tongues

---

34 2 Cor. 5.15.
35 2 Cor. 1.22, 55.
36 Ps. 38.8.
37 Phil. 3.21.
38 1 Thess. 4.16.
39 John 17.24.
40 Ps. 83.5.

with which they sing praises to their Lord and Creator, and give Him unceasing thanks, much more must the spiritualized bodies of men do so after the resurrection, since all the members of their glorified flesh will have tongues in their mouths, and they will give voice to their speaking tongues, and thus they will utter divine praises, the outpouring in words of their love and of the joys that fill even their senses. Doubtless, the Lord will add this to the grace and glory of His saints in the time of His kingdom, that the more perfectly they attain to this blessed condition of body by a happy transformation, the more fully will they sing with tongue and voice, and, being established in their spiritual bodies, they may speak, perchance, not with the tongues of men but with those of angels, such as the Apostle heard in paradise![41] And for this reason, perhaps, he bore witness that man had this indescribable form of speech, because, among other kinds of rewards being prepared for the saints, are new languages. But men of this world are not yet permitted to make use of them, so that, when they are immortal, they may speak in a language befitting their glory, of whom it is undoubtedly said: 'Yea they shall shout and they shall sing a hymn,'[42] among the dwellers in heaven. There they shall be with the Lord,[43] and 'shall delight in abundance of peace,'[44] rejoicing in the sight of the throne, casting down their phials and crowns before the feet of the Lamb[45] and singing to Him a new canticle, joined with the choirs of Angels, of Virtues, of Dominations and of Thrones, as these also with the Cherubim and Seraphim,[46] and those four living creatures, and

---

41 2 Cor. 12.4.
42 Ps. 64.14.
43 1 Thess. 4.16.
44 Ps. 36.11.
45 Apoc. 4.6; 10.5-9.
46 Col. 1.16. These, with the Archangels, Powers, and Principalities, are the names of the nine choirs of angels.

singing with everlasting voice, they say: 'Holy, holy, holy, the Lord God of Hosts,'[47] and the rest which you know.

This, then, is what I ask, needy and poor as I am, that foolish little one of yours, whom you, like a truly wise man, are wont to bear with, that you teach me truth on this matter, or give me your opinion, for I know that you are enlightened with the spirit of revelation by Him who is guide and fountain of the wise,[48] and, as you know things past, and see things present, so as to be able to form a judgment of things to come,[49] tell me what you think of these everlasting voices of heavenly beings, who even above the heavens, in the sight of the Most High, give praise. With what organs of speech do they express themselves? Although, when the Apostle says: 'If I speak with the tongues of angels,'[50] he shows that they have a certain speech, peculiar to their nature, or shall I say to their race, as much superior to human senses and speech as the nature itself and rank of the angels excels mortal inhabitants and earthly abodes, nevertheless he may have said 'tongues of angels' with the meaning of varieties of voices and speech, as when, discoursing of the diversity of supernatural gifts, he lists among the gifts of grace 'kinds of tongues.'[51] By this he doubtless meant that it was given to some to speak in the language of many peoples. But the voice of God, often manifested out of a cloud to the saints, shows that there can be speech without tongue, if, indeed, the tongue is a member of the body, both small and great.[52] But, perhaps that is why God gave the name tongue to the speech and voices of the incorporeal nature of the angels, because he located

---
47 Isa. 6.2,3.
48 Eph. 1.17; Wisd. 7.15; Prov. 18.4; Eccli. 1.5.
49 Wisd. 8.8.
50 1 Cor. 13.1.
51 1 Cor. 13.28.
52 James 3.5.

the faculty of speech in that member, just as the Scripture is accustomed to assign the names of parts of the body to God, according to the nature of His activity. Pray for us and teach us.

Our dearest and sweetest brother, Quintus,[53] is as quick in hurrying back from us to you as he was slow in traveling from you to us. This letter, with more erasures than lines, bespeaks his urgency in demanding a reply, and the papyrus shows the excessive haste of the above-mentioned slave-driver, for he came to us on May 14th for his answer, and he succeeded in getting away on the 15th before noon. See, then, whether this document is a commendation or an accusation of him. Perhaps, or rather assuredly, he will be judged worthy of praise rather than of blame, because he was in haste—and with the best of reasons—to go from the darkness, which we are in comparison to your light, 'to his light.'[54]

95. *Augustine gives greeting in the Lord to Paulinus and Therasia, most beloved and devoted lords, holy and desirable and venerable brothers, fellow disciples under our Master, the Lord Jesus (408)*

When the brethren, our most intimate friends, see you constantly, and you frequently return their greetings, mutually desirous of each other's company, it is not so much an increase of good fortune for us as an assuagement of ill fortune. Naturally, we do not like the reasons and necessities which force them to go overseas, in fact, we hate them, and

---
53 The deacon, mentioned at the beginning of the letter, who brought Augustine's letter to Paulinus.
54 1 Peter 2.9.

we try to avoid them as much as we can, but somehow or other—I suppose it is what we deserve—such exigencies cannot be avoided. Yet, when they visit you and see you, the words of Scripture are realized: 'According to the multitude of my sorrows in my heart, thy comforts have given joy to my soul.'[1] Therefore, when you hear from brother Possidius[2] of the sad reason which drove him to the joy of your company, you will realize that I speak the absolute truth. Still, if anyone of us crossed the sea for no other reason than to enjoy being with you, what better or more laudable excuse could he have? But our duty, which keeps us here in the service of the weak, would not allow that, nor could we go away and leave them, unless the same duty should impel us to it, by reason of a more threatening and more dangerous emergency. It would be hard to say whether I am occupied in these matters or bowed down by them, except that 'He does not deal with us according to our sins, nor reward us according to our iniquities,'[3] but He mingles great comfort with our sorrows, and treats us with a wonderful remedy so that we neither love the world nor are we overlooked by the world.

I asked you in previous letters what sort of eternal life you thought the saints enjoyed, and you answered me truly that it is the condition of this present life which we ought to consider. However, your desire to consult me was not good, because you either share my ignorance, or we both know the answer, or, more likely, you know better than I do, since you said so truly that we must first die the death

---

1 Ps. 93.19.
2 Bishop of Calama, pupil and friend of Augustine, whose life he wrote. Cf. *Fathers of the Church* 15 (New York 1952). The sad cause of his journey to Italy was a riot stirred up by the pagans in June 408, in which he almost lost his life, and in which damage was done to his church. He was presumably going to ask government protection in this state of disorder. Cf. Letters 91, 93.
3 Cf. Ps. 102.10.

of the Gospel, 'in which we anticipate our fleshly dissolution by a voluntary separation—not actual, but by intention—withdrawing from the life of this world.'⁴ There is a straightforward course of action, undisturbed by any storms of doubt, that we should so live in this mortal life as to fit ourselves somehow for our immortal life. But the whole question, which troubles active and inquiring persons such as I am, is this: how to live among people or near people who have not yet learned to live by dying, not by a fleshly dissolution, but by deliberately turning the mind away from the enticements of the flesh. On the whole, it seems to me that we shall not be able to succeed with them, unless we yield to them a little in those things from which we wish to detach them. Yet, when we do this, a certain pleasure in such things steals over us also, and we often enjoy speaking useless words and listening to them, and smiling at them, or even being overcome by laughter. Thus we are dragged down by these dusty and earthy desires, and we have a hard time lifting up our sluggish hearts to God, so as to live the life of the Gospel by dying the death of the Gospel. And if at any time anyone succeeds in doing this, at once he hears: 'Good! Good!'—not from men, for no man has such intuition of the mind of another, but in that sort of interior silence, that 'Good! Good!' is shouted, and that is the temptation to which the great Apostle referred when he said he was buffeted by an angel.⁵ This is why 'the life of man upon earth is [all] a warfare,'⁶ since man is tempted in the very act of fitting himself, to the best of his ability, to the likeness of the heavenly life.

What shall I say about punishment or non-punishment, since this is something we intend for the good of those who

---
4 These words are quoted from Letter 94, by Paulinus.
5 2 Cor. 12.7.
6 Job 7.1.

are to be punished or not punished according to our judgment? And, in setting the limit of the punishment, are we to proportion it to the kind and degree of the offenses, as well as to the endurance of the individual soul? It is a deep and difficult matter to estimate what each one can endure and what his limit of endurance is, so as to help him without doing him harm. And I doubt that many are saved from worse conduct by fear of impending punishment, at least of such penalties as are inflicted by men. And here is a dilemma which often occurs: If you punish a man, you may ruin him; if you leave him unpunished, you may ruin another. I admit that I make mistakes in this matter every day, and that I do not know when and how to follow what is written: 'Them that sin, reprove before all, that the rest also may have fear,'[7] and this: 'Rebuke him between thee and him alone,'[8] and this: 'Judge not [anyone] before the time,'[9] and this: 'Judge not, that you may not be judged'[10] —and here it does not add, 'before the time'—and this: 'Who art thou that judgest another man's servant? To his own Lord he standeth or falleth; and he shall stand for God is able to make him stand,'[11] which proves that he is speaking of what is within. And again he orders them to be judged when he says: 'For what have I to do to judge them that are without? do not you judge them that are within? Put away the evil one from among yourselves.'[12] But, when it is evident that this has to be done, how much anxiety and fear arises about the length to which it must go if we are to avoid what he is clearly urging us to avoid in the second Epistle to the same Corinthians:

---
7 1 Tim. 5.20.
8 Matt. 18.5.
9 1 Cor. 4.5.
10 Matt. 7.1; Luke 6.37.
11 Rom. 14.4.
12 1 Cor. 5.12,13.

'Lest . . . such a one be swallowed up with overmuch sorrow,'[13] and, lest anyone think that this does not matter much, he says: 'that we be not overreached by Satan, for we are not ignorant of his devices.'[14] What trembling in all this, my dear Paulinus, holy man of God! What trembling, what darkness! Of these it must have been said: 'Fear and trembling are come upon me, and I said: Who will give me wings like a dove and I will fly and be at rest? Lo I have gone far off, flying away, and I abode in the wilderness.' Truly, in that very wilderness he experienced what he adds: 'I waited for him that hath saved me from pusillanimity and storm.'[15] Obviously, then, 'the life of man upon earth is a warfare.'[16]

Do you not agree with me that those divine words of the Lord are actually felt rather than expounded by us when we are more eager to seek in them what ought to be felt about them than to have a fixed and settled opinion about them? And, although that self-distrust brings us much anxiety, it is far better than a rash statement. In many things, if a man is not wise according to the flesh, which the Apostle says is death,[17] he will be a great stumbling-block to the man who is still wise according to the flesh, when it will be dangerous to say what you think, extremely irksome not to say it, and deadly to say what you do not think. Furthermore, when there is something we do not approve in the speech or writings of 'those within'[18] and we do not conceal our opinion, because we believe this part of the liberty of fraternal charity, what an injustice is done us if

---

13 2 Cor. 2.7.
14 Ibid. 2.11.
15 Ps. 54.6-9.
16 Job 7.1.
17 Rom. 8.5,6.
18 The Vienna text indicates a lacuna here, but the sentence as given seems complete in meaning.

we are judged to be acting not through kindness but through ill-will! And, equally, when others criticize our statements, and we suspect that they are more anxious to wound than to correct us, what an injustice we do to others! Surely this is the source of the enmities which frequently come between the dearest and most intimate persons, and while 'one is puffed up against the other, above that which is written,'[19] while they bite and gnaw at one another, it is to be feared that they will devour each other. 'Who,' therefore, 'will give me wings like a dove and I will fly and be at rest?'[20] Whether it is that the dangers in which I am involved seem worse than those untried, or whether it is really so, 'pusillanimity and storm in the wilderness' seem to me less trying than these troubles which I either suffer or fear in the midst of the throng.

Hence, I strongly approve of your sentiment about the need of dealing with the condition of this life—or, perhaps, course rather than condition—and I add something to it: that this must first be sought and held before we get to the other question of the nature of the place to which the course leads us. And, indeed, I asked what you thought as if I were completely secure in keeping and observing the right rule of this life, whereas I realize that I am in dangerous straits in so many matters, and especially in those which I have referred to as briefly as I could. All this ignorance and difficulty seem to me to arise from the fact that we administer the government not of an earthly and Roman people, but of the heavenly Jerusalem. And my flock are all different in character and mind, and subject to all the secret weaknesses of men, and that is why I wanted to speak with you rather of what we shall be than of what we are. We may not know what good fortune awaits us

---
19 1 Cor. 4.6.
20 Ps. 54.7.

there, but we have no small assurance that misfortune will not exist there.

Therefore, in leading our temporal life in such wise as to attain to eternal life, I know that our fleshly desires must be curbed, and only so much indulgence must be granted to sensual pleasures as may be needed to sustain and carry on this life, and that all temporal troubles must be borne with patience and fortitude, for the truth of God and our own and our neighbor's eternal salvation. I know, too, that we must treat our neighbor with all consideration and love, so that he may live this life uprightly in view of his eternal life; that we must sacrifice the carnal to the spiritual, the transitory to the unchangeable; and that man can do all these things more or less in proportion as he is more or less helped by the grace of God through Jesus Christ our Lord. But, why this one or that one is so helped or not helped I do not know; this I do know, that God acts with a sovereign justice known to Himself. So, after all this that I have told you, if you have any light as a result of your experience, let me have it, please; and if these anxieties disturb you as they do me, talk them over with some kindly physician of the soul, either someone in the place where you are living, or someone at Rome when you go there for your yearly visit. Then write me what the Lord makes known to you through his words to you, or your speech together.

You asked me in your turn what I think about the resurrection of the body and the future functions of its various members in that state of incorruptibility and immortality: here it is in a few words, and, if that does not satisfy you, it can be discussed more at length, with the Lord's help. It is the true and clear pronouncement of Holy Scripture, and one to be held with firmest faith, that the visible and earthly body, which is now called animal, will be spiritual in the resurrection of the faithful and the just. But how that spiritual kind of body, which is outside our experience, can be grasped or thoroughly understood, I do not know. It is certain that there will be no corruption there, nor will the body then have need of that perishable food which now it does need. However, it will be able to take food and truly eat it, as a matter of ability not of necessity; otherwise, the Lord would not have taken food after His Resurrection,[21] when He showed us the type of the resurrection of our body, as the Apostle says: 'If the dead rise not again, neither is Christ risen again.'[22] But, when He appeared with all the parts of His Body and made use of their functions, He also showed the place of the wounds.[23] I have always held that these were scars, not the actual wounds, and that He retained them as a mark of power, not through necessity, for He especially showed the easy use of this power when He appeared in another form, or when He showed Himself in His true form, in the house where the disciples were gathered together, although the doors were closed.

A question akin to this is one about the angels, whether they have bodies adapted to their duties and intercourse, or whether they are wholly spirits. If we say they have bodies, we are reminded that 'He maketh His angels spirits,'[24] but, if we say they have not, we meet a more knotty question: how it is written that they showed themselves to the bodily senses of men without a body, that they had their feet washed and received hospitality of food and drink.[25] It will be easier to believe that the angels are called spirits as men are called souls, as it is written that so many

---
21 Luke 24.30, 43; John 21.13.
22 1 Cor. 15.16.
23 Luke 24.15-43; John 20.14-29; Mark 16.5-14.
24 Cf. Ps. 103.4.
25 Gen. 18.2-9; 19.1-3.

souls went down into Egypt with Jacob[26]—not that they had no bodies—rather than that all those actions were performed without bodies. Then there is a certain angel of great stature mentioned in the Apocalypse,[27] defined by a measure that can only be used of bodies, which in their appearances to men is not to be considered deception, but is to be attributed to the power and ease of spiritual bodies. But, whether the angels have bodies or whether anyone can show how they can do all these things without having bodies, nevertheless, in that City of saints, where those redeemed by Christ 'from this generation forever'[28] will be joined to the thousands of angels, their corporeal voices will show forth their souls, now no longer hidden, because in that divine society no thought will be hidden from anyone else, but there will be a harmonius oneness in praising God, and this praise will be expressed not only by the spirit but also by the spiritual body.

This is how it seems to me now. If you have an opinion which is more fitting and true, or if you hear anything from more learned men, I most eagerly look forward to hearing it from you. Be sure to read over my letter again. I am not complaining of your great haste in answering it, which you blamed on the deacon's hurry, but I am reminding you to answer what you then passed over. Look back and see what I want to learn from you: what you think about the Christian's leisure to learn and disseminate Christian wisdom, and about the leisure which I thought you had until your unbelievable activities were related to me.

Remember us in your happy life, our great joy and comfort, holy ones to God.[29]

---
26 Gen. 46.27.
27 Apoc. 10.1-3.
28 Ps. 11.8; Heb. 12.22.
29 The final sentence is in another hand.

96. Augustine to his most beloved lord and son Olympius,[1] worthy of honor and affection among the members of Christ (408; early September)

Whatever place you may hold in this world's affairs, we write with complete confidence to our dearest and most upright fellow servant, our Christian Olympius. We know that this is more prized by you than any other distinction, and that it is rated by you as higher than any honor. Rumor indeed brings us word that you have attained a higher office, but we have as yet no confirmation of the truth of the report at the time of this present writing. However, since we know that you have learned from the Lord not to mind high things, but to consent to the humble,[2] we feel sure that, whatever pinnacle of promotion you reach, you will receive our letters as you are wont to do, beloved lord, my son to be cherished with honor among the members of Christ. We have not the slightest doubt that you will make a prudent use of your temporal good fortune to secure an eternal gain, and that, the more influential you become in this earthly government, the more earnestly you will work for that heavenly City which has begotten you in Christ. May you be abundantly rewarded in the land of the living and in the true peace of assured and unending joys.

I commend again to your Charity the petition of my holy brother and fellow bishop, Boniface,[3] that what could not happen before may not happen now. For, since he was able

---

[1] On the death by violence of Stilicho, Olympius had been named Master of the Offices, a position of power and authority in Numidia. He is accused by some of having betrayed Stilicho, who had become virtual master of the West under Honorius. The Donatists and pagans hoped that the change of masters would bring the abolition of the penalties decreed against them by the emperor.

[2] Rom. 12.16.

[3] Bishop of Cataquas, a small town near Hippo.

to hold, in his own name and without any doubt, a property which his predecessor had bought—although under another name—and had begun to hold it under the name of the Church, I should not like to have a weight on my conscience about it, since he was in debt to the treasury. But that defect of ownership did not arise from his tax delinquency. Indeed, Paul,[4] after he became bishop, seeing the accumulated arrears of unpaid taxes, was willing to give up all his property, with the special guarantee that a certain amount of money would be reserved for him, with which he bought, as if for the Church, those few acres to support himself, but under the name of a very influential family, and following their custom, although he could not pay his taxes, he was not to suffer any seizure of that land by bailiffs. But his successor, who was ordained to that Church after Paul's death, shrank from taking possession of that land, and although he could have asked the emperor's clemency to remit the unpaid part of the taxes which his predecessor had agreed to subtract from the above-mentioned poor possessions, he preferred to tell the whole story: that Paul, still in debt to the treasury, had bought this land at auction with his own money. So now he asks that the Church may hold possession of it, not by reason of the underhanded action of a bishop, but through the generosity of a Christian ruler. But, if this cannot be, it will be better for the servants of God to suffer the pressure of want rather than to have their necessities supplied through an avowed dishonesty.

We ask that you be so kind as to add your support to this request, because he did not wish to put forward the former answer lest he should shut the door to further possibility of petition. As a matter of fact, he did not get the desired answer. But now, through your accustomed kindness and increased influence, we hope that this may easily be granted,

---
4 Predecessor of Boniface at Cataquas.

in consideration of your services. Surely, even if you asked for the same property and presented it in person to the aforementioned church, no one would criticize you; on the contrary, they would highly commend your request as due to Christian piety rather then to worldly covetousness. May the mercy of the Lord our God keep you ever happy in Christ, my honored son.

97. Augustine gives greeting in the Lord to his son, Olympius,[1] illustrious and deservedly renowned lord, greatly to be honored in the charity of Christ (408)

We have lately heard that you have received a well-deserved promotion, and, although the report has not yet been confirmed, we assume that your attitude toward the Church of God—of which we rejoice that you are truly a son—is the same as that you have recently shown in your letter. Moreover, we write to you with greater confidence, excellent and deservedly renowned lord, son greatly to be honored in the charity of Christ, after reading your letter in which you went so far as to send us, of your own accord, when we were feeling diffident and downcast, a very kind encouragement of our lowly efforts to point out to you how the Lord, whose goodness makes you what you are, may ever more and more succor His Church through your religious obedience.

Indeed, many of the brethren, my holy colleagues, in this time of serious trouble for the Church, have started out almost as refugees for the honorable court, and, even if you have seen them or received letters from them from Rome,

---
1 A general of Vandal origin, advanced to high military rank by Theodosius. Cf. Letter 96 n. 1.

through some favorable circumstance, although I have not been able to talk over any plan with them, I cannot forego the opportunity offered by this brother and fellow priest. He is forced by the grave danger to the safety of a fellow citizen of his to travel in mid-winter, in whatever way he can, to that part of the world, and through him I greet you and I urge that charity of yours which you have in Christ Jesus, to press on your good work, with the most immediate attention. Thus, the enemies of the Church will know that those laws concerning the destruction of idols and the restraining of heretics, which were enforced in Africa during the lifetime of Stilicho, were really enacted by our most devout and faithful emperor. Whether they deceitfully pretend or actually think so, they claim that these were passed without the knowledge and consent of the emperor, and they thereby stir up the ignorant to great violence, and make them so hostile that they are very dangerous to us.

In making this request or suggestion to your Excellency, I am sure I am acting conformably to the wish of all my African colleagues. I think that some action can very easily be taken, and should be taken at the earliest opportunity that presents itself, to let those foolish men, whose salvation we seek in spite of their opposition to us, know that the laws which were passed for the protection of the Church of Christ were the work of the son of Theodosius,[2] not Stilicho. That is why the above-mentioned priest, the bearer of this letter, a resident of the neighborhood of Milevis, has come through Hippo Regius, where I am, on the orders of his bishop, my revered brother, Severus,[3] who joins me in sending greetings to your most sincere Charity, because during the time we were together in bearing the great trials and

---
2 Honorius.
3 Mentioned by Augustine in Letters 22, 25, 29, 38. Severus was one of Augustine's oldest and dearest friends, at one time a member of his monastic community, afterwards, Bishop of Milevis.

disturbances of the Church we never found an opportunity of writing to your Excellency, although we often sought one. It is true I have already sent one letter[4] about the affair of my holy brother and colleague, Boniface, Bishop of Cataquas, but that was before these heavier tidings had reached us, which now exercise us so deeply. As to the plan by which we can best be helped to suppress and remedy these evils according to the way of Christ, the bishops[5] who are traveling to you for that very purpose can more satisfactorily take it up with the great goodness of your heart. In spite of the limited time, they have succeeded, by consulting together, in drawing up a carefully considered plan to submit to you. But that other matter, of letting the province know the sentiment of our most gracious and devout prince toward the Church, should emphatically not be delayed, and I recommend, I beg, I beseech, I implore you to hasten it on, even before you see the bishops who are on their way, as speedily as your most estimable care can act for the protection of the members of Christ, weighed down by the greatest suffering. The Lord has granted us no slight comfort in these trials, in willing you to have much more power now than you had before, although even then we rejoiced in your many great and good deeds.

We find great solace in the firm and steadfast faith of some —not a few, in fact—who have been converted to the Christian religion or have returned to Catholic unity, by reason of these very laws, and for their eternal salvation it would give us joy to imperil our own temporal welfare. On their account we now suffer more violent outbreaks of hatred from men who are hardened in their extreme perversity. Some of these converts bear these attacks most patiently

---

[4] Letter 96.
[5] Restitutus and Florentius, delegated by the Council of Carthage, October 13, 408, to carry an appeal to the emperor, to enforce the decrees against pagans and heretics.

with us, but we are much concerned for their weakness until such time as they learn and are helped by the most merciful grace of the Lord, to despise this present world and the day of men, with greater steadfastness of heart. I am enclosing a set of instructions for my brother bishops; if they are not yet there, as I suppose, I ask your Excellency to give it to them when they arrive. We put such trust in your most upright heart that we wish, with the help of the Lord our God, to have you not only as our benefactor, but even as the partner of our plan.

98. *Augustine gives greeting in the Lord to Boniface,[1] the bishop (408)*

You ask me whether parents do harm to their baptized babies when they try to cure them by means of sacrifices to demons, and, if they do not harm them, how the faith of parents is beneficial to their children when they are baptized, whereas their infidelity cannot harm them. To this I answer that the power of the sacrament—that of saving baptism—is so great in the structure of the Body of Christ that a person born once through the carnal pleasures of others, and reborn once through the spiritual will of others, can thereafter not be bound by the fetters of another's sin, unless he consents to it by his own will. 'Both the soul of the father is mine,' he says, 'and the soul of the son is mine: the soul that sinneth the same shall die.'[2] The soul does not sin itself when its parents or anybody else, without any knowledge on its part, have recourse to the sacrilegious worship of demons, but it does derive guilt from Adam— which is washed away by the grace of that sacrament—be-

---
1 Undoubtedly the bishop referred to in Letter 96.
2 Cf. Ezech. 18.4.

cause it was not yet a soul living a separate life, that is, another soul, of which it is said: 'Both the soul of the father is mine and the soul of the son is mine.' Therefore, when a man has a separate existence and becomes other than the one who begot him, he is not responsible for another's sin without his own consent. So, then, he inherits guilt because he was one with him and in him[3] from whom he derived it, at the time when it was committed, but, otherwise, no one contracts guilt from another so long as each one lives his own life. Hence it is said: 'The soul that sinneth the same shall die.'

It is one Spirit that makes it possible for a man to be reborn through the agency of another's will when he is offered for baptism, and through Him the one offered is reborn. For it is not written: 'Unless a man be born again through the will of his parents' or: 'through the faith of his godparents or the ministers,' but: 'Unless a man be born again of water and the Holy Spirit.'[4] The water, therefore, manifesting the sacrament of grace exteriorly, and the Spirit, effecting the benefit of grace interiorly, loosing the bond of guilt, restoring good to his nature, both regenerate in one Christ the man who was begotten of one Adam. The regenerating Spirit is, then, equally present in the elders offering and in the child offered and reborn; therefore, through this sharing of one and the same Spirit, the will of those offering is beneficial to the child offered for baptism. But, when the elders sin by offering the child and trying to subject him to the accursed bonds of devils, the same mind is not in both, so they cannot share the guilt. Guilt is not communicated by the will of another, as grace is communicated by the unity of the Holy Spirit. The same Holy

---

3 The Church teaches that all men sinned in Adam, and that all are born with the guilt of original sin on their souls. 1 Cor. 15.22. Baptism is the sacrament by which this guilt is removed.

4 John 3.5.

Spirit can be in this man and in that one, even if they do not know each other, because through Him each one has the same grace, but the spirit of a man cannot be in this one and in that, so as to make both share the guilt if one sins and the other does not. It follows from this that a child born of his parents' flesh can be born again of the Spirit of God, so that the taint contracted from them is washed away, but one born again of the Spirit of God cannot be reborn of the flesh of his parents so as to contract again the taint that has been washed away. Therefore, the child does not lose the grace of Christ once conferred, except by his own sinful act, if he turns out badly as he grows older. Then, indeed, he will begin to have his own personal sins which are not taken away by baptism, but may be healed by another remedy.

Truly can one give the name of spiritual murderers to those parents or other older people who try to subject their sons and any other baptized children to the accursed rites of demons. They do not actually commit murder, but as far as they are concerned they are murderers. Rightly is it said to them to deter them from this crime: 'Do not kill your little ones'; as the Apostle says: 'Extinguish not the spirit';[5] not that He can be extinguished, but, as far as it lies in them, they are truly said to extinguish Him when they act so as to wish Him to be extinguished. In that sense we can properly understand what the most blessed Cyprian wrote in his epistle about the lapsed, when he blames those who offered sacrifice to idols in time of persecution. He says: 'And to cap the climax of their crime, babies were brought by their parents or led there by the hand, to lose in their tender youth the sacramental grace they had received at the dawn of their existence.'[6] They lost it, he said, as far as it

---

[5] 1 Thess. 5.19.
[6] Cyprian, *De lapsis* (ed. Hartel, p. 243) 9-11, 12-18.

could be lost through the fault of those by whom they were forced to lose it: they lost it according to the will and intention of those who committed that crime against them, but, if they had lost it in themselves, they would have been left by the divine decree without any defense against damnation. If St. Cyprian had thought this, he would not in the next sentence have undertaken their defense by saying: 'When the day of judgment comes, will they not say: "We have done nothing, we have not voluntarily forsaken the food and drink of the Lord to hasten to pagan gatherings; it was the infidelity of others that destroyed us, we bear witness that our parents were murderers: they refused us the Church for mother and the Lord for father; little and inexperienced and unconscious as we were of their great crime, we became accomplices of it, we were involved in the apostasy of others." ' He would not have devised this defense for them if he had not thought it most just and most likely to benefit the little ones at the judgment of God. If then they can say with truth: 'We have done nothing,' 'the soul that sinneth, the same shall die,'[7] then they will not perish by the just judgment of God, since it was the parents, by their own crime, who tried to destroy their children, as far as it rested with them.

There is an incident, related in that same letter,[8] of a baby girl whose parents, frightened into flight, left her with a nurse. By this nurse she was taken to the idolatrous rites of demons, and was afterward carried into a church and given the Eucharist.[9] Under some strange influence, she spat it out, and I believe this was divinely permitted so that the elders might not think they had committed no wrong against their children by that sinful act, but might under-

---

7 Ezech. 18.4.
8 Cyprian, *op. cit.*, p. 25, 1-24.
9 It was not uncommon in the early centuries of the Church to allow babies in arms to be given a small particle of the Blessed Sacrament.

stand that significant physical gesture of speechless infants as a warning to them of what they ought to do: instead of rushing to the sacraments of reconciliation after their act of apostasy, they ought rather to refrain from them through penitence.[10] But, when Divine Providence acts thus through little children, we are not to believe that these latter act consciously or deliberately, any more than we are to marvel at the wisdom of asses because God willed to restrain the folly of a certain Prophet by making an ass speak.[11] Moreover, if God used an irrational animal to utter sounds like those of a man—something to be attributed to a divine miracle, not to the nature of the ass—in like manner the Almighty through the soul of an infant, in whom reason was not lacking but merely dormant, could reveal by a physical act what ought to be done by those who had sinned against Him and against their little ones. But, since the infant does not return into its parents, so as to be one person with them, but is an entirely separate being having its own body and soul, 'the soul that sinneth, the same shall die.'

Do not be troubled because some do not bring their children to receive baptism, through faith, that they may be reborn to eternal life, by spiritual grace, but because they think it is a medicine for retaining or regaining bodily health. The children are none the less regenerated even if they are not presented for that purpose, because the required actions and words of the sacrament are performed, without which the child cannot be consecrated. The Holy Spirit, who dwells in the saints, out of whom that peerless dove covered with

---

10 The question of the amount of penance required of the *'lapsi'*—those who had apostatized under persecution—was one that troubled the Church deeply for some time after the era of persecution had ceased. Public penitents at this and later periods were debarred from the sacraments of Penance and the Holy Eucharist for long periods.
11 Balaam. Cf. Num. 22.28.

silver[12] is molded by the fire of charity, does His work sometimes through the agency not only of the merely ignorant, but even of the utterly unworthy. Surely, the little ones are offered for the reception of the spiritual grace, not so much by those in whose arms they are carried—although they are offered by them if they are good and faithful—as by the whole company of the saints and believers. We rightly understand that they are offered by all who consent to the offering, and by whose holy and indivisible charity they are helped to share in the outpouring of the Holy Spirit. Mother Church who is in the saints does this wholly, because she wholly brings forth all and each. The sacrament of Christian baptism, being one and the same, is valid, even among heretics, and has its effect of consecration, although it does not bring the one conferring it to a share in eternal life—in fact, this conferring brings guilt upon the heretic as long as he is outside the flock of the Lord, which has its master's brand-mark. True doctrine advises that the heretic is to be brought to a right mind, but is not to be baptized a second time. If this is so, how much more effectively is the work of winnowing the good grain carried out by the agency of the chaff, so that it may be added to the quantity of the whole pile in the center of the threshing floor!

I do not want you to make the mistake of thinking that the bond of guilt derived from Adam cannot be loosed in any other way than by the parents presenting their children to receive the grace of Christ, for you write in these words: 'As their parents were responsible for their punishment,[13] so let the faith of their parents bring them likewise to be justified.' But you know that many are not presented by their parents, but by persons who are not even related to them, as young slaves are sometimes brought for baptism by their masters.

---

12 Ps. 67.14.
13 That is, the penalty due to original sin, remitted by baptism.

And, not infrequently, when the parents are dead, children are brought to be baptized by those who have the opportunity of doing this work of mercy. Sometimes, even children who have been exposed[14] by their parents are rescued and fed by others, often enough by the consecrated virgins,[15] and then they are brought to baptism by them, although these certainly have no children, since they have renounced the prospect of having any. In this you see the same thing happening which is written in the Gospel, when the Lord asked who had been a neighbor to the man wounded by robbers and left half-dead on the roadside, and received the answer: 'He that showed mercy to him.'[16]

That is a very difficult question which you seem to have thought up for yourself at the end of your list, obviously inspired by your customary and vigorous hatred of untruth. You say: 'If I were to set a baby before you and ask you whether he will be chaste when he grows up or whether he may not become a thief, no doubt you will answer: "I do not know." And if I ask you whether a child of that tender age thinks anything, either good or bad, you will say: "I do not know." If, then, you do not venture to make any promise about his future behavior, or any guess about his present thoughts, how is it that the parents, when they carry their children to be baptized, answer and profess the faith for them, and say that the children do what that age cannot even think of, or, if it can, we do not know it? For we question those who carry the children and we say: "Does he believe in God?" And they answer in behalf of

---

14 This desertion of unwanted children, who were put out to die, was only too common in the Roman world.
15 From earliest times the Church allowed women to take the vow of virginity, and to devote their lives to good works. These virgins did not necessarily live in religious communities, especially in the earlier ages.
16 Luke 10.37.

infants who do not know if there is a god: "He believes." And they answer similarly to each of the other queries. I marvel that parents answer so confidently for their child in these matters, and say he does these great things which the baptizer asks at the time of baptism, but, if at the same time I should add: "Will he be chaste or will he not be a thief?" I doubt that anyone would venture to say whether he will or will not be any of these things. Yet he answers unhesitatingly that the child believes in God.' You end your letter by adding these words: 'I ask you to be so kind as to answer these objections briefly, not in a formal manner, but so as to give me an explanation.'

After reading and rereading your letter, and thinking it over in the limited time at my disposal, I recalled my friend Nebridius,[17] who was a most persistent and most eager searcher into obscure questions, especially those referring to learning and piety, but who hated above everything a short answer to an important question. And if anyone had asked such an answer, he took it very ill, and if he knew who the person was, he showed his displeasure by expression and voice, esteeming him a poor sort of man who asked such things without knowing how much could or ought to be said in reply. But I am not angry with you as he used to be, for you are a bishop, weighed down with many cares, as I am; you will not easily find time to read long explanations nor I to write them. For he was then young when he disliked hearing serious subjects disposed of briefly, and he used to put many questions to me in our conversation —both of us with plenty of leisure—but you are aware both of who asks and who is asked, and you bid me to answer this difficult question in a few words. So, then, I

---

17 This was the dear friend of Augustine's youth, who used to ask such complicated questions. He followed Augustine in his conversion, and died soon afterward. Letters 3, 4, 7, 9, 10, 11, 12, 13, 14 are addressed to him; Letters 5, 6, 8 are his to Augustine.

do your bidding, to the best of my ability; may the Lord help me to do what you ask.

When we speak of the approach of Easter, it is usual for us to say that the Lord's Passion is tomorrow or the next day, although He suffered so many years ago, and the Passion itself happened once and for all. It is usual also for us to say of Easter Sunday: 'Today the Lord has risen!' although so many years have gone by since His Resurrection. No one would be so foolish as to accuse us of lying when we speak thus, knowing that we name those days in memory of the events that happened on similar days, and that, when the day is mentioned, not itself but one like it in the passage of time is meant, and it is so called because we recall the mystery which happened on it so long ago. Was not Christ offered in His Person only once, yet in the sacred mysteries He is offered for mankind not only on every Easter Sunday but every day? If the sacred rites had no resemblance to the things which they represent, they would not be sacred rites; they generally take their names from the mysteries they represent. As, then, in a certain manner the sacrament of the Body of Christ is the Body of Christ, and the sacrament of the Blood of Christ is the Blood of Christ, so the sacrament of faith[18] is faith. To believe is the same as to have faith. That is why the response is made [in baptism] that the child believes, although he has as yet no conscious knowledge of faith; the answer is made that he has faith because this is the sacrament of faith, that he turns to God because this is the sacrament of conversion. And that same response belongs to the administration of the sacrament, as the Apostle said of baptism itself: 'We are buried together with Christ by baptism unto death.'[19] He does not say: 'We symbolize burial,' but says plainly: 'We are buried

---
18 The sacrament of baptism is meant.
19 Cf. Rom. 6.4.

with Him.' Therefore, he calls the sacrament, which is the sign of so great an effect, by the same name as the effect.

So, then, although the child has not yet that faith which resides in the will of believers, the sacrament of that faith makes him one of the believers. And, as the answer is given that they believe, so they are called faithful because they receive the sacrament of faith, even if they do not assent to the faith by a mental act. When a man begins to acquire knowledge he does not receive the sacrament again, but he understands it, and adapts himself to its truth by an appropriate attitude of his will. But, as long as he is unable to do this, the sacrament will be his protection against adverse powers, and it will prevail so strongly that, if he departs from this life before attaining the use of reason, he is freed by this Christian remedy, through the loving recommendation of the Church, from that condemnation 'which by one man entered into the world.'[20] He who does not believe this, and thinks it cannot be so, is plainly an unbeliever, even though he has received the sacrament of faith, and the child is far better off than he, since he may not yet have accepted the faith by deliberate thought, but he offers no obstacle of a contrary thought, and therefore he receives the sacrament to his own benefit. I think I have answered your questions in a way that will probably not satisfy the unintellectual and the quarrelsome, but will more than satisfy the peaceable and the intellectual. I have not alleged as an excuse to you my strongly held custom, but, as best I could, I have given an account of a custom that is very useful.

---

20 Rom. 5.12.

99. Augustine gives greeting in the Lord to the most devout servant of God, Italica,[1] most worthy of holy praise among the members of Christ (late 408; or early 409)

I had received three letters from your Benignity when I began to write this: the first asking for a letter from me; the second acknowledging the receipt of mine, and the third proving your kind consideration for us in regard to the house of the noble and illustrious youth, Julian,[2] which adjoins our walls. I am answering this last letter at once, as your Excellency's agent writes that he can send it promptly to Rome. I was deeply troubled that your letter gave us no hint of what is happening[3] there in or around the city, nor did it confirm what we were loath to believe on mere rumor. Some letters of the brethren which reached us earlier described a dangerous and difficult situation, but less serious than we feared. I am more surprised than I can say that our brothers, the holy bishops, did not take advantage of the journey of your messengers to write to us, and that your letter gave us no news of your great trials, which are also ours because of the kinship of charity. But perhaps you thought you ought not to let us know, either because it would do no good, or because you did not want us to be saddened by your letter. But it does some good, according to my way of thinking, even to know of sad things: in the first place, because it is not right to be willing to 'rejoice with them that rejoice,' and not to be willing to

---
1 Cf. Letter 92.
2 No other reference is found to this young man, but it appears that he was a relative or a ward of Italica, who owned property in Hippo, and could be influenced by her to transfer the property to Augustine.
3 The siege of Rome by Alaric and the Goths. At this first appearance he was bought off, but returned two years later to sack the helpless city.

'weep with them that weep';[4] and in the second place, because 'tribulation worketh patience, and patience trial, and trial hope; and hope confoundeth not because the charity of God is poured forth in our hearts by the Holy Spirit who is given to us.'[5]

Far be it from us, then, to refuse to hear what is bitter and sad to those we love. It is not possible for one member to suffer without the other member suffering with it.[6] And the relief from sorrow is not given by sharing the disaster, but by the comfort of affection. Thus, although some suffer by bearing the trouble and others share it by knowing of it, the sorrow is common to all who share in the trial, the hope, the love of the Spirit. May we all receive the comfort of the Lord who foretold these temporal evils and promised eternal life after them. He who aims at being crowned with victory after the battle must not be cast down while the fight goes on, for He who prepares prizes beyond telling for the victors furnishes strength to the fighters.

You must not let this answer of mine affect your confidence in writing to me, because you had an especially good motive in lightening my anxiety. We send greetings again to your children, and we pray that they may grow great for you in Christ. Even at this early age they know by experience that the love of this world is dangerous and sinful. It is to be hoped that the young and tender will be warned by the overthrow of the great and long-established. I hardly know what to say about the house, except to thank you for your very kind consideration. They do not want the house we can give, and we cannot give the one they want. The report they had heard of its being left to the church by my

---

4 Rom. 12.15.
5 Rom. 5.3-5.
6 1 Cor. 12.26.

predecessor is not true; it is part of the long-standing estate of that ancient church, and is attached to it as the house which is now in question is attached to the other church.[7]

100. Augustine gives greeting in the Lord to the excellent lord, Donatus,[1] his deservedly honored and pre-eminently praiseworthy son (late 408; or early 409)

I should prefer that the Church in Africa, beset as it is with trials, should not have to depend on the help of any temporal power. But the Apostle says: 'There is no power but from God';[2] hence, when help is given to the Church by the most devoted sons of our Catholic mother, such as you are, there is no doubt that 'Our help is in the name of the Lord, who made heaven and earth.'[3] Anyone can see, excellent Sir, deservedly honored and pre-eminently praiseworthy son, that no slight comfort has been sent us by Providence in these great troubles, when a man like you, a great lover of the name of Christ, is raised to the high office of proconsul, for no other purpose than to restrain the accursed and sacrilegious attempts of the enemies of the Church, by the combined use of your power and your good will. But, there is one thing only about which I have grave misgivings, when you administer justice; namely,

---
7 Two churches in Hippo are mentioned by Augustine: the Basilica of St. Leontius (Letter 29) and the Basilica of Peace (Letter 213). There was also a Donatist basilica in Hippo, and three other Catholic churches or chapels. Houses attached to churches were probably in demand by religious communities.

---
1 Not the founder of the Donatists, but proconsul of Africa. Augustine knew several men of this name, a common one at that time.
2 Rom. 13.1.
3 Cf. Ps. 120.2.

that you decide to apply the penalty with more regard for the gravity of their crimes than for the exercise of Christian clemency, for it is certainly true that of all crimes committed by impious men, devoid of all feeling, those against a Christian commonwealth are more monstrous and more revolting than acts committed against any other group. We beg you by Christ Himself not to act thus rigidly. We are not looking for vengeance on earth over our enemies, and our sufferings should not reduce us to such anguish of soul that we forget the teachings of Him for whose name and truth we suffer; we do love our enemies, and we do pray for them.[4] Hence, in applying the deterring effect of judges and laws, we wish them to be restrained, but not put to death; otherwise, they might incur the punishment of everlasting judgment. At the same time we do want public authority to act against them, but not to make use of the extreme punishment which they deserve. Act against their offenses so that some of them may repent of having sinned.

In hearing these Church cases, then, even when you discover that the Church has been outrageously attacked and injured, we ask you to forget that you have the power of life and death, but not to forget our request. Do not consider what we ask as a light or insignificant thing, my honorable and beloved son; it is that those whose conversion we pray for should not be put to death. Passing over the fact that we ought never to depart from the rule of overcoming evil by good,[5] let your Prudence also consider that only churchmen have the duty of bringing these Church cases before you. Consequently, if you think the death penalty should be inflicted on these men, you will frighten us off, and no such cases would come to your court by our

---
4 Luke 6.27,28.
5 Rom. 12.21.

agency. If that becomes known, those enemies of ours will work for our ruin with a sort of legalized boldness, while the necessity is imposed on us of choosing to be put to death by them rather than to bring them to death by the verdict of your court. I beg you not to despise this warning, this request, this entreaty of mine. I am sure you recall that I could have had as much trust in you even if I were not a bishop, and you were raised to a much higher office than the one you now hold. Meanwhile, let the Donatist heretics know by your Excellency's proclamations that the laws passed against their false doctrine are still in force. At present, they imagine and boast that these laws are inactive, and if that were so they would not spare us in any way. You will help to make our toils and dangers fruitful if you would provide for the repression of that sect of theirs, so false and so full of impious pride, by means of the imperial laws, in such wise that they do not appear to themselves or their followers to be enduring any kind of suffering for truth and justice. Allow them, when they appeal to you, to be convinced and instructed by the clearest proofs of well-known facts, either in the proceedings before your Excellency or in those before lesser judges, to the end that those who are kept in custody by your order may bend their own obstinate will, if possible, to the better course, and may read these proofs to others for their amendment. When men act by compulsion, not by conviction, the attempt to make them give up a great evil and hold to a great good is productive of more labor than profit.

101. Augustine gives greeting in the Lord to the most blessed and reverently dear lord, Memorius[1] his most upright and longed-for brother and fellow bishop (late 408; or early 409)

I really ought not to answer the letter of your holy Charity without sending you the books[2] which you requested of me by the most insistent claim of holy love, but in this at least I can obey you by answering the letters by which you were so kind as to load me rather than to laud[3] me. Still, when I am bowed down under my load, I am equally lifted up by your love. And I am not so loved, lifted up, and chosen by just anybody, but only by that man and priest of the Lord who is so pleasing to God, I think, that, when you raise your good heart to the Lord, you raise me with it, since you have me in it. So, I ought to have sent the books which I had promised to revise, but I did not send them because I have not revised them; and not because I would not but because I could not, weighed down as I am with so many and such pressing duties. But it would be an altogether ungracious and heartless thing to do to let this holy brother and colleague, Possidius[4]—and you will find no small part of me in him—either miss knowing you and your great affection for me, or come to know you without any letter from me. As far as my slender resources have allowed, he has been nourished by my efforts with the bread of the Lord, not by those studies which are called liberal by those slaves of all sorts of passions.

---

1 Bishop of Capua. His son, Julian, later Bishop of Eclanum, became one of the strongest promoters of the Pelagian heresy.
2 Augustine's treatise *On Music*, written while he was living a monastic life after his conversion. Cf. *Fathers of the Church* 4 (New York 1947).
3 It is not always possible to reproduce Augustine's puns in English; the Latin here has *onerare* and *honorare*.
4 Cf. Letter 95 n. 2.

What else is to be said to those who think themselves liberally educated, however immoral and irreligious they are, but what we read in a truly liberal book: 'If the son shall make you free, you shall be free indeed'?[5] By Him it is granted us to know how much of the liberal there is in those studies which are called liberal by men not called to liberty. For, they have nothing that resembles liberty unless they have something that resembles truth. Hence, the Son Himself said: 'and the truth shall make you free.'[6] So, then, neither the numberless irreligious tales with which the works of futile poets are filled, nor the high-flown, carefully styled lies of the orators, nor even the wordy hair-splitting of the philosophers themselves have anything in common with our liberty, since they obviously either did not know God, or, 'when they knew God, they have not glorified him as God, or given thanks; but became vain in their thought, and their foolish heart was darkened: professing themselves to be wise, they became fools, and they changed the glory of the incorruptible God into the likeness of the image of a corruptible man; and of birds and of four-footed beasts and of creeping things.'[7] Even if they were not given up to the worship of such representations, or not too much given up to them, they nevertheless 'worshipped and served the creature rather than the Creator.'[8] As for the futilities and false fancies, the airy nothings and proud lies of such obviously ill-fated men who knew nothing, even in what they felt to be true, of the grace of God through Jesus Christ, our Lord, by which alone we are delivered from the body of this death,[9] surely these are not properly to be called liberal studies. Their history might perhaps have some claim

---

5 John 8.36.
6 John 8.32.
7 Rom. 1.21-23.
8 Rom. 1.25.
9 Rom. 7.24, 25.

to consideration from us who are free, especially as their writers show a certain respect for reliability in their narrative, since they give us a true account whether they speak of the good or evil deeds of men. Yet, I simply do not see how men who lacked the help of the Holy Spirit in recognizing the truth, and who were forced by the very limitations of human weakness to rely on hearsay, could have failed to go wrong in many of their facts. Still, they have some semblance of liberty, if they do not deliberately falsify their narrative, and do not deceive men except in so far as they are themselves misled by their informants through human proneness to error.

Since the pervasive influence of rhythm is more easily studied in speech, and an analysis of it leads by gradually mounting steps to the highest secrets of truth, in the ways in which 'wisdom showeth herself cheerfully to her lovers and meeteth them with all providence,[10] I planned, at the beginning of my retirement, when my mind was free from greater and more pressing duties, to try out my strength on those writings which you have requested of me, and I wrote six books on rhythm alone,[11] with the intention—I admit —of doing perhaps another six on music, when I should have some hoped-for time. But, once the burden of ecclesiastical authority was laid on me, all those sweet delights slipped from my hands, with the result that I can scarcely find the manuscript now, when I feel bound to respect your wish and request, or, rather, your command. If I succeed in sending you my treatise, you will be the one to regret having insisted so strongly on having it, not I for having yielded to you. Five of its books are very hard to understand unless you have personal direction about the different

---
10 Wisd. 6.17.
11 Augustine's estimate of the relative importance of these books has been endorsed by posterity.

characters of the dialogues, and help in pronouncing the syllables so as to give them the right quantity, thereby expressing the nature of the metre, and impressing it on the ear. Besides, there are in some of the feet specially contrived pauses, which cannot be noticed at all unless the speaker notifies the listener.

But I am sending the sixth book to your Charity at once. I have found a revised copy of it and it contains the essence of all the other books. Perhaps your serious mind will find it worth your while. As for the other five, they will hardly seem worth reading to our son and fellow deacon, Julian,[12] who is now engaged in the same warfare with us. I do not go so far as to say that I think more of him than I do of you, because that would not be true, but I do venture to say that I miss him more than I do you. You may wonder how I can love someone equally with you, yet miss him more; that is because I have greater hope of seeing him. For I think that if he comes to us at your bidding or sending, he will act as a young man should, especially one not yet hampered by heavier duties, and at the same time he will bring you yourself to me more speedily. I have not noted the metres in which the Psalms of David are composed, because I do not know them. A translator from the Hebrew language, which I do not know, would find it impossible to reproduce the verse forms, without being forced to deviate too widely, in his rendering, from the true sense of the passage, by being bound to the metre. However, on the authority of those who are versed in that tongue, I believe that they are written in definite metres, for that holy man[13] loved sacred music, and more than any other poet he rouses us to zeal for these studies. May you

---
12 Cf. above, note 1.
13 David.

all dwell forever 'in the aid of the most high,'[14] 'men of one manner who dwell in a house',[15] father and mother, brethren of your children, and all children of one Father. Be mindful of us.

102. Augustine gives greeting in the Lord to his most upright brother and fellow priest, Deogratias[1] *(c. 409)*

When you choose to refer to me the questions propounded to you, I imagine you are not actuated by sloth but by an excessive affection for me, which makes you want to hear me explain things which you know yourself. For my part, I would rather they were answered by you, because that friend of yours who asked the questions is timid about having anything to do with me, if I can judge by his failure to answer certain letters—only he can tell why. At least, I suspect it is so, and my suspicion is not unkind or unfounded, since you know very well how much I esteem him and what a grief it is to me that he is not yet a Christian. Consequently, I conclude with good reason that he does not want me to write to him, seeing that he would not answer me. I ask you, then, to do what I ask, as I have done what you asked, in yielding to you in the midst of most pressing duties, because I feared to go counter to a will so holy and so dear to me. This is what I want: that you make no difficulty about answering briefly all that he asks, just as you laid it before me, as if it was your

---
14 Ps. 90.1.
15 Ps. 67.7.

---
1 A priest of Carthage who hoped to convert a pagan friend by answering these questions. The name is reminiscent of some of those used by the Puritans in later times. The title of this letter is: 'One book in explanation of six questions raised by the pagans.'

own answer, and, indeed, you were well able to do it before you referred it to me. You will recognize when you read that I have said hardly anything that you did not know yourself, or that you could not know without me. I ask you to share this work of mine with others whom you know to be interested. But, let your friend have your own explanation—I insist on this, because it would be most acceptable to him and others, too, who take no little pleasure in the way you explain such things, as I do myself. Remember me always in Christ.

Six Questions Answered for Pagans

1. On the Resurrection

Some persons are disturbed and raise the question about the promise of resurrection, whether of the two resurrections it is typified by that of Lazarus or that of Christ. 'If it conforms to that of Christ,' they say, 'how can the resurrection of One who was born without any intervention of seed accord with that of the sons of his seed? And if it conforms to the resurrection of Lazarus, this does not seem appropriate, either, because the resurrection of Lazarus was accomplished with a body not yet corrupted, with that same body in which he was recognized as Lazarus,[2] whereas our bodies will be raised after having been scattered for many centuries. Besides, if the condition of the body after resurrection is that of blessedness, with no suffering, no subjection to hunger, why did Christ eat and show His wounds after His resurrection?[3] If He did this to overcome unbelief, He was merely pretending; if He showed real

---
2 John 11.39-44.
3 Luke 24.30, 39, 43; John 20.20; 27, 21.13.

wounds, then wounds once received will endure after resurrection.'

To this we reply that our promised resurrection will be conformed to that of Christ rather than to that of Lazarus, because Lazarus rose only to die again, but Christ, as it is written of Him, 'rising from the dead, dieth now no more' and 'death shall no more have dominion over Him.'[4] And this is the promise made to those who will rise again at the end of time and will reign with Him forever.[5] The difference between Christ's birth and ours—that He was born without male seed, but we are formed of man and woman—has no bearing on resurrection, just as it had no bearing on His death. Although He was not born of male seed, His death was none the less a real death. In like manner, although the body of the first man had an origin different from ours, since he was formed from the earth without parents, while we are born of parents, that does not cause any difference in the manner of death, so that he should die one way and we another. Thus, the different kind of birth affects neither death nor resurrection.

But, if unbelievers refuse to accept what is written about the first man, let them examine or take notice—if they can do that much—how many kinds of animals are generated by the earth without parents, whereas others produce offspring like themselves by mating, yet there is no difference of nature between those begotten of the earth and those who are born of mated pairs. They live and die in the same way, although they have different origins. So, it is not contrary to reason that bodies differently born should have the same sort of resurrection. But men of that sort, unable to distinguish when a difference applies and when it does not, maintain that all the consequences must be

---
4 Rom. 6.9.
5 Apoc. 20.6; 22.5.

different if they observe different origins. Such people might imagine that oil extracted from fat would not float on water as olive oil does, because they are derived from completely different sources: the latter from a tree, the former from flesh.

Turning to that other point of difference, that Christ's body rose on the third day, untouched by decay or decomposition, whereas ours will be gathered together after a long time from the unrecognizable parts into which they have been scattered, we see that either feat is impossible to human capability but very easy for divine power. The glance of our eye does not reach nearer objects more quickly and distant ones more slowly, but lights on both with equal speed; in like manner, when, as the Apostle says, the resurrection of the dead is effected 'in the twinkling of an eye,'[6] it is as easy for the omnipotence of God and His awe-inspiring authority to raise the recently dead as those long since fallen into decay. To some minds, these things are hard to accept because they are outside their experience, yet the whole universe is full of wonders which seem to us hardly worth noticing or examining, not because they are easily penetrated by our reason, but because we are accustomed to seeing them. But I, and those who join me in striving to understand the 'invisible things of God by the things that are made,'[7] wonder neither more nor less at the fact that in one tiny seed all that we praise in the tree lies folded away, than that the great bosom of the earth will restore whole and entire, at the future resurrection, all that it consumes of human bodies when they fall into decay.

That Christ took food after His resurrection is not inconsistent with the fact that there will be no need for food in our promised resurrection, since we read that angels

---

6 1 Cor. 15.52.
7 Rom. 1.20.

took food of the same kind and in the same manner; not by some visionary illusion but in real truth, and not because they needed it but because they had the ability to take it. The thirsty earth drinks in water in a far different way from that of the sun's shining ray—the earth acts through need; the sun, through power. So, then, the happiness of the body after the resurrection will be as incomplete if it cannot take food as it will be if it needs food. I could make a long argument about the changes of physical qualities, and the overwhelming superiority of our future bodies over our present ones, but I had decided to answer briefly, and this is written for those who need only a reminder.

Let the man who proposed these questions know that after His resurrection Christ showed scars, not wounds, as a proof to doubters, and for the same reason He also took both food and drink, not once but several times, to prevent them from thinking that He was a spirit instead of a body, or that His appearance was visionary instead of real. Those scars would not have been real unless there had been wounds to account for them, yet they would not have been there if He had not willed them to be there. By the favor of a certain dispensation, He willed to show to those whom He was strengthening in unfeigned faith that it was not another body, but the same one which they had seen crucified, that had risen again. What is the use, then, of saying: 'If He did this to overcome unbelief, He was merely pretending?' If some brave man, fighting for his country and receiving many deep wounds, should tell a very skilled doctor, who could cure them so completely that no scars remained, that he preferred to be cured so as to leave the traces of his wounds as badges of honor, would you say that the doctor had counterfeited the scars because he used his skill—for a good reason—to leave them, although he could have used it to obliterate them? As I said above, they could only be proved counterfeit scars if there had been no wounds to heal.

2. Of the Time When the Christian Religion Appeared

Again, they raise other objections which they make more weighty against the Christians by saying that they are quoted from Porphyry.[8] They say: 'If Christ says He is the way, the grace, and the truth, and He places in Himself alone the approach of believing souls to Him, what did the men of so many centuries before Christ do? To pass over, he says, the times before the kingdom of Latium, let us trace the beginning of the human name from Latium itself. In Latium, before the foundation of Alba,[9] there was a cult of gods. In Alba, religion and worship were equally in honor. In the long stretch of centuries—not a few—Rome itself existed without the law of Christ. What, he says, became of the innumerable souls, who were entirely guiltless, if He in whom they could believe had not yet lent His presence to men? The world, also, as well as Rome, was devoted to the religious rites of its temples. Why, he says, did He who is called the Savior, hide Himself for so many ages? But, he says, let them not say that the human race was saved by the ancient Jewish law, since the Jewish law appeared and flourished in a small part of Syria, a long time after, and still later it made its way into the Italian lands, after the reign of Gaius Caesar,[10] or probably during his reign. What, then, became of the souls of Romans or

---
8 Porphyry (233-303), a Neo-Platonist, follower of Plotinus, noted for the bitterness of his attack on Christianity.
9 The predecessor city of Rome. According to legend, it was founded by Ascanius, son of Aeneas, 1152 B.C., and was destroyed by Tullus Hostilius, the third king of Rome, 665 B.C. Cf. Livy 1.29.
10 Known to history as Caligula, successor to Tiberius, reigned 37-41.

Latins who were deprived of the grace of Christ not yet come until the time of the Caesars?'

The answer to this objection is that they themselves should first say whether the worship of their own gods, which was established at definite times, was beneficial to men. If they say it contributed nothing to the salvation of their souls, they are one with us in destroying that worship and admitting its futility. We will go further and prove that it was harmful, but it is no slight matter that they now admit its previous futility. But, if they defend their religion, and claim that it was wisely and usefully ordained, then I ask what became of those who died before it was established; surely they were cheated of its salvation and benefit. And if these were able to be cleansed of sin in some other way, why was this way not handed down to their descendants? What was the use of setting up new religious rites which had not existed of old?

If they say at this point that the gods themselves always existed, and had always been equally able to save their worshipers everywhere, but that on account of changes of temporal and earthly circumstances, which they knew accorded with certain times and places, they willed to be served under one name or another, in one way in one place, in another in another, why do they introduce this question into the Christian religion? It is a matter in which they either cannot answer us about their gods, or, if they can, by that very fact they would answer themselves about our religion, and they would agree that it makes no difference with what various rites a worship is carried on, according to diversities of time and places, so long as what is worshiped is holy, just as it makes no difference with what various sounds speech is uttered, according to diversities of language and hearers, so long as what is said is true. But it does make a difference that by a common agreement men are able to select the sounds of the language by which they communicate their meaning to each other, and that those who are truly wise follow the will of God in selecting the acts of worship which befit the Divinity. What is needed for salvation has never been wanting to the goodness and devotion of men, and, if the forms of worship are carried out in different ways by peoples in one or another place, though joined by one and the same religion, in so far as this happens it is very important that human weakness be supported or tolerated, and that the divine authority be not opposed.

Therefore, when we say that Christ is the Word of God, through whom all things were made,[11] we say also that He is the Son because He is the Word; not a word spoken or uttered, but Himself unchanged remaining unchangeably with the unchangeable Father, by whose authority every creature, spiritual and corporeal, is governed in a manner suitable to its time and place. In guiding and governing creatures, He knows and understands what should happen and when and where, and, obviously, before He raised up the Hebrew nation, through which He foreshadowed the revelation of His coming by appropriate ceremonies; and in the times of the Israelite kingdom, and later, when He showed Himself a man among men, taking flesh from a virgin; and now when He fulfills all that He foretold by the Prophets; and in time to come, to the end of the world when He shall separate the good from the wicked, and render to each his due, He is the same Son of God, co-eternal with the Father, the unchangeable Wisdom by whom the whole universe was created, and who becomes the happiness of every rational soul.

Therefore, from the beginning of the human race, all those who believed in Him and knew Him and lived a

---
11 John 1.1-3.

good and devout life according to His commands, whenever and wherever they lived, undoubtedly were saved by Him. Just as we believe in Him, both as remaining with the Father and as having come in the flesh, so the ancients believed in Him, both remaining with the Father and about to come in the flesh. We should not think that there are different kinds of faith, or more than one kind of salvation, because what it now spoken of in the course of time as something accomplished was then foretold as something to come; and, because one and the same thing is foretold or preached by diverse rites or ceremonies, we are not to think that they are different things or that there are different kinds of salvation. Let us leave to God the choice of when anything is to happen, which tends to the salvation of souls of the faithful and the good, and for ourselves let us hold to obedience. Thus, religion has been outwardly expressed and carried on under one set of names and signs in times past and another set now; it was more secret then and more open now; it has had fewer worshipers in olden times, more afterward, yet it is one and the same true religion.

We do not reproach them that Numa Pompilius[12] gave the Romans gods to be worshiped, different from those that had been adored by them or by the Italians before that time; nor that in the time of Pythagoras[13] a philosophy was in use which had either not existed before or had been kept as a secret by a very small number who had the same

---

12 Second king of Rome, successor to Romulus. He is supposed to have organized the Roman religion and to have reformed the calendar. Cf. Livy 1.18-22.
13 A Greek philosopher, founder of the school which bears his name. He lived between the late seventh and early fifth century B.C., but the dates of his birth and death are uncertain. One of his tenets was that of transmigration of souls, and his disciples refrained from animal food, and, if we can believe Horace, from beans. He settled in Crotona, a city in southern Italy, then known as Magna Graecia.

intellectual views, but did not live by the same code. But we take up with them the argument whether those were true gods or worthy of worship, and whether that philosophy was profitable for the salvation of souls; this we call in question, over this we clash with them in debate. Let them, then, cease to bring against us what can be brought against every sect and against everything called religion. Once they admit that events are ruled not by blundering chance but by Divine Providence, human planning passes over the choice of what is fit and suitable for any given period, and attributes it to that source whence Providence itself watches over human affairs.

If they say that the Pythagorean school of philosophy did not exist always and everywhere because Pythagoras was a man and did not have that power, can they then say that all those who were able to hear him were willing to follow him, at the time when he lived and in those parts of the earth where that philosophy flourished? If Pythagoras had possessed the power to preach his doctrine where and when he wished, and if with that power he also had the supreme foreknowledge of events, he would have had the more reason not to appear anywhere or at any time except where and when he foreknew that men would believe in him. Therefore, since they do not raise this objection against Christ, that all do not follow His teaching, they themselves feel that it is not right to raise this objection against either the wisdom of their philosophers or the divinity of their gods. What will they answer, if for the sake of brevity in explaining this question we say only this, that Christ willed to appear among men, and to preach His doctrine to them at the time when and the place where He knew there would be souls to believe in Him? In this way we say nothing of the depth of the wisdom and the knowledge of God, where, perhaps, another purpose was veiled in deep secrecy, and we say it without denying the possibility of other causes which can be examined into by prudent men. Of those times and places in which His gospel was not preached, He foreknew that all would be such if it were preached to them, as they were at the time of His physical presence—if not all, at least many—when they refused to believe in Him, even after He had raised the dead to life. Indeed, even now, when the announcements of the Prophets about Him have such clear fulfillment, we see many such who are unwilling to believe and who would rather use their human cleverness to resist than to yield to a divine authority, so clear and compelling, so sublime and so sublimely revealed. As long as the mind of man is small and weak, it will not yield to divine truth. Is it any wonder, then, that Christ, knowing that the world was so full of unbelievers in the early ages, was justly unwilling to appear or to preach to them who He foreknew[14] would believe neither in His words nor in His miracles?[15] Is it not to be wondered at that all were then of the same sort as we see—to our surprise—that so many have been, from the time of His coming, and still are even to the present time?

Yet, from the beginning of the human race, sometimes obscurely, sometimes openly, as it seemed to His providence to suit the times, He did not cease to prophesy, and before He appeared in the flesh there were not lacking men to believe in Him, from Adam to Moses, among the people of Israel, which by divine ordinance was the prophetic race, and among other peoples. In the sacred books of the Hebrews there is mention of many from the time of Abraham, who were not of his stock, nor of the people of Israel,

---

14 This passage was used by the semi-Pelagians to prove their erroneous teaching on predestination. Augustine amplified and explained it in his treatise on *The Predestination of the Saints* 9.
15 In Letter 226, St. Hilary of Poitiers calls Augustine's attention to the use being made of this passage by heretics at Marseille, and it was in consequence of this letter that he explained his meaning.

nor were they joined by any chance alliance to the people of Israel, yet were partakers in His worship; so why should we not believe that sometimes there were other men, here and there among other races, who were worshipers of Him, although we do not find mention of them in the same sacred Books? The saving grace of this religion, the only true one, through which alone true salvation is truly promised, has never been refused to anyone who was worthy of it, and whoever lacked it was unworthy of it.[16] From the beginning of human history to the end, this is made known for the reward of some and the punishment of others. And that is why it is not made known at all to some, because it was foreknown that they would not believe, yet it is also made known to some who will not believe, as a warning of the former. As to those to whom it is made known and who do believe, they are being made ready for the kingdom of heaven and for the companionship of the holy angels.

3. *The Difference in Sacrifices*

Now let us look at the next question. He says: 'They censure the ceremonial of sacrifice, the victims, incense and the rest, which are used in temple worship, yet the same ceremonial was originated by themselves or by the god whom they worship, in primitive times, when a god was supposed to need their offerings of first fruits.'

As this question is evidently derived from that passage in our Scriptures, which tells of Cain making an offering to God of the fruits of the earth, and Abel of the firstlings of his flocks,[17] we answer that the conclusion to be drawn from it is that sacrifice is a very ancient custom, because our true and sacred Books warn us that it is not to be

---
16 *Retractations* 2.31.
17 Gen. 4.3, 4.

offered except to the one true God.[18] But God does not
need sacrifices, as is most clearly expressed in the same
sacred Books: 'I said to the Lord, Thou art my God, for
thou hast no need of my goods,'[19] because in accepting or
refusing or receiving them He is looking only to man's
good. God does not derive any benefit from our worship,
but we do. When He reveals or teaches how He is to be
worshiped, He does so in our own highest interest, with
absolutely no need of anything for Himself. All such sacrifices are symbolic; they are a representation of certain
things by which our attention is aroused to study or understand or reflect upon the realities represented by them. To
explain this point adequately, a longer discussion is called
for than the one we proposed in answering these questions,
but we have spoken of it at length in other works of ours,[20]
and those who have annotated the word of God before us
have treated fully of the symbolic sacrifices of the Old
Testament as shadows and figures of things to come.[21]

One point must not be omitted in our attempt at brevity,
namely, that the temple, the sacrifice, and other attendant
circumstances belong to the one true God alone, and, if
this were not known to the false gods, that is, the demons
who are fallen angels, they would never require the same
of their adorers whom they lead astray. When this worship
is offered to God, according to His inspiration and teaching,
we have true religion, but when it is offered to demons,
according to their wicked pride, it is deadly superstition.
Therefore, those who are versed in the Christian literature
of both Testaments do not censure the sacrilegious rites of
pagans because they build temples, set up priesthoods, and
offer sacrifices, but because they use these to honor idols

---
18 Deut. 6.13; Matt. 4.10.
19 Ps. 15.2.
20 *Against Faustus* 22.
21 Col. 2.17; Hab. 10.1.

and demons. Does anyone imagine that idols have any sense perception? Yet, when they are set in lofty shrines to be honored, and are waited on by those who pray and offer victims, dumb and lifeless as they are, they give the illusion of moving and feeling, and to the weak-minded they seem to live and breathe. This greatly increases the veneration of the crowd, on which their cult so greatly depends.

The divine Scripture aims to cure these unnatural and dangerous tendencies when it drives home the known truth by the remedy of a salutary warning, saying: 'They have eyes and see not; they have ears and hear not,'[22] and similar details. And the more these words are published and generally received as true, the more they strike a saving shame in those who fearfully offer divine worship to such images, looking on them as if they were alive, honoring, adoring, praying as if they were present, sacrificing victims, fulfilling vows, and all the while so abashed that they dare not think their idols are bereft of sense. And so that they may not think our Books wish to give the idea that this instinct is produced in the human heart by idols, it is openly written: 'For all the gods of the gentiles are devils.'[23] Hence, the apostolic teaching says what we read in St. John: 'Brothers, keep yourselves from idols,'[24] and also in St. Paul: 'What then, do I say that what is offered to idols is anything? or that the idol is anything? But the things which the heathens sacrifice, they sacrifice to devils and not to God, and I would not that you should be made partakers with devils.'[25] From this it can easily be understood that what is objected to by true religion in the superstitions of the heathens is not the act of offering a victim, for the earliest saints offered victims to the true God, but the fact

---

22 Ps. 113.13,14.
23 Ps. 95.5.
24 Cf. John 5.21.
25 1 Cor. 10.19,20.

that they sacrifice to false gods and wicked demons. Just as truth urges men to become companions of the holy angels, so impiety tempts them to join the company of the devils. For these latter everlasting fire is prepared, but an everlasting kingdom is made ready for the company of the saints.

The idolaters cannot excuse their vile sacrifices and idols on the ground that what they signify has a fine literary interpretation, because obviously, that whole interpretation refers to the creature, not to the Creator, to whom alone belongs the homage of religion, which is expressed in Greek by the single word *'latria.'* On the other hand, we do not say that the earth, the sea, the sky, the sun, the moon, the stars, and certain heavenly powers, which are not directly visible, are demons; but, as every creature is partly corporeal, but partly incorporeal, or as we say, spiritual, it is evident that acts of devotion and religion proceed from the attitude of the mind, which is a spiritual being and preferable to any corporeal one. We conclude from this that sacrifice is not to be offered to a corporeal being. There remains the spiritual being, which is either good or bad; it is good, of course, in faithful men and angels who serve God purely, but bad in wicked men and those fallen angels whom we call demons. From this it follows that sacrifice is not to be offered even to a spiritual being, however holy, because, the more devout it is and the more subject to God, the less it holds itself worthy of such honor, which it knows to be due to God alone. How debasing it is, then, to sacrifice to demons—to a degraded spiritual being, which has its abode in this near and dark part of the sky, as in an airy prison, doomed to everlasting punishment! Consequently, when men say that they worship the higher heavenly powers, which are not demons, and they think it is a question of names only, because they call them gods, but we call them angels, the only ones who do not oppose them, but mock at them with every kind of deceit, are the demons, who delight in human error and, in a sense, feed on it. But the holy angels do not approve of any worship except such as accords with the teaching of true wisdom and true religion, which is offered to the true God alone, whom their holy company serves. Therefore, as impious pride, either of men or of devils, demands and craves that divine honors be attributed to it, so devout humility, either of men or of holy angels, refuses such honors when offered, and shows to whom they are due. Of this there are very clear instances in our sacred writings.

The divine pronouncements show a distinction in sacrifice according to the times, with some offered before the revelation of the New Testament, which was made by that true victim of the one priest, that is, by the shedding of Christ's Blood, and we who are now called by the avowed name of Christians offer another, which is shown by the Gospel as well as by the prophetic writings to be appropriate to that revelation. This change, which is not in God or in religion itself, but in sacrifices and ceremonies, might seem to be based on a rash presumption if it had not been long ago foretold. If one and the same man offers one kind of sacrifice to God in the morning, and another at evening, suiting the victim to the time of day, he does not change God nor religion any more than he changes the concept of health[26] by using one greeting in the morning and another at evening. In the same way, over the long stretch of ages, when one kind of offering was made by the ancient saints and another is made by those of today, the sacred mysteries are celebrated in a manner befitting the time, by divine authority, not by human presumption, and there is no change either in God or in religion.

---

26 There is a sort of pun here, for the Latin word for greeting—*salutare*—was a wish for good health—*salus*.

4. On the Text: 'With what measure you mete, it shall be measured to you again'[27]

Let us now see what sort of misjudgment he makes of the Gospel, when he speaks about the measure of sin and punishment. He says: 'Christ threatens those who do not believe in Him with eternal punishment,[28] and elsewhere He says: "With what measure, you mete, it shall be measured to you again." ' This, he says, 'is quite silly and contradictory, for if He is to render punishment according to measure, and every measure is limited by the end of time, what is the meaning of His threat of everlasting punishment?'

It is hard to believe that this objection is proposed by any sort of philosopher, especially where he says: 'Every measure is limited by time,' since that measurement is only applied to time in the case of hours and days and years, or to quantity, as when we say that a short syllable has one pulse of time as compared to a long syllable. But I think that pecks, and financial guarantees, and water jars, and wine jars are measures, but not of time. How, then, is every measure limited by time? Do they themselves not say that the sun is eternal? They even dare to examine by geometrical measurements how it compares with the earth, and to announce their findings. Whether this can be or not, it is a fact that it has a measure conformable to its circumference, and so, if they understand how large it is, they understand its measurement, and, if they do not grasp this, they certainly do not understand its measurement, but not on that account does it lack measurement because men cannot know it. Consequently, something can be eternal, and can have a definite measurement according to its kind. I have used their own form of speech about the eternity of

---
27 Matt. 7.2.
28 John 3.18; Matt. 25.46.

the sun, so as to convict them out of their own mouth and prove that there can be something eternal which is measurable. So, there is no reason for them to think that Christ's threat of eternal punishment is not to be believed because He also said: 'With what measure you mete, it shall be measured to you again.'

If He had said: 'What you shall mete, the same shall be measured to you,' even so it would not necessarily imply that the words should refer to the same thing in every way. We can say correctly: 'What you plant, that you shall gather,' although no one plants an apple, but a tree, yet he gathers an apple, not a tree. In this we are speaking according to the kind of tree, because we do not plant a fig tree and gather a nut from it. It could also be said: 'What you do, the same you shall endure,' not to mean that if anyone commits debauchery he shall suffer debauchery, but what ever a man does against the law by that sin, the same the law does against him. This means that, as he has removed from his life the law forbidding such things, the same law removes him from the life of men which it controls. In like manner, if He had said: 'As much as you mete, so much shall be measured to you,' it would not follow that we should understand exactly identical penalties for sins. So, for example, wheat and barley are not identical, so that we could say: 'As much as you mete, so much shall be measured to you,' meaning as much wheat as barley. Again, if it were question of suffering, and the saying were applied: 'As much suffering as you have inflicted, so much shall be inflicted on you,' it could happen that such suffering might be equal in intensity, but it might be of longer duration, that is, it might be more long-drawn-out. And if, in speaking of two lamps, we were to say: 'This light is as bright as that one,' it would not be untrue because one of them happened to go out sooner.

So, then, if a thing is equal to another in one respect, but not equal to it in another, or not equal to it in every respect, the degree in which it is equal is not thereby falsified.

Therefore, since He says: 'With what measure you mete, it shall be measured to you again,' and since it is clear that the measure by which a thing is estimated is one thing, and the object measured is something else, it is possible that the measure by which men weigh a peck of wheat, for instance, with that they could weigh thousands of pecks, and so there could be that much difference in the quantity of wheat, and none at all in the measure. I say nothing of the variety of substances, because not only could it happen that with what measure someone weighs barley, with the same, wheat might be measured out to him, but also with what measure he weighs grain, with that same, gold might be measured out to him, and that there might be one peck of wheat but any number of gold. Thus, without an equalizing of the substance measured, both the kind and quantity may differ, yet it can be said correctly: 'With what measure he used, it was measured out to him in turn.' What Christ meant when He said this is clear from His previous words: 'Judge not,' He said, 'that you may not be judged, for with what judgment you judge, you shall be judged.'[29] But then, if they judge by an unjust judgment, shall they be judged unjustly? By no means, because there is no injustice in God.[30] But the words: 'with what judgment you judge, you shall be judged,' are used in the same way as one might say: 'With what will you do good, you shall be saved,' or: 'with what will you do wrong, you shall be punished.' So, if anyone used his eyes for a lustful purpose, and he were ordered to be blinded, he might rightly hear: 'With what eyes you have sinned, with them you have deserved punish-

---
29 Matt. 7.1,2.
30 Rom.9.4.

ment.' Each one uses the judgment of his mind well or ill, either to do good or to commit sin. Hence, it is not unjust that he should be judged as he has judged, that is, that he should suffer the penalty in that same judgment of his mind, when it suffers those evils which follow upon a wrongly judging mind.

There are other manifest punishments which are prepared for the life to come, and these, too, are derived from the same source of the evil will, but in the mind itself, where the tendency of the will is the measure of all human acts, the penalty follows close upon the fault, and it is often greater through the blindness of refusing to reflect. Therefore, when He said: 'With what judgment you judge, you shall be judged,' He added at once: 'And with what measure you mete, it shall be measured to you.' Thus, a good man, by his own will, will measure out good deeds, and by it he shall have happiness measured out to him; and, equally, a bad man, by his own will, will measure out evil deeds, and by it wretchdness shall be measured out to him; since the one is good by the good acts of his will, as the evil man is bad by the bad acts of his will. Thus, it follows that a man will be happy or wretched according to the tendency of his own will, which is the measure of all his acts and all his deserts. Thus, we measure either our good deeds or our sins, by the bent of our wills, not by periods of time. Otherwise, it would be considered a greater sin to cut down a tree than to kill a man, because the former act would take a longer time and would require many blows, whereas the latter could be done in an instant, by a single blow. If a man were punished by perpetual exile for so great a sin, it would still be said that he was treated more mildly than he deserved, although there is no comparison, in length of time, between the duration of the punishment and the little time it took to commit the crime. If, then, there should be equally long or even eternal punishments, but some less and some more severe than others, so that where the duration is equal the degree of severity should not be equal, because the measure of sin is not in the extent of time, but in the will of the sinner, is that contradictory?

Now, the will is itself punished by suffering either of mind or of body, and what gives it pleasure in sinning is involved in the punishment. Thus, he who judges without mercy is judged without mercy.[31] And in this sense only is the 'same measure' to be understood, that the mercy which he did not show is not shown to him, and that the judgment which he makes will be eternal, although the thing judged could not be eternal. Therefore, eternal punishments are measured out to him in turn, although his wrong-doing was not eternal, and because he wished to have enjoyment of his sin he finds eternal severity in his penalty. As I intended this reply to be brief, I am not able to gather all or even many examples which the sacred Books contain on the subject of sin and punishment of sin. From these I would draw one completely unambiguous statement, if the strength of my mind sufficed for this, or even if I could find the requisite time. But now I think it has been conclusively proved that there is no contradiction between eternal punishment and the rendering of punishment according to the measure of the sins committed.

5. Of the Son of God according to Solomon

After this question the objector, who was taking his difficulties from Porphyry, added this one. 'Surely,' he says, 'you will be kind enough to tell me whether Solomon truly said, "God has no son."' This is quickly answered: not only did he not say it, but he did say that God has a Son.

---
[31] James 2.13.

Wisdom speaking through him says: 'Before all the hills, he begot me,'[32] and what is Christ but the wisdom of God?[33] Again, in a certain passage in Proverbs, he says: 'God hath taught me wisdom, and I have known the science of the saints. Who hath ascended up into heaven and descendeth? Who hath held the wind in his bosom? Who hath changed the water as a garment? Who hath held all the borders of the earth? What is his name? and what is the name of his son?'[34] Of these two lines which I have quoted at the end, he referred one to the Father, that is: 'What is his name?' and for that reason he said: 'God hath taught me wisdom.' The other is obviously referred to the Son, when he says, 'Or what is the name of his son?' because the rest of the passage is better understood of the Son, that is: 'Who hath ascended up into heaven and descendeth.' Paul expresses it thus: 'He that descended is the same also that ascended above all the heavens.'[35] The words, 'Who hath gathered the winds into his bosom?' refer to the souls of those who believe in him secretly and hiddenly, to whom it is said: 'For you are dead, and your life is hid with Christ in God';[36] and the words, 'Who hath changed water as a garment?' can be referred to: 'For as many of you as have been baptized in Christ, have put on Christ';[37] and 'Who hath held the borders of the earth?' is He who said to His disciples: 'You shall be witnesses unto me in Jerusalem, and in all Judea and Samaria, and even to the uttermost part of the earth.'[38]

---

32 Cf. Prov. 8.25.
33 1 Cor. 1.24.
34 Cf. Prov. 30.3 (Septuagint).
35 Eph 4.10.
36 Col. 3.3.
37 Gal. 3.27.
38 Acts 1.8.

6. About the Prophet Jonas

The last question is about Jonas, and it is not put as if it were taken from Porphyry, but as if it were a laughing-stock of the pagans. It is expressed thus: 'Pray tell me what we are to think about Jonas who is said to have been three days in the belly of a whale.[39] It is improbable and unbelievable that he should have been swallowed up with his clothing on and should have been inside the fish. If it is figuratively said, please explain it. Secondly, what does it mean that, after Jonas had been vomited out, a gourd-vine sprang up over him?[40] What reason was there for it to spring up? I have noticed that this sort of question is a matter of jest and much laughter to pagans.'

The answer to this is that either all the divine miracles are to be disbelieved, or there is no reason why they should not be believed. We should not believe in Christ Himself, and that He rose on the third day, if the faith of Christians feared the laughter of pagans. But, since our friend did not make a difficulty about believing that Lazarus was raised to life on the fourth day, or that Christ Himself rose again on the third day, I marvel greatly that he finds it impossible to believe what happened to Jonas, unless, perhaps, he thinks it easier to raise a dead man from the tomb than to keep one alive in the immense belly of a sea monster. I shall not go into detail on the great size of sea monsters as described by those who know, but the skeleton which had upheld the body of such a one was displayed in public for the people at Carthage, and eveyone knows how many men could be enclosed in that space. What an immense opening that mouth had, like the gateway of a cave! But, perhaps,

---
39 Jonas 2.1.
40 Jonas 4.6.

as he puts it, the clothing would prevent Jonas from being swallowed unhurt, as if he had to squeeze through a narrow passage! In reality, he was hurled through the air and swallowed so quickly that he was inside the monster before he could be crushed by its teeth. Although the Scripture does not mention whether he was naked or clothed when he was hurled into that cavern, it would be possible to suppose that he entered there naked, if there were need for his clothing to be removed, as a shell from an egg, to facilitate swallowing. But people are as anxious about this Prophet's clothing as if the report were that he had crept through a small window, or had gone down into a bath, where, even if he had to go in fully clothed, it would be somewhat troublesome, but not remarkable.

But they have, as a matter of fact, something to disbelieve in the divine miracle, namely, that the heat of the stomach, by which food is softened, could have been diminished so as to preserve the life of a man. But, how much harder they would find it to believe that three men, thrown into a furnace by a cruel king, walked about unharmed in the midst of the fire.[41] Therefore, if they refuse to believe any of these divine miracles, they must be refuted by another sort of argument, for they ought not to pick out one special one as unbelievable, and call it in question, but they should disbelieve all of the others, which are either similar or even more remarkable. Yet, if what is written about Jonas were related as having happened to Apuleius of Madaura,[42]

---

41 Dan. 3.21, 24.
42 An African Latin philosopher and writer of the second century. He lived at Madaura, where his father was chief magistrate. His fictional work, *Metamorphoses*, or *The Story of the Golden Ass*, in which the author is supposed to have undergone a magical transformation, gave rise after his death to the belief that he had performed miracles. Pagans were quick to set these against the miracles of Christ.

or Apollonius of Tyana,⁴³ whose many extraordinary exploits are vouched for by no responsible authority—although the devils do some things like those done by the holy angels, in appearance, not in reality; by trickery, not by real knowledge—if, as I said, such a miracle were related of them, whom men praise as wise men and philosophers, no laugh would spread over their face, but proud elation. Let them so laugh at our Scriptures, let them laugh as hard as they can, so long as they see their numbers becoming fewer and smaller every day, either by death or by belief, while all that was foretold is accomplished. Those who laughed at them so long ago as destined to fight uselessly and bark vainly against the truth, and to fail little by little, these have not only left to us and to their descendants these prophecies to read, but have promised us to experience them.

But it is not foolish or unseemly to inquire into the meaning of these happenings, and when this has been explained they may believe that these things were not only done but also written with a certain significance. First, then, let him who wishes to examine why this happened believe that the Prophet Jonas was in the immense belly of a sea monster for three days; it did not happen without a reason, but it did happen. If men are roused to belief by what is merely said, but not done, as a symbol of something, how much more must they be roused by what is not only said symbolically, but also done! Human speech is wont to express itself by words, but divine power by deeds; and just as new or rare words, if used sparingly and with restraint, add splendor to human language, so divine eloquence be-

---

43 Born in Cappadocia at the commencement of the Christian era, and famous in the annals of ancient imposture, he was a Pythagorean, had a series of fabulous adventures, was worshiped as a god in some places and credited with many miracles. Like Apuleius, his supposed miracles were used by pagans in their anti-Christian propaganda.

comes, in a sense, more beautiful by miraculous deeds, which have an appropriate meaning.

Why, then, are we asked what was prefigured by the Prophet being swallowed by that monster and restored alive on the third day? Christ explained it when He said: 'An evil and adulterous generation seeketh a sign, and a sign shall not be given to it, but the sign of Jonas the prophet. For as Jonas was in the whale's belly three days and three nights, so shall the Son of man be in the heart of the earth three days and three nights.[44] But, how the reckoning is made of the three days of death of the Lord Christ, when part is taken for the whole on the first day and on the last, so that three whole days with their nights are counted, that is too long to discuss here, and it has been explained very often in other works. So, then, as Jonas went from the ship into the belly of the whale,[45] so Christ went from the tree[46] into the tomb, or into the abyss of death; and as Jonas was sacrificed for those endangered by the storm, so Christ was offered for those who are drowning in the storm of this world; and as Jonas was first commanded to preach to the Ninivites,[47] but his prophecy did not come to them until after the whale had vomited him out, so the prophecy made to the Gentiles did not come to them until after the Resurrection of Christ.

But, when Jonas made himself a booth and sat down opposite the city of Ninive, waiting to see what would befall it,[48] the Prophet played a part of different significance. He was a type of the carnal people of Israel, for he was sad over the preservation of the Ninivites, that is, over the redemption and salvation of the Gentiles. Hence, Christ

---
44 Matt. 12.39, 40.
45 Jonas. 1.11,12,15.
46 The Cross is often called the 'tree of the Cross.'
47 Jonas 1.2,3; 3.2,3.
48 Jonas 4.5.

came to call 'not the just but sinners to penance.'⁴⁹ But the shadow of the gourd-vine over his head was the promises of the Old Testament, or even those obligations in which there was manifestly, as the Apostle says, 'a shadow of things to come,'⁵⁰ offering shade from the heat of temporal evils, in the land of promise. But the worm in the morning, which gnawed at the vine and withered it,⁵¹ appears again as Christ, for, when the Gospel had been published by His mouth, all those things which made temporal prosperity for the Israelites, symbolized previously by the shade of the vine, withered and faded away. And, now, those people have lost the kingdom of Jerusalem, and their priesthood and sacrifice, all of which was a foreshadowing of the future; they are scattered abroad in captivity, and afflicted with a great flood of suffering, as Jonas—so it is written—suffered grievously from the heat of the sun.⁵² Yet, the salvation of penitent nations is preferred to his suffering and the shade which he loved.

Let the pagans go on laughing at this worm, symbolizing Christ, and let them mock with proud phrases at this interpretation of a prophetic mystery; little by little, imperceptibly, it will devour them. Isaias prophesied of all such men, and God speaking through him says: 'Hearken to me, you that know what is just, my people, who have my law in their heart: fear ye not the reproach of men and be not overcome by their detraction, nor think it of great moment that they despise you. For as a garment so shall they be consumed by time, and they shall be eaten up as wool by the moth, but my justice remaineth forever.'⁵³ Let us therefore recognize the worm in the morning, because in

---

49 Luke 5.32.
50 Col. 2.17; Heb. 10.1.
51 Jonas 4.7.
52 Jonas 4.8.
53 Cf. Isa. 51.7, 8.

that psalm whose title is inscribed 'for the morning protection,' He deigned to call Himself by that name when He said: 'I am a worm and no man, the reproach of men and the outcast of the people.'⁵⁴ And this reproach is the kind of reproach we are bidden not to fear in the words of Isaias: 'fear ye not the reproach of men.' By that worm, those are eaten as by a moth who marvel every day at their own insufficiency, falling under the tooth of His Gospel. But let us acknowledge Him and let us endure human reproach for the sake of divine salvation. He is a worm because of the lowliness of flesh; perhaps, too, because He was born of a virgin; for the worm, almost alone among animals, or earthly things generally, is born without any act of mating. He is 'of the morning' because He rose from the dead very early in the morning.⁵⁵ But that gourd-vine could equally well have withered away without any worm. In any case, if God had need of a worm for that purpose, why did He have to add 'in the morning,' except to make known that worm who sings 'for the morning protection': 'I am a worm and no man?'

What is clearer than that prophecy and its fulfillment in the sequence of events? But, if that worm was laughed at when He hung upon the Cross, as it is written in the same psalm: 'They have spoken with the lips and wagged the head: He hoped in the Lord, let him save him, seeing he delighteth in him';⁵⁶ when those things which He had foretold were fulfilled: 'They have dug my hands and feet; they have numbered all my bones: they have looked and stared upon me; they parted my garments amongst them and upon my vesture they cast lots,'⁵⁷ which is related in the new Gospel with as great detail as it was foretold in

---
54 Ps. 21.7.
55 Mark 16.2.
56 Ps. 21.8, 9.
57 Ps. 21.17-19.

the old Book, as something about to come—if, as I began to say, that worm is laughed at in this lowliness, is He still to be laughed at when we see these things fulfilled? For, the psalm gives us the following: 'All the ends of the earth shall remember and shall be converted to the Lord: and all the kindreds of the gentiles shall adore in his sight; for the kingdom is the Lord's and he shall have dominion over the nations.'[58] So the Ninivites remembered and were converted to the Lord.[59] Israel grieved over this salvation and repentance of the Gentiles, prefigured so long ago in Jonas, as it now grieves, deprived of its shade, and stricken with the heat. Anyone who likes may interpret in any other way he chooses—so long as it conforms to the rule of faith—the other details which are veiled in mystery in the Prophet Jonas, but that one fact, that he was in the whale's belly for three days, cannot be lawfully understood in any other way than the one revealed in the Gospel by the divine Master Himself, as we have related it.

I have explained what was asked as best I could, but he who proposed these difficulties had better become a Christian now; if he thinks to come to the end of all the obscure points in the sacred Books, he may come to the end of this life before he passes from death to life. What he asks about the resurrection of the dead could be settled before he receives the Christian sacraments, and we might perhaps satisfy him when he asks why Christ came so late in history, or other great or small points which depend on these. But, if he thinks to solve all such questions as 'With what measure you mete, it shall be measured to you,' or those about Jonas, before he becomes a Christian, he little knows the limitations of human life or of his own. For, there are numberless difficulties which cannot be settled before one

---
58 Ps. 21.28,29.
59 Jonas 3.5.

accepts the faith, for fear of ending life without faith; but, once the faith has been firmly grasped, these questions may be studied deeply by faithful souls, and they will find holy joy in them. Then, what they discover is to be shared without any puffing-up of pride, and what remains obscure is to be accepted without any loss of faith.

103. Nectarius gives greeting in the Lord to the truly estimable lord, Augustine, his most honorable brother (March, 409)[1]

I have received the letter of your Excellency, in which you have laid low the worship of idols and the ceremonial of temples, and in it I did not seem to hear the voice of that philosopher, whom rumor describes as sitting on the Lycean ground of the Academe[2] in its shaded corners, buried in some profound thought, with his forehead bowed upon his knees, so that some impoverished prosecutor could attack the finely developed theories of others, and, while defending no skilled arguments of his own, should belittle those of other men. But, summoned by your words, there appeared before my eyes Marcus Tullius, the consul,[3] crowned with

---

1 Eight months before this date, Nectarius had written to ask Augustine's help in securing pardon and remission of penalty for the unlawful and violent acts of his pagan fellow citizens of Calama. In the course of observing a pagan festival, forbidden by law, these pagans had damaged Christian property and endangered Christian lives. This appeal is found in Letter 90. In Letter 91 Augustine answered that if all penalty were remitted the people might not understand the gravity of their offense, and he gave a full description of the excesses committed. For Nectarius, cf. Letter 90.
2 Aristotle was the philosopher of the Lyceum, as Plato was of the Academe.
3 The figure used by Nectarius is an intricate one and not too clear. Cicero is the victorious warrior bringing back the captured standards of the enemy; he is the trumpeter, sounding the charge against traitors; he is the citizen in his toga—the dress of peace—which he metaphorically tucks up and folds back to simulate a military cloak. And the eloquence of Augustine's letter reminds Nectarius of all this!

the laurels of Greek learning, who brought to the numerous fellow citizens whom he had saved the victorious standards of the forensic field; who turned the breath of his tuneful voice and language into that trumpet on which he had blown the blasts of rightful indignation against proved criminals and murderers of their country; who, by his unrestrained pages, unfolded his toga and girded it up to imitate the appearance of a military cloak.

Therefore, when you were urging us to the worship and religion of the supreme God, I listened to you with pleasure; when you encouraged me to look up to a heavenly country, I assented gratefully. You did not seem to describe to me the sort of country which some encircling wall encloses, nor the earthly sort which the treatises of philosophers portray, and which they promise as a possession to all, but a country where the great God lives, and where the souls who have deserved it dwell with Him; that one which all laws seek to reach by different paths and ways, which we cannot express in speech, but may perchance find in meditation. I grant that this country is chiefly to be desired and loved, but I think that the other one should not be forgotten; the one in which we were begotten and born, which first bestowed on us the light of life, which nourished us, brought us up, and—to speak in a manner befitting my subject—the one from which, as learned men say, a home in heaven is made ready for well-deserving heroes after the death of the body. Those who have done great things for their native cities are rewarded by being raised up to the heights, and they are the ones who dwell with God, the ones who have brought security to their fatherland by their plans or efforts. But when you said—coming down to our level with a jest— that our city blazed with flames and fires,[4] not with arms, and that it produced thorns rather than flowers, I did not

---

4 Cf. Letter 91.

take that as much of a rebuke, because we know that flowers often spring from thorns. Does not everyone know that roses grow from thorns, and that even the harvest of wheat is hedged about with a rampart of spikes? Thus we find sweet and bitter things usually intermingled.

Finally, your Excellency's letter said that neither the death penalty nor physical punishment is being asked by the Church as satisfaction for injury, but only what men fear most to lose. If my opinion does not play me false, I think it is worse to be stripped of the means of living than to be put to death. If it is true, as you have often learned in your studies, that death puts an end to all consciousness of misfortune, but a needy life begets an eternal loss, then it is worse to live in poverty than to end misfortune by death. The nature of your endeavor proves this, because you support the poor, you relieve the sick by caring for them, you furnish remedies for ailing bodies, and you do everything you can to keep the afflicted from suffering too long a time. But, as far as sin is concerned, it makes no difference what sort of sin it is for which pardon is asked. In the first place, if repentance brings pardon and cleanses what has been confessed, then he who asks pardon and casts himself at your feet certainly repents, and if, as some philosophers think, all sins are alike, then there should be a universal pardon for all. If someone speaks too angrily, he sins; if he multiplies insults and false accusations, he sins equally; if someone steals another's property, that is rated among transgressions; if he has profaned shrines or sacred places, he is not to be shut out from pardon. Finally, there would be no reason for pardon if sin had not come first.

And now that I have answered you, more or less, as they say, according to my ability, rather than to the requirements of the case, I beg and beseech you—and how I wish you were here to see my tears—to think who you are, what you profess, what you are doing, and to reflect again and again on the condition of that city from which these men have to be dragged out to punishment. Think of the grief of their mothers, their wives, their children, their parents; how ashamed they would be to return to their native soil, freed, but chastised; and how the sight of their wounds and scars would renew the grief and tears of their dear ones. After reflecting on all this, think first of God and of the reputation of these men; win their friendly good will, or, rather, their intimate affection, and even their praise, by pardoning rather than by punishing. Let this be enough to say of men whom the true guilt of their own confession weighs down, but to whom you have granted pardon, with due regard for the law, something I cannot cease to praise. But it would be impossible to describe the cruelty of seeking out innocent people and involving them in the capital punishment of a crime, with which they evidently had nothing to do. But, if they are acquitted, think, please, of the envy of the accused when they are set free, if those who have lost their case dismiss the guilty and abandon the innocent. May the most high God guard you and preserve you as the support of His laws and our glory.

104. Augustine gives greeting in the Lord to the illustrious lord, Nectarius,[1] his worthy, honorable and cherished brother (409)

I have read the letter of your Benignity which you sent me as an answer a long time after I had sent you mine. I wrote to you while my holy brother and fellow bishop, Possidius,[2] was still with us, before he sailed, but this letter,

---
1 Cf. Letters 90, 91, 103.
2 Cf. Letter 95 n. 2.

which you were so kind as to give him for me, reached me on March 27, almost eight months after my answer to you. I have no idea why my letter was so late in reaching you, or yours in reaching me, unless, perhaps, your Prudence decided to write to me only now, after disdaining to do so sooner. If that is the case, I wonder why. Did you hear something—still unknown to us—to the effect that my brother Possidius had won his case against your fellow citizens, whom, with all due regard to you, he loves more profitably than you do, although he treats them more sternly? Your letter shows me that you fear this, when you urge me to set before my eyes the condition of that city from which those men have to be dragged out to punishment, and the grief of their mothers, their wives, their children, their parents; how ashamed they would be to return to their native soil, freed, but chastised, and how the sight of their wounds and scars would renew the grief and tears of their dear ones.[3] Far be it from me to insist that such things should be inflicted on any one of our enemies, either by us or by anyone at all; but, as I said, if rumor has brought you any such report, come out with it more openly so that we may know what to do to prevent such happenings, or to answer those who believe that they have happened.

Examine my letter carefully—the one you were reluctant to answer—in it I set forth clearly enough what I thought. But I imagine you forgot what I wrote, and you quoted to me other words, very different, and unlike what I wrote. As if recalling what I said in my letter, you put something in yours which I did not say at all. You said that at the end of my letter I had written: 'Neither the death penalty nor physical punishment is being asked by the Church as satisfaction for injury, but only what men fear most to lose.' Then, to show what a great misfortune this is, you

---
[3] Quoted from Letter 103.

go on and add that, unless your opinion plays you false, you think 'it is worse to be stripped of the means of living than to be put to death.' And to make clear what means of living you refer to, you go on and add that I have often learned in my studies that 'death puts an end to all consciousness of misfortune, but a needy life begets eternal loss.'[4] Then you conclude that it is worse to live in poverty than to end misfortune by death.

For my part, I do not ever remember reading that a needy life begets an eternal loss, either in our literature—to which I confess I devoted myself later in life than I could wish—or in yours, which I studied from my earliest youth. Burdensome poverty has never been a sin, and is, in fact, a restraint and restriction on the sinner. Consequently, there is no reason for anyone to fear that, after this brief life, he should merit the eternal loss of his soul because of a life of poverty in this world. Similarly, in the life which we live on earth, no loss can possibly be eternal, because the life itself is not eternal, however long it may be or however advanced an old age we may attain. What I have read in your literature is more like this: that the life itself which we enjoy is brief, yet you think and you maintain it as a common saying that there can be eternal loss in this life. It is true that some of your authors consider death as the end of all misfortune, but not all of them; it is chiefly the opinion of the Epicureans[5] and those who think the soul is mortal. But those whom Tullius calls philosophers of consular rank,[6] because he greatly values their authority, believe

---

4 *Ibid.*
5 Epicurus (352-270 B.C.) had a materialistic philosophy, denying the spirituality of the soul, the possibility of a life after death, and taking an agnostic attitude toward the gods. His theories are best known to us in Lucretius' *De rerum natura* and in Cicero's *De finibus* and *De natura deorum*.
6 These philosophers were the Academics, who affirmed the immortality of the soul, and whom Cicero calls aristocrats, as he calls all those who dissent from them plebeians (*Tusc. Disp.* 1.23).

that when we come to our last day the soul is not destroyed, but departs from the body, and that its deserts, for good or ill, await it for its happiness or sorrow. This is conformable to our sacred literature, in which it is my ambition to excel. Death is, then, the end of misfortune, but only for those whose life has been pure, upright, faithful, blameless; whereas those who coveted temporal trifles and futilities, thinking themselves happy in them, are convicted by the perversity of their own will, and after death are forced not only to believe in but to suffer still greater woes.

These thoughts are common to the more highly esteemed of your authors and to all of ours; hence, great lover as you are of your earthly fatherland, you should fear for your fellow citizens a life of self-indulgence, not one of want. But, if you do fear want, warn them to avoid that kind of want which abounds in the fullness of earthly goods, but leaves in them an insatiable craving, which, to quote one of your authors, 'is lessened neither by plenty nor by destitution.'[7] However, in that letter of mine to which you replied, I did not say that the enemies of the Church, your fellow citizens, should be punished by being reduced to such poverty as to lack the necessaries of life, because charity, which you believe is an obligation of ours, would help them in that case, and the nature of our good works proves this. It is true that we support the poor, relieve the sick by caring for them, and furnish remedies for ailing bodies; in spite of all that, it is better to be in want than to possess to the full everything that satisfies evil desire. I am far from thinking that the people in question should be reduced by our exactions to that degree of wretchedness.

Go over my letter again, if you thought it worth while to put it away, where it could be brought out when you asked for it, since you had to answer it, even if you did not

---

7 Sallust, *Cat.* 11.3

reread it; notice what I said, and you will admit, I think, that you have not really answered it. I now quote my words from that letter: 'We have no desire,' I said, 'to feed our anger by taking vengeance for the past, but we are anxious to provide for the future by mercy. There are ways in which evil men are open to punishment by Christians; but only out of kindness and to their own benefit and improvement. They have their bodily integrity; they have the means of livelihood; they have the means of living wickedly. Let the first two of these remain intact, so that there may be some to repent; this we pray for, this we work for with all our might. But, in the third, if God wills to cut it off like something rotten and decayed, He will show great mercy in His punishment.'[8] If you had examined these words of mine, when you so kindly wrote to me, you would have thought it more of an insult than a duty to appeal to us to save those under consideration from death or bodily mutilation, because I said we wanted them to be assured of living unmutilated, and you certainly did not have to fear for them, on our account, such a life that they should lack the necessaries which are shared in by others. I also said that we wished them to be secure in the second point I mentioned, that they should have the means of livilihood. But, as to the third, that they should have the means of living wickedly, such as—to cite only one instance—to have the means of making silver statues of their false gods, and of serving and adoring those gods, and of carrying their accursed worship so far as to throw fire upon the Church of God, to give what is used to support the devout poor as plunder to their followers, and to stir them to bloodshed, why do you, who have the interest of your city at heart, fear to have this cut off, when, if there is no punishment, their boldness will only be nourished and strengthened?

---

[8] Quoted from Letter 91.

Explain this to us; show us by careful argument what misfortune it could be; note carefully what we say, and do not, under pretext of asking a favor, make our words an excuse for indirect reproach.

Granted that your citizens are honorable men, of upright character, and not endowed with excessive wealth, we have no desire to put any compulsion on them to return to the plough of Quintius[9] or the hearth of Fabricius.[10] Yet, these leaders of the Roman state lost nothing of the respect of their fellow citizens by their poverty; on the contrary, they were held in higher esteem and considered fitter to rule their country because of it. We do not even ask or require that the rich men of your country follow the example of Rufinus,[11] twice consul, whose possession of ten pounds of silver was adjudged an offense by the rigorous but much-praised censorship of that time, and was made subject to confiscation. But the custom of a depraved age induces us to treat these too flabby souls with too great indulgence, and what seemed right in the censors of that time seems excessive in the kindly Christians of today. You see how much difference it makes whether the crime to be punished today is to possess so much wealth, or to allow someone to possess it, in order to avoid other very serious abuses. What was wrong then, we wish might at least be the penalty of

---

9 Lucius Quintius Cincinnatus, a gentleman farmer of early Roman times, was made dictator in order to carry on war against the Aequi, one of the neighboring tribes, won a victory and returned to his ploughing in fourteen days, although the office of dictator had a term of six months. Cf. Livy 3.26.
10 Caius Luscinus Fabricius lived in the latter part of the third century B.C. He was an example of extreme frugality and simplicity of life as well as of great probity and honor. In the war with Pyrrhus, he was the admiration of his adversary for his honesty and integrity.
11 P. Cornelius Rufinus was dismissed from the Senate by Fabricius, who was then censor, because he possessed ten pounds of silver plate. The censor, in the Roman republic, had authority to enforce sumptuary laws.

wrong now. But it is both possible and necessary that, on the one hand, severity should not go to such lengths, and, on the other, that a too carefree security should not rejoice and keep holiday and thereby lead other hapless men, by the force of imitation, into excessive and secret penalties. Agree, at least, that those who contrive to burn and plunder our necessities should fear for their own superfluities. Give us leave to do this favor to our enemies; by making them fear the loss of goods which it is not harmful to lose we prevent them from trying to commit acts which are harmful to them. And this is not to be called vengeance for an offense, but a measure of precaution; it is not to inflict punishment, but to prevent men from having punishment inflicted on them.

To prevent a reckless man with some sense of sorrow, but hardened by useless crimes, from suffering excessive penalties is to pluck hairs from a child to keep him from applauding serpents; no physical harm is done him by this unwanted affection, but life and health are endangered by that from which we protect him. We are not kind-hearted when we do what we are asked, but when we do what is not harmful to our petitioners. Generally speaking, we do good by not giving, when we would do harm if we had given. Hence that proverb: 'Do not give a sword to a child.' 'And you,' said Tullius, 'do not give one even to an only child.' The more we love anyone, the less should we give in to him in matters where it is dangerous for him to go wrong. And, if I mistake not, he was speaking of riches when he said that. Therefore, if it is dangerous to allow people to make a bad use of things, it is generally beneficial to deprive them of such things. When doctors see that corruption has to be cut or burned out, they show mercy in turning a deaf ear to copious tears. If we had been pardoned by our parents or schoolmasters every time we begged them to overlook our offenses when we were little, or even growing up, who of us would be bearable when he had grown up? Who would have learned anything useful? They act, then, with foresight rather than with cruelty. In this matter do not, I beg of you, look at only one side, namely, how you can get from us what your people are asking of you, but look at it carefully on all sides. If you are shutting your eyes to the past, which cannot now be undone, take some thought for the future; be wise, consider what is good for your clients, not what they desire and ask of you. Our love is proved to be not truly disinterested when we think only of doing what we are asked, for fear of being less loved by those who ask us; and where is it that your literature praises the ruler of his country who looks out for their interests rather than for their inclinations?[12]

'It makes no difference,' you say, 'what sort of sin it is for which pardon is asked.' You could say this with truth if there were question of punishing rather than of reclaiming men. The Christian must keep far from his heart any lust of vengeance when someone is subjected to punishment; he must try to forestall the request by pardoning the offense before he is asked, or at least by granting pardon as soon as it is asked. Above all, he must not hate the offender, nor return evil for evil, nor burn with a desire of injuring him, nor seek satisfaction in vengeance even when it is legally owed to him. On the contrary, he must look out for the interests of the offender, think of his future, and restrain him from evil. It is possible, by too vigorous opposition, to fail to bring about the amendment of a man whom one hates too deeply, and equally, by restraining someone he greatly loves, he may make him better by causing him vexation. Repentance, as you write,[13] does bring pardon, and cleanses away what has been confessed,

---
12 Cicero, *Pro Sulla* 8.25.
13 Letter 103.

but only that repentance which is practised in the true religion, which reflects on the future judgment of God. The other kind, which is for the time being, and is expressed or pretended before men, has no efficacy in purifying the soul from everlasting guilt, but is only intended to free this present life, so soon to end, from the fear of present inconvenience. That is why we believe that the Christians who were involved in that outrage,[14] either by not helping to save the church when it was set on fire, or by carrying off some of the accursed loot, but who now confess and deplore their sin, are cleansed from it by the sorrow of their repentance; and we judge that this is enough to bring about their amendment, provided faith is present in their heart and they are able to recognize the consequences they ought to fear from God's judgment. But, how can repentance cure those who not only refuse to acknowledge the very source itself of pardon, but even continue to deride and blaspheme it? Not that we hold any grudge in our heart against them, as God knows and sees us, since it is His judgment we fear, and His help we hope for, both in this life and in the next. But we feel that we are doing them a good turn by making them fear something, if they will not fear God, when we hurt their self-esteem, without endangering their means of support. Otherwise, God Himself, whom they scorn, would be deeply angered by acts made bold by their dangerous assurance, and that same assurance could furnish a dangerous example to others. Finally, we pray God for those for whom you pray us, that He may win them over to Himself, and may teach them a true and saving repentance, by strengthening their hearts in the faith.

See now how much more sincere and—with all due regard for you—how much more profitable is our love than yours for those with whom you think we are angry, since we pray that they may escape greater evils and attain greater

---

14 Cf. Letter 91.

good. If you loved them with the heavenly charity of God, not in the earthly manner of men, you would answer me truthfully that you consent to embrace the worship and religion of the most high God, as I urge you to do, and you would wish the same benefit for them, or, rather, you would lead them to the same. In that way all this matter of your request would end in great and true joy; in that way, from a real and filial love for the earthly country which gave you birth, you would win to that heavenly country which you said you would be glad to claim when I urged you to look upon it; and you would truly seek the welfare of your citizens by bringing them the boon of everlasting happiness rather than the emptiness of temporal joy through an escape from punishment which could bring them only danger.

This is a summary of my views on this matter and these are the wishes of my heart. What lies hidden in the designs of God I confess I do not know—I am only a man—but this I know with full certainty, that, whatever it is, it is more just, more wise, and more solidly based on incomparable perfection than all the judgments of men. What we read in our books is certainly true: 'There are many thoughts in the heart of a man, but the will of the Lord remaineth forever.'[15] What time will bring, from now on, what ease or obstacle we may find, what sentiment may suddenly arise from the rectifying of the present state of affairs, or from their hope; whether God is so incensed by these acts that He will inflict a greater and more severe penalty on them by allowing them to escape punishment, as they ask; whether He will decree that they be mercifully restrained in the way we desire; or whether by some sharper but more efficacious measure He may first correct and then truly convert them, according to His mercy, not that of men, and will then turn aside and change into joy whatever fear awaits them—all this He

---

15 Cf. Prov. 19.21.

knows, but we do not. Why, then, do we waste our time on this, your Excellency and I? Let us lay aside our anxiety for a little while, since this is not the time for it, and let us, if you will, do what is always timely. For, it is always time to act as we must and ought so as to please God, although in this life it is either impossible or extremely difficult to attain to such perfection that a man should be entirely sinless. Consequently we must put an end to all delays and fly for refuge to His grace. He is the one to whom these words can most truthfully be applied, which the poet addressed to an unknown hero, claiming to have taken them from some prophecy of the Cumaean seer: 'Under thy guidance, if any traces of our guilt remain, made harmless they shall free the world from endless fear.'[16] Under His guidance, by this road, when all our sins have been forgiven and washed away, we come to our heavenly country, where you rejoiced to think of dwelling when I had done my best to commend it to you.

But, since you said that all the laws seek after that country by different paths and ways,[17] I am afraid you may happen to think that the way in which you are now established leads to it, and so you may be too slothful to turn toward the only way that does lead to it. Yet, when I think again of that word which you used, I imagine I find in it a meaning not unintended by you. For, you did not say that all laws, by different paths and ways, attain, or point out, or find, or enter into, or achieve, or anything of that sort, but, by saying seek after, a word well-chosen and carefully weighed, you meant a desire of attainment, not actual attainment. So, you did not exclude the meaning which is true, nor did you accept the others which are false, because, naturally, the way which leads to a place seeks for it, but not every one

---

16 Vergil, *Ec.* 4.13.
17 Cf. Letter 103.

which seeks does lead to it. Undoubtedly, a person is happy by being led along that way; we wish all to be happy; that is what we seek after. But, wishing is not the same as doing, that is, we do not attain what we seek after. The one who attains is the one who holds to the way by which he seeks after as well as attains, leaving others on their roads of seeking without reaching the goal of attainment. There would be no going astray if there were no seeking; no error would be held if truth were not being sought. If, then, when you said 'different ways' you did not mean opposite ones, as we speak of different teachings which all help to build up the good life, some on chastity, some on patience, some on faith, some on mercy and so forth, in that case the heavenly country is not only sought after but even found by different ways. In Holy Scripture we read both *ways* and *way*: *ways*, as in 'I will teach the unjust thy ways, and the wicked shall be converted to thee,'[18] and *way*, as in 'Conduct me in thy way and I will walk in thy truth.'[19] But the *ways* and the *way* are not different: they are all one, as the same Holy Scripture says in another place: 'All the ways of the Lord are mercy and truth.'[20] If these passages are carefully studied, they bring enrichment to one's speech and a most sweet understanding, but, if there is need of this, I shall postpone it to another time.

For the present I think I have gone far enough in carrying out my duty of answering your Excellency. Since Christ said: 'I am the way,'[21] all mercy and truth are to be sought in Him. If we should seek elsewhere, we should go astray by choosing a way that seeks but does not lead to the goal. So, for instance, if we insisted on holding that view from which you quoted something to the effect that all sins are

---
18 Ps. 50.15.
19 Ps. 85.11.
20 Ps. 24.10.
21 John 14.6.

equal, would not that way keep us in exile, far from that country of truth and blessedness? There could be nothing more ridiculous or more senseless than to say that someone who sometimes laughed extravagantly should be judged to have committed the same kind of sin as the one who wantonly set fire to his fatherland. That way, then, which you have thought fit to select from the opinion of certain philosophers —not because you believed it, but for the sake of your citizens—is not merely a different way, yet one which leads to the heavenly abode, but an obviously wrong one which leads to the most destructive error. According to that, we should extend the same forgiveness to the rioters who set fire to the church as to someone who assailed us with impudent abuse.

But, see how you introduce this idea. You say: 'And if, as some philosophers think, all sins are alike, then there should be a universal pardon for all.'[22] Then, as if you were trying to show that all sins are alike, you go on and say: 'If someone speaks too angrily, he sins; if he multiplies insults and false accusations, he sins equally.' This is not the way to prove anything, but to set forth a wrong point of view without any supporting authority. When you say: 'He sins equally,' the answer is quickly made: 'He does not sin equally.' Perhaps you want me to prove it, but what proof did you give that they were the same kind of sins? Or why should we have to listen to what you say next: 'If he steals another's property, that is rated among transgressions'? Here, indeed, you showed some diffidence; you were ashamed to say that the sinner committed the same kind of sin, so you said: 'It is rated among transgressions.' The question is not whether this offense is rated among transgressions, but whether this one is on a basis of equality with that other, or, if they are equal because they are both transgressions, then

22 Cf. Letter 103.

mice and elephants are equal because they are both animals, and flies and eagles are equal because they both fly.

You go even further, continuing: 'If he has profaned shrines or sacred places, he is not to be shut out from pardon.' Here, at last, in mentioning the profaning of sacred places, you have come to the crime of your countrymen, but even you have not likened it to an offense of impudent speech; you have simply asked for them the pardon which is rightfully asked of Christians on the plea of generous forgiveness, not that of equality of sins. I have written above: 'All the ways of the Lord are mercy and truth.'[23] They will meet with mercy if they do not hate truth. This is owed them by Christian right if they truly repent of a monstrous and impious crime, but not on the ground that it is the same kind of sin as if they had spoken too angrily. You are a man worthy of esteem, so do not, please, teach your Paradox[24] that the paradoxes of the Stoics[25] are fit to be followed. We hope and pray that he is growing up for you a truly devoted and happy young man. But, how could a well-born youth acquire knowledge more hatefully and with greater danger to yourself than by learning to make no distinction between an insult hurled at some stranger, and—I do not say murder—but the same insult directed against his father?

You make an appropriate appeal for your countrymen by reminding us of Christian compassion, but when you recall the severity of the Stoics, you win no support for the cause you have undertaken; you even do it much harm. The Stoics make of this compassion a weakness, to be

---

23 Ps. 24.10
24 This seems to have been the name of the young son of Nectarius, as the subsequent lines show.
25 The Stoics compressed their teaching into short epigrams which taught truth through apparent contradiction. Chesterton says of the paradox that it is a truth standing on its head to call attention to itself.

driven from the heart of the wise man, who is supposed to be hard and unyielding; but if we did not have it, we should be moved by no request of yours, by no appeals of theirs. A better quotation which might occur to your mind could be cited from your beloved Cicero, when he praises Caesar, saying: 'None of your virtues is more worthy of admiration or more pleasing than your compassion.'[26] How much more should this virtue shine out in our churches, since we follow Him who said: 'I am the way,' and we read: 'All the ways of the Lord are mercy and truth.' Have no fear, then, that we are plotting destruction for the innocent; we do not even wish the guilty to suffer a fitting punishment, restrained as we are by that mercy which, together with truth, we love in the Lord. Whoever shields and encourages the growth of vice for fear of crossing the offender is not being merciful, any more than the one who refuses to take a knife away from a child for fear of hearing his cries, yet does not fear to have to regret causing injury or death. You had better save for an opportune time the plea you make to us for those men—and with all due respect for you—you do not outstrip us in loving them, you do not even catch up with us. Write us, rather, your impression of this way on which we travel, and which we strongly urge you to take with us, so as to reach that heavenly country which we know, and rejoice to know, that you love.

Some of the citizens of your earthly country may be blameless, as you said, though not all, but if you will reread my letter, you must notice that you have not exonerated them. When I said that we had experienced thorns, not flowers,[27] answering what you had written, that you longed to leave your country in flower, you thought I was joking. As if anyone could joke about such disasters! Exactly so!

---
26 Cicero, *Pro Lig.* 12.27.
27 Cf. Letter 91.

The ruins of our burned-down church are still smoking and we joke about it! As far as I am concerned, I did not meet any blameless persons there, except those who were either away, or were victims of the outrages, or lacked strength or influence to prevent them. In my answer, I distinguished between the more and the less guilty, and I made one enumeration of those who feared to offend the powerful enemies of the Church, another of those who wanted violence done, another of those who did it, another of those who instigated it. But I did not wish to proceed against the instigators, because they could probably not be discovered without the use of physical tortures—something abhorrent to our way of life. Your friends, the Stoics, who hold that all sins are equal, admit that all offenders are equally guilty, and, applying their harshness which decries compassion to this verdict, they must think that all should be equally punished, not that all should be equally forgiven. Put them as far away as you can from the defense of this case; pray that we may deal with them as Christians, and that we may gain them, as we hope, by sparing them in Christ, not by sparing them to the danger of their eternal loss. May the merciful and true God deign to grant you true happiness.

105. Augustine, Catholic Bishop, to the Donatists (409)[1]

The charity of Christ, for whom we wish to gain every man, as far as in us lies, does not allow us to remain silent. If you hate us because we preach Catholic unity to you, we serve a Lord who says: 'Blessed are the peacemakers, for

---
1 This must have been a pastoral letter, intended for general circulation, but not addressed to any particular correspondent.

they shall be called the children of God,'[2] and it is written in the psalm: 'With them that hated peace, I was peaceable: when I spoke to them, they fought against me without cause.'[3] For that reason, certain of the priests of your sect sent us a message: 'Keep away from our flocks, if you do not want us to kill you.' With how much more reason do we say to them: On the contrary, do not you keep away, but be reconciled and draw near to our flocks, or rather His, to whom we all belong, but, if you will not, and you are still unreconciled, you are the ones to keep away from the flocks for which Christ shed His Blood. You wish to make them yours, so that they may not be Christ's, although you try to possess them in His Name, as if a thief should steal sheep from his master's flock, and, when young were born of them, should mark them with his master's brand, to keep his theft from being known. That is what your predecessors did: they separated people who had the baptism of Christ from the Church of Christ, and, whatever increase there was, they baptized with the baptism of Christ. But the Lord punishes thieves if they do not amend their lives, and He calls the sheep back from their wandering to His flock, without erasing His mark from them.

You say that we are betrayers, a charge which your ancestors could not prove against our ancestors, nor will you ever be able to prove it against us. What do you want us to do to you? We tell you to listen to us patiently while we plead your cause and ours, and you do nothing but rant and rage. We could certainly show you that the real betrayers were those who condemned Caecilian[4] and his co-workers on a fictitious charge of betrayal. And you say: 'Keep away from our flocks,' whom you teach to believe

---
2 Matt. 5.9.
3 Ps. 119.6.
4 Deacon of Carthage, whose consecration as bishop was the alleged excuse for the Donatist schism. Cf. Letters 43, 93, *et al.*

in you and not to believe in Christ. You tell them that because of betrayers—whom you do not produce—the Church of Christ exists only in Africa, in the sect of Donatus; and you do not give any authority for your statement, either from the Law, or from a Prophet, or a psalm, or an Apostle, or the Gospel, but only from your own feeling, and the false reports of your parents. But Christ says: 'And that penance and remission of sins should be preached in his name unto all nations, beginning at Jerusalem.'[5] Yet, you are not in communion with that Church which was announced by the word of Christ, and you do not want others, whom you drag down into your own ruin, to be set free.

If you are angry with us because you are forced by the decrees of the emperors[6] to rejoin us, you brought this on yourselves by stirring up violence and threats whenever we wished to preach the truth, and you tried to prevent anyone from listening to it in safety or choosing it voluntarily. Do not hiss and stir up your minds; think tolerantly, if you can, over what we say; call to memory the deeds of your Circumcellions and the clerics who have always been their leaders, and you will see what brought this on you. Your complaints are baseless because you forced the enactment of all these decrees. Not to go back over numerous past instances, consider, at least, your recent conduct. Mark, a priest of Casphaliana,[7] became a Catholic of his own free will, without compulsion from anybody; thereupon your people pursued him and would almost have killed him, if the hand of God had not restrained their violence by means of some

---

5 Luke 24.47.
6 These had been made in 405, and were a reaffirmation of earlier laws. At the death of Stilicho, military dictator of Africa, a rumor had spread that these laws were to be allowed to lapse.
7 Probably a small Numidian town or hamlet.

passers-by. Restitutus of Victoriana[8] came over to the Catholic faith without any compulsion, and was dragged from his house, beaten, rolled in the water, clothed in reeds,[9] kept in custody I don't know how long, and would probably not have been restored to liberty if Proculeianus[10] had not seen himself threatened with a show-down, largely on his account. Marcian of Urga[11] chose Catholic unity of his own free will, and, when he went into hiding, your clerics took his subdeacon, beat him almost to death, and stoned him. For this crime their houses were destroyed.

What is the use of saying more? Lately, you sent a herald to proclaim at Sinitus:[12] 'If anyone remains in communion with Maximinus,[13] his house will be burned down.' Why? Before he had been converted to the Catholic faith, when he had not yet returned from overseas, why else did we send there a priest of Sinitus, except to visit our people without troubling anyone, and, from his lawful dwelling, to preach Catholic unity to those who were willing to hear him? But your people expelled him, and did him a great wrong. What other purpose did we have when one of ours, Possidius,[14] Bishop of Calama, was traveling to the estate of Figulina,[15] to visit our flock, few as they were, and to give an opportunity to any who wished it to hear the word of God and return to the unity of Christ? But, while he was on his way, they lay in wait for him like a band of brigands and, failing to catch him in their toils, they attacked him

---

8 He may be the deacon to whom Letter 249 is addressed; Victoriana was another hamlet.
9 Cf. Letter 88.
10 Donatist bishop in Hippo.
11 Another Numidian hamlet.
12 A small town in the vicinity of Hippo.
13 Donatist bishop of Sinitus, who afterward became a Catholic, and remained in the same see. Augustine addressed Letter 23 to him.
14 Cf. Letter 95 n. 2.
15 Church congregations often owned estates and rented them out.

violently at the farm of Oliveta, left him half-dead and tried to burn down the house from which he had escaped. They would have done it, too, if the tenants of that same farm had not three times put out the flames which endangered their own safety. Yet, when Crispinus[16] was convicted in the proconsular court as a heretic of this very deed, he was let off the fine of ten pounds of gold, at the request of this same Bishop Possidius. He not only showed no gratitude for this kindly indulgence, but he even went so far as to appeal to the Catholic emperors.[17] This is what has brought down on you the wrath of God with greater force, and persistence, and you complain of it!

You see, you are suffering for your own evil deeds, not for Christ, when you stir up violence against the peace of Christ. What kind of madness is it to claim the glory of martyrdom when you are being justly punished for your evil life and your deeds of brigandage? If you, private citizens, so boldly and violently force men either to accept error or to remain in it, how much greater right and duty have we to resist your outrages by means of the lawfully constituted authority, which God has made subject to Christ, according to His prophecy, and so to rescue unfortunate souls from your tyranny, to free them from long-continued false teaching and let them breathe the clear air of truth! As for those who, according to you, are compelled to join us against their will, many of them wish to be compelled, as they admit to us both before and after conversion, for only thus can they escape your oppressive treatment.

Which, then, is the better course: to publish the decrees of the emperors in behalf of unity, or to proclaim a mistaken amnesty in behalf of heresy, as you have done, when you

---

16 Donatist bishop of Calama; Letters 51 and 66 are addressed to him. Cf. Letter 93 n. 4.
17 Honorius and Arcadius.

have suddenly filled the whole of Africa with your lies?[18] By this conduct you have proved nothing else except that the sect of Donatus, relying on falsehood, is tossed and tumbled about by all the winds, as it is written 'He that trusteth to lies, feedeth the winds.'[19] Thus, that amnesty was as true as the crimes of Caecilian and the betrayal of Felix of Aptunga,[20] by whom he was consecrated, and all the other charges which you commonly make against the Catholics, in order to separate unhappy souls from the peace of the Church of Christ and be yourselves unhappily separated from it. But, we on our side do not rely on any power of man, although, no doubt, it would be much more honorable to rely on the emperors than to rely on Circumcellions, and to rely on laws than to rely on rioting, but we recall what is written: 'Cursed be everyone who putteth his hope in man.'[21] So, then, if you want to know on whom we rely, think of Him whom the Prophet foretold, saying: 'All the kings of the earth shall adore him; all nations shall serve him.'[22] That is why we make use of this power of the Church which the Lord both promised and gave to it.

If the emperors were in error—perish the thought!—in accordance with their error they would issue laws against the truth, and through these the just would be both tried and crowned by not doing what was commanded because it was forbidden by God. Thus Nabuchodonosor had commanded his golden statue to be adored,[23] and they who refused to do it pleased God who forbade such acts. But, when the emperors hold to the truth, in accordance with

---

18 The Donatists had circulated the report that the imperial decrees against them had been abrogated after the death of Stilicho.
19 Prov. 10.4.
20 Cf. Letters 43, 88, 93, *et al.*
21 Cf. Jer. 17.5.
22 Ps. 71.11.
23 Dan. 3.1-18.

that truth they give commands against error, and whoever despises them brings down judgment on himself. He pays the penalty exacted by men and he has no standing before God, because he refused to do what truth itself commanded him by the 'heart of the king.'[24] Thus Nabuchodonosor himself was afterward moved by the miracle of the preservation of the three children, and, turning against error and toward truth, he published an edict that 'Whoever should speak blasphemy against the God of Sidrach, Misach and Abdenago, should be destroyed and their houses laid waste.'[25] And do you refuse to admit that Christian emperors should give like commands against you, when they know that Christ is mocked by you in those whom you rebaptize? If the commands of a king do not extend to the preaching of religion and the prevention of sacrilege, why do you single out the edict of a king giving such commands? Do you not know that the words of a king are 'signs and wonders [which] the most high God hath wrought toward me. It hath seemed good in my sight to publish how great and mighty is his kingdom, an everlasting kingdom, and his power to all generations.'[26] When you hear this, do you not answer 'Amen,'[27] and, making your reply in a loud voice, do you not enroll yourselves under the king's edict with sacred ceremony? But, because you have no influence with the emperors, you want to make trouble for us in that quarter; if you had influence, what would you not do, when, having none, you stop at nothing?

Know this, that your earliest predecessors appealed the case of Caecilian to Emperor Constantine. Challenge us on this; let us prove it to you, and, if we do not prove it,

---

24 Prov. 21.1.
25 Dan. 3.95,96.
26 Cf. Dan. 3.99,100.
27 In the office of Holy Saturday these words were chanted, and the congregation answered 'Amen.'

treat us according to your power. But, because Constantine did not dare to judge the case of a bishop, he assigned it to bishops to be discussed and settled. This was done at Rome with Melchiades[28] presiding as bishop of that Church, together with many of his colleagues. They declared Caecilian innocent, and gave a verdict against Donatus for having caused a schism at Carthage, whereupon yours went a second time to the emperor to denounce the verdict of the bishops, which had gone against them. But, can a guilty plaintiff ever praise the verdict of those by whom he is convicted? A second time our most clement emperor gave them a court of bishops, at Arles, a city of Gaul, and yours appealed from them to the emperor in person, and he personally examined the case and pronounced Caecilian innocent, and themselves guilty of false witness. Yet, they did not subside after this series of rebuffs, but wearied the emperor by daily appeals about Felix of Aptunga, by whom Caecilian had been consecrated, saying that he had been a betrayer and Caecilian therefore could not be a bishop because he had been consecrated by a betrayer. Finally, by the emperor's orders, the case of Felix was examined by Aelianus, the proconsul, and he was proved innocent.[29]

Thus, Constantine was the first to issue an extremely rigorous law against the sect of Donatus. His sons imitated him with similar edicts. They were succeeded by Julian,[30] a deserter and enemy of Christ, who yielded to the petition of your sectaries, Rogatian and Pontius,[31] by giving freedom to the sect of Donatus, to their own peril, and by giving back their basilicas to the heretics, while he was also restoring the temples to the demons. He thought that in this way the name of Christian could be blotted out from the

---

28 Pope at the time.
29 Cf. Letter 88.
30 Cf. Letters 91, 93.
31 Authors of a petition to Julian the Apostate.

earth, if he should attack the unity of the Church from which he had apostatized, and should allow the accursed forces of dissension to be free of restriction. This was his famous justice, which was praised by his petitioners, Rogatian and Pontius, who said—to an apostate!—that justice had found refuge in him alone. He was succeeded by Jovian, who died soon after his accession and gave no orders about such things. Then came Valentinian; read what he decreed against you. After him, Gratian and Theodosius; read when you will what they enacted against you. Why, then, are you surprised at the sons of Theodosius, as if they ought to have followed a different course in this matter than that prescribed by the verdict of Constantine, which was enforced so strictly by so many Christian emperors?

However, as we have said, and as we will show you whenever you wish, if you still do not know it, your ancestors took the case of Caecilian to Constantine of their own accord. Constantine died, but Constantine's decree remained in force against you. Your people had sent their case to him; they denounced the bishops' court to him; they appealed from the bishops' court to him; they wearied him with constant demands about Felix of Aptunga; however often they came away defeated and put to shame, they never gave up their desperate fury and hatred, but left it as a legacy to you, their posterity. The result is that you shamelessly display hatred for the commands of Christian emperors, and, if it were allowed, you would not now appeal to Constantine the Christian against us, but you would raise the apostate Julian from the dead, and, if any such thing really happened, it would bring great misfortune to nobody but you. Nothing can cause more complete death to the soul than freedom to disseminate error.

But, let us now put all that out of the way; let us love

peace, which everyone, learned and unlearned, recognizes as preferable to discord; let us cherish and maintain unity. The emperors command this, and it is what Christ also commands, because, when they command what is good, Christ gives the command through them. The Apostle also begs us all to say the same thing, and that there be no schisms among us; not to say: 'I indeed am of Paul, and I am of Apollo, and I am of Cephas, and I of Christ.'[32] But, at the same time, let us all be for none but Christ, for Christ is not divided; neither was Paul crucified for you, much less Donatus! We were not baptized in the name of Paul, much less of Donatus. The emperors say this because they are called Catholic Christians, not servers of idols like your Julian; not heretics, as certain ones have been and have persecuted the Church,[33] when true Christians have suffered the most glorious martyrdom for Catholic truth, not justly deserved penalties for heretical error.

Note with what perfectly clear truth God himself speaks through the 'heart of the king which is in the hand of God,'[34] by means of that very law which you say was promulgated against you. If you could understand, it was promulgated for your benefit. Note what the emperor's words say: 'If the rite of baptism, in the case of those who were first received into the Church, is considered invalid because those from whom it was received were deemed sinners, it will be necessary for the sacrament thus received to be renewed as often as the minister of the rite of baptism is found to be unworthy; and our faith will not be founded on the choice of our own will and the gift of divine grace

---

32 1 Cor. 1.10,12,13.
33 This is a reference to the emperors of the East, who were long tainted with Arianism, and who persecuted the Church.
34 Prov. 21.1.

but on the merits of priests and the character of clerics.'³⁵ Let your bishops hold a thousand councils, but let them give an answer to this one sentence, and we will agree to anything you wish. See now how wrong and wicked is that customary saying of yours that if a man is good he sanctifies the one whom he baptizes; if he is bad and the one baptized does not know it, then God sanctifies him. If this is true, men ought to pray to be baptized by bad men whose wickedness is unknown to them rather than by good men, known to be such, so as to be sanctified by God rather than by men. God forbid that we should accept such foolish beliefs! Why not speak truly and recognize that the grace is always God's and the sacrament is God's, but the ministry is man's? If the minister is a good man, he keeps close to God and works with God; if he is a bad man, God performs the visible action of the sacrament through him, but Himself gives the invisible grace. Let us all acknowledge this, and let us not have schism between us.

Be at peace with us, brothers. We love you; we wish the same for you as we do for ourselves. If you hate us so deeply because we do not allow you to go astray and be lost, say so to God, whose threats to the faithless shepherds we fear, when He says: 'That which was driven away you have not brought again, neither have you sought that which was lost.'³⁶ This is what God Himself does for you through us, either by beseeching or threatening or chastising; by loss or trouble; by His secret warnings or trials; or by the laws of secular powers. Understand what is being done to you: God does not wish you to be lost, cut off from your mother, the Catholic Church, in the midst of a sacrilegious dissension.

---

35 These are the words of the law of Constantine, Constantius, and Valentinian, on the subject of the non-repetition of baptism. *Cod. Theod.* 16.6.
36 Ezech. 34.4.

You have not at any time been able to prove anything against us. When your bishops were called together by us, would they confer peaceably with us, or did they avoid converse with us as if we were sinners? Could anyone endure such pride? As if Paul the Apostle did not converse with sinners, and with quite abandoned ones! Read the Acts of the Apostles and see. As if the Lord Himself did not hold speech with the Jews by whom He was crucified, and answer them courteously! Finally, the Devil is the chief of all sinners, since it will never be possible for him to be converted to goodness, yet the Lord Himself did not disdain to answer him about the Law,[37] by which you may know that the Donatists refuse to confer with us because they know that their case is lost.

We do not know why men make threats against themselves by rejoicing in lying dissensions. In the Scriptures we have learned Christ; in the Scriptures we have learned the Church. We both possess the Scriptures; why do we not both hold to Christ and the Church in them? Where we recognize Him of whom the Apostle said: 'To Abraham were the promises made and to his seed. He saith not: and to his seeds, as of many, but of one: and to thy seed, which is Christ,'[38] there we also recognize the Church of which God said to Abraham: 'In thy seed shall all nations be blessed.'[39] Where we recognize Christ prophesying of Himself in the psalm: 'The Lord hath said to me: Thou art my son, this day have I begotten thee,' there we recognize the Church in the words which follow: 'Ask of me and I will give thee the Gentiles for thy inheritance and the utmost parts of the earth for thy possession.'[40] Where we

---
37 Matt. 4.1-10.
38 Gal. 3.16.
39 Gen. 22.18.
40 Ps. 2.7,8.
41 Ps. 49.1,2.

recognize Christ in this which is written: 'The God of gods, the Lord hath spoken,' there we also recognize the Church in what follows: 'And he hath called the earth, from the rising of the sun even to the going down thereof.'[41] Where we recognize Christ in what is written: 'And he as a bridegroom coming out of his bride-chamber, hath rejoiced as a giant to run his way,' there we recognize the Church in the previous passage: 'Their sound hath gone forth into all the earth and their words to the ends of the world. He hath set his tabernacle in the sun.'[42] The Church itself is set in the sun; that is, it is made known by its manifestation to the ends of the earth. Where we recognize Christ in this that is written: 'They have dug my hands and feet, they have numbered all my bones, they have looked and stared upon me, they parted my garments amongst them, and upon my vesture they cast lots,'[43] there also we recognize the Church in what is said a little further on in the same psalm: 'All the ends of the earth shall remember and shall be converted to the Lord, and all the kindreds of the Gentiles shall adore in his sight. For the kingdom is the Lord's and he shall have dominion over the nations.'[44] Where we recognize Christ in what is written: 'Be thou exalted, O God, above the heavens,' there we recognize the Church in what follows: 'And thy glory above all the earth.'[45] Where we recognize Christ in what is written: 'Give to the king thy judgment, O God; and to the king's son thy justice,'[46] there we recognize the Church in the same psalm where it is said of it: 'He shall rule from sea to sea, and from the river unto the ends of the earth. Before him the Ethiopians shall fall down; and his enemies

---

42 Ps. 18.6.
43 Ps. 21.17-19.
44 Ps. 21.28-29.
45 Ps. 53.6.
46 Ps. 71.2.

shall lick the ground, the kings of Tharsis and the islands shall offer presents, the kings of the Arabians and of Saba shall bring gifts, and all kings of the earth shall adore him, all nations shall serve him.'[47] Where we recognize Christ in what is said of a stone cut from a mountain without hands, which broke all the kingdoms of the earth—doubtless, those that relied on the worship of demons—there we recognize the Church in what is said of this stone itself increasing and becoming a great mountain and filling the whole earth.[48] Where we recognize Christ in what is written: 'The Lord shall be terrible upon them, and shall consume all the gods of the earth,' there we recognize the Church in what follows: 'And they shall adore in his sight, every man from his own place, all the islands of the Gentiles.'[49] Where we recognize Christ in what is written: 'God will come from the south and the holy one from the shady mountain, his strength will cover the heavens,' there we recognize the Church in what follows: 'And the earth is full of his praise.'[50] Jerusalem was settled from Africa, as we read in the book of Josue, son of Nun; from there the name of Christ was spread abroad; there is the shady mountain, the Mount of Olives, from which He ascended into heaven, so that His strength might cover the heavens and the Church might be filled through all the earth with His praise.[51] Where we recognize Christ in what is written: 'He was led as a sheep to the slaughter and was dumb as a lamb before his shearer; so he did not open his mouth,'[52] and the rest which is there said of His Passion, there we recognize the Church in what is said: 'Give praise, O thou

---

47 Ps. 71.8,11.
48 Dan. 2.34,35.
49 Cf. Soph. 2,11.
50 Cf. Hab. 3.3.
51 Josue 15.8,18,14; Acts 1.2.
52 Cf. Isa. 53,7. The verbs are in the future in the prophecy.

barren, that bearest not; sing forth praise and make a joyful noise thou that travailest not with child, for many are the children of the desolate, more than of her that hath a husband, saith the Lord. Enlarge the place of thy tent and stretch out the skins of thy tabernacles, spare not; lengthen thy cords, and strengthen thy stakes. Stretch out again and again to the right hand and to the left, for thy seed shall inherit the Gentiles, and thou shalt inhabit the desolate cities. Fear not for thou shalt prevail, nor blush; for thou shalt not be put to shame; thou shalt forget shame forever, and shalt remember no more the reproach of thy widowhood. For I am the Lord who made thee, the Lord is his name, and he who redeemed thee, the God of Israel, shall be called the God of all the earth.'[53]

We do not know why you speak of betrayers when you have never been able to prove your charge, never even been able to point them out. I do not say this because it was rather your people who were found out, and who admitted their crime openly—what have we to do with the burdens of others, except those whom we are able to amend by chastisement or by some discipline applied in the spirit of mildness and the anxious care of love? As to those whom we are not able to amend, even if necessity requires, for the salvation of others, that they share the sacraments of God with us, it does not require us to share in their sins, which we should do by consenting to or condoning them. We tolerate them in this world, in which the Catholic Church is spread abroad among all nations,[54] which the Lord called His field, like the cockle among the wheat;[55] or on this threshing floor of unity, like chaff mingled with the good grain; or in the nets of the word and the sacrament, like the bad fishes enclosed with the

---
53 Cf. Isa. 54.1-5.
54 Matt. 13.38.
55 Matt. 13.24-30; 3.12; 13.47,48.

good. We leave them until the time of the harvest, or of the winnowing, or of the arrival on shore, so as not, on their account, to root up the wheat; or to winnow the good grain away from the threshing floor, before the time, not to store it in the granary but to throw it out, to be gathered by the birds; or, with our nets broken by schism, to swim out into the sea of dangerous freedom, in trying to avoid the bad fishes. For this reason the Lord strengthened the patience of His servants by these and other parables, to prevent them from thinking that their virtue would be defiled by contact with wicked men, and thus, through human and vain dissensions, they should lose the little ones, or these should perish. The heavenly Master went so far in forewarning them that He even warned His people against bad rulers, lest, on their account, the saving chair of doctrine should be forsaken, in which even the wicked are forced to utter truth; for the words they speak come not from themselves but from God, and He has placed the teaching of truth upon the chair of unity. Therefore, He, being truthful and the very truth itself, says of rulers, doing their own evil deeds but speaking the good things of God: 'What they say, do ye, but according to their works do ye not, for they say and do not.'[56] Doubtless He would not have said: 'according to their works do ye not,' if their works had not been manifestly evil.

Let us not destroy ourselves in evil dissension, because of evil men, although we can prove to you, if you will let us, that your ancestors were not denouncers of bad men, but accusers of innocent ones. But, whoever and whatever they may have been, let them bear their own burdens. Here are the Scriptures which we share; here we know Christ; here we know the Church. If you hold to Christ, why do you not hold to the Church? If, because of the truth

---
56 Matt. 23.3.

of the Scriptures, you believe in Christ, whom you read of, but do not see, why do you deny the Church which you both read of and see? By saying these things to you, and by forcing you to receive this good of peace and unity and charity, we have become enemies to you and to the laws, because you will kill us for speaking the truth to you and for preventing you, to the utmost of our power, from perishing in error. May God protect us from you; may he destroy your error, and may you rejoice with us in the truth. Amen.

106. Augustine to his beloved brother, Macrobius[1] (409)

I have heard that you are planning to rebaptize a certain deacon of ours. Do not do it: if you would live in God, if you would please God, if you would not make void the sacraments of Christ, if you would not be cut off forever from the body of Christ. I beg you, brother, not to do it; I beg it for your own sake. Pay attention for a little to what I say. Felician of Musti[2] condemned Primian of Carthage[3] and was himself also mutually condemned by him. For a long time Felician remained in the accursed schism of Maximian, and throughout his churches, as your bishop, he there baptized many persons, in the same manner as Primian did; but you do not baptize anyone after him. By what authority, then, do you think baptism ought to be repeated after us? Answer me this question and you can rebaptize me, but, if you cannot answer it, have mercy on another's soul, have mercy on your own. If you claim that

---

1 A Donatist bishop in Hippo, successor to Proculeianus. Cf. Letter 33.
2 One of the consecrators of Maximian who seceded from the Donatists, forming schism from schism. Cf. Letters 43, 51, 108 n. 1.
3 A Donatist bishop of Carthage, against whom Maximian rebelled. Each was condemned by a synod held by the other. Cf. Letters 43, 108 n. 1.

I have spoken falsely about Felician, oblige me to prove it, and then, if I do not prove it, do what you think best. I add that, if I do not prove it, may I not be a bishop of my communion, but, if I do prove it, do not be the enemy of your own salvation. I pray that you, my lord brother, may be at peace with us.

107. Maximus and Theodore[1] give greeting in the Lord to the most blessed lord, the venerable and much cherished father, Augustine (409)

According to the directions of your Holiness, we went to bishop Macrobius. When we delivered the letter of your Beatitude to him, he refused at first to allow it to be read to him. Then, somewhat later, he was influenced by our urging and agreed to have it read to him. After the reading, he said: 'I cannot but receive those who come to me and give them the faith which they ask.'[2] But, when he heard what was said about the conduct of Primian, he said that, as he was but recently ordained, he could not be a judge of his father, and he would stand by what he had learned from his predecessors. We thought we should report it in this letter to your Holiness. May the Lord keep your Beatitude for us, lord father.

---

1 Bearers of Augustine's letter (106) to Macrobius. From the following letter (108) where Augustine refers to them as 'my dearest sons, honorable men,' it would appear that they were members of his flock. As they are not given any clerical titles, they were probably prominent laymen of Hippo. The awkward style of their letter seems to prove that they were either not at home in the Latin tongue or they were not accustomed to writing letters.

2 That is, they would supposedly confer the faith by rebaptizing those who came to them. The point that Augustine makes is that a person once baptized has received the faith and cannot receive it again.

108. Augustine to the beloved lord, his brother, Macrobius[1]
(409)

When those honorable men, my dearest sons,[2] had delivered my letter to your Benignity, in which I urged and begged you not to rebaptize our deacon, they wrote back to me that you had answered: 'I cannot but receive those who come to me and give them the faith which they ask.' Yet, if someone who had been baptized in your communion should come to you after a long absence from you, and, through ignorance, should think that he ought to be bap-

---

1 For a better understanding of the arguments used by Augustine against the Donatists in this letter, it will be useful to recall a few facts. The chief argument turns on the inconsistency of the Donatists themselves, and on their own attitude toward separatists. The alleged reason for the Donatist schism was that the Catholic Church had been tainted by the *traditio*, i.e., the betrayal of sacred books or vessels under persecution of certain bishops, and therefore they could not transmit Holy Orders because they had lost the grace of God. This was the charge against Felix and Caecilian. Donatus set up a dissident group claiming to be the 'pure' Church, and said that all the rest of the Christian world was tainted by the supposed guilt of a few African clerics, even though they knew nothing of it. He demanded that all his adherents receive a second baptism from his ministers, and that 'converted' clerics be ordained anew. These are the claims that Augustine held up to ridicule in previous letters. In this letter he is dealing with contemporary developments. A Donatist bishop, Primian, excommunicated Maximian, one of his deacons. The latter had himself made bishop by a sympathetic group of twelve, and each prelate held a synod and excommunicated the other. Primian had himself acquitted by the Council of Bagai, in April 394; the Maximianists were condemned unheard, but were given until Christmas to return to Primian. After that time limit they were to be subjected to public penance. Maximian's church was destroyed, the laws against the Donatists were invoked by the Donatists against the Maximianists. All who returned were to be rebaptized, but, if a bishop and his flock returned, they were to be admitted without rebaptism. This happened in the case of two of the consecrators of Maximian, Praetextatus of Assur and Felician of Musti, who were received back to their rank and authority without penance, even after the proconsul had tried to expel them from their sees. It is this inconsistency of behavior that Augustine uses as a powerful weapon against the pretensions of 'purity.'
2 Theodore and Maximus. Cf. Letter 107.

tized again, and should ask for this, you would inquire
and find out when he had been baptized, and you would
indeed receive him when he came to you, but you would
not give him the faith which he asked. Instead, you would
show the man that he had what he was seeking, and you
would pay no attention to his mistake, but would apply your
efforts to his correction. His mistake shows up the wrongful
giving of what ought not now to be given, and the violation
of the sacrament which had already been given, but would
not excuse him for asking. Tell me, please, how could he
who asked it of you not have what he had already received from me? When Felician went over from you to the
sect of Maximian, he was called 'an adulterer of truth, a
bond of sacrilege,' as the report of your council[3] shows, and
if the reason for this was 'another's water, another's font,'
as those are wont to say who misunderstand what is written:
'Refrain thyself from another's water, and drink not from
another's font,'[4] and if he took your font away with him, in
what font did you baptize yours when he had left you? If
he had baptized in another's font, why did you not rebaptize
after him? Your bishop now sits with Primian, who was
condemned by him and who condemned him.

According to what ours, who went to see you on this
matter, reported to me in their letter, when they had asked
what you had to say about it, you answered that, since you
were but recently ordained, you could not be a judge of
the deeds of your father, but you would stand by what
you had learned from your predecessors. I have felt great
regret for this obligation of yours, because, from what I
hear, I judge you to be a young man of good parts. What
forces you, then, to this answer but devotion to a wrong
cause? But, if you would look into it, if you would think

---
3 Council of Bagai, in Numidia, 394.
4 Prov. 9.18 (Septuagint).

correctly about it, if you would fear God, you would find that no obligation forces you to persist in a wrong cause. This answer of yours has not solved the problem which I suggested to you, but it has freed our cause from any misrepresentation or false pretext on your part. You say that, since you were recently ordained, you could not be a judge of the deeds of your father, but you would stand by what you had learned from your predecessors. Why, then, do we not rather stand by the Church, which, as we have learned on the testimony of Scripture, beginning at Jerusalem, bears fruit among all nations and increases from the Lord Christ through the Apostles,[5] and why do we not simply refuse to judge the deeds of some father or other—deeds said to have been committed almost a hundred years ago? If you do not dare to judge of your father, who is still in this life, and of whom you can ask questions, why am I told to judge of a man dead long before I was born? Why are so many Christian peoples told to judge of the deeds of African betrayers, dead so many years ago, when so many Christians then living in such faraway lands were able neither to listen to them, nor even to know of their existence? You do not dare to judge Primian, still surviving, and known to you; then why would you lay on me the obligation of judging Caecilian, a man of a previous age and unknown to me? If you do not judge your fathers about their own deeds, why do you judge your brothers about someone else's deeds?

But, perhaps you do not admit that we are brothers? We do better to hearken to the Holy Spirit instructing us through the Prophet: 'Hear the word of the Lord, you that tremble at his word; say to those who hate you and detest you: "You are our brothers"; that the name of the Lord may be glorified and may appear to them for their joy, but let them be put

---
5 Luke 24.47; Acts 1.8.

to shame.'⁶ But, in truth, if the Name of the Lord were more joyful to men than the names of men, would Christ who said: 'My peace I give you,'⁷ be rent asunder in His members by those who say: 'I indeed am of Paul, and I am of Apollo, and I of Cephas,'⁸ and who are torn apart by the names of men? Would Christ be dishonored in this baptism, of which it is said: 'He it is that baptizeth;'⁹ of which it is said: 'Christ loved His Church and delivered Himself up for it, that He might sanctify it, cleansing it by the laver of water in the word [of life]'?¹⁰ Would He, then, whose baptism it is, be dishonored in His own laver if the name of the Lord were more joyful than the names of men of whom you say: 'What this one confers is holy, but not what that one does?'

In spite of that, your colleagues, when they chose, gave heed to the truth, and, because they rejoiced in the honor of the Lord, they deemed holy not only the baptism which Primian gave in your communion, but even that given by Felician in the accursed schism of Maximian. And the spiritual mark¹¹ which he had received from you and which, as a deserter outside your ranks, he had impressed on others, they did not dare to violate after his return to them, because they recognized its royal character. You are not willing to judge this good deed of theirs, in which you should laudably imitate them, but you support the judgment of them in which they deserve to be detested by all. You fear to judge of Primian, lest you be forced to hear something blameworthy; you would do better to judge, and therein you would rather find something to praise. We do not wish

---

6 Isa. 66.5.
7 John 14.27.
8 1 Cor. 1.12.
9 John 1.33.
10 Eph. 5.25,26.
11 According to the catechism definition: Baptism imprints on the soul an indelible spiritual mark, which remains there forever.

you to remember what wrong Primian did, but what good he did, when, in receiving back those whom his denouncer[12] had baptized in a most wickedly separated sect, he corrected the error of men without destroying the sacraments of God, recognized the good gift[13] of Christ even in bad men, and made amends for the wrong-doing of men without dishonoring the grace of Christ. If this conduct of his displeases you, take note at least of this; take note of it carefully, according to your good disposition: you refuse to judge Primian alone for the acts of Primian, but you judge the Christian world for the acts of Caecilian; you fear to be defiled by knowing what you cannot excuse; then you must free of guilt the nations which could not know what you blame.

But, this was not the only thing Primian did. You know —at least I think you do—that almost one hundred of your bishops conspired with Maximian in a damnably dissident group to condemn Primian, and that the council composed of 310 bishops held at Bagai decreed in the following words: 'The thunderbolt of our sentence has hurled from the bosom of peace Maximian, the foe of the faith, the adulterer of truth, the enemy of Mother Church, the agent of Dathan, Core and Abiron.'[14] The twelve who had taken part in his ordination, when he was set up against Primian, were subjected to an immediate condemnation, but for the rest a delay was granted in the time set for their return, to prevent too great a falling away, and they were allowed to retain their rank provided they returned within the time limit.[15] The 310 did not fear to welcome back to their ranks some who were accused of taking part in the great sacrilege of Maximian, in consideration, perhaps, of what is written:

---
12 Maximian.
13 The grace given in baptism.
14 Augustine, *Contra Cresc. Don.*, 3.22,24,59; 4.2,5,38.
15 By Christmas of that year.

'Charity covereth a multitude of sins.'[16] But, those who were allowed[17] an extension of time conferred baptism outside your communion on those whom they were able to baptize, and, if they had not been outside, they could not have been granted the delay in returning. Then, both before and after the extended time had elapsed, the twelve condemned with Maximian were charged before three or more proconsuls, that they might be expelled from their churches by judicial authority. Among these was Felician of Musti, whom I cite as an example, and also Praetextatus of Assur, lately deceased, in whose place, after his condemnation, another[18] had just been ordained. These two were reinstated, not only by Primian, but by many of your fellow bishops, who, with a great throng, were celebrating the anniversary of the ordination of Optatus of Thamugadi;[19] and those two were restored to their rank, in spite of their condemnation, without any time limit, after the time limit granted to the others had expired, and after their trial before so many consuls, published abroad with so much legal fanfare. And no one rebaptized after them. If there is any objection to this statement, or if any of these facts is denied, may I be required to stake my episcopacy on the proof of what I say.

The case is closed, brother Macrobius; God has done this; God has willed it; it was an act of His secret providence that a mirror of correction should be set before you in the case of Maximian, and that an end should be made of that false and evil charge brought against us, or, rather, against the Church of Christ, now increasing throughout the world.

---

16 1 Peter 4.8.
17 A lacuna in the text is here indicated by Goldbacher, but he offers a variant reading which has been followed in the translation.
18 Rogatus, who had been appointed to the see of Praetextatus.
19 Donatist bishop of Thamugadi, called Gildonianus because of his friendship with Gildo, Count of Africa (386-397). His cruelties were beyond description.

I do not blame that charge on you, not wishing to seem personally abusive, but it certainly was the work of your sectaries. Absolutely nothing remains of those objections commonly uttered against us, as if from the Scriptures, by men of no understanding. For they constantly have on their lips the words: 'Refrain thyself from another's water,'[20] and the answer is that the water is not another's, although it is found among strangers, just as that water was not Maximian's from which you did not refrain yourselves. They also quote to us: 'They are become to me as deceitful water that cannot be trusted,'[21] but the answer is that this was said of imaginary men, and does not refer to the sacraments of God, which cannot be deceitful even among deceitful men. No doubt, those men were deceitful who condemned Primian on false charges, as you yourselves admit, but the water was not deceitful with which those who broke away from you baptized whomever they could. For, when you accepted it in the case of those whom Felician and Praetextatus baptized outside your sect, you felt that it was true even among the deceitful. They quote to us: 'He that is baptized by the dead, what doth his washing avail?'[22] and we answer that, if this was written of the baptism administered by those whom the Church casts forth as dead, it does not say that it is not a washing, but that it does not avail, and we say the same. Indeed, when the baptism which was harmful to him outside comes with him into the Church, it will avail him there, not when the baptism itself is repeated, but when the baptized is converted. Thus, the Council of Bagai speaks of Maximian and his companions as dead, when they were expelled from your communion, saying:

---

20 Prov. 9.18. (Septuagint).
21 Cf. Jer. 15.18.
22 Cf. Eccli. 34.30.

'The shipwrecked bodies of some have been hurled against sharp rocks by the wave of truth, just as, in the case of the perishing Egyptians, the shore was filled with the dead, and the worst penalty of their death was that they found no burial after the avenging waves had torn away their lives.'[23] Out of this throng of dead you have received Felician and Praetextatus back to their rank like men risen again, and you did not rebaptize the persons baptized by them during that death, because you recognized that the baptism of Christ given outside [the Church] by the dead to the dead does not avail, but the same baptism does avail in the Church to those who rise again. You quote to us: 'But let not the oil of the sinner fatten my head,'[24] and we answer that this was written to be understood of the smooth and deceitful assent to a false flatterer, because the head is anointed and fattened when sinners are praised for the desire of their heart, and when those who act wickedly are blessed. This is clear from the first part of the verse: 'The just man shall correct me in mercy and shall reprove me, but the oil of the sinner shall not fatten my head.' He said he would rather be curbed by the truthful harshness of a merciful man than exalted by the deceitful praise of a liar. But, however you understand it, certainly in the case of those whom Felician and Praetextatus baptized in the sacrilege of Maximian, you either received the oil of sinners, or you recognized that the oil of Christ was given even by sinful ministers, since the Council of Bagai spoke of them in these words: 'Know that they are damned as guilty of an infamous crime, who, by their deadly work, glued together a dirty vessel with saved-up dregs.'[25]

---

23 Augustine, *Contra Crescon. Don.* 4.18; *Contra Gaudent. Don.* 1.54; *Contra Lit. Petiliani* 1.11; 2.16.
24 Cf. Ps. 140.5.
25 Augustine, *Contra Crescon. Don.* 3.22,59; 4.5; 15.39; *Contra Gaudent. Don.* 2.7.

This will be enough to say of baptism. But, the cause of your separation is usually glossed over by poorly understood testimony. It is written: 'Be ye not partakers of other men's sins,'[26] but we answer that the one who consents to evil deeds is a partaker in other men's sins, not the one who, though he be good grain, shares in the divine sacraments along with the chaff, until the threshing floor is swept. It is written: 'Go ye out from thence, touch no unclean thing'[27] and 'He that toucheth anything unclean is unclean,'[28] but that occurs by the consent of the will by which the first man was deceived,[29] not by the bodily contact by which Judas kissed Christ.[30] Undoubtedly, those good and bad fishes of which the Lord speaks in the Gospel,[31] as being within the same net, which gives unity to their group, swim about together in physical contact, but separation of kind, until the end of time, prefigured by the word shore. It is written: 'A little leaven corrupteth the whole lump,'[32] but this refers to those who consent to evil-doers, not to those who, according to the Prophet Ezechiel, 'sigh and mourn for the abominations of the people of God, that are committed in the midst thereof.'[33]

Daniel also groaned over that intermingling of evil, and the three men groaned over it[34]—the one testified to it in his prayer, the others in the fiery furnace; still, they did not withdraw themselves by bodily separation from their union with the people whose sins they confessed. What great things all the Prophets uttered against the same people among

---

26 1 Tim. 5.22.
27 Isa. 52.11.
28 Lev. 22.4-6.
29 Gen. 3.1-6.
30 Matt. 26.49; Mark 14.45.
31 Matt. 13.47-49.
32 1 Cor. 5.6.
33 Ezech. 9.4.
34 Dan. 9.5-16; 3.28.

whom they lived! But they did not separate themselves by a physical departure or withdrawal, nor did they seek out another people among whom they could live. The very Apostles, without any defilement to themselves, endured the company of the devil Judas until the end, when he destroyed himself with a halter, and the Lord spoke thus to them of his presence among them: 'And you are clean, but not all.'[35] Yet, in spite of his uncleanness, the lump was not corrupted by this leaven of dissimilar conduct among them. On the other hand, it cannot truthfully be asserted that his wickedness was unknown to them, except perhaps his coming betrayal of the Lord, for they even wrote of him that he was a thief, and carried off from the Lord's purse all that was put therein.[36] And no one alleged this testimony against them unjustly: 'Thou didst see a thief and didst run with him,'[37] because one runs with evil-doers by consenting to their deeds, not by sharing the sacraments with them. What great complaints the Apostle Paul makes of false brethren![38] Yet he was not defiled by their physical companionship, because he was set apart by the distinction of a pure heart. He rejoiced that Christ was likewise preached by some whom he knew as envious,[39] and assuredly envy is a diabolical vice.

Finally, there is Bishop Cyprian,[40] who is nearer to our time in which the Church is more widespread, by whose authority you sometimes try to support the repetition of baptism, although that council, or those writings of his—if they are really his, and not, as some think, falsely put out under his name—contain evidence of how much he loved

---

35 John 13.10.
36 John 12.6.
37 Ps. 49.18.
38 2 Cor. 11.23-27.
39 Phil. 1.15-18.
40 Cyprian: Saint, 210-258. A convert from paganism, became bishop of Carthage in 249. A vigorous apologist, he has left us thirteen works besides his Letters. He suffered martyrdom for the faith under Decius.

unity and how he advised, with most outspoken insistence, that those whose opinion differed from his were to be tolerated so as not to break the bond of peace. He held that if any human error crept in between two parties, and something appeared to one of them to be at variance with truth, if fraternal harmony is preserved, 'Charity covereth a multitude of sins.'[41] And he so held to this and so loved it that, if he had held a view about baptism contrary to the truth, God would have revealed this to him, also, as the Apostle says to the brethren walking in charity: 'Let us therefore, as many as are perfect, be thus minded, and if in anything you be otherwise minded, this also God will reveal to you. Nevertheless whereunto we are come, let us also continue in the same.'[42] In the end, the fruitful branch, if it had any need of pruning, was pruned by the glorious pruning knife of martyrdom, not because he was slain for the Name of Christ, but because he was slain in the bosom of unity for the Name of Christ. For, he himself wrote and steadfastly maintained that those who die outside the unity of the Church, even for that Name, can be killed but cannot be crowned.[43] Such is the force of this love of unity, either for taking away or for hardening in sin, according as it is either guarded or violated.

Therefore, when this same Cyprian was bemoaning the devastation wrought in the Church by the persecution of wicked pagans, and the many who fell away, he attributed this to their bad lives, because they lived with culpable laxity in the very Church, and, while mourning over the conduct of his own colleagues, he did not hide his lament in silence. He said that they had come to such an excess of avarice that they tried to keep their lavish store of money,

---
41 1 Peter 4.8.
42 Phil. 13.15-18.
43 Cyprian, *De Cathol. eccles. unitate* 14, ed. Hartel, p. 223.

even though their brothers in the Church were starving; they plundered Church estates by artfully contrived cheating, and increased their capital by frequent money lending at usury.[44] I am sure that Cyprian was not tainted by their avarice, plunder, and money lending, yet he was not separated from them by physical withdrawal, but by his different manner of life. With them he touched the altar, but he did not touch their impure life; when he thus blamed and reproved them, no doubt what was pleasing in them was touched, but what was displeasing was kept at a distance. Consequently, that excellent bishop did not withhold censure when it was a question of checking sin, nor was he lacking in prudence when the bond of unity was to be preserved. In one of his letters, which he wrote to a priest named Maximus, there is a clear and unmistakable sentence on this matter, where he emphatically lays down a prophetic rule, holding that the unity of the Church is never to be broken because of the admixture of bad men. He says: 'Even if there seems to be cockle in the Church, our faith and charity should not be shut off so as to make us leave the Church because we see that there is cockle in the Church. We must simply strive to be good grain.'[45]

That law of charity was pronounced by the lips of the Lord Christ, for those parables are His about the cockle scattered through the world in the unity of the field until the time of the harvest, and about the bad fishes which are to be left in the same net until the time for landing on the shore.[46] So, then, if your elders had kept that law of Christ in mind and if they had thought over it in the fear of God, they would not have separated themselves from the Church by a wicked schism, because of Caecilian and some obscure Africans, who were either, as you think, really guilty, or,

---

44 Cyprian, *De lapsis* 4.6.
45 Cyprian, Letter 54.3.
46 Matt. 13.24-43; 47-50.

as is more likely, were falsely charged. They would not have separated themselves from that Church which Cyprian himself described as spreading its rays over all peoples and stretching its branches with plentiful fruit over the whole earth,[47] nor would they have separated from so many Christian peoples who were completely ignorant of what accusations they made, or against whom they made them. This usually happens because of some personal grudge rather than for the sake of the general welfare, or by reason of that vice which Cyprian himself subsequently noted and pointed out as something to be avoided. For, when he laid down this principle that we are not to leave the Church because of the cockle found in the Church, he goes on and adds:[48] 'But we should strive so hard to be good grain that, when we begin to store the grain in the Lord's granaries, we may get some reward for our effort and labor. The Apostle says in his Epistle: "But in a great house there are not only vessels of gold and silver, but also of wood and of earth; and some indeed unto honor, but some unto dishonor." [49] Let us then make an effort and strive, as much as we can, to be the golden and the silver vessel. But only the master has the right to break the earthenware vessels, for he has the rod of iron. "The servant cannot be greater than his master."[50] And what the Father has reserved for the Son alone, let no one claim for himself, or imagine that he can carry the winnowing fan to clear off the threshing floor, and scatter the chaff; or by a human judgment to separate all the cockle from the grain.[51] That is an arrogant presumption and a profane obstinacy which misplaced ardor takes to itself; by always demanding for themselves more than kindness and justice require, they fall away from the

---

47 Cyprian, *De Cathol. eccl. unitate* 5.
48 Cyprian, Letter 54.3.
49 2 Tim. 2.20.
50 John 13.16; 15.20; Matt. 10.24.
51 Matt. 3.12.

Church, and lose the light of truth, vainly puffing themselves up, and blinded by their own swollen pride.'

Could anything be clearer or more truthful than the testimony of Cyprian? You see how luminous it is, with the strong light of the Gospel and of the teaching of the Apostles. You see that those who forsake the unity of the Church, who try to manifest their own sinlessness by pretending to be injured by the sins of others, are themselves the greatest offenders. You see that they who would not tolerate the cockle within the unity of the Lord's field are themselves the cockle outside of it; you see that those who would not endure the chaff in the unity of their great home are themselves the chaff outside it; you see how truly it is written: 'The wicked son calleth himself just, but he does not cleanse his going forth'[52]—the going forth, obviously, by which he goes out from the Church—and here he does not cleanse it, he does not excuse it, he does not defend it, he does not show that it is pure and free from stain. That is the meaning of 'he does not cleanse,' because, if he did not call himself just, but were truly and legitimately just, he would not withdraw from the good because of the wicked, but, with the utmost patience, he would bear with the wicked because of the good, until the Lord Himself, either in person, or through his angels, shall separate the cockle from the good grain, the chaff from the wheat, the vessels of wrath from the vessels of mercy, the goats from the sheep, and the bad fishes from the good, at the end of the world.

If you endeavor to receive that testimony of the Scriptures which your elders—to the division of the people of God—believed should be understood and quoted, in a sense different from that required by the meaning of the divine utterances, cease now, and, if you will acquire wisdom, look into that mirror which God has set before you by a most merciful

---

52 Prov. 24.35 (Septuagint); cf. **Prov. 30.12** (Vulgate).

dispensation. I mean the case of Felician, 'the foe of the faith, the adulterer of truth'—as the Council of Bagai pronounced—'the enemy of Mother Church, the agent of Dathan, Core and Abiron.' They added, further, that the earth did not open and swallow him up[53] because he was being saved for a greater punishment than that; 'He was carried out,' they say, 'and won his penalty at the expense of his funeral; he now collects the usury of a more fatal funeral, since he lives as a dead man among the living.'[54] I ask whether they then touched the unclean dead man when they joined with him in a conspiracy to condemn the innocent Primian? If they touched him, no doubt they became unclean by touching something unclean. Why, then, was a delay in returning granted to those who were enrolled in the same communion with him, and separated from yours, yet not innocent, so that they might 'recover their former rank and faith intact,' and those who merely took no part in the ordination of Maximian deserved to hear that 'those of the accursed branch did not defile the tree,'[55] though enrolled in the same sect, bound together in the same schism, separated from you, allied to them, organized at the same time in Africa, too well known, too friendly, too closely joined to them, and who, even if they were not present at the ordination, did condemn the absent Primian on account of him?[56] Why is the branch of Caecilian said to defile the Christian peoples of the world—innumerable, far-flung, completely unknown—many of whom could not have known his name, let alone his case? Those who not only knew the sin of Maximian, but promoted it by raising him up against Primian, do not share in the sins of others, but those do share in them who lived among faraway peoples and did

---
53 Num. 16.31,32.
54 Augustine, *Contra Crescon. Don.* 4.5.
55 *Ibid.*
56 Maximian.

not know that Caecilian had been made bishop; or who lived nearer by and only heard of it; or who in Africa itself knew that it had taken place simply and quietly; or who even in Carthage had raised up no one against him?[57] Yet, those who were in communion with him[58] were not running with a thief,[59] although the lawyer Nummasius, speaking in the presence and in behalf of Restitutus,[60] your bishop, said that by a secret and almost sacrilegious theft he had made an attack on the primacy of the bishop's title; nor were they sharing their lot with an adulterer[61] because they were in communion with the adulterer of truth; nor was their whole lump corrupted by a little leaven,[62] when they gave him their support, when they remained in his sect, cut off from you, but not in ignorance; and they took care that their sect should be severed from you and raised up against you. In the second place, you yourselves were defiled by no partnership in the sins of others, stained by no contact with uncleanness, corrupted by no leaven of evil, by the fact that you invited them to return to you, and said that they were not corrupted by the branch of sacrilege, though joined in such close alliance with Maximian; that you received Praetextatus also and Felician back with no loss of rank; that you agreed peaceably with them; that today you see Felician sitting amongst you! Yet, on the testimony of men like these, the charge of another's guilt is alleged against the Christian world, the rending of unity is defended by deadly schism, and the branch which has remained attached to the root of the true Mother is accused by the lopped-off branch of being a rotten branch!

57 The text is uncertain here.
58 Maximian.
59 Ps. 49.18.
60 Not the Restitutus referred to in Letter 97; this one was a Donatist, of the sect of Primian.
61 Ps. 49.18.
62 1 Cor. 5.6.

What reason have you for your usual boasts of suffering persecution? If martyrs are made by the penalty and not by the cause of their death, then it was useless to add the words 'for justice' sake' to the saying: 'Blessed are they that suffer persecution.'[63] Surely, the Maximianists easily surpass you in this claim to glory, since they not only suffered persecution with you afterwards, but they previously suffered it at your hands. The words which I quoted just above are those of the lawyer who accused Maximian in the presence of your colleague Restitutus, who had been put into the place of Salvius of Membresa,[64] and had been ordained before the time limit had expired. This Salvius had been condemned, along with the other eleven, with no time set for their return. Titianus[65] brought a charge against Felician and Praetextatus on the very day the time limit expired, and set forth the whole conspiracy against Primian in extremely severe words. The Council of Bagai was also mentioned more than once by the proconsular acts and later by the city records; the courts were roused to action; decrees of the most threatening import were secured; it was requested and prescribed that those who resisted should be restrained by force; the duty of enforcement was allotted; help was secured from the cities to carry out what the courts had decided. How, then, can you quarrel with us on the subject of suffering persecution, when you treated each other in that way, without law or justice? But, as the one who suffers persecution does not always persevere to the final

---

63 Matt. 5.10.
64 Salvius, Maximianist bishop of Membresa, was twice summoned by the proconsul to retire in favor of the Primianist Restitutus. As he was much respected by his people, and had their support, a mob was brought over from the neighboring town of Abitene to expel him; he was beaten and made to dance with dead dogs tied around his neck. But his people built him a new church, and this small town had three bishops: a Maximianist, a Primianist, and a Catholic.
65 Probably the proconsul who had to enforce the law.

suffering, so your clerics and Circumcellions arranged that you should suffer the persecution and we should bear the suffering. However, as I said, you vie with the Maximianists for that palm: they cite the court records against you when you roused the judges to persecute them,[66] yet it is clear that, when some of them had been punished, you afterward made arrangements with them, from which we conclude that peace between you and us is not to be despaired of, if God deigns to help us and to instill a peaceful mind in you. Your sect quotes against us, with more malice than truth, the words: 'Their feet are swift to shed blood,'[67] but we are rather the ones who have experienced that in such acts of brigandage at the hands of your Circumcellions and clerics, who butchered human victims with such horrible slaughter and stained so many places with the blood of our people. Meantime, they escorted you at your entry into this country, with their military squadrons, shouting praises to God with the voices which were like war trumpets when they were engaged in ravaging everything! On another day, shaken and goaded by the sting of your words, which you had hurled at them through a Punic interpreter, moved as you were by an honest and noble indignation, because you were more angered at their deeds than pleased with their service, they rushed out from the middle of the congregation with furious gestures—as we heard some who were present tell it—yet you did not wash the pavement with salt water[68] after their feet, swift to shed blood, as your clerics thought should be done after us.

---

66 By a strange contradiction, the Donatists turned against the Maximianists the laws enacted to restrain themselves, and they were strong enough in many places to carry these out with great violence.
67 Ps. 13.3.
68 In their excess of zeal for 'purifying,' the Donatists often destroyed altars in Catholic churches which they had seized, scraped walls and washed floors with salt water.

But, as I began to say, this passage from the Scriptures which you are wont to throw at us, more as a reproach than a proof: 'Their feet are swift to shed blood,' was poured out in a vehement attack even against Felician and Praetextatus, in that pretentious pronouncement of the Council of Bagai. For, when they had said what they thought had to be said about Maximian, they added:[69] 'Not only does he deserve a just death for his evil deeds, but many also whom the bond of sacrilege draws to a share in his crime, of whom it is written: "The poison of asps is under their lips; their mouth is full of cursing and bitterness, their feet are swift to shed blood,"'[70] and the rest. And after saying this, in order to show who those were whom the bond of sacrilege was drawing to a share in the crime, they condemned the companions of Maximian with equal severity, and they named 'guilty of that infamous crime' Victorian of Carcavia, to whom they joined the other eleven, among whom were Felician of Musti and Praetextatus of Assur. After speaking like this against them, they joined with them in such perfect union that they lost nothing of their rank; no one washed by them was judged to need washing again, after the feet of those washers swift to shed blood.[71] Why, then, should we despair of reaching an agreement? May God ward off the hatred of the Devil; 'may the peace of Christ prevail in our hearts,'[72] and, as the same Apostle says: 'let us forgive one another if any have a complaint against another, even as God hath forgiven us in Christ.'[73]

---

69 Augustine, *Contra Cresc. Don.,* 3.22,25,59; 4.5,12,15,38.
70 Ps. 13.3.
71 A reference to the rebaptism practised by the Donatists. In this case they showed their inconsistency by not rebaptizing Felician, Praetextatus, and those whom they had baptized while separated from Primian.
72 Cf. Col. 3.12.
73 Cf. Col. 3.13.

So that, as I have said before and must say often, 'Charity covereth a multitude of sins.'[74]

But, as for you, brother, with whom I now treat, and over whom I long to rejoice in Christ, as He knows, if you wish to undertake the defense of the Donatist sect in this matter of Maximian, using all the resources of your ability and eloquence, and acting sincerely, surely you will take refuge with the guardians of truth, since the memory of these things is fresh in the minds of those who are still in the flesh, and among whom the action took place, and also since the evidence is available in so many proconsular and municipal records, in which the Church has always been warned against you. You must then admit that the passage about another's water, and the water of deceit, and the washing of the dead, and other matters of this sort are not to be understood as you are accustomed to understand them, but in this sense, that the baptism of Christ given to the Church in order to admit all to a share in eternal life, is not to be esteemed of foreign origin outside the Church, nor is it to be considered as belonging to others among outsiders, but to both strangers and outsiders it brings destruction, while giving salvation to its own members. But even to the former it brings salvation when they are converted to the peace of the Church; their error is corrected, but the sacrament is not destroyed in punishing the error, with the result that what was dangerous to anyone persisting in error outside the Church begins to benefit him inside the Church, after his conversion. In the next place, you must not interpret in your usual fashion those passages about not taking part in the sins of others, about separation from evil, about not touching anything unclean or polluted, about being on guard against the corruption of a little leaven, and other such things;

---
74 1 Peter 4.8.

otherwise, you will involve yourselves groundlessly in the case of Maximian. If you are wise, you will affirm and hold to what sound doctrine approves, to what the rule of truth proves by the examples of Prophets and Apostles, namely, that we are to bear with the wicked, so as not to forsake the good, rather than to forsake the good so as to cut off the wicked. But, we must do this only to the extent that we refrain from imitating the wicked or agreeing with them or being like them in life and conduct; and this while growing with them, mingled in the same misfortune until the time of harvest and winnowing, or gathered with them in the net until the time of landing on the shore. In the matter of persecution, how are you going to defend what was done by your people in getting the courts to expel the Maximianists and drive them from their churches, except by saying that the more moderate among you did it with the intention of correcting them by a limited use of fear, but not of harming them? And if some exceeded the bounds of humanity, as is proved in the case of Salvius of Membresa, to whose sufferings the city itself bears witness, will you say that you have no control over these others, mingled like chaff with the grain in a common share in the sacraments, but distinguished from you by their different kind of life?

If that is the case, I welcome your defense. That will be your defense if it is true, and it will be overthrown by the truth if it is not that. I repeat, I welcome your defense, but you see it is also mine. Why, then, do we not strive together to be grain in the unity of the Lord's threshing floor; why do we not together bear with the chaff? I ask you why not, for what reason, what benefit, what advantage? Tell me. Unity is shunned and the peoples, ransomed by the blood of the one Lamb, are roused against each other by conflicting aims, and the sheep that belong to the Father of the family are divided among us as if they were ours; yet He said to

His servant: 'Feed my sheep,'[75] not 'Feed your sheep,' and it is said of them: 'that there may be one fold and one shepherd.'[76] He cries out in the Gospel: 'By this shall all men know that you are my disciples if you have true love one for another,'[77] and: 'Suffer both to grow until the harvest, lest perhaps gathering up the cockle, you root up the wheat also together with it.'[78] Unity is shunned so that the husband goes this way and the wife that—he says: 'Hold to unity with me because I am your husband,' and she answers: 'I stay where my father is.' The two on one marriage couch divide Christ, whom we would despise if they were to divide the couch. Unity is shunned, and, as a result, relatives and fellow citizens, friends and guests, and all who are mutually joined in some human relationship, but Christians all, agree together in sharing banquets, in giving and receiving in marriage, in buying and selling, in contracts and covenants, in salutations, in concessions, in conferences, in all their interests and transactions; and they disagree at the altar of God. Those who ought there to make an end of their disagreement, however great and from whatever source derived, and who should obey the Lord's command to go first and be reconciled with their brothers, and then offer their gift at the altar,[79] are in agreement everywhere else, but there they are at variance.

Unity is shunned, and we are forced to seek the protection of the civil laws against the excesses of your followers—I do not say your own excesses—and the Circumcellions are roused to arms against those very laws which were passed against you because of their fury, which they now treat with the same fury. Unity is shunned, and the peasants are

---

75 John 21.17.
76 John 10.16.
77 Cf. John 13.35.
78 Matt. 13.30,29.
79 Matt. 5.24.

emboldened to rise against their landlords; runaway slaves, in defiance of apostolic discipline,[80] are not only encouraged to desert their masters but even to threaten their masters, and not only to threaten but to plunder them by violent raids. All this they do at the suggestion and instigation, and with the authorization to commit crime, of those prize-winning confessors of yours, who magnify your rank 'for the glory of God,' and shed the blood of others 'for the glory of God,' so that you are forced by popular hatred for your followers, both severally and separately, to promise to restore the stolen properties to those from whom they were taken, yet you do not want to be able to keep your promise, because it would oblige you to offer too much opposition to that boldness which your priests have thought a necessary part of their[81] conduct. They even boast of their previous services to you, before the passage of that law which it pleases you to call the restoration of your liberty,[82] and they point out and count up how many places and basilicas your priests held through their action in plundering and expelling our people, so that, if you wished to be harsh toward them, you would seem ungrateful for their benefit.

Unity is shunned, and any of ours who refuse to submit to authority run to them for protection, and are presented to you to be rebaptized, like that subdeacon from the country, Rusticianus,[83] on whose account I have been obliged to write to you with great sorrow and fear. He was excommunicated by his priest on account of his reprobate and depraved conduct; he was in debt to many in that place,

---

80 St. Paul preached the duty of slaves to submit to their masters.
81 The Circumcellions.
82 This may refer to the liberty given by Julian to pagans and schismatics (Cf. Letter 105), but is more likely a reference to a recent attempt of Honorius (early in 409) to leave the schismatics free. The excesses of the Donatists brought about a renewal of restriction.
83 Cf. Letter 106. He is there referred to as a deacon.

and he found no other refuge from ecclesiastical severity, and from his creditors, than to be wounded a second time by you[84] and to be loved by them as one completely purified. Your predecessor[85] similarly rebaptized a deacon of ours who had also been excommunicated by his priest, and made him a deacon of yours, and a few days later he joined those same depraved men, as he had been longing to do, in a bold midnight raid, and in the midst of thieving and setting fires he was killed by a counter-attack of a crowd defending themselves. These are the fruits of that division, and you will not heal it by shunning unity. The division was what should have been shunned, because it is something foul and hateful of itself, even if such unspeakable and revolting deeds were not done in its name.

Let us, then, my brother, recognize the peace of Christ, and cling to it together; let us together work for the conversion of the wicked by such discipline as we can use within the bonds of unity; and for the sake of that unity let us bear with the wicked with what patience we can, lest, by wishing to gather the cockle before the time, we root up the grain together with it,[86] as Christ warned us. And blessed Cyprian bore witness that this cockle is to be seen and observed, not outside, but inside the Church. As a matter of fact, you do not possess such peculiar prerogatives of holiness, that our sinners should defile us, while your sinners do not defile you; that the ancient cowardice of betrayers, of which we knew nothing, should taint us, while the present lawlessness of abandoned men, which is before your eyes, does not taint you. Let us recognize that Ark which prefigured the Church; let us be the clean beasts in

84 He was rebaptized.
85 Proculeianus.
86 Matt. 13.29.

it, yet let us not refuse to allow the unclean ones[87] to be carried in it with us until the end of the deluge. They were together in the Ark, but they were not equally pleasing to the Lord as a savor of sacrifice, for, after the deluge, Noe offered sacrifice to God of the clean, not of the unclean.[88] But the Ark was not on that account abandoned before the time by any of the clean because of the unclean. It is true that the raven left it and separated itself from contact with it before the time, but the raven was of the two unclean, not of the seven clean.[89] That act of separation alone makes reprobate those of otherwise praiseworthy character, because: 'The wicked son calleth himself just, but does not cleanse his going forth,'[90] although he is so puffed up with insolence and so blinded by his own swollen pride that he dares to say what the Prophet in vision held in horror: 'Touch me not, for I am clean.'[91] Consequently, whenever anyone, because of the alleged uncleanness of some, leaves this gathering of unity, which is an ark carrying the clean and the unclean during the deluge, he shows that he is rather the sort of creature that flies away. The Lord has willed that your people in this city should [hear] this from the mouth of a certain one . . .[92]

---

87 Gen. 7.2-3; 8.
88 Gen. 8.20.
89 Gen. 7.2,3. God commanded Noe to save seven each of clean beasts and two each of unclean ones.
90 Cf. above, n. 52.
91 Cf. Isa. 65.5 (Septuagint).
92 Apparently, some lines have been lost from the end of the letter. A spurious line has been expunged as belonging to another letter.

109. Severus[1] to the venerable and esteemed bishop, Augustine, worthy of being cherished with the most intimate embrace of charity (409)

Thanks be to God, brother Augustine, who gives us whatever good joys we have. I confess that my well-being is from you, and I read you much. I will say something wonderful, but absolutely true: as much as your presence is usually absent to me, so much has your absence become present. No disturbing interruptions of temporal affairs come between us. I do as much as I can, although I am not able to do as much as I wish. Why should I say as much as I wish? You know well how greedy of you I am, yet I do not complain of not doing as much as I wish, since, on the other hand, I do not do less than I am able. Thanks be to God, then, sweetest brother, my well-being is from you; I rejoice at being closely joined to you, at being, so to speak, one very person with you, as far as that can be. I draw strength by clinging to you and sucking the abundance of your milk.[2] May I thus be enabled to penetrate and explain those thoughts of yours, and may they deign to pour out to me whatever secret and hidden meaning they guard within them, even their very vitals, if possible, when I have removed the outer skin which is between my lips and the source of milk. I desire, I say, that their very vitals may be poured for me, their vitals rich with heavenly marrow and stored with all spiritual sweetness; your vitals, pure vitals, simple vitals, except that they are bound around with the double cord of twofold charity; your vitals suffused with the light of truth, and reflecting truth. I place myself under that overflow and reflection that my night may fade in your light, and that we

---
1 Bishop of Milevis, a very close friend of Augustine. Cf. Letters 42,62,63.
2 Severus had been reading Augustine's *Confessions* and other devout works, and he uses this—to us—extraordinary comparison of mother's milk to represent the sweetness and nourishment he derived from them.

may walk together in the brightness of day. O truly skillful bee of God, building a honeycomb filled with divine nectar, overflowing with mercy and truth, whereby my soul is refreshed in its flights, and with which life-giving food it strives to restore and support whatever it finds or feels in itself to be weak or inferior!

The Lord is blessed by the praise of your mouth and your faithful ministry, and by the fact that you make us sing with you and answer you as you sing to the Lord. Thus, whatever flows out from His fullness upon us is made more joyful and more pleasing by your graceful service and your concise elegance, your faithful and chaste and sincere ministry, which shines so brightly through your wit and your insight that it would dazzle our eyes and focus them on itself, if you did not intimate to the Lord that we attribute to Him and recognize as His all that delightful brilliance of yours. You are good with His goodness, and pure and simple and beautiful with His purity and simplicity and beauty; and we give thanks to Him for all that is good in you, praying Him to deign of His bounty to yoke us to you, or in some way to put us under your yoke, that we may be more completely subject to Him, by whose guidance and direction we rejoice that you are such as to rejoice in us also. I do not doubt that this will happen if you help me with your prayers, since I have made some progress in imitating you, at least to the extent of wishing to be like you. You see what you do by being so good, and how you hurry us along into the love of our neighbor, which is for us the first step to the love of God, and also the last step and pathway, so to speak, of love of God and neighbor, by which we are bound to each other. Standing together on this pathway, we are touched with the warmth of both loves, and we burn with love of both. But in proportion as love of neighbor burns within us and purifies us, so it drives us into that purer love of God in which no limit of love is laid upon us, since the limit itself is to love without limit. Hence, we have not to fear that we may love our Lord too much, but must dread loving Him too little.

This later letter presents me to you in more joyful mood, with my sadness washed away by the opportunity, arising from a generous spell of leisure, of taking up with you what I have been able to take up in this country retirement of mine. It was written as a sort of goal post to those joys, before the venerable bishop was pleased to visit us, and, what was truly remarkable, he came on the very day I wrote. Why is this, my soul, I ask you, unless perhaps it is because what gives us pleasure, however worth while it is, is still not quite advantageous to us because it exists only in part? Meantime, it is allowable that we strive to render this part, which is ourselves, more polished and more fit to be joined to the whole,[3] if you will allow me the word, at least as far as the stuff I am made of allows, considering my sins, or, rather, as far as I allow it myself. Here is a letter too long for my littleness, but not for your greatness; by it I should like to challenge you to send me one measured not by my littleness but by your greatness. But, whatever and however long it may be, it will not be long to me, because the whole time spent in reading you is short. Write me when or where I am to meet you, in connection with that matter about which you told me to come to you.[4] If the matter is

---

3 These two words refer to books: the pages were *smoothed* with pumice, and fastened together. The passage is not clear, but the writer is evidently comparing himself to a book. The word *compaginabiliores* seems to be an invention of his own, and he apologizes for saying something like 'more joinable together.'
4 In Letters 62 and 63 Augustine had reproached Severus for allowing a certain deacon Timothy to leave Augustine's diocese and attach himself to that of Severus, which was bad for Church discipline. As Timothy is mentioned by Augustine in his answer to this letter (110), the matter referred to here may have been his case.

unchanged and you have perhaps reached no other decision, then I will come; if it is otherwise, I ask you not to call off my journey, for that course of action alone seems good to me which I set before myself. I long to see all the brethren, who are our fellow servants in the Lord, and I greet them.

110. Augustine and the brethren who are with me give greeting in the Lord to the most blessed and sweet and revered and much longed-for lord, his brother and fellow priest, Severus, and the brethren who are with you (409)

The letter which my dearest son, our fellow deacon, Timothy,[1] brought to you, was ready for his departure, when our sons, Quodvultdeus[2] and Gaudentius, came to us with your letter. Hence it happened that he did not take you my answer, because he was on the point of starting off, and he stayed so short a time after their arrival that he seemed about to go from hour to hour. But, even if I had sent my answer by him[3] I should still be in your debt. Even now, when I seem to have answered you, I am in debt, I do not mean for your love, but for that letter of yours. As to love, the more we have paid of that the more we owe, and the Apostle says: 'Owe no man anything, but to love one another.'[4]

---

1 The deacon who caused the trouble outlined in Letters 62, 63.
2 Literally, what God wills. These compound and descriptive names were common in Africa, as they were later among the Puritans. The holder of this name wrote to Augustine in Letters 221, 223, and was answered in Letters 222, 224.
3 There is some inconsistency here, and it seems as if there were two letters in question: the one Timothy took and this one. In that case, where is the first and who delivered this one? Or did he substitute this one for the first? He seems to imply that Timothy's hurry to be off prevented him from answering Letter 109, yet in this letter he does answer that one.
4 Rom. 13.8.

And after reading the letter, when can I make a return to your sweet friendship and the intense longing of your heart which it expressed? It brought me word of something in you well known to me, yet, though it was a messenger of nothing new, it was new in dunning[5] me for an answer.

You wonder, perhaps, why I speak of being unable to pay this debt, when you, who know me as my own soul knows me, have such a high opinion of me. This is the very thing that makes it difficult for me to answer your letter, namely, that you heap such praise on me, while I refrain—out of regard for your modesty—from telling you how high you are in my esteem. And, when I say so little about you, how can I be anything else but your debtor? I should not mind this if I did not know that what you say of me to me is dictated by the most sincere affection, and not by flattery which is the bane of friendship. In the latter case I should not be your debtor, because I have no obligation to repay such things, but, the better I know that you speak your true sentiments, the more deeply I sink in my debt to you.

See now what a predicament I am in; by saying that you were sincere in praising me I have, in a sense, given praise to myself. But, what can I say other than what I have suggested about you, as you know? There! I have raised another difficulty for myself, one which you did not propose, but which you probably expect me to solve. As if I were not already sufficiently in debt, here I am piling up even more debt for myself! Still, it would be easy for me to point out —and if I do not point it out, it will be easy for you to see—that it is possible to speak the truth dishonestly, and to speak untruth honestly. For, if a person speaks as he thinks,

---

5 The *exactor* was a tax-collector as well as the executioner who carried out sentences of physical punishment, inflicted for non-payment of debts. In the parable of the unforgiving servant (Matt. 18.23-35) the debtor is delivered to the 'torturers' or exactors until he paid all the debt.

he speaks honestly even if what he says is untrue, but he who does not speak as he thinks speaks dishonestly, even if what he says is true. Have I any reason, then, to doubt that you believe what you wrote of me? But, as I do not perceive those qualities in myself, it is possible that you have spoken untruly of me in all honesty.

However, I do not want you to be led astray, even by your kindness of heart. I am indebted to that kindness because I could say what is true about you as honestly and as kindly, except that I respect your modesty, as I said above. But, for my part, when I am praised by one so near and so dear to my heart, I feel as if I were being praised by myself. You see how awkward it is, even if what is said is true, but even more so when you are my other self—or, rather, your soul and mine are one—that you should be wrong in thinking that I have qualities which I do not possess, just as a single person can be wrong about himself. This is something I do not want to happen to you, not only to keep one whom I love from being deceived, but even more to keep him from relaxing in his prayers for me, that I may be what you now think me. But I am not indebted to you in such a way as to try to outdo you in kindness by believing in and speaking of good qualities which you know you do not yet possess, but, with a kindness to match yours, I should speak of your good points which I am sure you have, as the gifts of God. If I do not do this, it is not through fear of being wrong about it, but so that you may not seem to have praised yourself, when you were praised by me. That is simple justice, since I should not want it to happen to me. If this is something I ought to do, then I choose to be a debtor to you for as long as I think I ought not to do it; if it ought not to be done, then I am not in debt.

But I know what answer you can make to this: 'You

say that as if I had wanted a long letter from you, full of my own praises.' Perish the thought that I could believe this of you! But your letter, full as it was of my praises—I will not say how true or how untrue—did ask for some repayment from me, even if that was not your intention. If you wanted me to write something else, you wanted a free gift, not a payment; whereas the order of justice requires that we should first pay what we owe, and then, if we like, give something extra to the one whom we have repaid. Yet, even in the sort of thing you wanted me to write, we pay rather than give, if we think carefully over the command of the Lord that we should owe no man anything except that we love one another. Such love undoubtedly creates the obligation that we observe fraternal charity by helping our brother, as much as we can, when he has the sincere desire to be helped. But, my dear brother, I am sure you know how much business I have in hand, how many cares this state of bondage lays upon me, and how very few are the little drops of time which trickle on me. If I use those on other things, I feel that I am failing in my duty.

I admit that I ought to write you a long letter, as you wish; I owe it indeed to your sweet, sincere, upright desire. But you are a good lover of justice, hence I warn you to listen willingly to what I say about that virtue which you love. You see that what I owe to you and others together has priority over what I owe to you alone; that I have not sufficient time for everything, not even for those prior claims. So, all my dearest and most intimate friends—and in the Name of Christ, you are among the first of those—will do their duty, not only by refraining from imposing any more writing on me, but also by showing a holy kindness and using whatever authority they have to prevent others from writing me. I do not like to seem hard-hearted, when I do not yield to the requests of individuals, yet I do wish to pay first what I owe to all. Finally, I hope your Reverence will come to us, as we have your promise of doing, and then you will know how much occupied I am with certain literary works, and you will try harder to do what I ask, by keeping off others, as far as you can, who want to insist on my writing something more. May the Lord our God fill the vast and holy abyss of your heart, which He Himself created, my most blessed lord.

111. Augustine gives greeting in the Lord to the most beloved lord, his most cherished brother and fellow priest, Victorian[1] (November 409)

Your letter filled my heart with deep sorrow, but to your request that I answer you at some length I can only say that prolonged tears and grief are more appropriate to such sorrows than lengthy books. Indeed, the whole world is afflicted with such great disasters[2] that there is scarcely a part of the earth where such things as you have described are not being committed and lamented. A short time ago the brothers were massacred by the barbarians in the deserts of Egypt, where the monasteries, cut off from all disturbance, existed in a relative security. I am sure you know what cruelties were perpetrated in parts of Italy and Gaul, and reports are beginning to come in now from many of the Spanish provinces, which had long seemed immune to these calamities. But why go so far afield? Right here in our neighborhood of Hippo, which the barbarians have not touched, the brigandage of Donatist clerics and Circumcellions[3] has so ravaged our churches that the deeds of bar-

---
1 Apparently an Italian priest who had written to Augustine of the terrors caused by barbarian invasions.
2 The invasions of Vandals, Alans, and Suevi.
3 Cf. Letter 108.

barians might be less destructive. What barbarian could have thought up the idea of throwing lime and vinegar, as they do, into the eyes of clerics, after inflicting horrible blows and wounds on other parts of their bodies? They plunder and burn certain houses; they carry off the stored crops and trample down the growing ones; by threatening to do the same to others, they force many to be rebaptized. The day before I dictated this letter to you, I had word that forty-eight persons had been rebaptized in one place, under the influence of this kind of terror.

These are sorrows to be mourned over, not wondered at, and we must cry out to God to deliver us from such evils, according to His mercy, not according to our merits. But, what else was to be expected for mankind when these evils were foretold long ago by the Prophets and the Gospel? We ought not to be so inconsistent as to believe when they are read, but complain when they are fulfilled. Rather, those who were unbelieving when they read or heard these things in the sacred Books should now at last believe when they see them being fulfilled. It is as if the oil press of the Lord, by this great anguish, forces out the dregs of murmuring and blaspheming infidels, but at the same time it is constantly pressing out the good oil of praying and praising faithful. There are some who never stop uttering impious complaints against the Christian faith, saying that mankind never suffered such evils before that doctrine was preached to the world, but it is easy to answer them from the Gospel, for the Lord says: 'The servant that knew not the will of his lord and did things worthy of stripes, shall be beaten with few stripes, but the servant who knew the will of his lord and did things worthy of stripes, shall be beaten with many stripes.'[4] What wonder, then, if that world in Christian times, like the servant now knowing the will of his lord and doing

---

4 Cf. Luke 12.48,47.

things worthy of stripes, should be beaten with many? They notice how quickly the Gospel is spread, but they do not notice how obstinately it is despised. But the humble and holy servants of God who suffer doubly when temporal evils befall, because they suffer with the wicked as well as at their hands, have their own consolations and the hope of the world to come. Hence, the Apostle says: 'The sufferings of this time are not worthy to be compared with the glory to come which shall be revealed in us.'[5]

Therefore, dearly beloved, when those whose words you say you cannot bear say to you: 'Granted that we sinners have deserved such things, but why are the servants of God massacred by the sword of the barbarians, and why are the handmaids of God made captives?' answer them humbly and truly and devoutly thus: However great virtue we practise, however great obedience we show to the Lord, can we be better than those three men who were thrown into a fiery furnace for defending the law of God?[6] Read what Azarias, one of the three, says on that occasion. Opening his mouth in the midst of the fire, he said: 'Blessed art thou, O Lord, the God of our fathers, and thy name is worthy of praise and glorious forever; for thou art just in all that thou hast done to us, and all thy works are true, and thy ways right, and all thy judgments true. For thou hast executed true judgments in all the things that thou hast brought upon us, and upon Jerusalem, the holy city of our fathers; for according to truth and judgment, thou hast brought all these things upon us for our sins. For we have sinned, and have not obeyed the law; we have not hearkened to thy commandments, that it might go well with us: and all that thou hast brought upon us, thou hast done in true judgment; and thou hast delivered us into the hands of our enemies

---
5 Rom. 8.18.
6 Cf. Dan. 3.13-23.

that are unjust and most wicked and prevaricators; and to
a king unjust and most wicked beyond all the earth. And
now we cannot open our mouth and we are truly become
a shame and reproach to thy servants and to them that worship thee. Deliver us not up forever, O Lord, for thy name's
sake, and take not away thy mercy from us, for the sake of
Abraham thy beloved, and Isaac thy servant, and Israel
thy holy one, to whom thou hast spoken promising that thou
wouldst multiply their seed as the stars of heaven and as the
sand that is on the sea shore. For we, O Lord, are diminished more than any nation and are brought low on earth
this day for our sins.'[7] You see, surely, dear brother, what
sort of men these were, how holy, how strong in the midst
of trial, and although the very fire spared them and feared
to touch them, still they confessed their sins, on account of
which they knew that they were being worthily and justly
humbled, and they were not silent.

Could we be better than Daniel himself, concerning whom
the Lord said to the prince of Tyre by the Prophet Ezechiel:
'Behold thou art wiser than Daniel?'[8] He is unique in being
included among the three just men, whom God says He will
deliver, doubtless showing three special types of just men,
when He says He will so deliver them as not to deliver their
sons with them, but they only shall be delivered: namely,
Noe, Daniel and Job.[9] But, read also the prayer of Daniel
and see how, when he was taken into captivity, he confessed
his own sins as well as those of his people, and admitted that
the justice of God had brought him, on account of his sins,
to that chastisement and disgrace of captivity. Thus it is
written: 'I set my face to the Lord God to pray and make
supplication with fasting and sackcloth. And I prayed to the

---
[7] Dan. 3.25-37.
[8] Ezech. 28.3.
[9] Ezech. 14.14-16.

Lord my God, and I made my confession and said: O Lord God, great and terrible, who keepest thy covenant and mercy to them that love thee and keep thy commandments; we have sinned, we have transgressed against thy law; we have done wickedly and have revolted, and we have gone aside from thy commandments and thy judgments. And we have not hearkened to thy servants, the prophets, that have spoken in thy name to our kings and to all the people of the land. To thee, O Lord, justice, but to us confusion of face, as at this day to the man of Juda, and to the inhabitants of Jerusalem, and to all Israel, to them that are near and to them that are far off, in all the countries whither thou hast scattered them for their iniquity, because they have sinned against thee, O Lord. To us confusion of face; to our kings, to our princes, and to our fathers that have sinned. But to thee, O Lord our God, mercy and forgiveness, for we have departed from thee, and we have not hearkened to the voice of the Lord our God, to walk in the commandments of his law, which he set before us by the hands of his servants, the prophets. And all Israel have transgressed thy law, and have turned away from hearing thy voice, and the malediction and the curse which is written in the book of Moses, the servant of God, is fallen upon us, because we have sinned. And he hath confirmed his words which he spoke against us and against our judges that judged us, to bring upon us great evils such as never were under all the heaven, according to that which hath been done in Jerusalem. As it is written in the law of Moses, all these evils are come upon us, and we entreated not the Lord our God, that he might turn our iniquities from us, and that we might think upon thy truth. And the Lord God hath watched upon all his holy ones and hath brought those things which he hath done upon us, since the Lord our God is just in all his world which he hath made, and we have not hearkened to his voice. And now, O Lord our God, who hast brought forth thy people out of the land of Egypt with a strong hand, and hast made thee a name, as at this day, we have committed iniquity against thy law. O Lord, in all thy justice, let thy wrath and thy indignation be turned away from thy city, Jerusalem, and from thy holy mountain. For by reason of our sins and the iniquities of our fathers, Jerusalem and thy people are a reproach to all that are round about us. Now therefore, O God, hear the supplication of thy servant, and his prayers, and show thy face upon thy sanctuary, which is desolate. For thy own sake, incline, O Lord, my God, thy ear and hear; open thy eyes and see our desolation, and that of thy city Jerusalem, upon which thy name is called, for it is not for our justification that we present our prayers before thy face, but for thy mercy, which is great. O Lord, hear; O Lord, be appeased; hearken and do, O Lord; delay not for thy own sake, O my God, because thy name is invoked upon thy city and upon thy people. Now while I was yet speaking and praying and confessing my sins and the sins of my people'[10]—see how he mentions his own sins first and afterward those of his people. And he commends this justice of God, and speaks this praise of God, because He chastises even His holy ones, not unjustly, but for their sins. If such things are said by men whose holiness was so sublime that it made fire and lions harmless, what ought we to say from the depths of our lowliness, we who are so inferior to them, whatever degree of justice we may seem to attain?

But, in case anyone should think that those servants of God whom you mentioned as having been put to death by barbarians ought to have escaped that death, as the three men were delivered from the flames, and Daniel from the lions, let him know that such miracles were wrought to make the kings who had handed them over to torment believe

---

10 Cf. Dan. 9.3-20.

that the Hebrews worship the true God. Thus it was the hidden judgment and mercy of God to grant salvation in that way to those kings. But He did not do so for King Antiochus, who put the Macchabees to death with cruel torments; on the contrary, He inflicted a more severe punishment on the hard heart of the king by reason of their glorious martyrdom. For so it is written. Read what was said by one of them who was the sixth to suffer: 'After him, they brought the sixth, and when he had been racked and tortured, and was about to die, he said: Be not deceived; we suffer these things for ourselves, for having sinned against our God, and these are worthy things which are done to us. But do not think that thou shalt escape unpunished for that thou hast willed by thy laws to fight against God and his law.'[11] You see how humbly and how truly wise they were in confessing that they were being chastised by the Lord for their own sins, as it is written: 'For whom the Lord loveth, he chastiseth, and he scourgeth every son whom he receiveth.'[12] So the Apostle also says: 'But if we would judge ourselves, surely we would not be judged by the Lord; but while we are judged, we are chastised by the Lord, that we be not condemned with the world.'[13]

Read these passages faithfully, preach them faithfully, and as far as possible beware and teach others to beware of murmuring against God in these trials and tribulations. You say that good and faithful and holy servants of God have fallen by the sword of barbarians. What difference does it make whether they are set free from the body by fever or by the sword? What God looks for in His servants is not the circumstances of their departure, but what they are like when they come to Him. It is true that a lingering illness causes

---
11 Cf. 2 Macch. 7.18.
12 Heb. 12.6; Prov. 3.12.
13 1 Cor. 11.31,32.

more suffering than a speedy death, yet we read of that lingering and dreadful illness which Job suffered, although God Himself, who cannot be deceived, bears witness to his holiness.[14]

Certainly, that captivity of chaste and holy women is a terrible and grievous thing, but their God is not a captive, and He does not forsake His captives, if He knows them for His. Those holy men whose sufferings and confession I have quoted from the Holy Scriptures were led away by enemies and forced into captivity, but we read the report of what they said, and we learned that the captive servants of God are not forsaken by their Lord. How do we know what miracles the almighty and merciful God wills to perform in the very land of the barbarians by means of these virgins? Only you must not cease to lament for them before God, and to ask what has become of them, or what comfort they are able to have from you—all this to the extent of your power, and as far as He permits, since He has given the time and opportunity. The niece of Severus,[15] Bishop of Sitif, was captured while a nun a few years ago, by the barbarians, but by the wonderful mercy of God she was restored to her parents with great respect. For, when she entered the house of the barbarians as a captive, her masters suddenly were stricken with illness, and all of those barbarians, three or more brothers, if I am not in error, fell ill of a dangerous malady. Their mother noticed that the girl was consecrated to God, and believed that her sons might be saved from the imminent danger of death through the virgin's prayers, so she asked her to pray for them, promising that, if they recovered, they would restore her to her parents.[16] She fasted and prayed, and her prayer was heard at

---
14 Job 18.2,3.
15 Not the Bishop of Milevis, writer of Letter 109.
16 Many consecrated virgins lived a religious life in their own families at this period, before the conventual life had been widely organized.

once, and the outcome shows what happened. They recovered their health, by the sudden bounty of God, and with admiration and respect they fulfilled the promise made by their mother.

Pray, then, to the Lord for them, and ask Him to teach them such words as holy Azarias poured forth to God among others in his prayer and confession, as I have noted above. These virgins in the land of their captivity are like the Israelites in that land where they could not offer sacrifice to God, as they were accustomed to do. These, also, cannot make an offering at the altar of God, nor find there a priest to make their offering to God for them. May the Lord grant them to say what Azarias said in the sequel of his prayers: 'Neither is there at this time prince or prophet or leader or holocaust or oblation or supplication or place for sacrifice in thy sight, that we may find mercy; nevertheless in a contrite heart and humble spirit let us be accepted. As in holocausts of rams and bullocks and as in a multitude of fat lambs, so let our sacrifice be made in thy sight this day, to perfect those who serve thee. And now we follow thee with all our heart, and we fear thee, and seek thy face. Put us not to confusion, but deal with us according to thy meekness, and according to the multitude of thy mercy, and deliver us according to thy wonderful works, and give glory to thy name, O Lord! And let all them that show evil to thy servants fear, and let them be confounded in all thy might, and let their strength be broken, and let them know that thou art the Lord, the only God, and glorious over all the world.'[17] God, who is wont to hear His own, will surely hear them making such appeals and laments to Him, and He will either not permit any violence of hostile lust to be done to their chaste persons, or, if He permits it, He will not attribute it to them. For, when the mind is not defiled by any

---

17 Cf. Dan. 3.38-45.

guilty consent, it protects even its own flesh from guilt, and whatever the will of the victim refuses to consent to or permit toward itself, that will be the sin of the perpetrator alone, and all that violence will be counted as a wound suffered, not as the defilement of guilt. So great is the force of purity of mind that, so long as it is inviolate, the chastity of the body cannot be violated even though it be physically overpowered. May this letter satisfy your Charity; though too short for your desire, it is too long for my duties, and it is hurried because of the haste of the bearer. The Lord will console you much more abundantly, if you read His Scriptures with great attention.

112. Augustine gives greeting in the Lord to the excellent lord, his brother Donatus,[1] revered with sincere affection (late 409 or early 410)

I had a great desire to see you while you were in office, but I was not able to, even when you came to Tibilis.[2] I suppose that happened so that I might enjoy communication with your mind, free from public cares, rather than a mere greeting, while I, at leisure, might be with you while you were engaged, which, however satisfactory it might be, would not curb the longing of either of us. Recalling the sincerity and uprightness of your character from an early age, I think you have a heart large enough for Christ to pour Himself generously into it, so that you may bring forth for Him fruits more worthy of eternal and heavenly glory than of transitory and worldly distinction.

I have learned from many—or, rather, from all those

---
1 The former proconsul or civil governor of Africa, who had recently been relieved of his office. He was the recipient of Letter 100.
2 Also called Thibilis, a town in Numidia.

whom I have either been able to question or whom I have heard offering voluntary testimony—of the purity and strength of your administration, which they constantly praise and universally extol, without any trace of dissent or difference, and I believe it more confidently because they knew of no bond of affection between us, nor did your admirers positively know whether I was even slightly acquainted with you. So, I have no reason to think that they were flattering my ears rather than spreading the truth about you. When praise is free from vanity, reproof is safe from offense. But, indeed, excellent brother, honored with most sincere affection, it is not now a question of teaching you, but of warning you, perhaps, that all that glory and popular acclaim do not derive their satisfaction from the mouth of the people, but from the circumstances that gave rise to them; even if these were displeasing to the people, they would still be precious in their own right, having their own brilliance and importance, irrespective of the approval of ignorant men. Whoever disapproves of such actions is to be pitied, but he who is disapproved of by such men is not to be deemed unfortunate. On the other hand, when such actions are pleasing and are popularly extolled with the praise due to them, they do not, for all that, become greater and better by the verdict of others, since they are grounded on their own inner truth, and supported by the strength of conscience alone. Hence, an increase of joy from this source belongs to men of good principles rather than to the one whom the people esteem.

Since you know this so well, my good sir, gaze, as you have begun to do, with the greatest intensity of your heart, upon our Lord Jesus Christ; detach yourself entirely from all empty pomp; mount up to Him who comforts with more than words those who turn to Him, and places those who strive to climb up with the steps of faith on the eternal heights of heavenly and angelic honor. Through Him I beg you to write me in reply, and to urge, with friendly kindness, all those of your household, whom you have in Sinis[3] or in Hippo, to join in communion with the Catholic Church. I know that your worthy and excellent father has been begotten by you in the bosom of that Church, and I ask you to greet him for me with the respect which he deserves. And do not make a difficulty about coming to see us. I ask this without hesitation, because it is intended to improve your standing with God, such as you have here. May the mercy of God enfold you, and preserve you from all evil.

113. Augustine gives greeting in the Lord to the beloved lord, Cresconius,[1] his deservedly honored and cherished brother[2]

If I were to let drop the case about which I am writing to your Holiness[3] this second time,[4] not only your Excellency, but even that individual, whoever he is, on whose account Faventius[5] was thus arrested, would justly blame me and rightly reprove me. He would surely think that, if he himself had fled to the church for sanctuary,[6] I would equally neglect him in his need and distress. In the next place, beloved lord

---

[3] Evidently a small place near Hippo.
[1] The tribune or official in charge of the coast guards.
[2] Letters 113-115 are of uncertain date: some time after 409 and before 423.
[3] *Religio*, a title not confined to clerics, but used sometimes to laymen of high rank.
[4] The first letter does not seem to have survived.
[5] A tenant-farmer on the estate of Paratianis, the rest of whose story is related in Letter 115, but we are not told what act of his had aroused the animosity of the 'very rich man' who is spoken of as his adversary.
[6] The right of refuge or sanctuary, known to the pagan world, had been attached to churches by Constantine. Here, the innocent and oppressed could find protection for thirty days, if they remained in the church enclosure.

and revered son, if the opinion of men is to be despised, what shall I say to the Lord our God Himself, and what account shall I give Him, if I fail to do my utmost for the rescue of one who has trusted in the protection and help of the Church which I serve? Therefore I ask your Benignity —since it is hard to believe that you do not or cannot know on what charge he is held—to be so kind as to further my request to the arresting officer who is holding him to do what is prescribed by imperial law;[7] namely, to have him examined in the city court, to discover whether he wishes to be allowed to spend thirty days under light guard in that city in which he is held, so as to set his affairs in order, and provide for his expenses. If in that length of time, with the help of your Benevolence, we can reach an agreement on his case, by friendly discussion, we shall be thankful; if not, the verdict of the court will find him out, and he will please God according to the worthiness of his cause or the will of the almighty Lord.

114. Augustine gives greeting in the Lord to the lord, his beloved son, Florentinus[1]

By whose authority and command you carried off Faventius[2] is something for you to look to for yourself, but this I know, that all authority set up under the power of the emperor is subject to law. I sent a copy of the law by my brother and fellow priest, Caelestinus,[3] which you certainly

---

[7] The laws of Theodosius in 380, and of Honorius in 409.

---

[1] An officer of the Count of Africa, who at this time was Boniface, successor to the infamous Gildo. The office was a sort of military governorship.
[2] Cf. Letter 113.
[3] Evidently one of Augustine's diocesan priests. There is a Caelestinus addressed in Letter 18, but by the address he appeared to be a layman.

ought to have known about, even before I sent it. According to it, those who are summoned by some official to appear in court are to be produced in the municipal court, and there asked whether they wish to spend thirty days under light guard, in the city where they are being held, so as to provide for their expenses, or to set their affairs in order, if necessary. The above-mentioned priest brought me back word that this law had been read aloud to your Reverence. However, I am now sending it again in this letter, not to threaten you, but to ask you, as a man of feeling, exercising the mercy expected of a bishop, and to intercede with you, my lord and son, to the extent allowed by humanity and filial feeling, that you would kindly grant this favor to your own reputation and to my request, and not refuse to do, at my prayer and intercession, what the law of the emperor commands, since you are a public official in his service.

115. Augustine gives greeting in the Lord to the blessed lord, his revered and very dear brother and fellow priest, Fortunatus,[1] and the brothers who are with you

Your Holiness is well acquainted with Faventius, who was a tenant-farmer on the estate[2] of Paratianis.[3] He had some kind of reason to fear the lord of the estate, so he took sanctuary in the church at Hippo, and waited there, as refugees generally do, to see if his difficulty could be settled by our intervention. Then, as often happens, he grew less

---
1 Bishop of Cirta.
2 A *saltus* was an extensive estate, not unlike a medieval manor: the owner's house, or *villa* was surrounded by the houses of the workers, or *coloni*. The *conductor*, or tenant-farmer, held a position between the landlord and the *coloni*.
3 A Numidian town, some miles from Rusicade.

and less careful as time went on and, as if his adversary had given up, went out to dinner with a friend, and was suddenly abducted, as he was coming out, by one Florentinus, said to be an officer of the count, and with him a band of armed men, as many as seemed necessary to them.[4] When word of this was brought to me, and I still did not know where or by whom he had been carried off—although my suspicion fell on the man against whom he had taken refuge in the church—I sent at once to the tribune in charge of the coast guards. He sent soldiers; no one could be found. But by morning, we knew what house he was in, and that his captor had decamped with him after cockcrow. I also sent to the place where he was said to have been taken, but when the aforementioned officer had been found he would not allow the priest whom I had sent even to see him. On the next day I sent a letter requesting for Faventius the privilege which the emperor prescribed for such cases: namely, that those who were summoned to appear in court should be asked in a municipal session whether they were willing to spend thirty days under light guard, in that city, so as to set their affairs in order and provide for their expenses. My idea was that, during those days, we might perhaps settle his case by friendly discussion. But he had already gone off in the custody of that officer, and there is reason to fear that he may suffer some harm if he is brought before the governor's tribunal. Although the judge has the highest reputation for honesty, he has to deal with a very rich man. So, to prevent his money from influencing the court, I beg your Holiness, my beloved lord and revered brother, to be so kind as to take my letter to the honorable governor and read it to him, because I do not think it necessary to go into detail on the same case twice. Ask him to put off the hearing of the case, since I do not

[4] Cf. Letter 114.

know whether he is guilty or innocent. And ask him not to make light of the fact that the laws were not observed in regard to the man, since he was carried off in that manner and not taken, as the emperor prescribed, to the municipal court to be asked whether he wished to take advantage of the postponement, and thus give us a chance to reach an agreement with his opponent.

116. Augustine gives greeting in the Lord to the excellent lord, his deservedly famous, honored and dear son, Generosus[1]

Although the praise and esteem awarded your governorship and your own high reputation have always given me great joy, in proportion to the affection which we owe to your merits and your goodness, my dearest lord and revered son, I have never before found it hard to appeal to your Excellency to ask a favor. But now, when your Excellency finds out what happened in the city in which I serve the Church of God from the letter which I have given to my revered brother and fellow bishop, Fortunatus, your Benignity will perceive what necessity forced me to interrupt you in your duties by presenting my request. Doubtless, you will do what an upright judge, not to say a Christian one, ought to do, with that same good feeling toward us on which we had to rely in the name of Christ.

---
1 Consul or Governor of Numidia, before whom Faventius was to appear.

117. Here begins the letter of Dioscorus to the holy bishop, Augustine[1] *(410 or 411)*

A ceremonious preface is both useless and annoying to you, interested as you are in things rather than words, so listen to this simple request. The Elder, Alypius,[2] after many petitions from me, promised that he would join with you in answering a few little questions about the *Dialogues*,[3] and, since I hear that he is today in Mauretania, I beg and implore you with all my strength, please answer me, yourself alone, as unquestionably you would have done if your brother were present. If you had money or gold, you would undoubtedly give it to help anyone, but now you have only to speak, to give, without effort, what I ask. I could make this request more persuasive by sending it through many of your dear friends, but I know your mind: you do not want to be coaxed to do service to all, so long as there is nothing discreditable, and in this matter there certainly is not. However that may be, I ask you to help a wayfarer. You know how much I hate to be a burden to anyone, much less to your Sincerity, but God knows what extreme compulsion I am under in doing this. With the help of God, I am about to set out on a journey, while you are safe at home; you know what men are like, how prone they are to criticize, and you see how uncouth and stupid a man is considered if he cannot answer their questions. I ask you, then, to answer everything at once, and not to put me off with a disappointing rebuff. As I hope to see my parents, I have sent Cerdo for this sole purpose, and I am only waiting for him to return. Brother Zenobius, the

---
1 The letter has no formula of address. Dioscorus was an earnest young student of Cicero's works who, setting out on a journey, wanted to be able to appear skilled in his favorite author.
2 Augustine's close friend. The use of the title Elder shows that he was not yet a bishop.
3 The *Tusculan Disputations* of Cicero.

magistrate,[4] has sent us a permit to travel, and to buy provisions. If I do not deserve an answer to my little questions, at least have regard for the provisions! May the most high God keep you safe for us for a long age. My tutor sends cordial greetings to your Worthiness.

118. Augustine to Dioscorus[1] *(410 or 411)*

You thought to besiege or, rather, to take me by storm with a sudden throng of endless questions. But, even if you believed that I was free and at leisure, when could I, even in unlimited leisure, solve so many knotty points for someone in such a hurry, and, as you wrote, on the eve of a journey? I should be entangled by the very number of the points, even if the knots were easy to undo, but they are so involved in obscurity, and so complicated and difficult, that even though they were few and I were completely free they would weary my attention by keeping me busy for a great length of time, and wear down my finger-nails.[2] But I should like to tear you from the midst of your delightful inquiries, and set you down among my cares, so that you might learn not to be vainly curious, or not to venture to impose the task of feeding and nourishing your curiosity on those who have as one of their most pressing duties to curb and restrain the curious. If time and effort are to be spent in sending you letters, how much better and more fruitfully will they be spent in cutting

---

4 *magister memoriae*, an imperial officer who took note of all public pronouncements, published them, and sent replies to petitions. He also issued letters of recommendation to travelers going to the provinces, permits to travel by public conveyance, and licenses to buy provisions. He seems to have been a passport officer who also issued ration cards.

---

1 There is no formula of address.
2 A modern equivalent would be 'to wear one's fingers to the bone' with constant writing.

away your vain and deceitful ambitions, which are to be the more carefully avoided the more easily they lead you astray, veiled and cloaked as they are in some image of honorable pursuit, or under the name of liberal studies. How much better this, than that your ambitions should be stirred up, by my help, or under my escort, so to speak, to tyrannize over that good mind of yours.

All those *Dialogues* read, and what good are they if they have not helped you to consider your end, and to direct all your actions to it? Tell me. You give me plenty of information in your letter about the purpose you have in all this too ardent study, useless to you, and troublesome to me. For, when you importuned me in the letter which you sent with the questions you wanted answered, you wrote: 'I could make this request more persuasive by sending it through many of your dear friends, but I know your mind; you do not want to be coaxed, but to do service to all, so long as there is nothing discreditable, and in this matter there certainly is not. However that may be, I ask you to help a wayfarer.'[3] In these words of your letter you express a correct opinion of me: I do desire to be of service to everyone, provided there is nothing discreditable. But I am not sure there is nothing discreditable in this matter. Does not an unseemly aspect of the matter touch my imagination, when I picture a bishop, straitened and harried on all sides by the clamorous cares of the Church, suddenly turning a deaf ear to all of them, and shutting himself off, while he explains some of the fine points of Tully's *Dialogues* to one lone scholar? You do see how unseemly that would be, although you are so carried away by your eagerness for study that you refuse to consider it. Nothing else shows this so plainly as your having added: 'However that may be, I ask you to help a traveler,' after you had said that there was certainly nothing unseemly in this matter. This

---

[3] Quoted from Letter 117.

sounds as if you thought there were nothing unseemly in this request, but that, in case there were, you still wanted me to do this favor, because you were going on a journey. But why, I should like to know, did you add the detail about going on a journey? Ought I perhaps not do you a discreditable service, unless you were going on a journey? You probably thought that the defect would be washed clean by sea water. But in that case, the defect on my side would remain unforgiven because I was not going on a journey.

You write that I know how much you hate to be a burden to anyone, and you assert that God knows what extreme compulsion you are under in doing this. At this point, indeed, when I read your letter, I tried to discover this compulsion of yours, when, lo and behold, you gave yourself away by saying: 'You know what men are like, how prone they are to criticize, and how stupid and uncouth a man is considered if he cannot answer their questions.' At this point I was truly on fire with longing to answer you; by that soul malady you pierced my heart and broke in among my cares, so that I could not refuse to cure you, as far as God helps me to do so. However, I am not thinking of solving and explaining your problems, but of freeing your precarious happiness, which depends on the tongues of men, from such wretched fetters, and fastening it to some completely stable and unshaken foundation. But, my dear Dioscorus, do you not recall your friend Persius,[4] who mocks at you in a tortured verse, lays about your childish head with a proper blow, and sets you in your place, if you take in his meaning: 'Is it naught to know a thing is yours, unless you know another knows it too?' As I said above, you have read so many dialogues, you have enslaved your heart to the arguments of so many philosophers! Tell me, please, who of them made popular fame or the opinion of men, however good and wise, the object of their actions? But you—and

---

4 *Sat.* 1.27.

this is something rather to be ashamed of—as you are setting off on a journey, testify that you have made profit in Africa, when you lay this burden of explaining Cicero to you on care-laden bishops, who are occupied with far different matters, for no other reason than that you fear being thought stupid and uncouth if you do not answer the questions of men who are prone to criticize. A worthy object of the toils and midnight labors of bishops!

As I see it, you think of nothing else day and night but of being praised by men for your studies and your learning. I have always thought this a dangerous tendency even in those whose aim is sure and upright, but I see it proved in you. Because of that evil tendency, you did not see what motive could influence us to give you what you asked. You are so carried away by that perverted desire to learn what you asked, so as to be praised, or at least not blamed by men, that you think an equally perverted motive could make us answer your request, for the reasons you allege. My wish is that you also could be brought to be influenced not at all by the empty and deceitful boon of human praise, when we show you that our motive is not to yield to what you ask, when you write such things about yourself, but to convert you. 'You know what men are like,' you say, 'how prone to criticize.' What next? 'If a man does not answer their questions he will be considered stupid and uncouth.' See now, I do not ask you anything about Cicero's books, which readers are perhaps unable to interpret, but something from your own letter, and about the meaning of your own words. I ask why you did not say: 'If a man does not answer he will be proved stupid and uncouth,' rather than what you did say: 'he will be thought stupid and uncouth'? Doubtless it was because you understood well enough that anyone who did not answer such things was not really stupid and uncouth, but was only thought to be so. But I warn you that anyone who fears to be cut by the pruning-hook tongues of such supposers is dry wood, and therefore he is not merely thought to be stupid and uncouth, but he truly is and is proved to be such.

Perhaps you will say: 'But when I am not stupid in mind, and I particularly strive not to be, I don't want to be thought stupid in mind.' That is right, but I am asking why you do not want to be, when you did not hesitate to lay on us the burden of solving and explaining those questions for you, and it was so important that you called it an extreme necessity, not to be thought stupid and uncouth by men prone to criticize, whose questions you could not answer. But I should like to know whether this is the whole reason why you want this favor from us, or whether you do not want to be thought stupid and uncouth for some other reason. If this is the whole reason, you see, I think, that this is the purpose of that eager intensity of yours which makes you a burden to us, as you admit. But what burden could come to us from Dioscorus except the burden which weighs on Dioscorus himself, all unknowing? He will not feel it until he tries to rise, and I hope his burden is not fastened so tight that he will try in vain to shake his shoulders free of it! I do not say this because of his trying to learn those questions, but because of his purpose in learning them. Surely, you now see that this purpose is worthless, empty, conceited; it causes a swelling, under which corruption gathers, and spreads out over the eye of the mind to prevent it from seeing the richness of truth. As I hope to find you, my Dioscorus, in that disposition, and in the grandeur of truth, from whose shadow you turn away, believe me, it is so. I do not see any way but this to make you believe me in this matter. You do not see the truth, nor can you see it at all, so long as you build your edifice of deadly joys on the tongues of men.

But, if this is not the object of your acts and endeavor,

and you have another reason for not wanting to be thought stupid and uncouth, I ask what it is. If it is in order to have a freer opportunity of acquiring temporal riches, of winning a wife, of attaining to high office, and other things of this sort, which flow along with headlong current and swallow in their depths those who fall into them, then it is not fitting for us to help you to that goal; on the contrary, we ought to turn you from it. We shall not prevent you from making the uncertainty of fame your object in life, as if you were moving from the Mincius[5] to the Po, but in such wise as that the Mincius could still touch you even if you had not moved there. Since the vanity of human praise will not satisfy the hungry spirit, because it gives it nothing to eat but emptiness and air, by that very hunger it is forced to turn to something fuller and more profitable; and since it is none the less carried along by the stream of time, it is as if a river led into another river, and there is no end of wretchedness, so long as the object of our striving has no sure foundation. That is why we wish to attach you to some strong and unchangeable good, as the home of your most enduring effort, and the most sure rest for your every good and honorable action. But, perhaps you think to turn that same earthly happiness which I mentioned into some true and sure and complete good—always supposing you are able to attain it by setting your sails to the wind and breezes of favorable rumor? It does not seem so to me, and truth itself denies absolutely that happiness, which is close by, is arrived at by such a winding course, or that what is freely given is to be bought at such a price.

Or, perhaps you think that human praise is to be used as a tool with which you are to gain entrance to the minds of men, to convince them of what is true and useful, and you want to prevent them from thinking you stupid and uncouth,

---

[5] A river in northern Italy, tributary of the Po.

so they will not judge you unworthy of their most careful and patient hearing, when you are either encouraging someone to right conduct, or reproaching the malice and wickedness of a sinner? If, in asking those questions you had this virtuous and kindly motive in mind, then you did us a poor service when you did not put that motive in your letter, so that we might either willingly give you what you asked, or refuse it because some other reason prevented us, but not because we would be ashamed to yield to your vain ambition or at least not to resist it. It is much better and more profitable for you to learn the rules themselves of truth, as I ask you to do, and through them you will more surely and more quickly gain what you need to refute for yourself all sorts of false arguments. This will keep you from thinking yourself learned and intelligent—a false and shameful thing—because you have learned the hoary and worn-out falsehoods of so many philosophers, with a zeal more boastful than prudent. I do not think you believe that, because we have surely not been wasting our labor in setting forth for Dioscorus so many truths for so long a time—ever since we began on this letter.

Let us now look at this other point, since you do not judge yourself stupid and uncouth because of your ignorance of those things, but of the truth itself. In regard to what anyone has written or will write about those topics, either they are as you now securely hold them to be, or, if they are false, you are safe in not knowing it, and in not tormenting yourself with baseless anxiety lest you continue to be stupid and uncouth by not knowing the variation of others' opinions. Since all this is so, let us look, if you will, at this other point, whether the wrong opinion of others—who are, as you write, so prone to criticize that, if they perceive your ignorance of these things, they think you stupid and uncouth—ought so to influence you that you think it not inappropriate to ask to have these points explained to you by bishops. We truly believe you want to know these things with the object of doing a favor to those who hold you stupid and uncouth, as to Cicero's works, by winning them to the truth and amending their way of life, although they would think it beneath them to gain for themselves any useful and profitable knowledge from anyone like you.

Believe me, it is not as you think. In the first place, in those lands[6] where you fear to appear unskilled and not up to the mark, I do not know of any persons who would ask you anything about those problems. Certainly you experienced in this place, where you came to learn these things, and at Rome, how little attention is paid to them, and for that reason they are neither taught nor studied; and in Africa you would be so far from being exposed to questions on these points that you would not find anyone who would let you ask questions yourself. Because of that lack, you are forced to send your questions to bishops to be explained. But, even if those bishops had been carried away in their youth by the same eagerness or, rather, wrong purpose as you are, and if they were interested in learning such things as if they were something great, they would not likely allow them to remain in memory until as hoary-headed prelates they occupied the bishops' throne. In case they wished to do so, greater and heavier cares would shut them out of their hearts, whether they wished it or not, or, if some traces of these studies remained in their minds through excessive preoccupation with them, they would indeed prefer to bury what they remembered in forgetfulness rather than to answer foolish questions. As a result, to the superficial mind of the

---

6 Dioscorus was apparently intending to travel in Greece and Asia Minor.

scholar, and to teachers of rhetoric,[7] they seem so stupid and sleepy that they are supposed to think they have to send from Carthage to Hippo to get an answer. But, in this place, such topics are so unusual and so foreign that, if I were inclined to answer you, and if I wanted to look into the work in question to see what comes before the statement I am supposed to interpret and what argument develops from it in what follows, I should doubtless not be able to find a copy. But, if those same Carthaginian rhetoricians have been deficient in this study, I not only do not blame them, I actually praise them if, as is likely, they now recall that such contests of wits are not common to the Roman forum but to Greek schools. And when you had submitted your thoughts to the schools and you found them barren and cold to such ideas, the Christian basilica of Hippo came to your mind as a place where you could lay down your cares, because it is now presided over by a bishop who once sold such wares to little boys.[8] But, now, I do not want you to be a little boy any longer, and it is not fitting for me to be either a seller or a giver of childish toys. And since it is a fact that two great cities, Rome and Carthage, molders of Latin literature, have neither troubled you by asking you such things, nor cared to listen to you so as to relieve your trouble when you ask, I wonder, more than I can say, why a youth of such good intellect as you fears to find someone in Greek or Oriental cities who might be so troublesome as to ask you questions. Indeed, you will be more likely to hear jackdaws in Africa than that sort of utterance in those places.

In the second place, if I am wrong, and someone over

---
7 Rhetors were traveling lecturers, also called Sophists, who prided themselves on being able to give an extemporaneous talk on any subject. They used the exotic literary style of the day known as the *elocutio novella*. African scholars led the way in this development, but their interest was in literature, not in philosophy.
8 Augustine was a teacher of rhetoric in his young manhood.

there does appear as a questioner of that sort—more objectionable because more unskilled in that part of the world—are you not more afraid that Greeks should much more easily come forward and, finding you settled in Greece, and versed in the Greek language, as if it were your own, should question you on certain points taken from the works of their philosophers which Cicero did not treat in his writings? What will you answer if that happens? Will you say that you preferred to study those things in the works of Latin authors rather than Greek ones? By that answer you will first insult the Greeks—and, as you know, they are men who do not tolerate that—and then, when they are offended and angered, they will quickly judge you stupid—which you particularly do not want—because you preferred to learn the theories of the Greek philosophers, or, rather, some scraps of theories parceled out and scattered through the Latin dialogues, and not the whole, carefully developed theories in the Greek words of the original authors. And they will judge you uncouth because you are ignorant of so much in your own language, yet go around picking up crusts of the same thing in a foreign tongue! Will you perhaps answer that you did not undervalue the Greek works on these subjects, but you gave your attention first to learning the Latin authors, whereas now, as you are versed in the Latin, you want to study the Greek authors? If you, a Greek, are not ashamed to have learned Latin as a boy, and to wish to learn Greek as a grown man, will you not at least be ashamed of not knowing certain things among the Latin authors themselves? You know how many learned Latins share this ignorance with you, and you experience it by the admission you made to us of being weighed down by a great necessity while you were settled at Carthage in the midst of a great crowd of learned men.

Finally, suppose that you have been able to answer all the

questions you referred to us. Lo! you will now be called learned and adept! Lo! the Grecian air raises you to the sky on a wind of praise! But, remember your own worth; remember what purpose you had in wishing to deserve that praise, namely, that you might impart some supremely worthwhile and valuable instruction to those who so light heartedly admire your trifling talk, and hang with such good-will and eagerness upon your words. This is what I should like to know: Whether you possess and are able to impart anything supremely valuable and worth while. For it is absurd that you should have learned so many useless things for the express purpose of preparing men's ears to receive the necessary truths from you, if you do not know the necessary truths yourself, for the receiving of which you have prepared them by useless talk; and that you should be so busy learning how to get their attention that you have no desire to learn what to teach them when you have it. But, if you now say that you do know this, and you answer that it is Christian doctrine, and that you prefer it to all else, as we know, and that you place in it alone all your hope of eternal salvation, then for that there is no need of securing hearers by a knowledge of Cicero's *Dialogues* and by a list of other people's contradictory opinions brought into agreement. Let those who are going to hear anything of the sort from you first observe your conduct. I do not want you to learn something first which has to be unlearned in order that you may teach the truth.

Now, if the knowledge of the dissenting and contradictory opinions of others is any help to a teacher of truth, that he may know how to destroy the false arguments of opponents, at least to this extent, that no one arguing against him can fix his gaze on anything except on refuting your words, then let him carefully hide his own views. For, the knowledge of truth is well fitted to distinguish and demolish all false doctrines, even those previously unheard, provided only they are expressed. But, if there is need of knowing the errors of others in order not only to strike down open falsehoods, but even to root up hidden ones, lift up your eyes and ears, I beg of you; listen and see whether anyone brings any objection against us out of Anaximenes[9] or Anaxagoras.[10] Why, the ashes of much more recent and more vocal Stoics and Epicureans are not warm enough to strike out a spark against the Christian faith. But the groups and assemblies—some in hiding, some boldly in evidence—of the Donatists, the Maximianists, the Manichaeans, or even of the Arians, the Eunomians, the Macedonians, the Cataphrygians, and other pests among whose disturbing sects you are about to enter, are numberless and vociferous.[11] If it wearies you to search out all their errors, what use is it to us, in defending the Christian religion, to find out what Anaximenes thought, or to stir up the dead embers of controversy, out of idle curiosity, while we pass over in silence the quarrels and controversies of certain heretics who boasted the name of Christians, such as the Marcionites, the Sabellians[12] and many others besides? However, as I said before, if there is need to

---

9 Greek philosopher, born 556 B.C., who identified the divinity with air.
10 Greek philosopher, contemporary with Pericles (6th century B.C.), who gave a moral explanation of the myths of Homer and an allegorical interpretation of the names of the gods.
11 The Donatists, Maximianists, and Manichaeans were African schisms or heresies of Augustine's day. The Arians, founded by Arius (321), denied the divinity of Christ. The Eunomians, founded in the East (350-381), followed an extreme form of Arianism. The Macedonians, also called Pneumatomachi, denied the divinity of the Holy Spirit, and were found in countries around the Hellespont (4th and 5th centuries). The Cataphrygians, or Montanists, were an adventist sect of the 2nd century and after. They claimed to be prophets, and their teachings were secret. Tertullian was a Montanist.
12 The Marcionites (2nd century) attempted to repudiate the Old Testament and to 'purify' the Church through the writings of St. Paul. The Sabellians (3rd century) were heretical regarding the distinction of Persons in the Trinity.

have some acquaintance with the adversaries of truth, and some explanation of their opinions, we ought to think of the heretics who call themselves Christians, rather than of Anaxagoras and Democritus.[13]

But, whoever that person may be who asks you the questions you ask us, let him hear from you that you consider it the part of both learning and prudence not to know those things. Themistocles[14] did not mind being considered ignorant when he refused at a banquet to play the lyre, and said he did not know that sort of thing; when they asked him: 'What do you know, then?' he answered: 'How to make a small state great.'[15] Do you, then, shrink from saying you do not know those things, and, when your questioner asks what you do know, can you not answer that you know how a man can be happy without all that philosophy? But, if you have not yet reached that state of mind, then you are as wrong in seeking out those questions as you would be if you were ill of a dangerous ailment and should ask for exquisite and delicate garments instead of for medicines and doctors. You should not put off any longer acquiring that knowledge of the happy life, nor prefer the other to it, especially at your age, and in view of the order you have followed in your studies. See how easily you could learn this if you wished. He who seeks the way to attain happiness seeks nothing else but the right purpose in life, that is to say, where the supreme good of man is to be found, and this is based on a sure and unalterable truth, not on some rash and perverted opinion. And if anyone wants to know the foundation of this, it is not found except in the body, or in the soul, or in God, or in any two of these, or even in all of them. But, if you have

---

13 Greek philosopher of the 5th century B.C., a master of speculative and physical science, from whom Epicurus borrowed the principal features of his system.
14 Celebrated Athenian statesman and leader (514-449 B.C.).
15 Quoted from Cicero, *Tusc. Disp.* 1.2.4., and Plutarch, *Themis.* 2.

learned that neither the supreme good nor any part of the supreme good is to be found in the body, there will be left two alternatives, the soul and God, and it will be either in one of these or in both. And if you go further, and learn that the same holds true of the soul as of the body, what else will be left but God, in whom the supreme good is to be found? That is not to say that other things may not be good, but that one is called supreme to which others are referred; a man attains happiness by enjoying that, and he wishes for other goods on account of it, whereas the supreme good is not loved for anything else but for its own sake. For that reason it is called man's final end, because now he has no longer any need to run back and forth; there is his rest from seeking, there is his certainty of happiness, there the most peaceful joy of the upright will.

Give me, then, someone who will see at once that the body is not intended for the good of the soul, but, rather, the soul for the good of the body, and there will be an end of inquiring whether that supreme good or any part of it is in the body. The soul is superior to the body—something it would be extremely foolish to deny—and it would be equally foolish to deny that he who gives happiness or any part of it is superior to him who receives it; therefore, the soul does not receive from the body either the supreme good or any part of the supreme good. Those who are blinded by the attraction of carnal joys do not see this, and they do not perceive that such attraction arises from a defect in soundness. But, perfect soundness of body will be that final immortality of the whole man. God has made the soul of such a powerful nature that from its perfect bliss, which is promised to the saints at the end of time, there will flow out over the lower nature, namely, the body, not the particular happiness of enjoyment and understanding, but the fullness of physical integrity, which is the strength of incorruption. Those who do not see this, as I have said, wage a war of restless strife, of varying intensity, each one according to his own capacity, and by placing the supreme good of man in his body they also rouse up a host of unruly carnal passions. Among these, the Epicureans[16] had the greatest influence over the ignorant mob.

Give me, also, one who will see at once that the soul itself does not find its happiness in its own good; otherwise, it would never be unhappy, and there will be an end of inquiring whether that supreme and, so to speak, blissful good, or any part of it, is found in the soul. For, when it takes pleasure in itself as if it were its own good, it is proud, but, when it sees that it is subject to change, at least to the extent that it changes from foolish to wise, and that wisdom is unchangeable, then it must necessarily perceive that wisdom is something superior to its own nature, and that by sharing in and being enlightened by wisdom it finds a richer and surer joy than it could find in itself. Thus, by ceasing from its boasting and subsiding from its swollen self-importance, it strives to cling to God, and to be remade and reformed by His immutability. It now grasps the truth that not only does every species of all creation come from Him, both what is perceived by the bodily senses and what is inferred by the understanding, but also the very power to create, which exists before the act of creating, as is clear from our calling something formless which can be formed. Therefore, the less the soul clings to God, the Supreme Being, the less steadfast it feels itself to be, and God is precisely the Supreme Being because He neither advances nor falls back by any change. But, the soul sees that one change is beneficial to

---

16 Followers of Epicurus (341-270 B.C.). He was a materialist and a disbeliever in the pagan gods. He taught that happiness is found in the satisfaction of desire.

itself, when it advances so as to cling to God perfectly, but the other change, which consists in falling back, is harmful, and every falling back tends to destruction. Whether anything reaches that extreme may not be evident, but it is evident that all defect brings destruction with it for everything, so that it no longer is what it was. Hence we conclude that things can and do decline for no other reason than that they were created from nothing. Consequently, what is in them, what they are and remain, and even the fact that in proportion to their deficiencies all is arranged so that they can be joined to the totality of things, is a mark of God's goodness and almighty power. He is the supreme Creator who is able out of nothing to make not merely something, but even something great. But the first sin, that is, the first voluntary falling away, was an act of taking pleasure in man's own power; he took pleasure in something less than if he rejoiced in the power of God, which is certainly greater. Those who do not see this, and who fasten their gaze on the powers of the human mind, and on the great beauty of its deeds and words, who might be ashamed to place the supreme good in the body, have nevertheless, by assigning it to the mind, placed it lower than it should be placed by human reason acting with absolute honesty. Among the Greek philosophers who hold this opinion, the Stoics[17] are outstanding, both in numbers and in cleverness of argument. But, because they hold that all that exists in nature is corporeal, they distinguish the soul from the flesh rather than from the body.

But, among those who say that our sole and supreme good consists in the enjoyment of God by whom we and all things

17 A school of philosophy founded by Zeno (366-264 B.C.), named from the *stoa* or porch in which Zeno held his discussions. He taught that happiness is found in the denial of desire. His theories were expressed in so-called paradoxes; he practised and preached personal austerity.

were made, the Platonists[18] held first place, because they thought, quite properly, that it was their duty to offer the greatest and almost the only opposition to the Stoics and Epicureans. The Academics held the same views as the Platonists, as the continuance of their followers proves. Arcesilas, the first to make a secret of his own theory, determined to do nothing more than refute the Stoics and Epicureans; ask whom he succeeded, you will find Polemon; ask whom Polemon followed, you will find Xenocrates, but Plato left his school, the Academy, to his disciple, Xenocrates. Abstract from these personalities in so far as they deal with the question of the supreme good of man, and take up the debate itself; at once you will find two conflicting errors confronting each other: the one establishing the supreme good in the body, the other in the soul—whereas the doctrine of truth, by which our supreme good is understood to be God, opposed both of these, as well by teaching the true theory as by refuting the wrong one. Now, resume this survey by adding the individual teachers: you will find the Epicureans and the Stoics bitterly opposing each other, and the Platonists, while concealing their true opinion, striving to settle this quarrel by showing up and refuting the vain confidence of these others in their false ideas.

But the Platonists have not been able to play the part of true reason as fully as the others have been able to play their role of error. For, all of them lacked the model of divine humility, which enlightened us at the most fitting time through our Lord Jesus Christ. Before this peerless Model, all the pride of the most fiercely arrogant mind yields, is

---

18 Plato (429-310 B.C.) laid the foundation for Christian philosophy. His followers met in a grove or academe, and were called Academics. Arcesilas (316-244 B.C.) was the founder of a school called the Middle Academy, in which he attempted to develop and purify some of Plato's theories. Polemon, a 4th-century-follower of Plato, became director of the Academy after the death of Xenocrates (400-316 B.C.).

broken and expires. Therefore, the Platonists are not able by their authority to lead the mob, blinded by the love of earthly things, to faith in the unseen, when they see them so strongly enticed by Epicurean claims to drain the cup of carnal pleasures to the dregs—something they are naturally drawn to—and even to advocate this so strongly that they place in it the supreme good of man. And when they also see that those who are moved to oppose this kind of pleasure through their esteem of virtue behold it more easily in the minds of men, from which good deeds originate, as far as they can judge of them, if they should attempt to suggest to them some divine being, above all forces of change, apprehended by no bodily sense, understood by the mind alone, but transcending the nature of the mind itself, and should state that this being is God, who is offered for the enjoyment of the human soul, purified of all taint of human passions, in whom alone is the term of all our good, they would not understand, and would much more easily give the palm either to the Epicureans or to the Stoics in this contest than to themselves. Thus the true and saving doctrine would fall into disrepute through the contempt of untaught peoples— a most dangerous result for the human race. This is the case in the field of ethics.

In the problems of cosmology, if the Platonists should say that uncreated wisdom is the creating force of the whole of nature, the Epicureans and the Stoics would not admit anything outside the physical world, for some of them postulate atoms[19] as the original matter of the universe, while others assign it to four elements,[20] among which they attribute to fire the primal force of creation. In this case, who could fail

---

19 These were particles of matter out of which everything was formed by their chance combinations, according to Epicurus.
20 According to Empedocles (5th century) everything was formed of earth, air, water, or fire.

to see that the greatest following of fools is on the side of the materialist view, into which opinion one is dragged along since he cannot see an uncreated power as the creator of all things?

There remains the section on logic. As you know, everything that is inquired into for the sake of gaining knowledge is a question either of ethics or of natural philosophy or of logic. Therefore, when the Epicureans said that the bodily senses were never deceived, while the Stoics granted that they were sometimes deceived, although both placed the test of acquiring truth in the senses, would anyone listen to the Platonists over the opposition of these two? Who would recognize their right to be included in the list of men, much less of wise men, if they had forthrightly declared that not only was there something which could not be perceived by bodily touch or smell or taste, or by those ears or eyes, but, if they even claimed that it was the sort of thing which could not be apprehended nor even formulated by any mental image, that, moreover, it was the only true being, and the only one which could be perceived, but, because it is unchangeable and eternal, it is perceived by the understanding alone, the only way in which the one truth is apprehended, as far as it can be apprehended?

Since, then, the Platonists held such opinions as could not be taught to men addicted to fleshly pleasures, and since they had not sufficient authority among the people to induce them to believe such doctrines, until their minds should be adapted to such belief, they chose to conceal their own opinion and to argue against those who boasted of having found the truth, which truth they located in the senses of the body. And what good does it do to inquire into the nature of their system? It was certainly not divine nor endowed with any divine authority. But, note this one point, that Plato has been very clearly proved by Cicero[21] to have been gifted not with a human wisdom, but with an evidently divine one, from which the human is, in a sense, enkindled, when he placed the supreme good, and the origins of the universe, and the bases of certitude in that same unchangeable wisdom and that truth which remains ever the same. Note, too, that those who were attacked by the Platonists, under the name of Epicureans and Stoics, were the ones who placed the supreme good and the origins of the universe and the bases of certitude in the nature of either the body or the mind. This question continued in the course of centuries until at the beginning of the Christian era, when faith in things invisible and eternal was being advantageously preached by visible miracles, to men who could neither see nor think of anything beyond the body, yet these same Epicureans and Stoics are found in the Acts of the Apostles[22] to have contradicted the blessed Apostle Paul, who was sowing the same faith among the Gentiles.

I think, then, that I have sufficiently proved that the errors of the Gentiles have persisted even into Christian times, in spite of attack and refutation by learned men, endowed with great subtlety and fluency, and that this is true whether they concerned ethics or natural philosophy or the rules for discovering truth, and that, however many or manifold they may have been, they are most conspicuously shown in these two schools of thought. But now, in our time, we see that they have so far fallen silent that the schools of oratory hardly mention what their opinions may have been, and that their debates have been abolished and suppressed in even the most wordy of Greek schools, to such an extent that if now any partisans of error arise against the

---
21 Cicero, *De finibus* 5.15.43.
22 Acts 17.18.

truth—that is, against the Church of Christ—they dare not come forth to the fight except under cover of the name of Christian. From this it is clear that the philosophers of the Platonic school, making the few changes which Christian teaching requires, should bow their heads devoutly before Christ, the one unconquered King, and recognize the Word of God made man, who commands and is believed, being the Word which they feared even to utter.

To Him, my dear Dioscorus, I wish you to submit with complete devotion, and to construct no other way for yourself of grasping and holding the truth than the way constructed by Him who, as God, saw how faltering were our steps. This way is first humility, second humility, third humility, and however often you should ask me I would say the same, not because there are not other precepts to be explained, but, if humility does not precede and accompany and follow every good work we do, and if it is not set before us to look upon, and beside us to lean upon, and behind us to fence us in, pride will wrest from our hand any good deed we do while we are in the very act of taking pleasure in it. It is true that other defects have to be feared in our sins, but pride is to be feared in our very acts of virtue; otherwise, those praiseworthy acts will be lost through the desire of praise itself. And so, just as that famous orator[23] who was asked what he considered the fundamental rule of public speaking is said to have answered 'delivery,' and when asked the next important, he again said 'delivery,' and, for the third, the same 'delivery,' so, if you should ask, and as often as you should ask, about the precepts of the Christian religion, my inclination would be to answer nothing but humility, unless necessity should force me to say something else.

Our Lord Jesus Christ was humbled in order that He

---

23 Demosthenes (385-325 B.C.).

might teach this most beneficial humility, and it is directly opposed, I repeat, to that sort of ignorant knowledge—if I may use that expression—which makes us take pleasure in knowing what Anaximenes, Anaxagoras, Pythagoras[24] and Democritus thought, and other things of that kind, for the sake of appearing learned and well informed. In reality, that is far removed from learning and erudition. Whoever has learned that God is not extended or diffused through space, whether limited or unlimited, as if He should be larger in one place and smaller in another, but that He is wholly present everywhere, knows that truth is the same. No one in his sane mind would say that part of truth is in this place and part of it in that, since truth is God; nor would he be at all impressed by what anyone thinks about the unbounded air, in case anyone thinks that is God. It is of no importance to him if he does not know what bodily shape they assign to God—and they do indeed assign one which is limited on all sides—or whether it was for the purpose of refuting Anaximenes that Cicero[25] spoke as an Academic in protesting that God must necessarily have form and beauty, thinking in terms of physical appearance, because the former said that God was a corporeal being, and that His body was the air. Or did he himself think that truth had form and the incorporeal beauty which gives form to the mind, and through which we judge that all the actions of a wise man are beautiful, and, in that case, did he say

---

24 Pythagoras (581-496 B.C.) left works on geometry, music, and arithmetic. He enjoined an austere life on his disciples, and kept much of his philosophical teaching secret. He believed in the transmigration of souls.
25 *De natura deorum* 1.10.26. According to Cicero, Anaximenes had identified air with God, had said that He was produced from it, that it was vast and infinite and always in motion. Cicero then goes on to say: 'As if God could be air without any form, when it is especially fitting that God not only has form, but has the most beautiful form.' (Translated by H. Rackham, in Loeb Classical Library.)

with perfect truth—and not just to refute the other—that God must necessarily have an appearance of absolute beauty, because nothing is more beautiful than comprehensible and unchangeable truth? But when Anaximenes says that the air, which he thinks is God, came into being, he does not convince this man who understands, for He is not produced like air —that is, brought into being by any cause—for then He would not be God at all. But, the Word of God was begotten in such a different manner, God of God, that no one will understand unless God Himself reveals it to him. Who would not see how foolish that philosopher is with his various bodies when he says that air comes into being and that it is God; and who would not say that He is God by whom the air is created and who cannot be created by any other being? But, when the air is said to be always in motion, that is nothing to upset a man into thinking it is God, when he knows that all bodily activity is inferior to the activity of the mind, and that the activity of the mind is far more sluggish than the activity of the supreme and unchangeable Wisdom.

Likewise, if Anaxagoras, or anybody else, says that the mind is truth and wisdom, why should I quarrel with the man about a word? It is evident that the orderly disposition of the universe[26] comes about through a mind, and that it can be appropriately called infinite, not in spatial relations, but in a power which cannot be understood by human thought, yet not in the sense that wisdom is something formless, for it is a characteristic of bodies that those of them which are infinite are also formless. But, Cicero, it seems, in the zeal of his rebuttal, because his opponents were thinking in corporeal terms, asserts that nothing can be added to the infinite, because in that part where something is added to bodies there must necessarily be some limit to them. There-

---
26 Quoted from *De natura deorum* 1.11.

fore, he says[27] that the philosopher[28] failed to see that 'there can be no such thing as sentient and continuous activity,' that is, a contact by continuous union—'in that which is infinite,' that is, an infinite thing, as if he were treating of bodies to which nothing can be added except by spatial relations. Thus, he goes on: 'that sensation in general can only occur when the whole subject becomes sentient by the impact of a sensation.' As if Anaxagoras had said that the mind, which was the creator and regulator of the universe, had sensation such as the mind has through the body. It is evident that the whole mind becomes sentient when it perceives something through the body, for, surely, the whole mind is not kept in ignorance of whatever sensation there is. But, to this he said that the whole subject became sentient, so that he seems to deny something to what he calls the infinite mind. For, how is it wholly sentient if it is infinite? Sensation in the body begins at a particular spot; it does not pervade the whole, but reaches its own proper organ, which cannot be said of what is infinite. But, he had not spoken of bodily sensation, and that which is incorporeal is elsewhere called complete, because it is understood to be free of space limitation; consequently, it can be called both complete and infinite: complete because of its wholeness, infinite because it is not confined by spatial boundaries.

'Furthermore,' he says, 'if he intended this infinite mind to be a definite living creature, it must have some inner principle of life to justify the name,' so that this mind should be like a body and should have within it a principle of life, which should give it the name of living creature. Note that he speaks in corporeal terms, according to the mode of appearance of living creatures, on account of the thick wit, I suppose, of those against whom he is arguing. Yet, he stated

---

27 *De natura deorum* 1.11.26,27.
28 Anaxagoras.

a fact which would give them enough enlightenment if they could be made aware of it, namely, that, as every living body is in contact with a soul, it should be considered to have a principle of life and to be a living creature rather than to be a principle of life. This is what he says: 'There will be some inner principle of life to justify the name,' but he adds: 'but mind is itself the innermost principle.' Therefore, mind cannot have an inner principle of life whereby it is a living creature, because it is itself the inner principle. Suppose, then, that it has a body exteriorly, to which it is the inner principle, so as to be a living creature. This is what he says: 'Mind, therefore, will have an outer integument of body,' as if Anaxagoras said that, unless it was part of a living creature, it could not be a mind—in case he was thinking that supreme wisdom was pure mind. But, truth is not an innate quality of any living creature, because truth is universally ready to gather fruit from all living minds. Therefore, see how cleverly he concludes: 'But this he will not allow'—that is, Anaxagoras will not allow that the mind, which he calls God, should have an outer integument of body, so as to be a living creature—'yet mind naked and simple, without any material adjunct to serve as an organ of sensation,' that is, not joined to a body through which it could become sentient, 'seems to elude the capacity of our understanding.'

Nothing is more true than that this eludes the capacity of the understanding of Stoics and Epicureans, who can imagine nothing without a bodily form. When he says 'our understanding,' he means 'human understanding,' and he is careful not to say 'it eludes,' but 'it seems to elude,' for it seems to them that no one can understand it, and therefore they think there is no such thing. But, there are some whose understanding it does not elude—in so far as it is granted to man—that there is a naked and simple wisdom and truth, which is not the innate characteristic of any living being, but through which every mind everywhere, according to its ability, becomes wise and true. If Anaxagoras recognized this as a fact, and saw that it was God, and called it mind, his name does not thereby make us learned and wise, any more than does the knowledge by which he knew that this was true. And his name, because of its literary antiquity, is readily puffed up by the language-peddlers,[29] if I may speak like the soldiers. Nevertheless, truth ought not to be dear to me because it did not elude Anaxagoras, but because it is truth, even if none of them had known it.

So, then, if the knowledge of this man who may have seen the truth should not puff us up so as to make us seem learned by knowing it, but should rather strengthen us in the real truth through which we can be truly learned, how much less can the names and theories of those men whose ideas were false help our teaching and throw light on hidden truths! Indeed, if we are men, we ought to be saddened at the errors of so many famous men, if it falls to our lot to hear of them, rather than to inquire eagerly into them for the express purpose of being carried aloft on the breeze of empty ostentation among those who are ignorant of such things. How much better for me not even to have heard the name of Democritus than to reflect with sorrow that someone was considered great in his own times who thought that the gods were images which were emitted from solid substances, although they themselves were not solid, and that they, by circling around this way and that, of their own motion, and by sliding into the minds of men, make them think the image is a divine force, while the substance from which the image was given off was deemed excellent in proportion to its solidity! Therefore his theory wavered, as they say, and varied, so that sometimes

---

29 He uses the word *litteriones*, a contemptuous expression for teachers of language.

he said that a certain substance from which the images streamed was god, yet, that substance cannot be conceived except through the images which it emits and gives off, that is, those which come from that substance, which he somehow thinks is corporeal and eternal and therefore divine, while the images are carried along by a constant emanation like mist, and they come and enter into our minds so that we can think they are a god or gods. Those philosophers hold that there is no other cause for any thought of ours except these images which, when we think, come from those substances and enter into our minds; just as if there were not many, almost innumerable, thoughts of incorporeal things, such as wisdom and truth, which are comprehensible to those who know how to engage in such thinking! If those thinkers do not have such thoughts, I wonder how they can even discuss them; if they do, I wish they would tell me from what substance the image of truth is emitted, or what it is like when it comes into their minds.

However, Democritus is said to differ from Epicurus in his natural philosophy, in that he thinks there is a certain living and breathing force present at the coming together of atoms, by which force, I believe, he says[30] 'the images are endowed with divinity'—not the images of all things, but those of gods—and 'that the elements from which the mind is compounded' exist in the universe, and to these he attributes divinity, and that these are 'animate images which are wont to exercise a beneficient or harmful influence over us.' But Epicurus postulated nothing as the beginning of the world but atoms, that is, certain particles of matter so minute that they cannot be divided or perceived by either sight or touch, and by the chance meeting of these particles he says that innumerable worlds, and living beings, and the principle of life itself were produced, as well as the gods whom he

---

30 Cicero, *De natura deorum* 1.43.120.

endows with human form, and locates, not in any world, but beyond and between the worlds. He refuses absolutely to consider anything but material substances, but, in order to be able to think even about these, he says that images are given off by the very things which he supposes to be formed by the atoms, that they enter the mind, and that they are finer than the other images which appear to the eyes—for he says that this is the cause of our sight—but that they are 'vast images of such a size as to envelop and enfold the entire world.' You understand now, I think, what they mean by those images.

I wonder that Democritus did not notice that what he says is false, from the very fact that these vast images, coming into our limited mind, if it is corporeal, as they hold, are enclosed by such a very small substance but cannot touch it from every part. For, when a small object is enclosed in a large one, it cannot possibly be touched by every part of it at once. How, then, can the whole of these images be comprehended at once, if only as much of them at a time can be thought of as can come, enter into, and touch the mind, and if the whole image cannot enter into such a small object, or touch the small mind with every part of itself? Remember, I am speaking of this according to their way of thinking—for I do not believe that the mind is like that —and if Democritus thinks the mind is incorporeal, Epicurus, indeed, is the only one who can be met with that argument, but even he should have seen that it is neither necessary nor possible for an incorporeal mind to think by means of the approach and impact of corporeal images. Surely, both are equally refuted concerning the sense of sight; such vast corporeal images cannot touch our very small eyes in their totality.

But, when we ask them why one image of a certain object is seen, when innumerable ones are given off by it, they answer that it is because of the very frequency of the images as they stream and pass off, and that thus one image out of many happens to be seen by reason of their—so to speak—close crowding together. Cicero refutes this fallacy and proves that their god cannot be considered eternal by the very fact that he is imagined to consist of these innumerable images flowing and ebbing. And, when they say that the forms of the gods are eternal because there is an innumerable supply of atoms, they do not admit that the divine nature is disintegrated by that succession which occurs when some particles detach themselves from the divine body so that others may take their place. In that case, Cicero says, everything would be eternal, because that continual supply of atoms would not be lacking to anything, but would at once make good the ever-recurring losses. Then he goes on:[31] 'How could that god fail to be afraid of destruction, since he is subjected, without a moment's respite, to the buffeting and jostling of a horde of atoms that eternally assail him?' —for he says that body is buffeted which is beaten upon by the onrushing atoms and jostled by those that penetrate it. He continues: 'and since from his own person a ceaseless stream of images is given off,'—and this is enough about the images—'how can he be sure of immortality?'

There is one thing to be especially regretted in all the fantastic dreams of those who hold these opinions, that it is not enough for them to be stated, so as to be rejected by any chance argument, but the minds of the most brilliant men have undertaken this task of refuting them fully, whereas their theories should have been laughed at and repudiated by even the slowest wits. For, if you agree that there are atoms, if you agree that they buffet and jostle each other in their chance encounters, then is it right to agree with those philosophers that the atoms, rushing together by chance,

---

31 *Ibid.* 1.41.114.

fashion an object, shape it with a form, distinguish it by an appearance, beautify it with symmetry, adorn it with color, and vivify it with the breath of life? Anyone who loves to see with his mind rather than with his eyes, and who seeks the answer to this from Him by whom he was created, sees that all these things come about uniquely by the skill of Divine Providence. But, it is not to be granted in any wise that those atoms exist; see how easily this can be shown according to their own theory, leaving out the 'fineness' which, from the teaching of their authorities, is caused by the division of particles. It is true they say that all of nature is comprised of matter and space, and whatever takes place in them—by this I suppose they mean motion and contact and consequent forms. Let them say, then, in which class they would include the images which, as they think, stream from solid substances, without themselves being at all solid, and by their impact on the eyes cause us to see; on the mind, to think. They could not possibly be perceived if they are themselves substances. But, these men think that the images are able to stream from an object and make contact with the eyes or the mind, which they still say is corporeal. I ask whether the images stream from the atoms themselves. If they do, how do they continue to be atoms after some of these particles are detached? If they do not, is it possible to think something without atoms—which they vigorously deny—or how do they know about the atoms which they cannot think about? I am ashamed at this time to refute those theories, although they were not ashamed to hold them, but when they are so bold as to defend them, I am ashamed not so much of them but of the whole human race whose ears could tolerate such things.

Since the blindness of our minds is so great, by reason of the gluttonous excess of our sins, and the love of the flesh, that even those monstrous ideas could make learned men waste their time discussing them, will you, Dioscorus, or anyone gifted with an alert mind, doubt that there was any better way to seek the welfare of the human race than that Truth Itself should have ineffably and miraculously become man and, playing His part on our earth by teaching right principles and performing divine actions, should persuade us to believe, for our own advantage, what could not yet be understood by human wisdom? This is the glory we serve, this is He in whom we urge you to believe steadfastly and unswervingly. Through Him, not merely a few, but whole people who cannot make these distinctions by mere reason mock at the faith until they find the support of His saving doctrine, and by it escape from their snare into the air of the purest and clearest truth. We owe the more faithful submission to His authority when we see that no error dares today to gather its following of unlettered folk, without putting on the habiliments of Christianity, and that those only of the ancients outside Christianity get somewhat better attendance at their meetings who have writings in which they pretend to understand and foresee the coming of our Lord Jesus Christ. Moreover, those who boast of being Christians, although they are not members of Catholic unity and communion, are forced to oppose true believers, and dare to lead away the unlearned by plausible reasoning. Then the Lord comes with His great remedy of imposing faith on the nations. But, they are forced to do this, as I said, because they feel that they have an extremely low rating when their authority is compared with Catholic authority. Therefore, they try to counter the supremely strong foundations of the authority of the Church by the specious title and appeal to reason. That is the usual shameless method of all heretics. But that most clement emperor[32] has done two things: he has both strengthened the Church in her citadel of authority by widespread meetings of peoples and tribes,

---

32 Honorius, who had recently issued edicts against heretics and pagans.

and in the very sees of the Apostles has armed her with the abundant weapons of invincible reason by means of a smaller group of learned, devout, and truly spiritual men. But, the noblest course of action is for the weak to be received into the citadel of the faith as freely as possible, so that, once they are safe in its shelter, the fight may be waged for them with the strongest possible claims of reason.

But the Platonists, at the time when the errors of false philosophers were raging around them, had no divine person in whose name they could demand faith, so they chose to hide their true belief as something to be sought out rather than exposed to dishonor; when at length the Name of Christ became well known, to the wonder and consternation of earthly powers, they began to show themselves and to publish and expound Plato's doctrines. That was when the school of Plotinus[33] flourished at Rome, and had as disciples many extremely shrewd and clever men. But some of them were led astray by an attraction for the practices of magic, while others learned that the Lord Jesus Christ is the embodiment of absolute truth and unchangeable wisdom, and they came over to His service. Thus, the whole sum of authority and the light of reason is found in that one saving Name, and in His one Church, set up to restore and reform human nature.

I have not the slightest regret for having spoken to you at such great length in this letter, although you would probably prefer to hear something different. But, the more progress you make in truth, the more you will appreciate what I have said, and then you will regard as good this advice of mine which you now think is not directed to your advancement in studies. However, I have answered by brief notations, as best I could, not only those of your questions which I have treated in this letter, but almost all the others, marking them on the parchment sheets on which you sent them. If you think

---

[33] Philosopher of the Neo-Platonic school (205-270).

I have dealt too briefly with some of them, or have treated them otherwise than as you wished, you have not the right idea of the one from whom you asked these things. I have passed over all the questions about oratory and the books *On Oratory.* I should seem a queer kind of trifler if I went on to explain those. It would not be inconsistent with my position to be questioned about those other matters, if anyone proposed those difficulties to be analyzed and solved, not out of the books of Cicero, but in their own right; of the rest, such things are not in accord with our profession. Indeed, I should not have done all these if your man, at his coming, had not found me away from Hippo, where I had gone after an illness which I had. In fact, on those same days I had a return of fever and ill health. That accounts for this letter being sent to you later than it might have been. I ask you to send me back word how it has reached you.

119. Consentius[1] to the holy lord and blessed prelate, Augustine (410)

Some time ago, in a short conversation, I reminded the holy Bishop Alypius, your brother, a man esteemed by me for all his gifts of mind, of the nature of my request, hoping that he would do me the favor of helping on my prayer to you. But, as the circumstance which has forced you to go to the country has cheated me of your company,[2] I thought it better to put my request into a letter than to suffer suspense of mind. If you

---
1 If he is the same as the addressee of Letter 205, the latter was living in 420 among Priscillianists, who were numerous in Spain. He may have been a monk at Lerins or St. Victor, monasteries founded on islands off the south coast of France. (He speaks of 'these islands.') To him Augustine addressed the treatise *Contra Mendacium*; Cf. *Fathers of the Church* 16 (New York 1952).
2 Augustine mentioned his ill health, at the end of Letter 118.

see fit to grant me what I ask, I think the very quiet of the place where you are now staying will be a help to your understanding, as you search into the highest of mysteries. To be exact, I had laid down for myself the principle that a divine truth is to be grasped by faith more than by reason, for, if the faith of the holy Church were attained by the exercise of reason and not by the virtue of belief, no one but philosophers or orators would possess eternal happiness. But, because it has pleased God, 'Who hath chosen the weak things of this world that He may confound the strong, by the foolishness of our preaching to save them that believe,'[3] it is not so much a question of asking a reason of God as it is of following the authority of the saints. Surely, the Arians[4] who think the Son is younger—where we confess Him begotten—would not persist in this impiety, nor would the Macedonians,[5] as far as in them lies, expel the Holy Spirit from the citadel of Divinity—whom we believe to be neither begotten nor unbegotten—if they were willing to adapt their faith to the Holy Scriptures rather than to their own reasoning. But, if our Father, who alone knows the secret of hearts, who has the key of David,[6] has granted you, admirable man that you are, to pierce through the framework of the heavens by the luminous contemplation of your heart, 'with open face' as it is written, 'to behold the glory of the Lord,'[7] do you, as far as He shall give you the gift of utterance, as He has given you depth of thought, set forth for us in words some part of His ineffable substance, and strive to draw a likeness of Him, to the extent of your ability and with His help. Without you as leader and master in this great undertaking, our mind would shrink from looking upon such,

---

[3] 1 Cor 27.21.
[4] Cf. Letter 118 n. 11.
[5] *Ibid.*
[6] Apoc. 3.7.
[7] 2 Cor. 3.18.

and its, so to speak, inflamed eyes would be struck blind by the splendor of such great light. Enter, then, into that dark cloud of the mysteries of God, which shrouds Him from our sight, and set me right, first in my own mind, and then in my writings, in regard to those points which I know I have explained incorrectly; for, indeed, I would rather follow the authority of your Holiness than be led astray by a false concept of reason as formed in my heart.

For myself, in my still cautious simplicity, hearing and believing that the Lord Jesus is light of light, as it is written: 'Show forth his salvation from day to day,'[8] and in the Book of Wisdom of Solomon: '[He] is the brightness of eternal light,'[9] although I believed of God what it is lawful to believe, I was not able to believe, as is fitting, that the greatness of any unimaginable light is infinite, something of which the human mind, however lofty its thought, can neither judge the nature, nor measure the extent, nor picture the appearance. Nevertheless, I believed that there is something, whatever it may be, of which the form is incomparable, the beauty unimaginable, which Christ at least beholds with even bodily eyes; and toward the end of my first book—as you, no doubt, condescend to remember—wishing to prove that the Lord Jesus Christ, in becoming man, possesses such divine power that the mortal flesh which He assumed became immortal, I taught that in His vital organs only His mortality had died, whereupon the knotty point of the question was thus proposed to me: 'If,' he said, 'the manhood which Christ assumed was changed into God, it should not have a locality. Why, then, after the Resurrection, did He say: "Do not touch Me for I am not yet ascended to my Father'?"[10]

For this reason I strove to prove that Christ is everywhere—

---
8 Ps. 95.2.
9 Wisd. 7.26.
10 John 20.17.

in His power, but not in His Body; in His divinity, but not in His flesh—and I wrote in this wise about the unity of God and the Trinity of Persons: 'God,' I said, 'is one, the Persons are three. God is undivided, the Persons are distinct; God is within all things and beyond all things; He surrounds the outermost, He fills the middle, He surpasses the highest; He fills all space beyond the universe and throughout the universe; the Persons, however, are always distinct from each other by their special character; they are not confusedly intermingled. There is, therefore, one God and He is everywhere, both because there is none other than He, and because there is no empty space where another could be. All things are filled with God, and there is nothing outside God. He is in the Father, He is in the Son, He is in the Holy Spirit; yet not for this are the Father and the Son and the Holy Spirit several gods, but there is only one God, and the Son is not the Father, the Holy Spirit is not the Son. The Father is in the Son, the Son in the Father, the Holy Spirit in both, because the one indivisible God dwells in the Three, who are distinct in number, not in rank; in Person, not in power. All that the Father has the Son has, and what the Son has the Father has, and what both have the Holy Spirit has, because they possess the substance of Godhead which is one, not divided; the same, not equal. Therefore, one does not excel the other in majesty or age, because what is entire cannot be divided, and there is nothing in plenitude which can divide plenitude, so as to allot a larger portion to one and a lesser to the other. But in the Persons it is not thus, because the Person of the Father is not that of the Son; the Person of the Son is not the same as that of the Holy Spirit. There is one power which the triune power possesses, one substance in which these that are Three subsist. Therefore, the Father and the Son and the Holy Spirit are everywhere in majesty, because They are one; but in Person They are only in Themselves because They are three. And developing the rest in this manner, I brought my argument to the point where I asserted that the Persons are everywhere, but in that majesty which is one and the same above the heavens, and across the seas, and below the depths of hell. From this I showed how we should understand that the manhood which Christ assumed, when changed into God, did not lose the nature it had taken, so that we could not believe there was a fourth person.

But it is allowed to you, good sir, to enter heaven itself, I think, by the penetrating power of your thought—for he speaks truly who says: 'Blessed are the clean of heart for they shall see God,'[11]—and as you lift up your pure heart above all the stars to that height of contemplation, you say that God must not be thought of in the terms of a material body, for, if anyone were to form an image in his mind of a light, a thousand times brighter and more intense than our sun, he could not thereby achieve any likeness of God, because all that can be seen is material. But, just as we cannot conceive of justice or piety in corporeal terms—unless, perhaps, we picture them to ourselves in some female form as the pagans foolishly do— so God is to be thought of without the representation of any mental image, as far as it is possible for us to do so. However, for my part, I can scarcely as yet grasp the fine point of your argument, and it seemed to me that justice has no living substance, and therefore I cannot think of God, whose nature is living, as anything like justice, because justice does not exist in itself but in us; rather, we live according to justice. Yet, justice has nothing like self-existence, unless, perhaps, we affirm that justice is not a part of this human excellence, and that only that which is God is justice.

Therefore, I should like to be reassured, not only in these words, but in a really long letter, for it is not right that only my feet should be turned back by your warning from the path

---

11 Matt. 5.8.

of error on which many of us have entered. For, many in these islands in which we live, while making for the road by a straight embankment, run into the twisting bypath of error, and will there be any Augustine whose authority they would respect, whose teaching they would believe, by whose genius they would be overcome? Or would you, perhaps, in your fatherly affection, prefer to guide me by a private warning rather than rebuke me as one of the company on the wrong path? But, as I wish to run rather for the advantage of my soul than for the praise of the world, your refutation is not without use to me, just as it is also not unpleasant, especially as it is likely to win for me and others life and praise at the same time. No one could be so unjust a judge that he would choose to rate me as a fool because at one time I followed the wrong road, rather than shrink from judging me because I followed the right road. They are not to be adjudged fools whom the Apostle Paul warns not to run as at an uncertainty, saying: 'So run that you may obtain.'[12] Therefore, that wrong road on which we run is not only to be abandoned by us but is to be blocked and cut off by you, lest it deceive men by the false pretense of attraction. If I am not deceived, you have been chosen, not to read the books published by me, but to correct those in need of approval. In that letter which I prefixed to my books as a sort of brief preface, words of this tenor are found: 'A sentence of the blessed bishop Augustine,' I said, 'has been pleased to steady the tossing bark of my faith.' Then why, sir, pillar as you are of the doctrine which is in Christ, do you hesitate to give an open refutation to your son, who stands in need of correction about the rest of the question? Indeed, the anchor of your sentence cannot steady us securely unless it grips more deeply. The question is not a slight one, nor is the fault, by which we have not only failed to do good, but even—as you so strongly pointed out—my

---
12 1 Cor. 9.26,24.

thought, by its blindness, risks the guilt of a sort of idolatry. I should like this to be discussed by you carefully and skillfully, so that the clear light of your learning and genius may so drive the cloud from my mind that what I cannot now understand I may be able to see with the eyes of my heart, once it has been illumined by the brightness of your intellect. May you be safe and happy, holy lord, most blessed prelate, and may you be mindful of us when you possess the heavenly kingdom.

120. Augustine gives greeting in the Lord to Consentius, his most beloved brother, worthy of honor in the heart of Christ (c. 410)

I asked you to come to us because I have found much pleasure in your natural ability as shown in your books. For that reason I wanted you here with us, not far away from us, to read certain works of mine which I thought indispensable to you, so that you could easily ask me in person about what you might not have understood completely, Thus, from my explanation and our mutual exchange of views—as far as the Lord should grant me to give and you to receive—you should personally recognize and correct anything in your books that might need correction. Indeed, you are a man of such ability that you are able to express what you think, and you are, besides, so honest and so humble that you deserve to think what is true. But I am of the same opinion, and this should not displease you, as I was when I advised you to read privately what I have composed, to make notes of the passages which give you trouble, and to come to me and ask me about each of them. I urge you to do what you have not yet done. It would be allowable for you to draw back and feel some objection to doing this if you had once wished to do it and had found me hard to approach. In addition to that, when I had heard that you were wearing yourself out over very unreliable manuscripts, I also said that in reading my works you should use the best-edited copies you could find.

As to your request that I carefully and skillfully discuss the question of the Trinity, that is, of the unity of the Godhead and the distinction of the Persons, so that, as you say, the clear light of my learning and genius should so drive the clouds from your mind, that what you cannot now understand you may be able to see, in some sort, with the eyes of your heart,[1] see first whether this request is consistent with your earlier statement. In the first part of that same letter, in which you make the request, you say that you have laid down a principle for yourself that truth is to be grasped by faith more than by reason. 'For, if the faith of the holy Church,' you say, 'were attained by the exercise of reason and not by the virtue of belief, no one but philosophers or orators would possess eternal happiness. But, because it has pleased God,' you say, "Who hath chosen the weak things of this world that He may confound the strong, by the foolishness of our preaching to save them that believe," it is not so much a question of asking a reason as it is of following the authority of the saints.' See, then, according to these words whether you should not in this matter, which is the very heart of our faith, follow only the authority of the saints, and not ask me to make it intelligible to you by reason. For, when I begin to induct you, so to speak, into the understanding of such a great mystery—and if God does not aid us interiorly, I shall not be able to do so—I shall not do anything else in my discussion but give you such reason as I can. Consequently, if you are not unreasonable in asking of me or of any other teacher, to make you understand what you believe, you should change your statement of principle,

---
1 Quoted indirectly from Letter 119 by Consentius.

not to lessen the value of faith, but so that you may see by the light of reason what you now hold by faith.

God forbid that He should hate in us that faculty by which He made us superior to all other living beings. Therefore, we must refuse so to believe as not to receive or seek a reason for our belief, since we could not believe at all if we did not have rational souls. So, then, in some points that bear on the doctrine of salvation, which we are not yet able to grasp by reason—but we shall be able to sometime—let faith precede reason, and let the heart be cleansed by faith so as to receive and bear the great light of reason; this is indeed reasonable. Therefore the Prophet said with reason: 'If you will not believe, you will not understand';[2] thereby he undoubtedly made a distinction between these two things and advised us to believe first so as to be able to understand whatever we believe. It is, then, a reasonable requirement that faith precede reason, for, if this requirement is not reasonable, then it is contrary to reason, which God forbid. But, if it is reasonable that faith precede a certain great reason which cannot yet be grasped, there is no doubt that, however slight the reason which proves this, it does precede faith.

That is why the Apostle warns us that we ought to be ready to give an answer to anyone who asks us a reason for our faith and hope,[3] since, if an unbeliever asks me a reason for my faith and hope, and I see that he cannot accept it until he believes, I give him that very reason, so that he may see how absurd it is for him to ask a reason for things which he cannot grasp until he believes. But, if a believer asks a reason so that he may understand what he believes, his mental ability is to be considered and then, when the reason for his faith has been given according to it, he may draw as much understanding as he can, more if he is capable of more, less if

---

2 Isa. 7.9.
3 1 Peter 3.15.

he is less capable, but with the provision that, to the extent that he attains to the fullness and perfection of knowledge, he does not withdraw from the way of faith. On this point the Apostle says: 'And if in anything you be otherwise minded, this also God will reveal to you; nevertheless whereunto we are come, let us walk in the same.'[4] If, then, we are faithful now, we shall attain to the way of faith, and, if we do not leave it, we shall unfailingly come not only to a great understanding of incorporeal and unchanging things, such as cannot be reached by all in this life, but even to the height of contemplation, which the Apostle calls 'face to face.'[5] For, some have very little knowledge, yet by walking with great perseverance in the way of faith they attain to that most blessed contemplation; whereas others, although they know even now what the invisible, unchanging, and incorporeal nature is, and what way leads to the abode of such happiness, cannot attain to it because the way, which is Christ crucified, seems foolish to them, and they refuse to withdraw to the innermost chamber of that repose by whose light their mind is stunned as by a far-shining radiance.

There are, however, some things which we are not able to believe when we hear them, because we do not apply our faith to them, yet when a reason for them is given, we recognize it as true. Thus, none of the miracles of God is believed by infidels because the reason for them is not evident; as a matter of fact, there are things for which no reason can be given, but that does not mean there is none, for God made nothing in the universe without reason. Of certain of His wonderful works it is better sometimes for the reason to be hidden; otherwise, our minds, weighed down with weariness, might hold them cheap if we had knowledge of their causes. There are others, and they are many, who are more impressed

---

4 Cf. Phil. 3.15,16.
5 1 Cor. 13.12.

by wonder at the objects than by a knowledge of their causes, and, when miracles cease to be wonderful, they have to be roused to faith in the invisible by visible wonders. Thus they may be cleansed and purified by charity, and may return to the point they had left when they ceased to wonder, through familiarity with truth. In the theatre, men wonder at the rope-dancer, and take pleasure in the musicians: in the former case, the difficulty of the act rouses awe; in the latter, pleasure sustains and nourishes them.

I should like to say these things to rouse your faith to a love of understanding to which true reason leads the mind and for which faith prepares it. For, that reasoning which argues about the Trinity, which is God, that the Son is not co-eternal with the Father, or that He is of another substance, and that the Holy Spirit is unlike Him in some way and therefore inferior, and that reasoning which claims that the Father and the Son are of one and the same substance, but the Holy Spirit is of another, are to be avoided and detested, not because they are reasoning but because they are false reasoning; for, if the reasoning were true, it would surely not go wrong. Therefore, just as you ought not to give up all speech because there is false speech, so you ought not to turn against all reasoning because there is false reasoning. I would say the same of wisdom: that wisdom is not to be avoided because there is also false wisdom, to which Christ crucified is foolishness, though He is 'the power of God and the wisdom of God,' and, therefore, 'by the foolishness of our preaching it pleased God to save them that believe; for the foolishness of God is wiser than men.'[6] This truth could not be made acceptable to some of the philosophers and orators who followed a way that was not the true one, but an imitation of the true one, and who deceived themselves and others on it. But by others it could be accepted, and to those who could accept it Christ crucified was

---

6 1 Cor. 1.18,24,21,25.

neither a stumbling-block nor foolishness: among them are those that are called, both Jews and Greeks, 'to whom he is the power of God and the wisdom of God.'[7] In this way, that is, in the faith of Christ crucified, those who were able by the grace of God to embrace His upright code of conduct, even though they are called philosophers or orators, certainly confessed with humble piety that the fishermen[8] who preceded them were far superior to themselves, both in the steadfast strength of their belief, and in the unerring truth of their understanding. For, when they had learned that the foolish and weak things of the world had been chosen for this purpose that the wise and strong things might be confounded, and when they understood that their own wisdom was folly and their strength weakness, they were confounded for their own salvation and made foolish and weak, that by the foolish and weak thing of God, which is wiser and stronger than men, they might be chosen among the foolish and weak things and might become truly wise and effectually strong.[9]

But, the devout believer is ashamed of any but the truest reasoning; therefore, let us not be slow to overthrow a sort of idolatry which the frailty of human thought is prone to set up in our hearts, in consequence of our customary dealing with visible things, and let us not make bold to believe that the Trinity, which we worship as invisible, incorporeal, and unchangeable, is like three great living objects, which though immense and beautiful, are bounded by the proper limits of their own spaces, touching each other because they are ranged close together, either with one of them in the middle, so as to separate the two joined to it on either side, or in the fashion of a triangle, with each one touching the other two, and none separated from any. Let us not believe, either, that the huge

---
[7] 1 Cor. 1.24.
[8] The Apostles who were 'fishers of men.'
[9] 1 Cor. 1.27,29,25.

mass of these three great Persons, which are limited on however large a scale from above and below and round about, have a single godhead as if it were a fourth person, not like any one of them, whereas it is common to all as the divinity of all and in all, and wholly in each one; through which sole Godhead the same Trinity is said to be God. And we must not believe that His three Persons are nowhere but in heaven, while that Divinity is not in any one place but is present everywhere, and for that reason it would be right to say that God is in heaven and on earth, because of the Godhead which is everywhere and is common to the Three, but it would not be right to say that the Father is on earth or the Son or the Holy Spirit, since the abode of this Trinity is only in heaven. When true reasoning begins to break down that train of carnal thought, that vain imagining, with His interior help and light—since He does not dwell in our hearts with such idols—we make haste to shatter them and, so to speak, to shake our faith free of them, so that we do not allow even the dust of such fancies to remain there.

Therefore, should we not listen in vain to what is true, unless faith which clothes us with piety had preceded reason, through whose outward argument, together with the light of truth within us, we are roused to perceive that these idols are false? Thus, when faith acts in its own sphere, reason, following after, finds something of what faith was seeking, and true reason is to be preferred to false reason because it makes us understand what we believe, but faith in things not yet understood is undoubtedly even more to be preferred. It is better to believe in something true but not yet seen, than to take the false thing one sees for true. For, faith has its own eyes with which it sees, so to speak, that what it does not yet see is true, and with which it most certainly sees that it does not yet see what it believes. Moreover, he who now understands by a true reasoning what he only believed a while ago is emphatically to be preferred to the one who wishes to understand now what he believes, but, if he does not also have a desire for the things which are to be understood, he considers them an object of belief only, and he fails to grasp the advantage of faith, for a devout faith does not wish to be without hope and without charity. So, then, a faithful man ought to believe what he does not yet see, so as to hope for and love the fulfillment of vision.

As a matter of fact, we hold things visible but past by faith alone, since there is no hope of seeing again what has slipped away with time. They are regarded as finished and gone by, as it is expressed in the words: 'Christ died once for our sins, and rose again and dieth now no more: death shall no more have dominion over him.'[10] The things which are not yet in existence, but are to come, such as the resurrection of our spiritual bodies, are believed in such wise that we hope to see them, but they cannot be experienced now. And of the things which are such that they are neither past nor future, but remain forever, some are invisible, like justice and wisdom, and some are visible, like the Body of Christ, now immortal. But, 'the invisible things are clearly seen, being understood,'[11] and in that way they are also seen in a special and appropriate manner. And, when they are seen, they are much more certain than the objects of the bodily sense, but they are said to be invisible because they cannot, in any way, be seen by these mortal eyes. On the other hand, those living things which are visible and perpetual can be seen even by these mortal eyes, if they are made manifest; as the Lord showed Himself to the disciples after His Resurrection,[12] and even after His Ascension, to the Apostle Paul and to the deacon Stephen.[13]

---

10 1 Peter 3.18; Rom. 6.9,10.
11 Rom. 1.20.
12 Matt. 28.9,10; Mark 16.5,7,9; 12-14; Luke 24.4-7; 15.36; John 20.14,19; 26; 21.1.
13 Acts 9.3-5; 7.55.

Therefore, we believe in those visible and perpetual things in such wise that, even if they are not manifested to us, we hope we shall see them some day, and we do not make an effort to understand them by reasoning and thought, except that we make a distinction in our thought between these visible things and invisible ones, and we imagine to ourselves in thought what they are like, although we know quite well that they are not known to us. Thus, I think in one way of Antioch, a city unknown to me, and in another way of Carthage, which I do know; my mind makes an image of the former but recalls the latter. There is, however, no doubt in my mind that my belief about the former is based on the evidence of numerous witnesses, but about the latter on my own sense-impressions. Nevertheless, we do not form an image of justice and wisdom or anything else of this sort, in any other way, but we see them differently; we behold these invisible qualities by a simple intellectual attention of the mind and reason, without any forms or physical bulk, without any features or appearance of parts, without any locality, whether limited or of unbounded space. The light itself by which we distinguish all this, by which we are made aware of what we believe without knowing it, what we hold as objects of knowledge, what physical shape we recall, what one we imagine, what the sense-organ perceives, what the mind imagines in the likeness of a body, what is present to the intellect as certain yet totally unlike any physical object, this light by which all these mental acts are differentiated, is not diffused in any special place, like the brilliance of this sun or of any physical light, and does not illumine our mind as if it were a visible brightness, but it shines invisibly and indescribably, yet intelligibly, and it is as certain a fact itself as are the realities which we see as certain by means of it.

We have, then, three classes of objects which are seen: the first, of material things, such as heaven and earth and everything the physical sense-organ perceives or experiences in them; the second, of representations of material things, such as those we picture to ourselves in thought by means of our imagination, whether we behold them inwardly as remembered or as imagined objects. In this class are visions, such as occur either in sleep or in some state of ecstasy, and are presented in these spatial dimensions. The third class is different from both the former, and consists of things which are not corporeal and have no corporeal representation: for example, wisdom, which is perceived by the understanding and by whose light all these other things are correctly estimated. But, in which class are we to believe that the Trinity, which we wish to know about, is included? Obviously, in some one of them or in none. If in some one, it must be the one which is superior to the other two, namely, the one in which wisdom is included. But, if His gift is in us, and if it is a lesser thing than that supreme and unchangeable wisdom which is said to be of God—I suppose we should not rate the giver as lower than his gift—if some of His light is in us and is called our wisdom, in so far as we can grasp anything of Him, 'through a glass in a dark manner,'[14] then we must distinguish that wisdom from all material objects and from all representations of material objects.

But, if the Trinity is not to be included in any of those classes, and if it is so far invisible that it is not seen by the mind, we have no reason at all to believe that it is like either material objects or the representations of material objects. It is not in the beauty of its shape nor in its immensity that it surpasses material things, but in the difference and complete dissimilarity of its nature. It is also remote from any comparison with our spiritual goods, such as wisdom, justice, charity, chastity, and other like qualities, which we certainly do not value for their physical size, nor do we endow them in our

---

14 1 Cor. 13.12.

thoughts with bodily shapes, but, when we understand them properly, we behold them by the light of our mind without bodily attributes or any likeness of bodily attributes. How much more, then, must we refrain from any comparison of physical qualities and dimensions in thinking of the Trinity! But the Apostle is witness that our mind is not to shrink away from it entirely, when he says: 'For the invisible things of him from the creation of the world are clearly seen, being understood by the things that are made; his eternal power also and divinity.'[15] Consequently, since the same Trinity created both body and soul, it is evidently superior to both. And, if the soul so considered, especially the human, rational, and intellectual soul, which was made in His image, does not elude our thoughts and understanding; if, by mind and understanding, we are able to grasp its excellence, which is to say, the mind itself and the understanding, it will not perhaps be unreasonable for us to try to raise our soul to the understanding of its Creator, with His help. But, if it fails in that and falls back on itself, let it be satisfied with devout faith, as long as it is a wanderer from the Lord,[16] until He acts to fulfill His promise in man, as the Apostle says: 'Who is able to do all things more abundantly than we desire or understand.'[17]

In view of all this, I want you in the meantime to read the many works we have written on this question, and even those which we now have in hand, and which we have not been able to finish because of the importance of the matter and its extreme difficulty. At this time you must hold with unshaken faith that the Father, the Son, and the Holy Spirit are the Trinity, but they are only one God; not that the divinity, which they have in common, is a sort of fourth

---

15 Rom. 1.20.
16 2 Cor. 5.6.
17 Eph. 3.20.

person, but that the Godhead is ineffably and inseparably a Trinity; that the Father alone begot the Son, and the Son alone was begotten of the Father, but the Holy Spirit is of the Father and the Son. If any sort of corporeal image comes to your mind when you think these thoughts, repudiate it, refuse it, cast it out, reject it, put it to flight, for it is no slight approach to the thought of God if, before we are able to know what He is, we begin to know what He is not. Love this knowledge very deeply, for the Holy Scriptures themselves, which inspire us with faith, the forerunner of knowledge, can be of no use to you unless you understand them rightly. All the heretics who accept their authority think they are following them while they are following their own errors, and they are heretics precisely because they do not understand the Scriptures, not because they despise them.

But you, my dearest, pray ardently and faithfully that the Lord may give you understanding; thus, whatever you gain from without by the care of a teacher or master may be fruitful, since 'neither he that planteth is anything, nor he that watereth, but God that giveth the increase.'[18] He it is to whom we say: 'Our Father who art in heaven,'[19] not because He is there and not here, He is wholly everywhere by His incorporeal presence, but because He is said to dwell in those to whose filial devotion He is present, and these are especially in heaven, where our conversation also is,[20] if our mouth answers truthfully that we have lifted up our heart.[21] For, even if we should give a carnal sense to what is written: 'Heaven is my throne and the earth my footstool,'[22] we should believe that He is both here and there, although not

---

18 1 Cor. 3.7.
19 Matt. 6.9.
20 Phil. 3.20.
21 The response to *Sursum corda* (Lift up your hearts), in the Preface to the Mass, is *Habemus ad Dominum* (We have them lifted up to the Lord).
22 Isa. 66.1.

wholly there because His feet would be here, nor wholly here because the upper parts of His Body would be there. That carnal thought should be again shaken out of us by what is written of Him, that 'He hath measured the heaven with his palm, and the earth with his fist.'[23] Now, who could sit in the space of his own palm, or set his feet in as much room as his fist encloses? It might be, perhaps, that this carnal view goes only so far as to think it inadequate to attribute human limbs to the substance of God, without fancying them as something monstrous, such as a palm wider than the thighs, and a fist larger than the two feet together. But this is said so that, when such things are contradictory if we take them in a carnal sense, we may be warned thereby to think of them as ineffably spiritual.

For this reason, even if we think of the Lord's Body, which was raised from the tomb and ascended into heaven, only as having a human appearance and parts, we are not to think that He sits at the right hand of the Father[24] in such wise as that the Father should seem to sit at His left hand. Indeed, in that bliss which surpasses human understanding, the only right hand and the same right hand is a name for that same bliss. Consequently, those words which He spoke to Mary after His Resurrection: 'Do not touch me, for I am not yet ascended to my Father,'[25] are not to be taken in such a foolish sense that we should suppose Him willing to be touched by women after He had ascended, since He allowed Himself to be touched by men before He ascended. But, evidently, when He said this to Mary, who is a figure of the Church, He wished it to be understood that He had then ascended to His Father when the Church recognized Him as equal to His Father and touched Him by means of its

23 Cf. Isa. 40.12.
24 Mark 16.19.
25 John 20.17.

saving faith, because, if men thought Him to be only what He appeared in the flesh, they would not touch Him to their own good. Thus the heretic Photinus[26] touched Him when he believed that Christ was only man.

It may be that some better and more exact meaning can be read into those words of the Lord, but that opinion is to be unhesitatingly rejected by which it is held that the substance of the Father, whereby the Father is one Person of the Trinity, is in Heaven, but the divinity is everywhere and not in heaven only—as if the Father were one thing and His divinity something else, something which He shares with the Son and the Holy Spirit. Thus, the Trinity itself would be somehow corporeal and subject to corporeal space. For, if their nature existed—and God forbid that in the Father or the Son or the Holy Spirit the nature should be different from the substance—if their nature could exist, doubtless it could not exist more largely for anyone of Them than it does in their substance, but, if the substance is different from Themselves, it is another substance, and this plainly is a completely false belief.

If, perchance, you do not understand what difference there is between nature and substance, you surely grasp this more easily: that the divinity of the Trinity, which is thought to be something other than the Trinity—and the reason why we say there are not three gods but one God is that it is common to the Three—is either the substance or it is not the substance. If it is the substance, and it is different from the Father or the Son or the Holy Spirit, or the same Trinity all together, doubtless it is another substance; and truth recoils from this idea and rejects it. But, if that divinity is not the substance of God, yet is itself God because it is everywhere wholly

---

[26] Bishop of Sirmium, a disciple of Marcellus, bishop of Ancyra, whose doctrine verged on Sabellianism and was condemned at the synod of Sardica in 343.

present, it is not that Trinity, and therefore God is not a substance—would any Catholic say that? Likewise, if that divinity is not a substance, and the Trinity is one God according to it because it is one God in Three, we should not say that the Father and the Son and the Holy Spirit are of one substance, but of one divinity, which is not a substance. You know that in the Catholic faith it is the true and firm belief that the Father and the Son and the Holy Spirit are one God, while remaining a Trinity, because they are inseparably of one and the same substance, or, if this is a better word, essence. For, some of ours, and especially the Greeks, say that the Trinity, which is God, is rather of one essence than of one substance, thinking or understanding that there is some distinction between these two terms. But, there is no need of discussing that now, because, even if we say that the divinity, which is supposed to be distinct from the Trinity itself, is not substance but essence, the conclusion will be equally false. For, if it is something distinct from the Trinity, the essence will be another different thing, and God forbid that a Catholic should think that! It remains for us, then, to believe that the Trinity is of one substance and that the essence is nothing else than the Trinity itself. Let us make what progress we can in this life toward beholding the Trinity, which we shall see 'through a glass in a dark manner.'[27] But, when we begin to have a spiritual body as we are promised in the resurrection, let us see it even in the body, either by an intellectual vision or in some miraculous manner, since the grace of the spiritual body is indescribable. We shall then see it according to our capacity, without limitations of space, not larger in one part and smaller in another, since it is not a body and it is wholly present everywhere.

You said in your letter that it seems, or seemed, to you that

---
27 1 Cor. 13.12.

justice has no living substance and therefore you cannot think of God, whose nature is living, as anything like justice, because 'justice,' as you say, 'does not exist in itself but in us; rather, we live according to it. Yet, justice itself has nothing like self-existence.'[28] Look into this now and answer for yourself whether it is correct to say that life itself lives, which is the principle of life for everything which we rightly speak of as living. I think you now see how senseless it is to say that life makes other things live but does not live itself. Now, then, if life, the living principle of all living things, is itself preeminently alive, recall, please, what the divine Scripture says about dead souls; surely you will find that they are sinful, impious, unfaithful. We grant that these souls are the life-principle for the bodies of the wicked, of whom it is said: 'Let the dead bury their dead,'[29] and that it is there understood that even sinful souls are not without some sort of life; otherwise, their bodies could not derive life from them, if they did not have some sort of life, which they cannot be wholly deprived of, since they are rightly called immortal. However, these souls are called dead because they have lost justice, and because justice is a truer and greater life than any other sort of life in living souls however immortal; it is a sort of life of lives, and when it is found in bodies, the very bodies are alive, whereas they have no life of themselves. Therefore, if souls cannot live in any way soever except in themselves, because their bodies depend on them for life, and when abandoned by them they die, how much more truly is justice to be understood as living in itself, since souls live by it, and are said to be dead when they lose it, although they do not cease to live by some inferior life.

This justice, moreover, which lives in itself is undoubtedly God, and has an immutable life. Thus, while life is self-

---

28 Quoted from Letter 119.
29 Matt. 8.22.

existent, but becomes life in us when we share in it in some way, so, while justice is self-existent, it becomes justice in us when we live virtuously by clinging to it, and we are more or less virtuous as we cling to it more or less strongly. Thus it is written of the only-begotten Son of God, since He is unquestionably the wisdom and justice of God and is always self-existent, 'who of God is made unto us wisdom and justice and sanctification and redemption, that, as it is written, he that glorieth may glory in the Lord.'[30] You saw this yourself when you added the words: 'Unless, perhaps, we affirm that justice is not a part of this human excellence, and that only that which is God is justice.' Indeed, that supreme God is true justice or that true God is supreme justice; meantime, our justice in this pilgrimage is to hunger and thirst for it,[31] and our full justice in eternity will be to be filled with it hereafter. So, then, we are not to think that God is like our justice, but we must think rather that we shall be more like God the more we are able to become just by a greater share in His justice.

If, then, we have to guard against thinking that God is like our justice, since the light which shines is incomparably superior to that which it shines upon, how much more must we guard against believing that He is something lesser and, in a sense, dimmer than our justice is. For, what else is justice when it is in us, or any virtue which makes us live well and wisely, but the beauty of the interior man? Certainly it is in this beauty, rather than in the body, that we are made to the image of God. Hence, we are told: 'Be not conformed to this world, but be reformed in the newness of your mind that you may prove what is the good and the acceptable and the perfect will of God.'[32] In differentiating or thinking about

---
30 1 Cor. 1.30,31.
31 Matt. 5.6.
32 Rom. 12.2.

corporeal objects we endow them with size and with separate parts, which occupy different spaces, but in speaking of the mind we endow it with an intellectual excellence, such as justice, by which we know or wish it to be beautiful. It is with this beauty that we are re-formed to the image of God, and the beauty of this God, who has formed and re-formed us to His image, is to have no supposition of corporeal size, but we are to believe that He is incomparably more beautiful than the minds of the just, as He is also incomparably more just. I have written to your Charity at greater length, perhaps, than you expected or than an ordinary letter requires, but in treating a subject of such importance this is no more than a brief summary, not intended to satisfy your learned mind, but enough to stimulate you to revise your own writings, after you have been carefully informed by reading and hearing other works, and this will be well done in proportion as it is humbly and faithfully done.

121. Paulinus[1] to Augustine (c.410)

The bearer of letters is in a hurry to get to his ship and has affected me with his hurry, so I am setting down in great haste a few points on certain matters which have come into my mind, so that you may not have to answer me without advance payment. If these thoughts are clear, whereas they seem obscure to me, let none of the wise sons—with, probably, some of ours—who stand around you at the hour of reading laugh at my foolishness; rather, let the kindness of fraternal charity do me the favor of enlightening me, so that I may become a partner of those who see, of those whose minds,

---

[1] The letter has no formal address. Paulinus, Bishop of Nola, also wrote Letters 25, 30, 32, 94, 347. Augustine answers this one in Letter 149.

illumined by your learning, 'Consider the wondrous things of the law,'[2] of the Lord.

Tell me, then, blessed master in Israel, what is meant by the words of Psalm 15: 'To the saints who are in his land, he hath made wonderful all his desires among them; their infirmities were multiplied, afterward they made haste.'[3] What saints does he mean, who are saints on the earth? Surely, he does not mean the Jews who, as 'children of the flesh' of Abraham, not 'children of the promise,' are shut out from the 'seed which was called in Isaac,'[4] but he calls them saints on earth because they are holy according to their physical origin, who are earthly in life and thought, who 'mind earthly things'[5] and grow old 'in the oldness of the letter,'[6] by their carnal observance; not reborn into a new creature, because they have not received Him through whom 'the old things are passed away and all things are made new.'[7] Perhaps He calls them saints in this psalm in the same way that He calls them just in the Gospel when He says: 'I am not come to call the just, but sinners,'[8] that is, those just who boast of the holiness of their race and the letter of the Law,[9] to whom it is said: 'Do not boast of your father Abraham, for God is able of these stones to raise up children to Abraham.'[10] This type is exemplified in the Pharisee[11] who recited his good works in the Temple, as if recalling them to an ignorant Lord, not praying to be heard, but demanding the reward due to his good conduct. Yet, this was displeasing to God because he

---

2 Ps. 118.18.
3 Cf Ps. 15.3,4.
4 Rom. 9.8,7.
5 Phil. 3.19.
6 Rom. 7.6.
7 2 Cor. 5.17; Apoc. 21.4,5; Gal. 6.15.
8 Matt. 9.13.
9 Rom. 2.23.
10 Matt. 3.9; Luke 3.8.
11 Luke 18.10-14.

tore down by his pride what he had built up by his justice; he did not do this silently, but at the top of his voice; and it is evident that he did not speak to divine ears, because he wished to be heard by men. Hence, he was not pleasing to God because he was pleasing to himself. 'For the Lord hath scattered the bones of men pleasing to themselves, they have been confounded,' he says, 'because He hath despised them,'[12] who 'does not despise a contrite and humbled heart.'[13]

Finally, in the same parable of the Gospel[14] in which the character of the Pharisee is compared with that of the Publican, the Lord clearly shows what He raises up in men, what He rejects, as it is written that 'God resisteth the proud, but giveth grace to the humble.'[15] Therefore, He testifies that the Publican went down from the Temple justified after his confession of sin, rather than the Pharisee after his recital of his supposed good works. Deservedly, then, did this panegyrist of himself go away from the presence of God rejected, because, by his very title, he boasted of his knowledge of the Law, but he had forgotten what the Lord said by the Prophet: 'Upon whom shall I dwell but upon him that is humble and peaceful, and that trembleth at my words?'[16] whereas the accuser of himself is received in a contrite heart, and obtains pardon after his confession of sin through the grace of humility, while that holy Pharisee—holy as the Jews are holy—carried away a load of sin after boasting of his holiness. Doubtless, he is a type of those Jews of whom the Apostle says that, 'seeking to establish their own justice,' which is of the Law, 'they have not submitted themselves to the justice of God,'[17] which is of faith. This faith was 'reputed to

---

12 Cf. Ps 52.6.
13 Ps. 50.19.
14 Luke 18.10-14. The Pharisee was called *legisperitus,* the 'title' referred to below.
15 James 4.6; 1 Peter 5.5; Prov. 3.34.
16 Cf. Isa 66.2.
17 Rom. 10.3.

Abraham unto justice,' not by his works, but 'because he believed God,'[18] by the power of God, before whom he is truly just, 'who liveth by faith';[19] who is not holy on earth but in heaven, because he walks not according to the flesh but according to the spirit;[20] 'whose conversation is in heaven';[21] not glorying in the circumcision of the flesh, but in the circumcision of the heart which is performed invisibly,' not in the letter but in the spirit, whose praise is not of men but of God.'[22]

Again, where he adds in the same verse: 'He hath made wonderful all his desires among them,'[23] I believe he speaks of the fact that he first lighted the lamp of the Law, and gave commandments for right living, for he says: 'He hath made his ways known to Moses, and his wills to the children of Israel.'[24] Then God worked that mystery of His godliness among them, when He was born in the flesh, of a Virgin, of their race and flesh, made man of the seed of David;[25] then He worked miracles of healing among them[26] and in their presence. Even so, He was not believed but was blasphemed by them, when they said: 'This man is not of God, who keepeth not the sabbath,'[27] and: 'This man casteth not out devils but by Beelzebub the prince of devils.'[28] On account of this mind, blinded and hardened by impiety, 'their infirmities were multiplied,'[29] and also their darkness.

But what does he mean by saying: 'Afterwards they made

---

18 Rom. 4.2.3.
19 Rom. 1.17; Heb. 10.38.
20 Rom. 8.5; Gal. 5.16.
21 Phil. 3.20.
22 Rom. 2.28,29.
23 Ps. 15.3.
24 1 Tim. 3.16.
25 Rom. 1.3.
26 Luke 13.22.
27 John 9.16.
28 Matt. 12.24.
29 Ps. 15.4.

haste'? Did they make haste to repent, as those did in the Acts of the Apostles who were struck with compunction at the preaching of blessed Peter, and believed in Him whom they had crucified, and, hastening to expiate so great a sin, ran to the gift of grace?[30] Or is it true that because the virtues of the soul are strengthened by faith and love of God, so, in those who are wicked and devoid of both, their infirmities are multiplied in the soul, overcome by deadly weakness induced by the twofold impiety of their crimes? Christ is the light and life[31] of believers, and 'health is under his wings.'[32] Hence, it is no wonder if their darkness and infirmities are multiplied to their destruction, since they have not received life and light, nor wished to dwell under His wings, of whom He bore witness in His Gospel, weeping that often He wished to gather them together under His wings, 'as the hen doth gather together her chickens under her wings,'[33] and they would not. Therefore, with multiplied infirmities, where are they making haste? Perchance to demand the cross for the Lord, and to wrest it from an unwilling Pilate,[34] by their criminal shouts, in order to fill up the measure of their fathers,[35] and themselves to kill the Lord of Prophets, as their fathers had killed the Prophets themselves, by whom the coming of the Saviour of the world had been foretold. Afterwards they made haste, for their feet are swift to shed blood; destruction and unhappiness are in their ways, and the way of peace they have not known,'[36]— the way that is Christ who says: 'I am the way.'[37]

In the following psalm I should like to have that passage explained to me where it says: 'Their belly is filled from thy

---

30 Acts 2.37-41.
31 John 1.9; 8.12; 11.34.
32 Mal. 4.2.
33 Matt. 23.37; Luke 13.34.
34 Luke 23.23.
35 Matt. 23.32; 1 Thess. 2.15.
36 Ps. 13.3.
37 John 14.6.

hidden stores. They are full of pork,' or, as I hear it is written in another version of the psalms: 'They are full of children, and they have left to their little ones the rest of their substance.'[38]

Again in another psalm, I am always struck with admiration, understanding that the Son is speaking to his Father—in Psalm 58—where he says of the Jews of whom he had spoken above: 'Behold they shall speak with their mouth, and a sword is in their lips,'[39] and a little further on he says: 'Slay them not, lest at any time my people forget thy law; scatter them by thy power and bring them down, O Lord.'[40] This we see fulfilled in them to the present day; they have been brought down from their ancient glory; they are living dispersed among all races, without a temple, without sacrifices, and without prophets. But why do we wonder that He was then praying through the Prophet that they should not be killed, when He prayed for them at the very time of His Passion while they were leading Him to be crucified, saying: 'Father, forgive them, for they know not what they do'?[41] But, I admit that it is not clear to me why He adds: 'Lest at any time they forget thy law,' as if on this account their life were a state of bondage even without the faith of the Gospel. How did it help them to salvation—since this is to be sought by faith alone—to pass their time in recalling and meditating on the Law, unless, perhaps, it added something to the honor of the Law itself and the race of Abraham that the letter of the old Law should endure, even in the earthly abode of his carnal seed, which seems to be reckoned like the sand of the sea?[42] Or was it to prevent some from being enlightened by faith in Christ through reading the ancient Law, since He

---

38 Ps. 16.14. The second version is St. Jerome's.
39 Ps. 58.5.
40 Ps. 58.12.
41 Luke 23.34.
42 Gen. 22.17; 32.12.

is the end of both Law and Prophets,[43] and He shines forth as prefigured and foretold in all their books? Or is it because from these impious ones a generation of elect is to come, who are chosen from the twelve tribes, and who will be signed to the number of 144,000,[44] to which the revelation of blessed John, speaking of the words of the angel, bears witness, that they will be the close companions of the eternal king, being pure of heart and innocent of human taint? Of these in particular he adds: 'They will follow the lamb whithersoever he goeth, because they were not defiled with women, for they are virgins.'[45]

In Psalm 66, this passage, among others, is most obscure to me, where it says: 'But God shall break the heads of his enemies, the hairy crown of them that walk on in their sins.'[46] What is the meaning of the hairy crown walking on in sins? For he did not say the crown of the head, but the crown of the hair, which makes no sense. Or does he wish to portray a man filled with sin? It is written: 'The whole heart is sad from the feet to the head,'[47] and a little further on he says: 'Of thy enemies the tongue of thy dogs . . . with the same.'[48] What same? And can the Gentiles be called the dogs of God, when He Himself names them dogs in the Gospel?[49] Or would He, perhaps, call dogs of God those who can be so rated because they have the name of Christians but live like Gentiles, whose lot is with unbelievers because, though they worship God in word, they deny Him by their deeds?[50]

---

43 Rom. 10.4.
44 Apoc. 7.5; 8.
45 Apoc. 14.4.
46 Ps. 67.22. This is Psalm 67, not 66, in the Vulgate. In the answer to these questions in Letter 149, Augustine corrects this and speaks of the passage as of Ps. 67.
47 Cf. Isa. 1.5,6.
48 Cf. 67.24.
49 Matt. 15.26: 'It is not good to take the bread of the children and to cast it to the dogs.'
50 Titus 1.16.

This is enough from the Psalms for the present: now I will bring up something from the Apostle. He says to the Ephesians, as he had said in another Epistle,[51] regarding the distribution of ranks and orders by the operation of the Holy Spirit of God, that there are diversities of graces: 'And he gave some apostles, and some prophets, and other some evangelists, and other some pastors and doctors for the perfecting of the saints,'[52] and the rest. I wish you would distinguish for me in this variety of names the peculiar gift and grace attached to each name. What is the special quality of apostles, of prophets, of evangelists, of pastors and of doctors? In all these different names I see that practically one and the same duty of teaching has been laid down. But the prophets whom he placed after the apostles are not the ones, I think, who preceded the Apostles in time, but those to whom, under the Apostles, the grace was given either to interpret the Scriptures, or to read minds, or to predict the future. Thus, Agabus saw and foretold a coming famine, and he declared by word and showed by the sign of his girdle what blessed Paul was to suffer in Jerusalem.[53] I wish to know what specific difference there is between pastors and doctors, because both names are regularly given to those who have authority in the Church.

Likewise, where he says to Timothy: 'I desire therefore, first of all, that supplications, prayers, intercessions and thanksgivings be made for all men,'[54] I ask you to explain for me what distinction there is in this diversity of words, because all of those exercises he recommends seem to me to be included in prayer.

I also ask and beg of you to expound for me what he says to the Romans, for I admit I have very poor sight for this

---
51 1 Cor. 12,28; 4.
52 Eph. 4.11,12.
53 Acts 11.22; 21.10-11.
54 1 Tim. 2.1.

opinion of the Apostle about the Jews, where he says: 'As concerning the Gospel, indeed they are enemies for your sake, but as touching the election they are most dear for the sake of the fathers.'⁵⁵ How can these same ones be enemies for our sake, now that we former Gentiles have become believers, as if Gentiles could only believe if the Jews had refused to believe? Is not God Himself the one Creator of all, 'Who will have all men to be saved and to come to the knowledge of the truth,'⁵⁶ and was He not able to gain both without dispossessing one for the other? Secondly, 'most dear for the sake of the fathers': how or why this 'most dear,' if they do not believe and if they continue to be enemies of God? 'O God,' he says, 'have I not hated them that hated thee, and pined away because of thine enemies? I have hated them with a perfect hatred.'⁵⁷ Certainly, I think the Father's voice speaks to His Son by the prophet in the same psalm where He spoke on behalf of believers: 'But to me thy friends, O God, are made exceedingly honorable; their principality is exceedingly strengthened.'⁵⁸ How can it be profitable for their salvation to be 'most dear to God for the sake of the fathers,' when salvation is only acquired through the faith and grace of Christ? What good does it do them to be loved, when they are inevitably to be damned because of their unbelief, because they have fallen away from the faith of the prophets and of the patriarchs, their fathers, and have become enemies of the Gospel of Christ? If they are most dear to God, how shall they be lost? And if they do not believe, how can they fail to be lost? If they are loved for the sake of the fathers, without any merit of their own, why will they not be saved for the sake of the fathers, too? 'And if Noe, Daniel and Job shall be in

---
55 Rom. 11.28.
56 1 Tim. 2.4.
57 Cf. Ps. 138.21,22.
58 Ps. 138.17.

the midst thereof, they shall not deliver the' wicked 'sons: they only shall be delivered.'[59]

There is another even more obscure passage about which I ask you to pull me up out of deep water and set me in the shallows. In the Epistle to the Colossians, I simply cannot see the connection where he says: 'Let no man seduce you willing in humility and religion of angels, walking in the things which he hath not seen; in vain puffed up by the sense of his flesh and not holding the head.'[60] What angels does he mean? If he means the rebel and wicked angels, what is their religion, or their humility, or who is the master of this seduction, who under cover of some angelic religion or other would teach what he does not see as something seen and experienced? Doubtless, the heretics, who follow the teachings of demons,[61] who think up false systems under the impulse of their spirit, who give out that they have seen visions which they have not seen, and by their deadly arguments sow their seed in foolish and credulous hearts—doubtless, these are the ones who do not hold the head, namely Christ, the source of truth. Whatever is opposed to His teaching is without sense, and these are the 'blind, leaders of the blind,'[62] of whom I think it is said: 'They have forsaken me, the fountain of living water, and have digged to themselves broken cisterns that can hold no water.'[63]

Then, in a subsequent chapter, he added: 'Touch not, taste not, handle not, which are all unto destruction by the very use according to the precepts and doctrines of men; which things indeed have a show of wisdom in superstition and humility, and not sparing the body, not in any honor to the filling of the flesh.'[64] What are these things in which the master of truth

---

59 Ezech. 14.14-16.
60 Col. 2.18,19.
61 1 Tim. 4.1,2.
62 Matt. 15.14.
63 Jer. 2.13.
64 Col. 2.21-23.

testifies that there is a show of wisdom, yet declares that the truth of religion is not in them? Does he perhaps speak of such as he described to Timothy: 'Having an appearance indeed of godliness, but denying the power thereof'?[65] I ask you to give me a word-for-word annotation of these two chapters, in particular from the Epistle to the Colossians, because it has hateful and laudable things intermingled. What is so praiseworthy as a show of wisdom, and what so detestable as the superstition of error? Humility, also, both pleasing to God and eminently praiseworthy in true religion, is given with a show of wisdom to those of whose teachings and actions we are told: 'Touch not, taste not, handle not, which are unto destruction,'[66] because they are not of God, and 'all that is not of faith, is sin.'[67] But, God 'casteth away the counsels of the wise'[68] of those who are foolish in God's eyes, by reason of the wisdom of the flesh, which cannot submit to the law of God,[69] for 'He knoweth the thoughts of men that they are vain.'[70] I wish to know what this humility is and this show of wisdom which he says is in their superstition, which comes from the doctrines of men. Again I fail to understand what he means by saying: 'not sparing the body, not in any honor to the filling of the flesh,'[71] because it seems to me there is strong distinction to be made in that sentence. I think he is speaking of a pretended and useless abstinence such as heretics usually strive after, when he says: 'not sparing the body'; but he adds: 'not in any honor' because they put on the appearance of a holy work, but, as they do not practice it in the fold of truth, they gain neither honor nor the reward of glory, and, transforming themselves into ministers of

---

65 2 Tim. 3.5.
66 Col. 2.21.
67 Rom. 14.23.
68 Cf. Ps. 32.10.
69 Rom. 14.23.
70 Ps. 93.11.
71 Col. 2.23.

justice,⁷² they achieve only the great reprobation of their depraved error. But, when he adds: 'to the filling of the flesh,' he seems to me to contradict his words: 'not sparing the body,' for he who tames the flesh by fasting does not seem to me to spare the body, as the Apostle says: 'I chastise my body and bring it into subjection.'⁷³ This practice seems to me contrary to the filling of the flesh, unless, perhaps, he means that the care of filling the flesh, which is supremely repulsive to those who aim at religious observance, is the same as not sparing the body, according to that precept of honor which he mentions elsewhere: 'that everyone of you should know how to possess his vessel in honor,'⁷⁴ 'that he present his body a living sacrifice and pleasing unto God,'⁷⁵ because the filling of the body is destructive of temperance and inimical to chastity.

It remains for me to submit to your Beatitude some passages from the Gospel, not, of course, such extensive ones as usually arise when one is engaged in leisurely reading—for at present I have time neither to look up scattered texts in books, nor to stir up my memory to recall them—but at least I shall present a few which come to mind during this hour of dictation. When I was spending the winter at Carthage,⁷⁶ you answered my second appeal about the form of the [body in the] resurrection, by a letter filled with faith and learning, although not a long one. If you have a copy of it among your papers, please send it to me, or at least rewrite it for

---

72 2 Cor. 9.27.
73 1 Cor. 9.27.
74 1 Thess. 4.4.
75 Rom. 21.1.
76 It is believed that this verb should be in the second person rather than the first, because Augustine was more likely to winter at Carthage than Paulinus was; moreover, the letter referred to in this passage seems to be *Ep.* 95, which was written at Carthage, and which contains an explanation of the nature of the glorified body after the resurrection.

me—that is easy for you to do. For, even if there is no written copy of it—and being short and hastily written, it might not have been thought worth keeping among your works—compose it for me again on the same theme, out of the treasure of your heart, and send it to me with the other answers which you will give me, I hope. Thus, if Christ grants to you and me a length of days, I may receive the answers to the questions on these passages from Scripture, about which I have consulted you; thus your labor will bear fruit in me; thus I shall hear what God speaks to me[77] in you or from you, for, indeed, you see things in God, if I may say so.

Thus I ask you to make clear for me how or by what means the Lord, after His Resurrection, was both recognized and not recognized either by the women who came first to the tomb, or afterward by those two on the road, and afterward by His disciples,[78] for He rose in the same Body in which He suffered. Why did His Body not have the same appearance as it had previously had, or, if it had, why was He not recognized by those who had known Him? I believe that there is a mystery here, because He who had not been recognized as they walked along the road was made known in the breaking of bread.[79] But I want your thought on this, not mine.

And when He said to Mary: 'Do not touch me for I am not yet ascended to my Father,'[80] if He would not let her touch Him when she was standing beside Him, how could she touch Him when He had ascended to the Father, except, perhaps, by the grasp of faith and the lifting-up of the mind, whereby God becomes remote from man or near to him. As she had doubted about Christ, whom she took for the gardener, that

---

77 Ps. 84.9.
78 John 20.14; Luke 24.37. The two on the road were the disciples going to Emmaus.
79 Luke 24.30-31.
80 John 20.17.

may be why she deserved to hear: 'Do not touch Me.' She was judged unworthy to touch Christ with her hand, because she had not yet grasped Him by faith; she had not understood that He was God when she thought He was the gardener. Yet, a short time before, she had heard the angels say: 'Why seek you the living with the dead?'[81] Therefore: 'Do not touch me, for I am not yet ascended to my Father,' and I seem to you still a man; afterward you shall touch Me when you have risen to the knowledge of Me by faith.

Please set forth for me what you think of those words of blessed Simeon, and I will follow your interpretation. I mean those words in which he spoke to Mary, when, by the Spirit, he had come into the Temple, to see Christ, according to the prophecy of God, and had taken the infant Lord into his arms and blessed Him, saying: 'Behold this child is set for the fall and for the resurrection of many in Israel, and for a sign which shall be contradicted, and thy own soul a sword shall pierce, that out of many hearts thoughts may be revealed.'[82] Are we not to believe that this is a prophecy of the passion of Mary, which is not written anywhere? Or at least a prophecy of her maternal love which afterward, at the time of His Passion, kept her standing beside the Cross to which her Son was fastened, when sorrow pierced her mother-heart, and the lance which struck through the flesh of her Son on the Cross as she watched penetrated her own soul? For I see that, as in the Psalms, this is said of Joseph: 'They humbled his feet in fetters, the iron pierced his soul,'[83] so, in the Gospel, Simeon said: 'And thy own soul a sword shall pierce.'[84] He does not say 'flesh,' but 'soul,' because there the feeling of mother-love resides, and there the sting of sorrow is felt like a sword. This is so when anyone suffers a physical injury, as Joseph did

---
81 Luke 24.5.
82 Luke 2.34,35.
83 Ps. 104.18.
84 Luke 2.35.

when he was sold into slavery, bound with fetters like a criminal, and cast into prison,[85] in which he bore the passion of insult, but not of death. It is also true when one suffers grief and sorrow in the innermost affections of the heart, as Mary did,[86] for her mother's heart had led her to the Cross of the Lord in whom she recognized the only Son of her body, but, when she saw Him dead, and while she mourned over Him with human weakness, and prepared Him for burial, she had no advance comfort in the thought of His Resurrection, for the pain of His Passion, set before her eyes, obscured her confidence in the wonder about to be accomplished. It is true the Lord consoled her as she stood beside His Cross, not with the trembling weakness of a dying man, but with the full strength of a living one, having full power over the death which He willed to undergo, and with the firm confidence of one who was to rise again, when He gave His charge to the blessed Apostle John, saying: 'Woman, behold thy son,' and in like manner to the Apostle standing by: 'Behold thy mother.'[87] By His death on the Cross He was now leaving behind the human weakness which He had taken on when He was born of a woman, and was returning to the eternal life of God, to be with the Father in glory, so He openly bequeaths to a man His human rights as a son; of His disciples He chooses the youngest, as nearer to His own youth, and He entrusts His virgin Mother to His virgin disciple. He reveals both these things in the same sentence, leaving us a pattern of filial devotion by showing His care for His Mother. It is true He was depriving her of His physical presence, but He was not giving up His care for her, and He was not even depriving her of His presence because she was to see Him risen whom she now looked upon in death. By a secret pur-

---

85 Gen. 37.28; 39.20.
86 John 19.25.
87 John 19.26,27.

pose of His plan He set before us that saving mystery of His filial love, which belongs to the faith of all, when He bequeathed His mother to another, who was to have her for his own, and to console her instead of her own Son; equally, He gave her a new son in the place of Himself. Nay, I might almost say He created one, to show that she neither had nor could have any other Son than the One who was born of her virginity; nor would the Saviour have to take such care of her if He had not been her only Son.

But, let us return to the words of Simeon, over the conclusion of which I confess that my mind grows dark: 'And thy own soul a sword shall pierce, that out of many hearts thoughts may be revealed.'[88] Taken literally this is completely unintelligible to me, because we do not read anywhere that blessed Mary was killed, which makes it seem clear that the holy man did not prophesy for her future suffering by a real sword. Then he added: 'that out of many hearts thoughts may be revealed,'—'the searcher of hearts and reins is God,'[89] he says—and the Apostle says of the judgment to come that then God 'shall bring to light the secrets of hearts and the hidden things of darkness.'[90] The Apostle, giving a spiritual description of the heavenly weapons with which we should be armed for the interior conflict, also says that the sword of the spirit is the word of God,[91] and to the Hebrews he says: 'the word of God is living and effectual and more piercing than any two-edged sword, and reaching' he says 'unto the division of the soul and the spirit,'[92] and the rest which you know. What wonder, then, if the fiery force of that word and the penetrating point of that two-edged sword should have pierced the soul of holy Joseph long ago,

---
88 Luke 3.35.
89 Ps. 7.10.
90 Cf. 1 Cor. 4.5.
91 Eph. 6.17.
92 Heb. 4.12.

and, later, of blessed Mary? For we know that no sword pierced either his body or hers. To make it more clear that the Prophet used the word steel for the sword of the word, he says at once in a subsequent verse: 'The word of the Lord inflamed him.'[93] The word of the Lord is both fire and sword, on the word of God Himself, when He says of both in speaking of Himself: 'I am come to cast fire on the earth, and what will I but that it be kindled?'[94] and, similarly, He says in another place: 'I come not to send peace but the sword.'[95] You see that He has expressed the single force of His doctrine under the different terms of fire and sword. But, how did passion or suffering come to Mary by the sword? So I wish to know this: What was it to Mary that 'out of many hearts thoughts should be revealed' or where did it appear that thoughts of many hearts were revealed because the sword pierced her soul[96] either physically by a real weapon, or spiritually by the word of God? Explain for me this phrase of the words of Simeon in particular, because I do not doubt that light shines on your holy soul which has deserved to be illumined by the Spirit of God, because of the purity of its interior eye, by which it can scan and examine the high things of God. 'May God have mercy on me' through your prayers, and 'may He cause the light of His countenance to shine on me,'[97] by the light of your word, holy lord, most blessed and dear brother in the Lord Christ, my master in the faith of truth and my support in the heart of the charity of Christ.

---

93 Ps. 104.19.
94 Luke 12.49.
95 Matt. 10.34.
96 Luke 2.35.
97 Ps. 66.2.

122. Augustine gives greeting in the Lord to his dearly beloved brethren, his fellow clerics, and all the people (c. 410)

First of all, I beg your Charity and I entreat you in the Name of Jesus not to grieve over my physical absence,[1] for I am sure you know that in spirit and in my heart's love I can never be parted from you. Still, I grieve more deeply, perhaps, than you do that in my weak health I cannot reach out to all the services which the members of Christ have a right to exact from me, and which my fear and love of Him press me to render to you. Your Charity knows that I have never been away for any selfish holiday, but for reasons connected with the duties of my office, such as have often obliged my holy brothers and fellow workers to undergo hardships on the sea and across the sea. From these latter I have been excused, not through any lack of zeal, but because my health was not robust enough. Therefore, my dearly beloved brothers, so act that, as the Apostle says, 'Whether I come and see you, or being absent may hear of you, you stand fast in one spirit, laboring together for the faith of the Gospel.'[2] If some temporal trial disturbs you,[3] it ought even more to warn you of your duty to set your thoughts on the life to come, where you may live free of toil, and may escape not the merely straitening burdens of fleeting time, but the dread pains of everlasting fire. If you exert such care, such effort, and such labor to escape a few transient pains, how anxious you should be to avoid unending torments! If death, which puts an end to temporal toil, is fearful, how much more dreadful is that death which consigns the soul to eternal sorrow! And if the pleasures of this world, so brief and

---
1 This letter was written from the country, where Augustine had gone, as he says in Letter 118, to convalesce after an illness.
2 Phil. 1.27.
3 No doubt, the terrifying news of the siege and sack of Rome by Alaric and the Goths in 410.

worthless, are so much loved, how much more ardently should we yearn for the pure and infinite joys of the world to come! Think of these things, and do not be sluggish in good works, so that in due time you may reap the harvest of your sowing.

I have had word that you have dropped your custom of clothing the poor, a work of mercy in which I always encouraged you, when I was with you; I still do urge you not to let the pressure of worldly life overcome you and make you slothful. You see the kind of things that are happening in the world, such as our Lord and Redeemer, who cannot lie, foretold would come upon it. You ought to be so far from lessening your works of mercy that you would perform even more than you were wont to do. Those who see their home about to collapse, with crumbling walls, move out very quickly to safer places; so should Christian hearts, the more they see the destruction of this world draw near with growing calamities, make haste to transform into heavenly treasure the riches which they were getting ready to bury in the earth. Then, if human disaster befalls anyone, he will rejoice that he moved away from the dangerous spot, but, if no such consequence ensues, inasmuch as he is going to die some time, he will not regret having entrusted his possessions to the immortal Lord before whom he is to appear. Therefore, my dearest brethren, according to each one's means—and each one knows what he has—do what you used to do with greater eagerness than you used to do it, and amid all the trials of this world keep in mind the Apostle's warning: 'The Lord is nigh; be nothing solicitous.'[4] Let me have such news of you, that you are doing what I know you used to do, not because of my presence, but because of God's commandment, for He is never absent. Indeed, you did do it for many years in my presence, and sometimes even in my absence. May the Lord keep you in peace, dearest brothers; pray for us.

---

4 Phil. 4.5,6.

123. Jerome announces certain tidings to Augustine enigmatically[1] *(410)*

Many people are lame on both feet, and go about with bent head though their necks are not broken, keeping their attachment to the old error, although they no longer have the same liberty to preach it. The holy brothers, who share our littleness, and especially your holy and venerable daughters, greet you humbly. I beg your community to greet your brothers, my lord Alypius and my lord Evodius, in my name. Jerusalem has been taken, it is held by Nabuchodonosor[2] and would not heed the warnings of Jeremias; it even longed after Egypt, to die at Taphnis,[3] and perish there in everlasting slavery.

---

1 This is a puzzling fragment, formerly included in Letter 195. It seems to have been written by St. Jerome, but, whether the first part refers to the condemnation of the Pelagians in Palestine, or whether the whole letter is about the capture of Rome, or whether it is about the Origenists, is not clear. All three views are held. There is no superscription. This title is given by Migne.
2 Jer. 43.2, 7-10. Some commentators think the Bishop of Jerusalem is meant, who was apparently in sympathy with the condemned Pelagians. Others think the capture of Rome by the Goths is meant, because Rome did not recognize the hand of God.
3 A city in Egypt, connected with the prophecy of Jeremias.

124. Augustine gives greeting in the Lord to Albina,¹ Pinian, and Melania, illustrious nobles, beloved brothers, cherished for their holiness (411)

Because of my constitution and my state of health, I have never been able to bear the cold, but never could I have felt storms more keenly than I did this last dreadful winter, because they made it impossible for me, I will not say to go, but to fly, to you, when you were so close to me, after you had had to cross the seas in your flight, and had come from such a distance to see me. But your Holiness may have thought that the bad weather of the winter was the only reason for my suffering. God forbid, beloved friends. Could those storms be too severe, or trying, or even dangerous for me to undergo and endure, when it was a case of coming to you, great comfort that you are in our great misfortunes, light so brightly kindled by the Supreme Light, in this confused and perverse generation, loftier for the lowliness you have embraced, brighter for the lustre you have scorned? At the same time I could have enjoyed being in my own natural birthplace,² with a happiness so spiritual because it had the honor of your presence. Although it had heard of you in your absence—of the rank you were born to and what you have become by the grace of Christ—and probably believed it out

---

1 Albina was the daughter-in-law of the elder Melania (cf. Letter 94) whose son, Publicola, she married. Her daughter, the younger Melania, was married at thirteen to Pinian. On the sack of Rome in 410, they left that city with Rufinus, who, however, died in Sicily. They then fled to Carthage, and ultimately to Tagaste, where they ardently hoped to see Augustine. As he was not able to go there for reasons given in this letter, they came to Hippo, and became involved in the difficulty described in the following letters. After the birth of their two children, Pinian and Melania made a vow of perpetual virginity; Pinian became a monk in a monastery on Mt. Olivet, and Melania became abbess of a convent nearby. Augustine dedicated his treatise, *Contra Pelagium et Coelestium, de gratia Christi et de peccato originali*, to these three friends.
2 Tagaste.

of charity, yet it shrank from publishing it for fear of not being believed.

I shall tell you, then, why I have not come, and what evils have kept me from so great a good, and I shall hope to deserve your pardon and, even more, through your prayers, mercy from Him who works in you because you live for Him. The people of Hippo, to whom the Lord has given me as a servant, and who are weakened to such a great and almost universal extent that the onset of even a slight trouble could put them into a serious illness, are now stricken with so grave a trouble that, even if they were not so weak, they could scarcely meet it with any health of mind. I found on my recent return that my absence had been a very dangerous stumbling-block to them. Your healthy palate—and how I rejoice in your spiritual strength!—will relish the meaning of the saying: 'Who is weak and I am not weak? Who is scandalized and I am not on fire?'[3] especially as there are many here who try to undermine in other souls the esteem in which I seem to be held by them, and to rouse them against me so as to make place for the Devil in them. But, when they rage against us while we are busy trying to save them, their great instrument of vengeance is a passion for dying, not in body but in soul, and the death is secretly disclosed by its own stench of corruption before we can forestall it by our own plan of action. I am sure you willingly find excuses for this anxiety of mine, all the more because you could probably find no greater punishment, in case you were angry and wanted to take vengeance on me, than what I actually suffer in not seeing you at Tagaste. I hope that, with the help of your prayers, it will be granted me at the earliest possible moment, when this emergency which now detains me has passed, to come to you in whatever part of Africa you may be, if this town in which I labor is not worthy of enjoying your presence with us—and I hardly dare think it is worthy.

---

3 2 Cor. 11.29.

125. Augustine, and the brothers who are with me, give greeting in the Lord to the most blessed lord, our reverend and most dear brother and fellow priest, Alypius, and the brothers who are with you (411)

I am deeply grieved, and it is not possible for me to make light of the fact, that the people of Hippo have protested loudly[1] against the injustice of your Holiness, but I find it much more grievous, my good brother, that such things should be thought of us than that they should be protested aloud. For, when we are suspected of wanting to keep the servants of God here, through the attraction of their wealth rather than through love of their goodness, is it not preferable that those who believe this should express their secret thought aloud, and thus allow of some more potent remedies being sought if possible, rather than perish in silence by the poison of their deadly suspicions? Therefore, as I said even before this happened, we must be more concerned about how we can convince men, to whom we are bound by precept to give good example, that what they suspect is false, than about how we can lay the blame on those who voice their suspicions aloud.

Consequently, I bear no grudge against the saintly Albina, and I judge that she is not to be blamed, but cured of such a suspicion. It is true she did not utter these words against me personally, but she made a complaint against the Hipponensians to the effect that they had displayed their avarice in wanting to keep with them a man so rich, so detached from his wealth, and so generous with it, and that their motive was not love of the priesthood but of money. Besides, she almost expressed what she thought of us, and not herself alone but her two saintly sons, too, who said this

---

[1] For this controversy, cf. Introduction.

that same day in the sanctuary.² I think, then, that they should be cured of suspicions of this sort rather than censured for them. When such thorns have been able to germinate in hearts so holy and so dear to us, where can protection from such be furnished or offered to us? Such suspicions have been engendered about you by the ignorant mob, but about me by the lights of the Church; you see, then, why we have more reason to grieve. But I still think that both sides should be cured, not accused; they are human, and about human beings it is not unbelievable that such suspicions, however false, should arise. Surely, such persons are not so completely foolish as to believe that the people covet their money, especially as they have already found out that the Tagastians have not received any of it—any more than the Hipponensians. Of a truth, all this ill will boils up only against the clergy, and more particularly against the bishops, because their influence seems to predominate, and they are believed to use and enjoy the property of the Church as if they were its owners and lords. Those who are ill of this disease should, if possible, not be encouraged by us, my dear Alypius, in this contagious and deadly avarice. Remember what we said before the occurrence of that temptation which has more force in this kind of case. Let us rather, by taking example from this happening, try to provide against it, with the Lord's help, and let us not be satisfied with the testimony of our own conscience, because this case is not such as can be satisfied by that alone. If we are not false servants of God, if there is in us a spark of that fire whereby 'charity seeketh not her own,'³ we certainly should make our good works

---

2 The semi-circular part of the church in which the altar was placed. It was separated then, as now, by a lattice or railing from the nave or body of the church. Honored guests were sometimes admitted to the sanctuary, which was generally higher than the nave, and they were thus visible to the congregation. In the early centuries of the Church the people often had a voice in the choice of both priests and bishops.
3 1 Cor. 13.5.

appear, not only before God, but even before men, lest, while drinking of quiet waters in our own conscience, we should be constrained by careless feet to drive the sheep of the Lord to drink the troubled waters.[4]

As to the suggestion you made in your letter that we should examine together the nature of an oath extorted by force, I beg of you, do not let our discussion turn crystal-clear matters into murky ones. If a servant of God were threatened with certain death, so that he should swear to do something forbidden and wicked, he still ought rather to die than to so swear, so as not to commit a crime in fulfilling his oath. But, in this case, when it was only the persistent shouting of the people that was forcing the man, not to any crime, but to what could lawfully be done, if it were done, and when the only thing to fear was that a few violent men, mingled with a crowd of mostly good ones, might seize the occasion to start a riot, under pretense of virtuous indignation, and might break out into some accursed disturbance to satisfy their passion for robbery, and when even this fear was unfounded, who would think that perjury could be committed even to avoid certain death, much less loss or some kind of physical injury? That individual called Regulus[5] had never heard what the holy Scriptures say about the wrongfulness of a false oath; he had learned nothing about the sickle[6] of

---

4 Jer. 2.18.
5 Cicero, *De off*. 1.13.39-40. This Regulus was much admired by the Romans. A consul, during the first Punic War, he was captured by the Carthaginians, but was allowed to return to Rome to arrange for an exchange of prisoners of war, after having sworn to come back to Carthage if he failed in his mission. He himself urged the Senate not to agree to the exchange, on the ground that they had some able Carthaginian generals among their prisoners, whereas the Roman prisoners did not deserve to be ransomed because they had let themselves be captured. He thereupon returned to Carthage in fulfillment of his oath, and was tortured and put to death, according to some accounts.
6 Zach. 5.1-3 (Septuagint); the Vulgate reads 'scroll.'

Zacharias, and obviously he had not sworn to the Carthaginians by the sacraments of Christ, but by the filthiness of demons, yet he did not so fear certain torture and a horrible sort of death as to take his oath under compulsion, but went to meet them to avoid perjuring himself, because he had sworn the oath of his own free will. The Roman censorship[7] of that time refused to include in the number of Senators—not saints—and on the roll of an earthly Senate—not in heavenly glory—those who chose to perjure themselves through fear of death and cruel punishments rather than return to their savage foes, and even excluded the one who thought himself absolved of the guilt of perjury because after his oath he had returned on some trumped-up necessity. Those who expelled him from the Senate did not take account of his intention in swearing, but of what those to whom he took the oath expected of him. They had not read what we commonly sing: 'He that sweareth to his neighbor and deceiveth not.'[8] We usually bestow high praise and admiration on this kind of fidelity, even in men who are strangers to the grace and Name of Christ, and are we to go so far as to think we should search the divine Books to find out whether it

---

7 The office of the Roman censor was one of great power and authority. It included keeping the lists of members of the two degrees of nobility: Senators and knights. By striking their names from the list the censors could deprive certain nobles of their rank. They also had supervision of public morals and sumptuary laws, and were in charge of such public works as road-building. Augustine's argument through here seems to be that Regulus was faithful to the literal words of his oath, namely, that he would return to Carthage if he failed in his mission, but the Carthaginians obviously expected him to urge the exchange of captives out of regard for his own safety. By not doing so he failed in the spirit of his oath. The reason of his removal from the rolls of the Senate would naturally have been the fact that he continued to be a Carthaginian prisoner rather than that he had failed in the spirit of his oath while keeping it to the letter. It is doubtful that the Romans made that distinction, and it is a fact that Roman writers always hold him up as an example of heroic fidelity to the pledged word.

8 Ps. 14.4.

is ever justifiable to commit perjury, when in them it is even enjoined on us not to swear at all,[9] lest, through too great ease of swearing, we fall into perjury?

I am sure it is perfectly correct to say that an oath is kept faithfully when it accords with the expectation of the one to whom the oath is sworn, not with the words of the one who swears, and the one who takes the oath knows this. For, it is very difficult to express a sentence, especially a brief one, in words which can convey the exact obligation of the one who takes the oath. Consequently, those who keep literally to the words, but cheat the expectation of the ones to whom they take the oath, commit perjury; those who do not keep literally to the words, but perform what is expected of them by those to whom they swear, do not commit perjury. Hence, as the Hipponensians wanted to have the saintly Pinian, not as a condemned man, but as a dearly loved dweller in their city, even if he cannot be entirely bound by his own words, it is so far evident what they expected of him that the fact of his departure after his oath does not trouble any of them, because they could understand that he might go away for a special reason, so long as he had the intention of returning. This will not make him a perjurer, nor will he be considered one by them, unless he cheats their expectation, but he will not cheat it unless he either changes his intention of living among them or goes off some time without making any arrangement to return; and this would be repugnant to his character and to the faith which he owes to Christ and to His Church. I will not recall—for you know it as well as I do—how dreadful is the divine judgment on perjury, but this I know well, that hereafter we shall never have grounds for being angry with anyone who refuses to trust our oath, if we think that the false oath of such a man is to be not only excused, but even accepted without objection. May this be

---
9 Matt. 5.34.

averted from us and from him by the mercy of Him who delivers from temptation those who hope in Him.[10] Therefore, as you wrote in your letter of instruction, let him keep the word by which he promised that he would not leave Hippo, but in the same way as I or the Hipponensians themselves do not leave, although we have full freedom to go and come, with this exception, that those who are not bound by oath have the power to go away entirely and not come back, without incurring the guilt of perjury.

Whether it can be proved that our clerics or the brothers who are members of our monastery shared in or encouraged the insults to you, I do not know. When I looked into this, I was told that only one Carthaginian from the monastery joined the people in shouting, when they demanded him for priest, but not when they hurled insults at you. I am adding to this letter a copy of his promise, transcribed from the paper which he signed, and which I have examined and verified.

126. Augustine gives greeting in the Lord to the holy lady and venerable servant of God, Albina (411)

Your letter tells me that the grief of your heart is indescribable, so the right thing for me to do is to relieve, not augment it; at the same time we wish, if possible, to allay your suspicions rather than add to the trouble of your soul, so revered and so devoted to God, by taking offense at them on our own account. Our holy brother, your son, Pinian, had no reason to fear death at the hands of the people of Hippo, although, perhaps, he did have some such fear. What we feared on our part was that some of the desperate characters, who often mingle with crowds for purposes of

---

10 Ps. 17.30; 2 Peter 2.9.

their own, might seize the opportunity to stir up the open violence of a riot, under pretense of venting their just indignation. From what I was able to gather afterward, no such attempt was either suggested or carried out, but it was a fact that they did shout many undeserved insults against my brother, Alypius. I hope that through his prayers they may win pardon for this great offense. For my part, I spoke to them at the outset of the commotion, and told them he could not be ordained against his will; that I had made a promise to this effect, and was bound by it; and I added that if, in violation of my word, they should have him as priest, they would not have me as bishop. After that I left the mob and returned to the throne.[1] At this unexpected reply of mine, they were somewhat disconcerted, and checked for a little while, like a flame blown back by the wind, but afterward they began to blaze up higher with excitement, thinking it might be possible either to force me to break my word, or to have him ordained by another bishop if I insisted on keeping my promise. When some of the more notable and more influential people had come up to me in the apse, I kept saying to those I could reach that I could not be turned from my pledged word, and that he could not be ordained by another bishop in the church entrusted to me, without my permission asked and given; that, if I gave that permission, I should still be going back on my pledge. I added, too, that they were aiming at nothing less than to drive him away after his ordination, if he were to be ordained against his will. They kept on believing that this could not happen, but their thoughts and plans were thrown into uncertainty by the mob which had now gathered in front of the steps, and which

---

1 *Subsellia*, or stalls. The bishop's chair, which he occupies during divine service, was, in Augustine's day, at the rear of the semi-circular apse, behind the altar. It was curtained, and offered some privacy to the bishop. Today, it is found at the left of the sanctuary and the curtains are always fastened back.

showed their persistence in the same design by a terrific and continual din. It was then that their insults were shouted against my brother, then that I feared more serious consequences.

Yet, though I was perturbed by this great outbreak of the people, and this great commotion in the church, I made no other answer to their collective insistence except that I could not ordain him against his will. I was not prevailed upon, either, to use some persuasion with him, to induce him to receive the priesthood—because, if I had persuaded him, he would not be ordained against his will. But this, too, I had promised not to do. I was faithful to both promises, not only the one I had by this time made known to the people, but even the other one to which I was bound by only one witness, at least as far as men are concerned. I was faithful, as I said, to a promise, not an oath, even in the presence of such great danger. And though the danger we feared turned out not to be real, as we found out afterwards, the threat of it, in case there were any, hung over all of us; the fear itself was shared by all, and I began to think of withdrawing, being especially fearful about the church in which we were. But, there was more reason to fear that their diminished respect and more vehement resentment would lead to some such outrage, if I were not present. Furthermore, if I left with brother Alypius, and passed through the throng of people, we should have had to guard against anyone daring to lay a hand on him; if I left without him, how could I face public disapproval if any accident befell him and I should seem to have deserted him with the intention of handing him over to the aroused populace?

In the midst of these anxieties of mine, and this deep concern, with no glimmer of a way out, behold our holy son, Pinian, suddenly and unexpectedly sends a servant of God to tell me that he is willing to swear to the people that, if he should be ordained against his will, he would leave Africa altogether; with the idea, I suppose, that the people would leave off shouting their useless importunities since he could not swear falsely, and they would only succeed in driving away a man whom we ought at least to have as a neighbor. I made no answer to this, but kept it to myself, because it seemed likely that we should have to fear more violent resentment on their part, because of such an oath. However, as he had, in the same message, requested me to come to him, I did not delay. He then repeated to me the same offer, and made this addition to the oath, which he had confided to another servant of God while I was making my way to him; namely, that he would stay here on condition that no one would impose the burden of priesthood on him without his consent. In the midst of these straits, this was as refreshing as a breath of fresh air; still, I did not give him an answer, but went with hurried step to brother Alypius, and related what he had said. But his reply was: 'Don't ask me anything about it,' because, I imagine, he wanted to avoid the responsibility of whatever he thought might offend you. On hearing this, I went back to the people, who were still in an uproar, and, after getting silence, I announced to them what Pinian had promised, as well as his promise to swear to it. However, they were still so strongly set on their single idea and wish of having him for a priest that they did not accept the offer as I expected, but, after muttering among themselves for a while, they requested this addition to the same promise and oath: that, if ever he decided to consent to receive Holy Orders, he would consent to receive it nowhere else but in the church at Hippo. I reported this to him; he accepted it without hesitation. I gave them his answer; they were overjoyed, and demanded the promised oath at once.

I went back to our son, and found him in a state of uncertainty about the formula of words by which he could make provision for such pressing necessities as might oblige him to leave. At the same time, he showed what he feared, namely, a hostile invasion,[2] which would have to be avoided by flight. The saintly Melania wanted to add the excuse of an unhealthy climate, but he gave her a reproachful reply. I said, however, that the reason alleged by him was a serious one, not to be lightly dismissed, because it might oblige the citizens to leave, too, but, if it were put to the people in these words, there was reason to fear that they would think us prophets of woe. On the other hand, if the plea of necessity were phrased in general terms, they would think it only a lying excuse. So we decided to try out the temper of the people on this point, and it turned out to be exactly what we had thought. For, when the words he had spoken were repeated by a deacon, and everything was agreeable, as soon as they heard the word 'necessity' which had been inserted, there was an immediate outcry and objection against this promise, with a renewed uproar, while the people concluded that they were being treated to nothing but a piece of double-dealing. But, when our holy son saw this, he ordered the word 'necessity' struck out, and the people returned again to their state of satisfaction.

Although I pleaded fatigue, he would not face the people without me, so we faced them together. He said that the words they had heard from the deacon expressed what he promised; he swore that he would do those things, and he at once repeated the whole thing in the same form in which he had dictated it. They answered: 'Thanks be to God!' and asked that the written formula be signed. We dismissed the catechumens,[3] and he signed the written oath at once.

---

2 Pinian had left Rome to escape the Vandals, and evidently had no great confidence that Africa would be able to hold them off.
3 Those not yet baptized, but under instruction for baptism. They were not allowed to remain for the solemn part of the Mass, and it can easily be seen that this peculiar happening might have disedified them.

Then they began to importune us bishops[4] to sign it, too, but this they did through the agency of certain honorable members of the faithful, not by the shouts of the people. But, when I began to add my signature, the saintly Melania objected. I wondered why she intervened so late, and whether she thought we could invalidate that promise and oath by not signing it. Still, I yielded to her, and so my signature remained incomplete, and no one thought any further pressure should be put on me to sign.

In my official report I have been careful to let your Holiness know, as fully as I thought wise, what the sentiments and remarks of the people were when they learned on the next day that Pinian had gone away. If anyone happens to tell you anything different from what I have told you, he either is a liar or has his information wrong. I am aware of having passed over certain details which seemed to me irrelevant to the subject of my anxiety, but not of having made any false statements. It is true, then, that our holy son, Pinian, took the oath in my presence and with my sanction; it is not true that he took it at my suggestion. He knows this himself; the servants of God know it—those whom he sent to me: first, the saintly Barnabas; next, Timasius, through whom he sent me word of his promise to live here. The people, too, were trying to force him by their shouts to become a priest, not to take an oath, but, when one was offered them, they did not reject it, with the hope that if he lived among us a willingness could spring up in him by which he might consent to be ordained, and that he would not go away, as he had sworn to do if he should be ordained against his will. Thus, even their outcries were motivated by a zeal for the work of God—for the ordaining of a priest is nothing else but the work of God—and it is quite evident that the people took no pleasure in his promise to live here, until he added that, if he should ever wish to consent to receive Holy

---
4 Alypius was evidently still there.

Orders, he would consent to receive it only in the church at Hippo. So, whatever hopes they had about his living among them, they did not give up that longing for the work of God.

How, then, can you say that they acted thus through a base craving for money? In the first place, this is no concern at all for the common people who made the demonstration, for, just as the people of Tagaste got nothing from the alms which you bestowed on the church of Tagaste, but their joy in your virtuous act, so with those at Hippo, or of any other place where you have followed out, or are going to follow out, the instructions of the Lord regarding the 'mammon of iniquity.'[5] So, then, when the people wanted such a man for the advantage of their church, there was no eager desire for their own pecuniary gain in what they asked of you, but what they esteemed in you was your contempt of money. For, if they loved in me what they had heard of my contempt for my few poor paternal acres, and my conversion to the free service of God, they did not on this account begrudge these to the church at Tagaste, which is my earthly birthplace, but, since Tagaste had not conferred the priesthood on me, they laid claim to have me as soon as they were able. How much more eagerly could they esteem in our Pinian his great conversion which has made him overcome and trample upon such worldly ambition, such wealth, such prospects! But, as far as I am concerned, in the opinion of many who 'compare themselves with themselves,'[6] I seem not so much to have left riches behind as to have come into riches. For, my patrimony can scarcely be reckoned as the twentieth part in comparison with the property of the church which I am now considered to possess as master. So, if this friend of ours were to become—I do not say a priest, but a bishop—in any one of the African churches especially, he will be

---
5 Luke 16.9.
6 2 Cor. 10.12.

extremely poor in comparison with his original wealth, even if he acts in the spirit of a proprietor. Thus, Christian poverty is esteemed in him much more purely and serenely, inasmuch as no greed of greater possessions can be imputed to him. This is what roused the feelings of the people; this is what stirred them up to that violent and continued uproar. Let us not accuse them over and above of a sordid avarice, but let us at least allow them, without imputing low motives to them, to love in others the good which they themselves do not possess. For, even if some needy persons or beggars were included in that crowd who, at the time they shouted, had some hope of help for their destitution from your honorable abundance, I do not consider that a sordid avarice.

We have to conclude, then, that the allegation of a sordid greed for money is indirectly aimed at the clergy and especially at the bishop, for we are the ones who are supposed to control the property of the Church; we are supposed to enjoy its wealth. In short, whatever we have received of those revenues, we either still possess them or we have disbursed them as we pleased; we have distributed nothing to the people who are not included in the clergy or the monastery, except to a very few paupers. I do not say, then, that those charges must necessarily have been made by you against us, but that they could plausibly have been made against us alone. What, then, are we to do? If we cannot clear ourselves with our enemies, is there not at least some explanation that will clear us with you? This is an affair of conscience; it lies within, far removed from mortal eyes; known to God alone. So, what is left but to call God to witness, since it is known to Him? Since you have that opinion of us, you do not prescribe the much better course of action, which you saw fit to reproach me with, as something blameworthy, in your letter, but you absolutely force me to take an oath, not by threatening me with the fear of death to my body, as the people of Hippo are supposed to have done, but with the threatened fear of death to my reputation, which is certainly to be set above the life of this body, because of the weak brethren to whom we try to give the example of good works,[7] in all our relations with them.

Nevertheless, although you force me to take this oath, we are not indignant with you, as you are with the people of Hippo. For, although in the manner of men judging men you believe things which are not in us, you do not believe things which cannot be in us. These are matters which we must remedy in you without censuring you; we have to clear our good name with you, since our conscience is clear before the Lord. Possibly, as brother Alypius and I said before this trial befell us, the Lord will make clearly known, not only to you, our beloved fellow members, but even to our very enemies, that we are tainted with no covetousness for money in our administration of Church affairs. But, until that happens, if the Lord grant it to happen, see now that I am doing in the meantime what I am forced to do, so as not to delay even the least little time this comfort for your heart. God is my witness that it is only because of the service which I owe to the love of my brethren and the fear of God that I bear with that whole administration of Church affairs over which I am supposed to love to exercise authority, but I am so far from loving it that I long to be free of it, if I could do so without failing in my duty. God is also my witness that I feel that the same is true about brother Alypius. Nevertheless, the people—and, what is worse, the people of Hippo—held a different opinion of him, and were carried away into violent abuse of him, while you, saints of God, filled with the deepest compassion, believed such things on the credit of the people who have nothing whatever to do with a charge of covetousness of this sort, and you wanted to

---
[7] Tit. 2.7.

touch us and reprove us, no doubt for our amendment, not through hatred—far be that from you! Consequently, I should not be angry but grateful, because you could not have acted more respectfully or more courteously; not abusively throwing blame on the bishop for what you thought, but allowing it to be understood indirectly.

Do not be hurt or feel yourselves burdened because I have taken an oath. For, the Apostle neither burdened nor failed to love those to whom he said: 'We have not used the language of flattery among you, nor taken an occasion of covetousness, God is witness.'[8] He made them his witnesses of what was clearly known, but of a hidden matter, what witness is there but God? If, then, he was right in fearing that human ignorance might think some such thing of him when his work was apparent to all, when he took nothing for his own benefit, except in cases of strict necessity, from the people to whom he dispensed the grace of Christ, working with his own hands to furnish what he needed for his own support, how much more effort should we make to maintain men's confidence in us, far removed as we are from the goal of sanctity and inner fortitude! Moreover, we can produce nothing with our own hands of what is needed to sustain our life, and, even if we could, we should never be allowed to do it, in the midst of such duties as I believe they did not have to perform. So, then, in this matter, do not let the charge of debased greed for money be made any more against the Christian people who are the Church of God. Such a charge is more tolerably made against us on whom the suspicion of this evil—false, indeed, but still probable—could fall, than against them who are manifestly incapable of such greed and such suspicion.

To refuse to keep an oath—I do not say assert something contrary to it, but even to hesitate about it—this for minds endowed with any sort of faith, much more the Christian

---
8 1 Thess. 2,5.

faith, is entirely wrong. On this point I have set forth my opinion clearly enough, I think, in the letter which I wrote to my brother bishop.[9] Your Holiness wrote to ask me whether I or the people of Hippo think an oath extorted by force should be kept. What do you think yourself? Do you agree that even in the face of certain death—which there was then no reason to fear—a Christian should take the name of the Lord his God in vain; that a Christian should make God his witness to a lie? Surely, if he were forced, by the threat of death, to bear false witness over and above his oath, he ought to have a greater fear of defiling his life than of ending it. Armed enemies clash in the line of battle, with the avowed purpose of dealing death to each other, yet, when they take a mutual oath, we praise those who keep their word, and rightly despise those who break it. But what made them take the oath except that each side feared being killed or captured by the other? Thus, if even such men as these are held back by the stigma of sacrilege and perjury, which they would incur if they had no respect for the oath extorted by fear of death or capture, if the word once given were not kept—for they are more afraid of committing perjury than of killing a man—are we, then, to raise the question, as if it were a subject of debate, whether an oath should be kept when taken through compulsion by servants of God, by religious men who run in the way of the commandments of God to the extent of distributing their goods?

Is that promised residence of his at Hippo made burdensome by the name of exile or deportation or banishment? I assure you I do not consider the priesthood a state of exile. Would our friend, then, choose this rather than that exile? God forbid that a saint of God, and one most dear to us, should be upheld by us in that point of view! God forbid, I say, that he should be reported to have preferred exile to the

9 Cf. Letter 125.

priesthood, or to have preferred perjury to exile! I might say this if the oath by which he promised to live here had really been extorted from him by us or by the people—actually, it was not extorted, although this is denied—when offered it was accepted, with the hope and belief, as we said above, that he might possibly yield to their desire by receiving the priesthood. Finally, whatever may be thought of us or of the people of Hippo, there is a great difference between the case of those may have who forced him to take the oath and those who, I do not say forced, but advised, him to break it. So, then, let him of whom we speak not refuse to consider whether an oath taken under the influence of any kind of fear is worse than the breaking of an oath when the fear has been removed.

Thank God, the people of Hippo regard his promise to them as fulfilled if he comes here with the intention of staying, and goes away where necessity takes him, with the purpose of returning. For, if they took his oath literally and exacted it to the letter, the servant of God ought no more to leave here than he ought to commit perjury. But, as it would be wrong of them to bind any person in this manner, not to mention a man of his type, they themselves have proved that they expected nothing else, since, when they heard that he had left with the intention of returning, they expressed satisfaction; thus, to them a true oath demands no more than what they expected of it. What point is there in saying that he made an exception of necessity in the oath pronounced by his own lips, when again with his own lips he ordered that to be stricken out? Obviously, he might have inserted it when he spoke to the people himself, but if he had, they would emphatically not have answered: 'Thanks be to God!' and they would have repeated that protest which arose when the deacon read it out in that form. But, has it really any bearing on the case whether the excuse of necessity for leaving was inserted in the oath or was not? Nothing else was expected of him than what I said above. Whoever cheats the expectation of those to whom he takes an oath cannot be anything but a perjurer.

So, then, let the promise be kept, and the hearts of the weak brethren healed; otherwise, those who approve of this conduct might be encouraged by such an example to imitate his perjury, while those who disapprove could say with perfect justification that none of us deserve to be believed whether we promise something or even swear to it. Still more should we guard against the tongues of our enemies, which that Arch-enemy makes use of like darts, to slay the weak. But, God forbid that we should hope from such a soul anything other than what the fear of God inspires, and its own high degree of sanctity demands. Although you say that I ought to have prevented the oath, I confess that I could not be so wise as to prefer to see the church I serve endangered by a great outbreak of disorder rather than accept what was offered by a man of such character.

127. Augustine gives greeting in the Lord to his son and daughter, Armentarius and Paulina,[1] illustrious nobles, deservedly honored and esteemed (411)

Your relative,[2] my son Ruferius, a worthy man, brought me back word of the vow you have made to the Lord. I was cheered by his report, but at the same time afraid that a counter-suggestion might be made to you by that tempter who of old has hated such good works; hence, I have thought it my duty to urge your Charity, my excellent lord

---
1 A man and wife who had made a vow of continence and wanted to be released from it.
2 The word *affinis* may mean a neighbor or a relative by marriage.

and deservedly honored and beloved son, to recall what is read in the divine words: 'Delay not to be converted to the Lord, and defer it not from day to day,'[3] and to be active and zealous in performing what you know you have vowed to Him who both demands what is His due and grants what He has promised. For this also is written: 'Vow ye and pay to the Lord our God.'[4] Even if you had not made the vow, what other advice could be given you, or what better thing can a man do than give himself back to the One who gave him life, especially when God has manifested and revealed such a great proof of His love for us in sending His only Son to die for us? It follows, then, Christ died, as the Apostle says, to accomplish this: 'that they who live, may not now live to themselves, but unto him who died for them and rose again.'[5] But, perhaps this world is still to be loved, broken down as it is by such destruction that it has lost even the semblance of attraction? Those who disdained success, when everything in the world succeeded, deserve praise and commendation, but, in equal measure, those who delight in death, when the world is falling to ruin, are worthy of blame and censure.

If the toils and dangers and calamities of this transitory life are undergone for the benefit of this same life which is doomed to die sometime, and not with the hope of removing death entirely, but only of postponing it for a little while, how much greater reason have we to undergo them in view of eternal life, where nature neither anxiously guards against death, nor does cowardice basely fear it, nor wisdom bravely face it! Doubtless, it will come upon no one there, since it will not exist there. Therefore, let eternal life count you among its lovers. Do you not see how this wretched and needy life makes its devotees violent and how it enslaves them

---
3 Eccli. 5.8.
4 Cf. Ps. 75.12.
5 2 Cor. 5.15.

to itself? Yet, those who are often perturbed by its dangers meet a speedier end by the very fact that they fear this end, and by trying to avoid death they hasten it; as if a man, running away from a thief or a wild animal, should plunge into a river and be carried away. When a storm rages at sea, the sailors often throw their food supply overboard; to save their lives they sacrifice what supports life, and they live a life of suffering to avoid an imminent death. What efforts are made to make sure of further effort! And, when death begins to draw near, it is warded off only to prolong fear, for amid so many mischances of human frailty how many deaths are feared! But, when one of them comes, as it surely will come, the others are no longer feared, yet one is warded off that all may be feared. With what sufferings are men tortured when they are treated and cut by doctors! Do they expect to prevent death entirely? They can only postpone death to a slightly later time. Many certain torments are endured by men to prolong life for a few uncertain days, and not seldom death comes to them at once, brought on by the very sufferings which they undergo through their fear of death. Because their choice is emphatically not death to avoid suffering, but suffering to avoid death, they end by enduring both suffering and death. Hence, not only do those who are cured come to the end of their life after their sufferings, since this life, prolonged by such pains, can neither be eternal because it is mortal, nor lengthy because the whole span of life is brief, nor sure of itself for even a short time because it is always uncertain, but these same ones who were willing to suffer to ward off death die eventually of their suffering.

Moreoever, the excessive love of this life has this great evil, which is something to be hated and dreaded, that many, wishing to live a little longer, grievously offend God 'with whom is the fountain of life,'⁶ and thus, while they vainly fear the inevitable end of life, they are cut off from the life which has no end. An additional fact is that a wretched life, even if it could be eternal, is in no wise to be compared to a life of happiness, however short. Yet these lovers of a too wretched and too short life lose the eternal life of endless happiness by wrongly loving the former and wishing to have in it what they lose in the latter. It is certain that they do not love the wretchedness of this life, for they wish to be happy, nor its shortness, for they do not wish to die, but, just because it is life, they love it so much that they often lose the blessed and eternal life.

In view of all this, what great command does eternal life lay upon its lovers when it demands to be loved as that other life is by its devotees? When men will sacrifice everything which is normally loved in the world for the sake of prolonging for some little time in the world a life doomed to end soon in any case, is it right or even bearable that they should not sacrifice the world to attain an unending life with Him by whom the world was made? Just lately, when Rome itself, center of the world's greatest power, was being laid waste by barbarian attacks, how many lovers of this temporal life gave everything they had been saving for the pleasure and adornment of life, not to mention its support and protection, in order to ransom it and to prolong its hapless and destitute existence! Lovers, indeed, are wont to bestow many gifts on those they love, so as to hold them, but these lovers could not have held their beloved unless they had made it needy by loving it, nor could they bestow many gifts upon it; on the contrary, they choose rather to throw everything away lest the enemy take away their beloved life. I do not blame their course of action, for who does not know that

---

6 Ps. 35.10.

life would have been lost if the things which had been stored up for life's sake had not been lost? Yet, some lost their possessions first and then their life, while others, though ready to lose everything to save life, lost life first. Let us learn from this what love we should have for eternal life, so that we may sacrifice all superfluous things because of it, seeing that the lovers of this transitory life have sacrificed even what was necessary to preserve that life.

But let us not despoil our beloved in order to hold her as they do. We can make our temporal life into an ever-ready handmaid to serve us in attaining eternal life, if we do not bind it with the fetters of useless adornment or load it with the burdens of harmful cares. So let us listen to the Lord, who most faithfully promises us eternal life as the object of our most ardent desire when He cries out to the assemblage of the whole world: 'Come to me all you that labor and are burdened, and I will refresh you. Take up my yoke upon you and learn of me, because I am meek and humble of heart, and you shall find rest to your souls; for my yoke is sweet and my burden light.'[7] This science of devout humility drives from the mind and, in a sense, blows away that windy and stormy covetousness, greedy of things set beyond our reach. Labor is found where many things are sought for and loved, things which the will is not adequate to grasp and hold, because it lacks the requisite opportunity. But the good life is near at hand whenever we wish, because goodness consists in wishing for itself in full measure, and requires for its perfection nothing but a perfect will. See if there is any labor when all you have to do is to wish. Hence this divine saying: 'Peace on earth to men of good will.'[8] Where there is peace, there is rest; where there is rest, there is an end of seeking and no reason for labor. But, if this will is to be complete, it

---

7 Matt. 11.28-30.
8 Luke 2.14.

must also be healthful, and it will be healthful if it does not shun the Physician by whose grace alone it can be healed of the disease of its baneful desires. Therefore, He is the Physician who cries out: 'Come to me all you that labor,' saying that His yoke is sweet and His burden light because when His 'charity is poured forth in our hearts by the Holy Ghost,'[9] what He commands will surely be loved, nor will it be hard or burdensome; and the less the neck which is bowed under this single yoke is proud, the more will it be free. This is also the one burden by which the bearer is not bowed down but lifted up. If riches are loved, let them be hoarded where they cannot be lost; if honor is loved, let it be kept where no one is honored undeservedly; if safety is loved, let it be desired and found where there is no fear of losing it when it is gained; if life is loved, let it be sought for where it is ended by no death.

Pay, then, what you have vowed because you are yourselves, and you pay to Him from whom you have your being; pay it, I beg of you. What you pay will not be diminished in the payment, but will be preserved and increased, for He is a kindly creditor, not a needy one; He does not gain anything from what is paid, but makes His payers grow wealthy in Him. What is not paid to Him, therefore, is lost, but what is paid is added to the payer's account; rather, the payer is himself preserved in Him to whom he makes the payment. Payment and payer will then be the same thing, because debt and debtor were the same thing. For, man owes himself to God from whom he has received his being, and, in order to be happy, he must be paid to Him. This is the meaning of what the Lord says in the Gospel: 'Render to Caesar the things that are Caesar's, and to God the things that are God's.'[10] For, He said this when a coin had been shown to Him and He had

---
9 Rom. 5.5.
10 Matt. 22.21.

asked whose image it bore. The answer was 'Caesar's,' and they were to understand thereby that God claims of man His own image in man himself, as Caesar claimed it on the coin. How much greater is the obligation of paying Him what is promised when it is owed to Him even without the promise.

Therefore, my dearest, as far as my poor little ability allows, I might be able to praise more copiously the reward of the holy promise which I hear you have made to the Lord, and to show what a difference there is between the Christians who love this world and those who despise it. Although both are called faithful, both have been cleansed in the water of the same sacred font, and have been inducted into and consecrated by the same mysteries; both have been not only hearers but even preachers of the same Gospel, yet both are not sharers in the light and kingdom of God, nor co-heirs of eternal life, which is the only happy one. The Lord Jesus did not distinguish between those who do not hear Him and those who do, but between the hearers of His words themselves, and this with no fine distinction but to the fullest extent, when He said: 'Whoever heareth these my words and doth them, I shall liken him to a wise man that built his house upon a rock, and the rain fell and the floods came and they beat upon that house, and it fell not, for it was founded upon a rock. But whoever heareth these my words and doth them not shall be like a foolish man that built his house upon the sand, and the rain fell and the floods came and they beat upon that house, and it fell, and great was the fall thereof.'[11] Therefore, to hear those words is to build; in this the two are alike, but in doing and not doing they are as unlike as the building solidly based on the rock is unlike the one without foundation which is thrown down by the ready shifting of the sand. But the one who does not hear the word of God at all cannot for that reason attribute

---

11 Matt. 7.24-27; Luke 6.47-49.

greater safety to himself, for the man who does not build, who has no roof over him, is much more easily exposed to be hurled down, carried off, and swept away by the floods and the winds.

I might, within my modest limits, make a distinction among those who have a claim to be on His right hand in the kingdom of heaven, according to their rank and merits, and I could show how the married life of fathers and mothers of families, who beget sons, however devout and holy they may be, differs from the life which you have vowed to God—I might do this if it were now a question of urging you to make that vow. But, as you have now made the vow, as you have now bound yourself, you are not free to do anything else. Before you incurred the obligation of the vow, you were free to choose the less perfect way, although such liberty deserves no credit when what is not owed is paid, to one's own gain. But, now that your promise binds you before God, I do not invite you to great perfection, I warn you to avoid a great sin. If you do not keep what you have vowed, you will not be the same as you would have been if you had not made the vow. For, in that case, you would have been less perfect, not worse; whereas now—which God forbid!—you will be as much worse off if you break your word to God as you will be more blessed if you keep it. So, then, do not regret having made the vow; rather, rejoice that you are no longer free to do what you might have done to your own great harm. Go forward boldly, then, and turn your words into deeds; He who inspired your vow will help you. Happy the necessity which forces us to better things!

There could be only one reason why we might not only advise you against carrying out what you have vowed, but even forbid you to do it: if by any chance your wife, through weakness of mind or body, should refuse to undertake it with you. For, such vows are not to be made by married people without a mutual will and agreement, and, if there has been inconsidered haste, there is question of making amends for rashness rather than of keeping a promise. God does not exact of us what is vowed at another's expense; rather, He forbids us to trespass on another's rights. A divine pronouncement has been made on this matter by the Apostle: 'The wife hath not power of her own body, but the husband. And in like manner, the husband also hath not power of his own body, but the wife.'[12] He called sex by the name of body. But, since I hear that she is so ready to promise continency to God that she is only prevented from it by her obligation to pay you the conjugal debt, do you both pay God what you both have vowed, so as to offer to Him what you refrain from demanding of each other. If continence is a virtue, as it is, why should the weaker sex be more ready to practise it, when the word virtue seems to be derived from *vir*, man, as the sound of the word indicates? As a man, then, do not shrink from a virtue which a woman is ready to undertake. May the offering of your consent at the supreme altar of the Creator, and the victory over concupiscence, be a stronger, as it is a holier, bond of love. May we rejoice over you in the fullness of the grace of Christ, excellent lords, deservedly honored and cherished sons.

---

12 1 Cor. 7.4.

128. Aurelius,¹ Silvanus,² and all the Catholic bishops to their honored and beloved son, the eminent and excellent tribune and legate, Marcellinus³ (411)

By this letter we hereby make known that we assent to the decree of your Excellency by which provision is made for securing the peace and harmony of our conference and for publishing and safeguarding truth, and we agree to all the details as you have condescended to advise us of them, namely, the place and time of the conference and the number of those who are entitled to be present. We agree also that those whom we choose as conferees shall sign their report, and in the document by which we lay this burden on them, and in which we promise to ratify whatever action they take, you may not only have the signatures of all of us after they have been written, but may even witness us writing them. We will also, with the Lord's help, warn the Christian people, for the sake of peace and quiet, to refrain from gathering near the place of the conference, to restrain their eagerness to hear what is going on while it is going on, and to wait to be informed by the published account, as you promised to make a report to all.

---

1 Archbishop of Carthage.
2 Primate of Numidia. These two prelates signed this letter, but it is believed to be the work of Augustine, although his name does not appear in it.
3 Brother of Apringius, proconsul of Africa, tribune and special legate named by rescript of Emperor Honorius to preside over the joint conference of Catholics and Donatists, and to judge between them. This was the conference which Augustine had been urging for years, in the hope of putting an end to the Donatist schism. It was held on June 1, 2, and 8, 411. Seven months later, after Marcellinus had passed sentence against the Donatists, Emperors Honorius and Theodosius published a decree disestablishing them, confiscating their property, and inflicting heavy penalties for non-compliance. Marcellinus met his death as a result of Donatist intrigue, during the revolt of Heraclian in 413. His name is found in the Roman martyrology under date of April 6. Augustine dedicated several works to him, including the first two books of the *City of God*.

Relying, then, on the truth, we bind ourselves to observe this condition, that, if those with whom we hold the discussion can prove to us that after the Christian peoples, according to the promises of God, had increased in every direction and filled a good part of the earth, and were still spreading out to fill other parts, the Church of Christ was suddenly stricken with the contagion of some obscure persons' sins and died out (according to the charges of these men), and survived only in the sect of Donatus; as was said, if they can prove that, we shall look for no honors of episcopal rank among them, but we shall follow their direction for the sake of our eternal salvation alone, and we shall owe them our gratitude for the great boon of revealing the truth to us. If, on the other hand, we are able to show that the Church of Christ occupies the territory of all the provinces of Africa, as well as those of overseas countries, and of many other races, with a most fruitful abundance of people; that it brings forth fruit and grows through the whole world, as it is written;[4] that it was not possible for it to die out because of the sins of certain persons in its midst; if, in the next place, we demonstrate that the case is closed for those who were more willing to accuse than able to convince (although the cause of the Church does not depend on them); that Caecilian[5] was innocent, while they were adjudged guilty of violence and calumny, by the very emperor to whose judgment they had submitted their charges and their gratuitous accusations; finally, if we prove by divine or human evidence—notwithstanding anything they may have said about anybody's sins—either that those who were indicted on false charges were innocent, or that the Church of Christ, whose communion we share, was not destroyed by any of their sins, then let them return to unity with us, and

---

4 Col. 1.6.
5 Cf. Letter 105 n. 4.

let them find the way of salvation without losing their episcopal rank.⁶ What we detest in them is not the mystery of divine truth but the vagaries of human error; once they have forsaken these, we are ready to embrace them and bind them to our heart in Christian charity, as we now grieve that they are severed from us by a diabolical dissension.

It will be possible for each one of us to occupy his see jointly with a selected partner of his episcopal dignity, with more distinction than he would if he sat with a foreign bishop as colleague. It is mutually agreed on by the basilicas on both sides, with each one outdoing the other in tokens of reciprocal respect—because, when the sentiment of charity dilates hearts, the possession of peace is not limited—that, when one of them dies, from then on individual bishops shall succeed each other in the usual way.⁷ This will not be anything new, for, from the beginning of this separation, Catholic charity has observed it toward those who have tasted the sweetness of unity, however belatedly, after casting off the error of their accursed schism. But, if it happens that Christian peoples set their heart on having only one bishop, and cannot bear the unusual state of affairs of having two in partnership, let us resign from the contest on both sides, and let single bishops be appointed in the places where it is needful to preserve the unity we have achieved, after the individual churches have cast off the state of schism, and have been organized in peaceful unity by other bishops, who shall be found presiding singly over their churches. Why should we shrink from offering this sacrifice of humility to

---

6 At the Council of Carthage (June, 407) it was agreed that if a bishop and his whole flock were converted from Donatism, the flock should keep their bishop, and that bishops who converted their flocks previous to the Imperial Decree of Unity (February, 405) should keep their flocks and churches.

7 That is, the disputed sees would be held jointly by a Catholic and an ex-Donatist bishop, but would revert to single occupancy upon the death of one of the two.

our Redeemer? He came down from heaven to dwell among His human members, that we might be His members, and shall we fear to come down from our episcopal throne to save His members from being torn by a cruel dissension? On our side, nothing is more needful than that we be faithful and obedient Christians; let us always be so. We are ordained bishops for the sake of Christian peoples; let us, then, use our episcopate to effect whatever may further Christian peace for Christian peoples. If we are profitable servants, why do we sacrifice the eternal gain of the Lord to our temporal advancement? The episcopal rank will bring us greater reward if we lay it aside to gather the flock of Christ together than if we hold it and see them scattered, for what right have we to hope for the honor promised by Christ in the next world if our regard for honor in this world has hindered Christian unity?

Our reason for having all this written down for your Excellency is that you may publish it for the benefit of all. We pray that by the help of the Lord our God, by whose inspiration we promise this, and by whose help we hope to fulfill it, that even before the conference, if possible, the hearts of men, however weak or obdurate, may be healed and subdued by a tender charity, that with minds set upon peace we may not resist the clearly evident truth, and that harmony may both precede and follow our discussion. We should not despair so long as they recall that the peacemakers are blessed,[8] and that it is much more appropriate and much easier for them to wish the sect of Donatus to be reconciled with the whole Christian world than that the whole Christian world should be rebaptized by the sect of Donatus. This is shown especially by their treatment of those who returned to them from the sacrilegious and accursed

---

8 Matt. 5.9.

schism of Maximian,[9] whom they had tried to bring back by invoking the decrees of secular powers upon them, but they sought them out with such affection that they did not venture to call in question the baptism conferred by them, and they received some of them back after their condemnation without any reduction of their clerical rank, and without considering that any of them had been contaminated by their participation in that separation. We do not begrudge them this harmonious agreement, but they ought surely to notice how lovingly and zealously the Catholic root[10] seeks after the branch broken away from it, when the branch itself strives equally hard to bring back the little twig cut off from it.

We wish you, son, health in the Lord. I, Aurelius, Bishop of the Catholic Church at Carthage, have signed this letter.[11]

I, Silvanus, elder of the Church at Summa, have signed.[12]

129. Aurelius, Silvanus, and all the Catholic bishops to their honored and dear son, the illustrious and excellent tribune and legate, Marcellinus (411)

We feel great anxiety over the notice or letter of our brothers, whom we wish to convert from their deadly schism to our Catholic peace, since they refused to agree to the edict of your Nobility, by which you made provision for the peaceful and quiet conduct of our discussion, for, even if all of them do not attend, some of them could cause confusion and disorder by crowding in to our conference, which should be a peaceful and orderly one. Let us hope that such is

---

9 Cf. Letter 105 n. 13.
10 Rom. 11.16.
11 In another handwriting.
12 In still another handwriting.

not their plan, and that our suspicion is groundless. It may be that they all wish to be present so that, when it seems good to them, after we have also gathered there, we may all come out together, of one mind, with our differences appeased, the separation of schism healed, and all of us joined in the fraternal bond of the unity of Christ, to the wonder and joy of all good men, and the sorrow of none but the Devil and his peers. May we then all go together in procession to the church to give praise and thanks to God with the most ardent and sincere love!

Leaving out of consideration all the human charges in that letter, whether true or false, is it any great thing if the eye of the man at peace notes, or the reasoning power of the Christian does not refuse to examine and see, that the Church to be sought for is the one where Christ Redeemer is known? For, as we do not listen to the enemies of Christ who say that His Body was stolen from the tomb by the disciples,[1] so we ought not to listen to the enemies of the Church who say that she is not found except among Africans and a very few allies of Africans. The Apostle certainly said that true Christians are the members of Christ.[2] So, then, as we do not believe that the dead Body of Christ disappeared from the tomb through someone's theft, we must not believe that His living members have disappeared from the world through someone's sin. Thus, it is not difficult, since Christ is the head and the Church is the body,[3] to see the Gospel defending the head against the false reports of the Jews, and, at the same, time the Church against the false accusations of heretics. For, the passage which we read: 'It behooved Christ to suffer and to rise again from the dead on the third day,'[4] was directed against those who say that His dead Body was

---
1 Matt. 27.64; 28.13.
2 Eph. 4.25.
3 Eph. 4.15; 5.23; Col. 1.18.
4 Luke 24.46.

carried off from the tomb, and what follows: 'And that penance and remission of sins should be preached in his name unto all nations, beginning at Jerusalem,'[5] is against those who say that the Church does not exist on earth. Thus, in one brief passage and in few words, the enemy of the head, as well as the enemy of the body, is put to flight; if he is faithful in paying attention, he may be set right.

Our grief that our brothers hold to their hostility is accentuated by the fact that they hold to the same Scriptures with us, Scriptures in which those most evident proofs are found. As for the Jews who deny the Resurrection of Christ, they at least do not acknowledge the Gospel, but these brothers of ours are bound by the authority of both Testaments, yet they insist on falsely accusing us of betraying the Gospel,[6] and they will not accept it when it is read. Now, it may be that they have studied the holy Scriptures more carefully as a preparation for undertaking this conference, and that they have discovered the numerous proofs of the promise that the Church will exist among all nations and throughout the whole earth, just as we see that it was handed down and presented from the beginning in the Gospel, and in the apostolic letters, and in the Acts of the Apostles. In these we read of the very places and cities and provinces in which the Church increased from its beginning at Jerusalem, and from there it spread into Africa, not by transferring itself there, but by growing there. But, they have not found there any divinely uttered testimony saying that the Church would die out in other parts of the world, and would survive in Africa alone, in the sect of Donatus, and they must have seen how ridiculous it would be for so much divine evidence to be read for a Church which, according to their way of thinking, was to be pleasing to the Lord. So,

---

5 Luke 24.47.
6 This charge was connected with the beginnings of Donatism.

perhaps, it was with these thoughts, suitable to put an end to their vain and deadly hostility, so adverse to their eternal salvation, that they wished to come in full numbers to the place of our conference, not to cause a new disturbance, but to put an end to a long-standing feud.[7]

Turning to that point in which they are commonly deeply angered against us, namely, that the kings of the earth—who, according to ancient prophecy, are to serve the Lord Christ[8]—enact laws against heretics and schismatics, to preserve Catholic peace, we believe that at one time they thought that was not reprehensible, because early kings, not only of the Hebrew nation, but even of a foreign one, overawed all the peoples of their realm with most threatening ordinances, enjoining them not even to utter, much less do, anything against the God of Israel, that is, the true God. Besides, their own predecessors referred the very case of Caecilian,[9] out of which the whole controversy arose, to the Emperor Constantine, forwarding their charges through the proconsul Anulinus, and obviously their only reason for doing this was to induce the Emperor Constantine to use his royal power and issue a decree against the defeated party but in support of the winning side. If they had read the public records—and perhaps they have been forced to do so by this conference—they could have found out that the whole question was settled long ago, after the ecclesiastical trials in which Caecilian was acquitted, by the decision of the same emperor, to whose consideration they referred the whole matter, both at the beginning and again when they appealed. In the public records they could also have found the case of

---

7 The Donatists wanted all their bishops, who had come to Carthage, to attend the conference, not merely selected delegates, as had been arranged by Marcellinus and agreed to by the Catholics, who had reason to fear Donatist violence.
8 Ps. 101.23; Dan. 7.27.
9 Cf. Letters 105,108.

Felix of Aptunga,[10] the consecrator of Caecilian, whom they named in their council as the source of all evils, and they could have learned that he was exonerated by the proconsul Aelian, who was appointed arbitrator by the emperor.

Still, even if they had taken note of this and—what would have been easy—if they had observed that in the holy Scriptures it was promised that the Church would survive to the time of the harvest, the winnowing and the selection of fish on the shore,[11] in spite of being intermingled with the cockle, the chaff, and the bad fish, they could have reflected that, even if Caecilian and his fellow bishops had been guilty as charged, they could not have been prejudicial to the Christian world. This world God promised long before to a few believers, and has now accomplished before many witnesses; unless, perhaps we are to think that a man, sinning, had more power against the Church than God, making oath, had in its favor, and that sin which destroyed was stronger than truth which promised. Perhaps they have now realized how foolish and wicked it is to think such things; they have also reflected that the Maximianists who condemned Primian were condemned by them, and that they called on the secular power to expel them from their basilicas. From a quite recent example of their own they must have learned more exactly that it is not a sin for the Church to call on such secular powers for some similar action against those who revolt against her. The fact that they later on received back some of those whom they had condemned; that they gave a period of grace to many others involved in participation in the same schism, at the very time when they were condemning them; that they said their period of sojourn in communion with the sacrilegious branch of Maximian had not contaminated them; that they did not dare to invalidate

---

10 Cf. Letters 43,88,93,108.
11 Matt. 13.24-30; 3,12; 13,47,48.

or confer again the baptism administered by the condemned or their partisans, even though such baptism had been given outside their sect in schism: all this shows how they must certainly have concluded that everything they said against us was proved wrong by their own example. So it is possible to believe that they now understand how shameful and how intolerable it is that peace should be found in the sect of Donatus, while the Christian world should be defiled because of Caecilian, and the unity of Christ should not enjoy peace while those who condemned Primian, as well as those condemned in his trial, should sit in the bishops' chairs with them and with Primian himself. The Christian world is to be branded with infamy, on account of Caecilian, to produce peace in the sect of Donatus, but the unity of Christ in not to live in peace.

It may be that they were thinking these thoughts, and were moved by the fear of God, when they all wished to be present at the place of the conference, and that their object was not disturbance but peace. According to their story, they were present in full strength so as to show how numerous they are, because their opponents often falsely claimed that they were few in number. If this claim was ever made by ours, it could be made with perfect truth of those places where the number of our bishops, clerics, and laymen is much greater than theirs, and especially in the proconsular province,[12] although, with the exception of consular Numidia,[13] we also easily outnumber them in the rest of the African provinces; certainly, in comparison with all the nations through which the Catholic communion has spread, we are absolutely right in speaking of them as a mere handful. But, if they were now really anxious to advertise their number,

---

12 This was the province in which Carthage was situated; it was called Proconsular Africa.
13 Consular, or Proconsular, Numidia was the part of Numidia along the coast. Hippo was in this province.

could they not do it in a more orderly and peaceful manner through their signatures, which your edict notified them to subscribe, in your presence, to their authorization of delegates? What do they mean by insisting on a full attendance of their membership at the place of conference? If their intentions are not peaceful, are they going to make a disturbance by speaking or are they going to take some action without speaking? For, even if there is no uproar, the mere whispering of so many will make enough noise to interfere with the conference.

Why do they think it necessary to add to their note of acceptance that they were justified in asking for a full attendance, because all had been summoned to attend, as if the few who had a right to attend could not be chosen, except by all who had come to subscribe to their election in your presence? Was it so that all should be included among the few, since the few had been chosen by the many? They are planning either an outbreak or peace. We are praying for the one and guarding against the other; consequently, we have agreed to allow them all to attend, in case they are planning what we are guarding against—which God forbid!—rather than what we are praying for. However, we stipulate that our number be as large as your Excellency approves; and, if any disorder breaks out because of the crowd, it is to be blamed on them with good reason, because their side had such a superfluous number present when the business was supposed to be transacted by a few. If, on the other hand, as we greatly desire, ardently hope for, and humbly beg of the Lord, their large number is necessary to bring about unity, when they are ready for it, we also shall be present and, with the help of Him who gives this great boon, we shall rush together with eagerness, saying: 'You are our brothers'—not to those who hate us, but to those who have put an end to hatred and who embrace us—'that the name of the Lord may be glorified and may appear to them in gladness,'[14] and also to those who now experience with us 'How good and how pleasant it is for brethren to dwell together in unity.'[15]

We wish you, sons, good health in God.

I, Aurelius, Bishop of the Catholic Church at Carthage, have signed.

I, Silvanus, primate of the province at Numidia, have signed.[16]

130. Augustine, bishop, servant of Christ and of the servants of Christ, gives greeting in the Lord of lords to Proba,[1] servant of God (c. 412)

Mindful of your request and my promise to write you something on prayer to God, whenever time and opportunity should be available by the bounty of Him to whom we pray, I should since have paid my debt and given my tribute to your loving desire in the charity of Christ. I have no words to express my joy on receiving your request, which showed me how much importance you attach to this great duty. For, what occupation is more fitting for your widowhood than to persevere in prayer night and day, according to the advice of the Apostle? As you know, he says: 'But she that is a widow indeed and desolate, has trusted in the Lord and

---

14 Isa. 66.5 (Septuagint).
15 Ps. 132.1.
16 These lines are in different hands.

---

1 A noble Roman lady, surnamed Faltonia, wife of Probus, praetorian prefect and one-time consul, grandmother of the virgin Demetrias, whose mother Juliana was Proba's daughter-in-law. She had fled into Africa to escape the barbarian invasion of Rome. Augustine refers to these ladies in his treatise on *Widowhood* (cf. *Fathers of the Church* 16, New York 1952), and St. Jerome (*Ep.* 8 to Demetrias) praises Proba in almost extravagant terms.

continues in prayers night and day.'² It might seem a strange thing, since you are noble according to this world, as well as rich and the mother of such a great family, and not desolate, although a widow, that the attraction of prayer should have taken hold of your heart, and laid strong claim to it, but you have a wise understanding of the fact that no soul can be free of danger in this world and in this life.

Therefore, He who gives you this inner knowledge surely does for you what He did for His disciples who were sorrowful, not for themselves but for the human race, and were in a state of doubt whether anyone could be saved, when they heard from Him that 'it is easier for a camel to pass through the eye of a needle, than for a rich man to enter into the kingdom of heaven.'³ With a marvellous and most merciful reassurance He answered that what is impossible for men is easy for God. He, then, to whom it is easy to make a rich man enter the kingdom of heaven, has inspired you with a devout anxiety about the proper way for you to pray, about which you thought fit to consult me. For, when He was still on earth, in the flesh, He opened heaven to Zacchaeus, a rich man,⁴ and after His Resurrection and Ascension He glorified many rich men by imparting the Holy Spirit to them, making them despise this world and thereby become the richer by having done with the craving for riches. How, then, could you thus long to pray to the Lord if you did not put your hope in Him? And how could you put your hope in Him, if you put it in the uncertainty of riches, despising that salutary warning of the Apostle? For, he says: 'Charge the rich of this world not to be high-minded, nor to trust in the uncertainty of riches, but in the living God (who giveth us abundantly all things to enjoy); to be rich in good works,

---
2 Cf. 1 Tim. 5.5
3 Matt. 19.24-26; Luke 18.25.27.
4 Luke 19.2-10.

to give easily, to communicate to others, to lay up in store for themselves a good foundation against the time to come, that they may lay hold on the true life.'[5]

Through love of this true life you ought, then, to consider yourself desolate in this world, no matter what happiness you enjoy. For, just as that is the true life in comparison with which this other, which is so much loved, is not to be called life, however pleasant and prolonged it may be, so that is the true comfort which God promised by the Prophet saying: 'I will give them true comfort, peace upon peace.'[6] Without this comfort there is more grief than consolation to be found in earthly comforts, whatever they may be. Certainly, as far as riches and high-ranking positions and other things of that sort are concerned—things which mortals think themselves happy to possess, because they have never partaken of that true happiness—what comfort can they bestow, when it is a far better thing not to need them than to excel in them, and when we are tortured by the craving to possess them, but still more by the fear of losing, once we do possess them? Not by such goods do men become good, but having become good otherwise, they make these things good by their good use of them. Therefore, there is no true comfort in these things; rather, it is found where true life is. A man's happiness necessarily must come from the same source as his goodness.

These good men seem to spread no small comfort about them, even in this life. For, if poverty pinches, if grief saddens, if physical pain unnerves them, if exile darkens their life, if any other misfortune fills them with foreboding, let there be good men at hand who know how to 'rejoice with them that rejoice,' as well as to 'weep with them that weep,'[7] who are skilled in helpful words and conversation, and in large

---

[5] 1 Tim. 6.17-19.
[6] Isa. 57.18,19 (Septuagint).
[7] Rom. 12.15.

measure those bitter trials are lessened, the heavy burdens are lightened, the obstacles are met and overcome. But He who makes them good by His Spirit[8] effects this in and through them. On the other hand, if riches abound, if no bereavement befalls them, if they enjoy health of body and live securely in their own country, with evil men for their neighbors, men whom no one can trust, yet at whose hands trickery, cheating, anger, discord, and treachery are to be met and feared, do not all those other goods become bitter and harsh, devoid of all joy and sweetness? Thus it is in almost all human affairs—they are not our friends if man is not our friend. But, where on this earth is such a one to be found, one whose mind and character give a sense of security? For, no one is known to another as he is to himself, yet neither is he so well known to himself as to be sure of his place of abode tomorrow. Hence, although many are known by their fruits,[9] and some give joy to their friends by their good lives, while others cause grief by their bad lives, there is so much about human minds that is unknown and unknowable that the Apostle warns us not to 'judge anyone before the time, until the Lord come who both will bring to light the hidden things of darkness, and will make manifest the counsels of the hearts, and then shall every man have praise from God.'[10]

Therefore, amid the shadows of this life in which 'we are absent from the Lord' as long as 'we walk by faith and not by sight,'[11] the Christian soul should consider itself desolate, and should not cease from praying and from attending with the eye of faith to the word of the divine and sacred Scriptures: 'as to a light that shineth in a dark place, until

---

8 Luke 11.13.
9 Matt. 7.16,20.
10 1 Cor. 4.5.
11 2 Cor. 5.6,7.

the day dawn and the day-star arise in our hearts.'[12] For, the ineffable source, so to speak, of this light is that brightness which so shines in the darkness that it is not comprehended by the darkness,[13] and our hearts must be purified by faith[14] if we are to see it. For, 'Blessed are the clean of heart, for they shall see God,'[15] and 'We know that when he shall appear, we shall be like to him, because we shall see him as he is.'[16] Then there will be true life after death, and true comfort after desolation. That life will 'Deliver our soul from death,' that comfort will 'free our eyes from tears,' and, since there will be no temptation there, the same psalm continues: 'He has delivered my feet from falling.'[17] Moreover, if there is not temptation, there is no longer any prayer, for the contemplation of fulfillment has replaced the hope of the promised good. Hence he says: 'I will please the Lord in the land of the living,'[18] where we shall then be, and not, as now, in the desert of the dead. 'For you are dead,' says the Apostle, 'and your life is hid with Christ in God. When Christ shall appear, who is your life, then you also shall appear with him in glory.'[19] This is the true life which the rich are charged to lay hold on by good works,[20] and there is the true comfort for the widow who is now desolate, even though she has children or grandchildren, and governs her own house virtuously, dealing with all her dependents so as make them place their hope in God,[21] and says in her prayer: 'For thee my soul hath thirsted, for

---

12 2 Peter 1.19.
13 John 1.5.
14 Acts 15.9.
15 Matt. 5.8.
16 1 John 3.2.
17 Ps. 118.8.
18 Ps. 14.9.
19 Col. 3.3,4
20 1 Tim. 6.17-19.
21 1 Tim. 5.4,5.

thee my flesh, O how many ways, in a desert land and where there is no way and no water.'[22] This is indeed a dying life, whatever mortal comfort it may shower on us, whatever companions may share it with us, whatever wealth of worldly goods it may lavish on us. I am sure you know how uncertain all those things are, and, compared to that promised happiness, what would they be, even if they were not uncertain?

You asked me for instruction on prayer, but I have said all this because you are a widow of wealth and high rank, and the mother of a large family who are still with you and who still reverence you, but I want you to feel that you are desolate, that you have not yet laid hold on that life where true and certain comfort is found, and where the words of the prophecy are fulfilled: 'We are filled in the morning with thy mercy, and we have rejoiced and are delighted all our days. We have rejoiced for the days in which thou hast humbled us, for the years in which we have seen evils.'[23]

So, then, that you may continue in prayers night and day, until that consolation comes to you, remember that you are desolate, however much you may abound in the good fortune of worldly wealth. The Apostle did not attribute this gift to just any widow, but he says: 'She that is a widow indeed and desolate, has trusted in the Lord, and continues in prayers night and day.'[24] But, note carefully what follows: 'But she that liveth in pleasures is dead while she is living,'[25] for a man lives in the things which he loves, which he chiefly seeks after, by which he believes himself happy. Therefore, what the Scripture says about riches: 'If riches abound, set

---

22 Ps. 62.2,3.
23 Ps. 89.14,15.
24 1 Tim. 5.5.
25 1 Tim. 5.6.

not your heart upon them,'[26] I say to you about pleasures: if pleasures abound, set not your heart upon them. Do not rely too strongly on the fact that they are not lacking to you, that they minister to your satisfaction abundantly, that they flow, so to speak, from a plentiful source of earthly happiness. All these things you must inwardly despise and reject; you must seek after no more of them than is needed to support your bodily health. Because of the necessary activities of this life, health is not to be despised until 'this mortal shall put on immortality,'[27] and that is the true and perfect and unending health which is not refreshed by corruptible pleasure when it fails through earthly weakness, but is maintained by heavenly strength and made young by eternal incorruptibility. The Apostle himself says: 'Make not provision for the flesh in its concupiscences,'[28] because our care of the flesh must be in view of the exigencies of salvation. 'For no man ever hated his own flesh,'[29] as he also says. This seems to be the reason why he rebukes Timothy for too great chastisement of the body, and advises him to 'use a little wine for his stomach's sake and his frequent infirmities.'[30]

These are the pleasures among which the widow is dead while she is living if she lives by them, that is, if her heart clings to them and lingers over the joy they give, but many holy men and women have been on guard in every way against riches, as the very source of pleasures, and have cast them aside by distributing them to the poor, thus, in another and better way, storing them up as treasure in heaven. If you feel yourself bound by your duty to your family not to do this, you know what account you must give of them to God. For no one 'knoweth what is done in

26 Ps. 61.11.
27 1 Cor. 15.54.
28 Rom. 13.14.
29 Eph. 5.29.
30 1 Tim. 5.23.

man, but the spirit of a man that is in him.'³¹ Therefore, we ought not to judge anything before the time 'until the Lord come, who will both bring to light the hidden things of darkness, and will make manifest the counsels of the heart; then shall every man have praise from God.'³² However, it is part of your duty as a widow, if pleasures abound, not to set your heart upon them, lest it wither away and die, whereas, in order to live, it ought to be lifted up on high. Number yourself among those of whom it is written: 'Their hearts shall live forever and ever.'³³

You have heard how you are to pray; hear now what you are to ask in prayer, since this is the point about which you especially wanted my advice, being deeply moved by what the Apostle said: 'For we know not what we should pray for as we ought,'³⁴ and you were afraid you might suffer more harm by not praying as you ought than by not praying at all. This can be summed up briefly thus: Pray for happiness; this is something all men wish to possess, for those who live the most wicked and depraved life would never live that way if they did not imagine themselves happy thereby. So, what else ought we to pray for except that which both bad and good desire, but which only the good attain?

You will probably ask me next: What is the nature of that happiness? Many philosophical minds have been occupied, and much time has been spent, on that question, and those who have been less successful in answering it are the ones who have paid least honor and given least thanks to its Author. First, then, note whether one should agree with those who place happiness in the following of their own will. God forbid that we should think that true! For what would happen if a man willed to live wickedly? Could we not

---
31 Cf. 1 Cor. 2.11.
32 1 Cor. 4.5.
33 Ps 21.27.
34 Rom. 8.26.

prove him to be wretched in proportion to the ease with which his evil purpose was fulfilled? Even those who practise philosophy without recognizing God have rightly repudiated that opinion. For, the most eloquent man of them all says: 'Look, now, at some others, not exactly philosophers, but fond of debating, who say that all those are happy who live according to their own inclination. But they are wrong, for it is essentially a most unhappy thing to wish for what is not proper, yet is it not more unhappy to wish to obtain what is not proper than not to obtain what you wish?'[35] What do you think of those words? Were they not spoken by Wisdom herself through the lips of a man? We can then say what the Apostle says of a certain prophet of Crete, whose opinion he accepted: 'This testimony is true.'[36]

He, then, is happy who has everything he wants, but does not want what is not proper. Accepting that conclusion, note now what men may wish for without impropriety. One wishes to marry; another, having lost his wife, chooses to live thereafter in continence; another, though married, chooses not to enjoy any of the fruits of marriage. Even if anything better is found, here or elsewhere, we cannot say that any of these wish what is not proper; thus, to desire sons as the fruit of marriage is obviously to desire life and health to those one has brought forth, and even the chaste widow is commonly absorbed in that wish. Those who reject marriage and no longer wish to beget sons still wish life and health to the sons they have begotten. The chastity of virgins is free from all this care; still, they have all their dear ones for whom they can quite properly wish temporal welfare. But, when men have attained that welfare for themselves and for those whom they love, shall we be able to say that they are

---
35 Cicero, *Hortensius*, the dialogue, now lost, which Augustine says (*Conf.* 3.7-9) aroused in him a love of wisdom.
36 Tit. 1.13.

now happy? They have something which it is proper to wish for, but, if they have nothing else, either greater or better or more to their advantage and personal distinction, they are still far from happiness.

Is it agreed, then, that over and above that temporal welfare men may wish for positions of rank and authority for themselves and their families? Certainly, it is proper for them to wish for these things, not for the sake of the things themselves, but for another reason, namely, that they may do good by providing for the welfare of those who live under them, but it is not proper to covet them out of the empty pride of self-esteem, or useless ostentation, or hurtful vanity. Therefore, if they wish for themselves and their families only what is sufficient of the necessaries of life, as the Apostle says: 'But godliness with contentment is a great gain. For we brought nothing into this world, and we can carry nothing out; but having food and wherewith to be covered, with these we are content. For they that will become rich fall into temptation, and the snares of the devil and into many unprofitable and hurtful desires, which drown men into destruction and perdition. For the desire of money is the root of all evils, which some coveting have erred from the faith and have entangled themselves in many sorrows'[37]—this sufficiency is not an improper desire in whoever wishes this and nothing more; whoever does wish more does not wish this, and therefore does not wish properly. He wished this and prayed for it who said: 'Give me not riches [or] beggary; give me only enough of the necessaries of life; lest being filled I should become a liar and say: "Who seeth me?" or become poor, I should steal and forswear the name of my God.'[38] Surely you see that this sufficiency is not to be coveted for its own sake, but to provide for health of body and for clothing

---

37 1 Tim. 6.6-10.
38 Prov. 30.8,9 (Septuagint).

which accords with man's personal dignity, and which makes it possible for him to live with others honorably and respectably.

Among all these objects, man's personal safety and friendship are desired for their own sake, whereas a sufficiency of the necessaries of life is usually sought—when it is properly sought—for the two reasons mentioned above, but not for its own sake. Now, personal safety is closely connected with life itself, and health, and integrity of mind and body. In like manner, friendship is not confined by narrow limits; it includes all those to whom love and affection are due, although it goes out more readily to some, more slowly to others, but it reaches even our enemies, for whom we are commanded to pray. Thus, there is no one in the human race to whom love is not due, either as a return of mutual affection or in virtue of his share in our common nature. But, those who love us mutually in holiness and chastity give us the truest joy. These are the goods we must pray to keep when we have them, to acquire when we do not have them.

Is this, then, the whole of happiness, and are these all the goods which are comprised in it? Or does truth teach us something else which is to be preferred to all of these? As long as that sufficiency and that personal safety—either our own or that of our friends—is a merely temporal good, it will have to be sacrificed to secure eternal life; whatever may be true of the body, the soul is certainly not to be considered sane if it does not prefer eternal to temporal goods. For, our temporal life is lived profitably only when it is used to gain merit whereby eternal life is attained. Therefore, all other things which are profitable and properly desired are unquestionably to be referred to that one life by which we live with God and by His life. Inasmuch as we love ourselves in God, if we really love Him, so also, according to another commandment, we truly love our neighbors as ourselves, if, as far as we are able, we lead them to a similar love of God. Therefore, we love God for Himself, but ourselves and our neighbor for His sake. But, even when we live thus, let us not think that we are established in happiness, as if we had nothing left to pray for. How can we find happiness in life when the one incentive to a good life is still lacking to us?

And what use is there in spreading ourselves out over many things and asking what we should pray for, fearing that we may not pray as we ought, when we should rather say with the Psalmist: 'One thing I have asked of the Lord, this will I seek after, that I may dwell in the house of the Lord all the days of my life; that I may see the delight of the Lord, and may visit his temple?'[39] In heaven all these days are not accomplished by coming and going; and the beginning of one is not the end of another; they are equally without end, since the life of which they are the days has no end. That true Life taught us to pray[40] to attain this blessed life, and not to pray with much speaking, as if we were more likely to be heard, the more words we use in our prayer, for He knows, as the Lord Himself said, what is needful for us before we ask Him. For this reason it may seem strange, although He cautions us against much speaking, that He still urges us to pray, since He knows what is needful for us before we ask for it. Yet, He said: 'We ought always to pray and not to faint,'[41] and He used the example of a certain widow who wished to be avenged of her adversary, and who petitioned an unjust judge so often that she made him listen to her, not through any motive of justice or compassion, but through weariness of her importunity. In this way we were to be

---

39 Ps. 26.4.
40 Matt. 6.7,8.
41 Luke 18.1-8.

taught how surely the merciful and just God hears us when we pray without ceasing, since the widow, because of her continual petition, could not be treated with contempt even by an unjust and wicked judge, and how willingly and kindly He satisfies the good desires of those by whom He knows that others' sins are forgiven, since she who wished to be avenged obtained her desire. The man, too, whose friend came to him off a journey[42] and who had nothing to set before him, wishing to borrow three loaves from a friend—and perhaps the Trinity of one substance is symbolized by this figure—woke him, as he slept in the midst of his servants, by begging insistently and importunately, so that he gave him as many as he wished. By this we are to understand that if a man, roused from sleep, is forced to give unwillingly in answer to a request, God, who does not know sleep, and who rouses us from sleep that we may ask, gives much more graciously.

The following passage bears on the same thought: 'Ask and you shall receive, seek and you shall find, knock and it shall be opened to you. For everyone that asketh receiveth, and he that seeketh findeth, and to him that knocketh it shall be opened. And which man of you if his son ask for bread, will he give him a stone? or if he asks a fish will he give him a serpent? or if he asks an egg will he reach him a scorpion? If you then, being evil, know how to give good gifts to your children, how much more will your Father from heaven give good things to them that ask him?'[43] Of those three things which the Apostle commends,[44] faith is signified by the fish, either because of the water of baptism, or because it remains unharmed by the waves of this world; and the Serpent is opposed to it, because it craftily and deceitfully

---

42 Luke 11.5-13.
43 Luke 11.9-13.
44 1 Cor. 13.13.

persuaded man not to believe in God. Hope is symbolized by the egg, because the chick is not yet alive but it will be, it is not yet seen but it is hoped for—'for hope that is seen is not hope;'[45]—and the scorpion is opposed to it because whoever hopes for eternal life forgets the things that are behind and stretches himself forth to those that are before,[46] since it is dangerous for him to look backward, and he is on guard against the rear of the scorpion, which has a poisoned dart in its tail. Charity is symbolized by bread, for 'the greater of these is charity,'[47] and among foods bread certainly surpasses all others in value; the stone is opposed to it because the stony-hearted cast out charity. It may be that these gifts signify something more appropriate; nevertheless, He who knows how to give good gifts to His children urges us to ask and to seek and to knock.

Since He knows what is needful for us[48] before we ask Him, our mind can be troubled by His acting thus, unless we understand that our Lord and God does not need to have our will made known to Him—He cannot but know it—but He wishes our desire to be exercised in prayer that we may be able to receive what He is preparing to give.[49] That is something very great, but we are too small and straitened to contain it. Therefore it is said to us: 'Be enlarged, bear not the yoke with unbelievers.'[50] Thus we shall receive that which is so great, which eye hath not seen because it is not color, nor ear heard because it is not sound, nor hath it entered into the heart of man,[51] because the heart of man has to enter into it; and we shall receive it in fuller measure

---
45 Rom. 8.24.
46 Phil. 3.13.
47 1 Cor. 13.13.
48 Matt. 6.8.
49 1 Cor. 2.9.
50 2 Cor. 6.13,14.
51 1 Cor. 2.9.

in proportion as our hope is more strongly founded and our charity more ardent.

Therefore we pray always, with insistent desire, in that same faith and hope and charity. But, we also pray to God in words at certain fixed hours and times, so that we may urge ourselves on and take note with ourselves how much progress we have made in this desire, and may rouse ourselves more earnestly to increase it. The more fervent the desire, the more worthy the effect which ensues. And that is why the Apostle says: 'Desire without ceasing'.[52] Let us, then always desire this of the Lord God and always pray for it. But, because that desire grows somewhat lukewarm by reason of our cares and preoccupation with other things, we call our mind back to the duty of praying at fixed hours, and we urge ourselves in the words of our prayer to press forward to what we desire; otherwise, after our desire has begun to grow lukewarm, it then becomes entirely cold and is completely extinguished unless it is frequently rekindled. Consequently, that saying of the Apostle: 'Let your petitions be made known to God,'[53] is not to be taken in the sense that they are actually made known to God, who certainly knew them before they were uttered, but that they are made known to us before God, through our patience, but not before men through our boasting. Or, perhaps they might even be made known to the angels who are with God, so that they may, in a sense, offer our prayers to God and consult Him about them, and bring us back His answer, either openly or secretly, according as they know what He wills, as it befits them to know. Thus, an angel said to a man: 'And now, when thou didst pray, thou and Sara, I offered the remembrance of your prayer in the sight of the splendor of God.'[54]

---

52 Cf. 1 Thess. 5.17.
53 Phil. 4.6.
54 Tobias 12.12 (Septuagint).

In view of this, it is not reprehensible or useless to pray at length when one is free, that is, when the obligations of other good and necessary works do not prevent us, although even in those, as I said, we must always pray by that desire of the heart. But, to pray at length does not mean, as some think, to pray with much speaking.[55] Continual longing is not the same as much speaking. For, it is written of the Lord Himself that He passed the night in prayer and that 'He prayed the longer.'[56] In this He had no other object than to show Himself to us on earth as our ready Advocate, and with the Father as our eternal Benefactor.

It is said that the brothers in Egypt have certain prayers which they recite often, but they are very brief, and are, so to speak, darted forth rapidly like arrows, so that the alert attention, which is necessary in prayer, does not fade and grow heavy through long-drawn-out periods. By this practice they show quite well that, just as this attention is not to be whipped up if it cannot be sustained, so, if it can be sustained, it is not to be broken off too quickly. Prayer is to be free of much speaking, but not of much entreaty, if the fervor and attention persist. To speak much in prayer is to transact a necessary piece of business with unnecessary words, but to entreat much of Him whom we entreat is to knock by a long-continued and devout uplifting of the heart. In general, this business is transacted more by sighs than by speech, more by tears than by utterance. For, He sets our tears in His sight[57] and our groaning is not hid from Him[58] who created all things by His Word and who does not look for human words.

Words, then, are necessary for us so that we may be roused and may take note of what we are asking, but we are not to

---

55 Matt. 6.7.
56 Luke 6.12; 22.43.
57 Ps. 55.9.
58 Ps. 37.16.

believe that the Lord has need of them, either to be informed or to be influenced. Therefore, when we say 'Hallowed be thy name,'[59] we rouse ourselves to desire that His Name, which is always holy, should be held holy among men also, that is, that it be not dishonored, something which benefits men, but not God. Likewise, when we say 'Thy kingdom come,' it will come inevitably whether we wish it or not, but we stir up our desire for that kingdom, that it may come in us, and that we may deserve to reign in it. When we say 'Thy will be done on earth as it is in heaven,' we ask of Him that obedience for ourselves, so that His will may be done in us as it is done in heaven by His angels. When we say 'Give us this day our daily bread,' by 'this day' we mean 'at this time,' when we either ask for that sufficiency, signifying the whole of our need under the name of bread, which is the outstanding part of it, or for the sacrament of the faithful, which is necessary at this time for attaining not so much this temporal as that eternal happiness. When we say 'Forgive us our debts as we also forgive our debtors,' we warn ourselves both what to ask and what to do that we may deserve to obtain mercy. When we say 'Lead us not into temptation,' we warn ourselves to ask not to be deprived of His help, not to consent to any temptation through deception, not to yield through tribulation. When we say 'Deliver us from evil,' we warn ourselves to reflect that we are not yet in that happy state where we shall suffer no evil. And the fact that this petition is placed last in the Lord's Prayer shows plainly that the Christian man, beset by any kind of trouble, utters his groans by means of it, pours out his tears in it, begins, continues, and ends his prayer by it. By these words it was fitting to recall the truths thereby implied to our mind.

For, whatever other words we may say, whatever words

---

59 Matt. 6.9-13.

the fervor of the suppliant utters at the beginning of his petition to define it, or follows up afterward to intensify it, we say nothing that is not found in this prayer of the Lord, if we pray properly and fittingly. But, whoever says anything in his prayer which does not accord with this Gospel prayer, even if his prayer is not of the forbidden sort, it is carnal, and I am not sure it ought not to be called forbidden, since those who are born again of the Spirit[60] ought to pray only in a spiritual manner. For instance, he who says: 'Be sanctified among all men, as thou hast been sanctified among us,'[61] and: 'May thy prophets be found faithful,'[62] what else does he say but 'Hallowed be thy name'? And he who says: 'O God of hosts, convert us and show thy face, and we shall be saved,'[63] what else does he say but 'Thy kingdom come'? He who says: 'Direct my steps according to thy word, and let no iniquity have dominion over me,'[64] what else does he say but 'Thy will be done on earth as it is in heaven'? He who says: 'Give me neither beggary nor riches,'[65] what else does he say but, 'Give us this day our daily bread'? He who says: 'O Lord remember David and all his meekness,'[66] or: 'Lord, if I have done this thing, if there be iniquity in my hands, if I have rendered to them that have repaid me evils,'[67] what else does he say but 'Forgive us our debts as we also forgive our debtors'? He who says: 'Take from me the greediness of the belly and let not the lusts of the flesh take hold of me,'[68] what else does he say but, 'Lead us not into temptation'? He who says: 'Deliver me from my enemies,

---

60 John 3.5.
61 Eccli. 36.4.
62 Eccli. 36.18.
63 Ps. 79.4.
64 Ps. 118.133.
65 Prov. 30.8.
66 Ps. 131.1.
67 Ps. 7.4,5.
68 Eccli. 23.6.

O God, and defend me from them that rise up against me,'[69] what else does he say but 'Deliver us from evil.'? And if you were to run over all the words of holy prayers, you would find nothing, according to my way of thinking, which is not contained and included in the Lord's Prayer. Hence when we pray, it is allowable to say the same things in different words, but it ought not to be allowable to say different things.

These are the things we must ask without fail for ourselves, for our families, for strangers, and for our very enemies; although one may pray for this one and another for that one, according as a near or remote kinship stirs or raises up affection in the heart of the suppliant. But, if anyone, for instance, says in his prayer: 'Lord, multiply my wealth,' or: 'Give me as much as You have given to this one or that one,' or: 'Increase my rank in life, make me influential and well known in this world,' or anything else of this sort, and if he says it because he covets these things, and does not bear in mind that they are given him to help his fellow men according to God's will, such a one, I think, does not find in the Lord's Prayer any words which he can adapt to these petitions. Therefore, he ought at least be ashamed to ask for what he is not ashamed to covet, or, if he is ashamed, but covetousness has the mastery over him, how much better for him to ask to be freed from that evil of covetousness, addressing his prayer to Him to whom we say: 'Deliver us from evil!'

Now, you know, I think, not only the nature of your prayer, but its object, and you have learned this, not from me, but from Him who has deigned to teach us all. Happiness is what we must seek and what we must ask of the Lord God. Many arguments have been fashioned by many men about the nature of happiness, but why should we turn to the many men or the many arguments? Brief and true is the word in

---

[69] Ps. 58.2.

the Scripture of God: 'Happy is the people whose God is the Lord.'[70] That we may belong to that people and that we may be able to attain to contemplation of Him and to eternal life with Him, 'the end of the commandment is charity from a pure heart and a good conscience, and an unfeigned faith.'[71] Among those same three, hope is put for a good conscience. 'Faith therefore, and hope and charity,'[72] lead the praying soul to God, that is, the believing and hoping and desiring soul who attends to what he asks of the Lord in the Lord's Prayer. Fasting and abstinence from other pleasures of carnal desire—with due regard for our health—and especially alms-giving are great helps to prayer, so that we may be able to say: 'In the day of my trouble I sought God with my hands lifted up to him in the night, and I was not deceived.'[73] How is it possible to seek an incorporeal God who cannot be felt with the hands, unless He is sought by good works?

Perhaps you have still some grounds for asking why the Apostle said: 'We know not what we should pray for as we ought.'[74] We must on no account believe that either he or those to whom he spoke those words were unacquainted with the Lord's Prayer. We think that his reason for saying it, since it was not possible for him to speak impulsively or untruthfully, was because temporal trials and troubles are often useful for curing the swelling of pride, or for proving and testing our patience, and, by this proving and testing, winning for it a more glorious and more precious reward; or for chastising and wiping out certain sins, while we, ignorant of these benefits, wish to be delivered from all trouble. The Apostle shows that he himself was not untouched by this ignorance, unless, perhaps, he did know what to pray

---

70 Ps. 143.15.
71 1 Tim. 1.5.
72 1 Cor. 13.13.
73 Ps. 76.3.
74 Rom. 8.26.

for as he ought, when, lest he should be exalted by the greatness of his revelation, there was given to him a sting of the flesh, an angel of Satan, to buffet him. On account of this he thrice besought the Lord that it might depart from him,[75] but, certainly, he then knew not what to pray for as he ought. At length, he heard the answer, explaining why that could not be which so great a man asked, and why it was not to his advantage that it should be: 'My grace is sufficient for thee, for power is made perfect in infirmity.'[76]

Therefore, in these trials which can be both our blessing and our bane, 'we know not what we should pray for as we ought,' yet, because they are hard, because they are painful, because they go against the feeling of our infirmity, by a universal human will, we pray that they may depart from us. But, this meed of devotion we owe to the Lord our God, that, if He does not remove them, we are not to think that we are thereby forsaken by Him, but rather, by lovingly bearing evil, we are to hope for greater good. This is how power is made perfect in infirmity. To some, indeed, who lack patience, the Lord God, in His wrath, grants them what they ask, just as, on the other hand, He refused it to His Apostle, in His mercy. We read what and how the Israelites asked and received, but, when their lust had been satisfied, their lack of patience was severely punished.[77] And when they asked, He gave them a king, as it is written, according to their heart, but not according to His heart.[78] He even granted what the Devil asked, namely, that His servant should be tested by trial.[79] He also heard the unclean spirits when they asked that the legion of devils should enter into the herd

---

75 2 Cor. 12.7,8.
76 2 Cor. 12.9.
77 Num. 11.1-34.
78 1 Kings 8.5-7.
79 Job 1.12; 2.6.

of swine.[80] These things are written that no one may think well of himself if his prayer is heard, when he has asked impatiently for what it would be better for him not to receive, and that no one may be cast down and may despair of the divine mercy toward him if his prayer has not been heard, when he has, perhaps, asked for something which would bring him more bitter suffering if he received it, or would cause his downfall if he were ruined by prosperity. In such circumstances, then, we know not what we should pray for as we ought. Hence, if anything befalls us contrary to what we pray for, by bearing it patiently, and giving thanks in all things, we should never doubt that we ought to ask what the will of God intends and not what we will ourselves. For, our Mediator gave us an example of this when He said: 'Father, if it be possible, let this chalice pass from me,' then, transforming the human will which He had taken in becoming man, He added immediately: 'Nevertheless not as I will but as thou wilt, Father.'[81] Thence He merited that 'By the obedience of one, many are made just.'[82]

Whoever asks that one thing of the Lord and seeks after it[83] asks with certainty and security, without fear that it will do him harm when he obtains it. Without this, no other thing which he asks as he ought will do him any good when he obtains it. That one thing is the one true and solely happy life, that we may see forever the delight of the Lord,[83] made immortal and incorruptible in body and soul. Other things are sought for the sake of this one thing, and are asked for with propriety. Whoever possesses it will have everything he wishes, and will not be able to wish for anything in that state, because it will not be possible for him to have anything

---

80 Matt. 8.30-32; Luke 8.32.
81 Matt. 26.39.
82 Cf. Rom. 5.19.
83 Ps. 26.4.

unbecoming. Truly, the fountain of life is found there,[84] which we must now thirst for in our prayers, as long as we live in hope, because we do not see what we hope for[85] under the covert of His wings, before whom is all our desire. We hope to be inebriated with the plenty of His house, and to drink of the torrent of His pleasure, since with Him is the fountain of life, and in His light we shall see light.[86] Then our desire shall be satisfied with good things and there will be nothing more for us to seek by our groaning, since we possess all things to our joy. Truly, since that life is the 'peace which surpasseth all understanding,'[87] even when we ask that in our prayer, 'We know not what we should pray for as we ought.' Certainly, we do not know what we are unable to conceive in our thought, and, when any thought comes to our mind, we cast it out, reject it, despise it; we know that what we seek is not this, although we do not yet know exactly what it is.

Therefore, there is in us a certain learned ignorance, if I may say so, but it is learned in the Spirit of God, who helps our infirmity. For, when the Apostle said: 'But if we hope for that which we see not, we wait for it with patience,' he added: 'Likewise the Spirit also helpeth our infirmity, for we know not what we should pray for as we ought, but the Spirit himself asketh for us with unspeakable groanings. And he that searcheth the hearts knoweth what the Spirit desireth, because he asketh for the saints according to God.'[88] But, this is not to be understood in a sense to make us think that the Holy Spirit of God, who is unchangeable God in the Trinity, one God with the Father and the Son, asks for the saints like someone who would not be what God is. No

---
84 Ps. 35.10.
85 Rom. 8.25.
86 Ps. 35.8-10; 37.10.
87 Phil. 4.7.
88 Rom. 8.25,27.

doubt it is said: 'He asketh for the saints' because He makes the saints ask, as it is said: 'The Lord your God trieth you that he may know whether you love him,'[89] that is, that He may make you know. Therefore He makes the saints ask with unspeakable groanings, breathing into them the desire of this great thing, as yet unknown, which we await in patience. For, how could it be put into words when what is desired is unknown? On the one hand, if it were entirely unknown, it would not be desired; and on the other, if it were seen, it would not be desired or sought with groanings.

Think over all this, and if the Lord gives you any other idea on this matter, which either has not occurred to me or would be too long for me to explain, strive in your prayer to overcome this world, pray in hope, pray with faith and love, pray insistently and submissively, pray like the widow in the parable of Christ. For, although the obligation of prayer rests on all His members, that is, all who believe in Him and who are joined to His Body, as He taught, a more particular and more earnest devotion to prayer is enjoined on widows, as we see in His Scripture. There were two women with the honored name of Anna: one married, who gave birth to holy Samuel;[90] the other a widow, who recognized the Saint of saints when He was still an infant. The married one prayed with grief of soul and affliction of heart, because she had no sons. In answer to her prayer Samuel was given to her, and she offered him to God as she had vowed in her prayer to do. It is not easy to see how her prayer agrees with the Lord's Prayer, except, perhaps, in those words, 'Deliver us from evil,' because it seemed no slight evil to be married and to be deprived of the fruit of marriage, when the sole purpose of marriage is the begetting of children. But, note what is written of the widow Anna,

---
89 Deut. 13.3.
90 1 Kings 1.2-28.

that 'she departed not from the temple, by fasting and prayers, serving night and day.'[91] And the Apostle, as I said above, speaks in the same tenor: 'But she that is a widow indeed,' he says, 'and desolate, hopes in the Lord, and continues in prayers night and day.'[92] And when the Lord exhorted us to pray always and not to faint,[93] He told of the widow whose continual appeal brought a wicked and impious judge, who scorned both God and man, to hear her cause. From this it can easily be understood how widows, beyond all others, have the duty of of applying themselves to prayer, since an example was taken from widows to encourage us all to develop a love of prayer.

But, in a practice of such importance, what characteristic of widows is singled out but their poverty and desolation? Therefore, in so far as every soul understands that it is poor and desolate in this world, as long as it is absent from the Lord,[94] it surely commends its widowhood, so to speak, to God its defender, with continual and most earnest prayer. Pray, then, as the widow praised by Christ, not yet seeing Him whose help you ask, and however wealthy you may be; pray like a poor woman, for you have not yet the true wealth of the world to come, where you need fear no losses. And, although you have sons and grandsons and a numerous family, pray as a desolate widow, as was explained above, for all temporal things are uncertain, even though they last, for our consolation, to the end of this life. But, for your part, if you seek and relish the things that are above,[95] if you sigh for the things that are eternal and certain, as long as you do not possess them, even though all your family are safe and devoted to you, you ought to look on yourself as desolate,

---

91 Luke 2.36-38; 2.37.
92 Cf. 1 Tim. 5.5.
93 Luke 18.1-5.
94 2 Cor. 5.6.
95 Col. 3.1,2.

and so also should your most devout daughter-in-law,[96] as well as the other holy widows and virgins gathered safely under your care. For, indeed, the more religiously you conduct your household, the more earnestly should all of you persevere in prayer, free of preoccupation with worldly affairs, except inasmuch as family affection requires.

Surely, you will also remember to pray attentively for me, for I do not wish you, out of regard for the position which I occupy, to my own peril, to deprive me of a help which I recognize as necessary. By Christ's household prayer was made for Peter, prayer was made for Paul;[97] you rejoice to belong to His household, and there is no comparison between my need of the help of fraternal prayers and that of Peter and Paul. Vie with each other in prayer, in a mutual and holy rivalry, for you will not vie against each other, but against the Devil, who is the enemy of all the saints. Let each one of you do what she can in fasting, in watching and in every bodily chastisement, all of which is a help to prayer.[98] If one can do less, let her do what she can, so long as she loves in another what she does not do herself because she cannot. Thus, the weaker will not hold back the stronger, and the stronger will not press the weaker. You owe your conscience to God, 'owe no man of you anything but to love one another.'[99] May the Lord hear your prayer, 'Who is able to do more abundantly than we desire or understand.'[100]

---

96 Juliana, wife of Olibrius and mother of Demetrias.
97 Acts 12.5; 13.3.
98 Job 12.8.
99 Rom. 13.8.
100 Eph. 3.20.

www.ingramcontent.com/pod-product-compliance
Lightning Source LLC
Chambersburg PA
CBHW032023290426
44110CB00012B/651